Longman New Junior English Dictionary

Longman

Guide to the dictionary

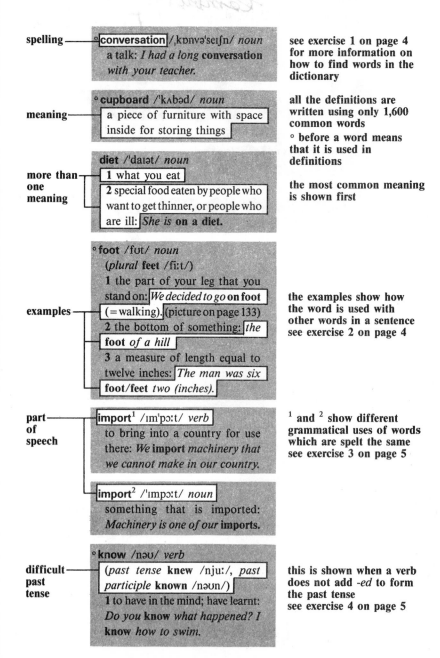

spelling — °**conversation** /ˌkɒnvəˈseɪʃn/ *noun*
a talk: *I had a long* **conversation** *with your teacher.*

see exercise 1 on page 4 for more information on how to find words in the dictionary

meaning — °**cupboard** /ˈkʌbəd/ *noun*
a piece of furniture with space inside for storing things

all the definitions are written using only 1,600 common words
° before a word means that it is used in definitions

more than one meaning — **diet** /ˈdaɪət/ *noun*
1 what you eat
2 special food eaten by people who want to get thinner, or people who are ill: *She is* **on a diet.**

the most common meaning is shown first

examples — °**foot** /fʊt/ *noun*
(*plural* **feet** /fiːt/)
1 the part of your leg that you stand on: *We decided to go* **on foot** (= walking). (picture on page 133)
2 the bottom of something: *the* **foot** *of a hill*
3 a measure of length equal to twelve inches: *The man was six* **foot/feet** *two (inches).*

the examples show how the word is used with other words in a sentence
see exercise 2 on page 4

part of speech — **import**¹ /ɪmˈpɔːt/ *verb*
to bring into a country for use there: *We* **import** *machinery that we cannot make in our country.*

import² /ˈɪmpɔːt/ *noun*
something that is imported: *Machinery is one of our* **imports.**

¹ and ² show different grammatical uses of words which are spelt the same
see exercise 3 on page 5

difficult past tense — °**know** /nəʊ/ *verb*
(*past tense* **knew** /njuː/, *past participle* **known** /nəʊn/)
1 to have in the mind; have learnt: *Do you* **know** *what happened? I* **know** *how to swim.*

this is shown when a verb does not add *-ed* to form the past tense
see exercise 4 on page 5

related words

rain² noviation *noun*
(*no plural*)
water falling
from the sky:
*There was rain
in the night.*

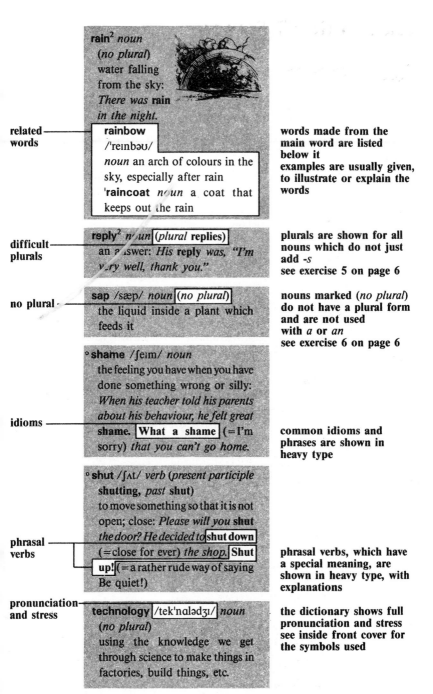

rainbow
/ˈreɪnbəʊ/
noun an arch of colours in the
sky, especially after rain
ˈraincoat *noun* a coat that
keeps out the rain

words made from the
main word are listed
below it
examples are usually given,
to illustrate or explain the
words

difficult plurals

reply² noun (*plural* **replies**)
an answer: *His* **reply** *was, "I'm
very well, thank you."*

plurals are shown for all
nouns which do not just
add *-s*
see exercise 5 on page 6

no plural

sap /sæp/ *noun* (*no plural*)
the liquid inside a plant which
feeds it

nouns marked (*no plural*)
do not have a plural form
and are not used
with *a* or *an*
see exercise 6 on page 6

idioms

°**shame** /ʃeɪm/ *noun*
the feeling you have when you have
done something wrong or silly:
*When his teacher told his parents
about his behaviour, he felt great*
shame. **What a shame** (=I'm
sorry) *that you can't go home.*

common idioms and
phrases are shown in
heavy type

phrasal verbs

°**shut** /ʃʌt/ *verb* (*present participle*
shutting, *past* **shut**)
to move something so that it is not
open; close: *Please will you* **shut**
the door? He decided to **shut down**
(=close for ever) *the shop.* **Shut
up!** (=a rather rude way of saying
Be quiet!)

phrasal verbs, which have
a special meaning, are
shown in heavy type, with
explanations

pronunciation and stress

technology /tekˈnɒlədʒɪ/ *noun*
(*no plural*)
using the knowledge we get
through science to make things in
factories, build things, etc.

the dictionary shows full
pronunciation and stress
see inside front cover for
the symbols used

1

Alphabetical order: how to find a word in the dictionary quickly

The words in the dictionary are listed in alphabetical order. Above is the alphabet.

A word which begins with **b**, like **book,** will be near the front of the dictionary, but one which begins with **t**, like **table**, will be near the back, and one which begins with **m**, like **make**, will be near the middle of the dictionary.

First practise putting these words into alphabetical order, without using the dictionary:

road	far	see
ask	house	turn
box	zoo	careful

Now look at these words:

and	August	asleep
about	agree	aim
atom	allow	address

All these words start with the letter **a,** so to put them into alphabetical order you must look at the second letter of the word. **b** comes before **n,** so you will find **about** before **and** in the dictionary. Now put the other words above into alphabetical order.

If the first two letters of the words are the same, you have to look at the third letters, and so on.

To help you to find the words quickly, the first or last word on each page is shown at the top of the page.

2

Using the examples

The examples tell you more about what a word means and how it is used in a sentence. For example, look at:

° **foot** /fʊt/ *noun*
(*plural* **feet** /fiːt/)
1 the part of your leg that you stand on: *We decided to go* **on foot** (= walking). (picture on page 133)
2 the bottom of something: *the* **foot** *of a hill*
3 a measure of length equal to twelve inches: *The man was six* **foot/feet** *two (inches).*

From the examples we see that **on foot** means "walking", that the bottom of a hill is called the **foot** of a hill, and that when foot means "a measure of length" the plural can be **foot** or **feet**.

Now look at these entries in the dictionary, read the examples, then write different sentences yourself using the words:

usual	imagine	regret
give	quite	what
job	accident	before

example: **usual**
Peter went to school at the **usual** *time today.*

3
Noun, verb, adjective

When you hear or read a new word, you need to know what sort of word it is before you can use it in a sentence. Look at the words below, and see which sentence you can use them in:

table	new	small
eat	red	teacher
goat	sleep	work

1. *I can see the . . .*
2. *I . . . at home.*
3. *My house is . . .*

example: **table**
  *I can see the **table**.*

The words which can be used in the first sentence are all names of a person, place, animal, or thing: they are **nouns**. The words which can be used in the second sentence all tell us what someone or something does or is: they are **verbs**. The words which can be used in the third sentence all describe something: they are **adjectives**.

Now look at these words in the dictionary. Write them in three lists: nouns, verbs, and adjectives. Then use each one in a sentence:

sell	grow	make
door	lovely	river
common	want	work

example: **sell**
  *My father **sold** his car.*

4
Verb endings

Most verbs add **-ing** to form the present continuous, and **-ed** to form the simple past tense and the past participle.

For example: **walk**
  *Peter **is walking** home from school.*
  *He **walked** home from school yesterday.*
  *He **has walked** home from school every day this week.*

Some verbs change their endings, or have completely different forms in the past tenses.

For example: **drive**
  *Peter's father **is driving** home from work.*
  *He **drove** home from work yesterday.*
  *He **has driven** home from work every day this week.*

Now look at these verbs in the dictionary and make sentences with them, like the ones above:

eat	fly	swim
drop	leave	take
catch	read	teach

example: **eat**
  *Anna **is eating** a banana.*
  *She **ate** a banana yesterday.*
  *She **has eaten** a banana every day this week.*

5
Plural forms of nouns

Most nouns add **-s** to form their plurals (like **dog**: a **dog,** some **dogs**). Some have different plural forms (like **man**: a **man,** some **men**). This dictionary tells you when you do not just add **-s** to form the plural.

For example:
> **sheep** /ʃiːp/ *noun*
> (*plural* **sheep**)

Look at the entries in the dictionary for the nouns listed below. Write sentences with the words, using the plural form:

child	foot	shelf
box	leaf	thief
enemy	mouse	zebra

example: **child**
> *There are thirty* **children** *in my class.*

6
Uncountable nouns

Some nouns do not have a plural form (like **water**). This means that they are never used with **a** or **an**. This dictionary tells you when a noun does not have a plural form.

For example:
> **traffic** /ˈtræfɪk/ *noun*
> (*no plural*)

Look at the entries in the dictionary for the nouns listed below. Then decide if they fit in sentence 1 or sentence 2:

cup	bread	spoon
milk	flour	tea
bottle	mango	yam

1. *I bought three . . . s from the shop.*

2. *I bought some . . . from the shop.*

examples: **cup, milk**
> *I bought three* **cups** *from the shop.*
> *I bought some* **milk** *from the shop.*

7
Using the pictures

To help you to understand the words in this dictionary, there are many pictures. There are also four pages full of pictures, showing:

animals	on page 17
human body	on page 133
objects and shapes	on page 185
space	on page 259

Aa

a /ə; *strong* eɪ/
1 one; any: *I gave him* **a** *pencil.* **A** *bird has two legs.*
2 for each; in each: *The sweets cost 10 cents* **a** *bag. three times* **a** *year*

an /ən; *strong* æn/ is used instead of **a** before a word that starts with the sound of a, e, i, o, or u: **an** *apple and* **an** *orange*

abandon /ə'bændən/ *verb*
to leave or give up completely: *The baby was* **abandoned** *by its mother. We* **abandoned** *our holiday because we had no money.*

abbreviation /əˌbriːvɪ'eɪʃn/ *noun*
a short way of writing a word or name: *Mr is the* **abbreviation** *for Mister.*

ability /ə'bɪlɪtɪ/ *noun* (*no plural*)
the power or knowledge to do something: *She has the* **ability** *to do it, but she is lazy.*

able /'eɪbl/ *adjective*
having the power or the knowledge to do something: *Is he* **able to** *swim?*

aboard /ə'bɔːd/
preposition, adverb
on or onto a ship or aeroplane: *"Are all the passengers* **aboard?***" asked the captain.*

abolish /ə'bɒlɪʃ/ *verb*
to stop (something that is happening); get rid of completely: *The new government* **abolished** *the tax on clothing.*
abolition /ˌæbə'lɪʃən/ *noun* (*no plural*)

about /ə'baʊt/ *preposition, adverb*
1 concerning; of: *What are you talking* **about?** *a book* **about** *birds*

2 a little more or less than: *Come* (*at*) **about** *six o'clock.*
3 here and there: *The children were kicking a ball* **about.** *They walked* **about** *the town.*

above /ə'bʌv/ *adverb, preposition*
at a higher place; higher than; over: *The lamp hangs* **above** *the table. We watched the birds in the sky* **above. Above all** (= more than anything else) *I like learning English.*

abroad /ə'brɔːd/ *adverb*
in or to a foreign country: *My brother is studying* **abroad.**

abrupt /ə'brʌpt/ *adjective*
1 sudden: *an* **abrupt** *knock at the door*
2 not polite: *an* **abrupt** *answer to his question* **abruptly** *adverb*

absent /'æbsənt/ *adjective*
not there; not present: *He was* **absent** *from work last Tuesday.*
absence *noun* (*no plural*): *Her* **absence** *was noticed by the teacher.*
absent-'minded *adjective* forgetful

absolute /'æbsəluːt/ *adjective*
complete: *Are you telling me the* **absolute** *truth?*
abso'lutely *adverb*

absorb /əb'sɔːb/ *verb*
1 to take in liquid slowly: *The cloth* **absorbed** *the water in the bowl.*
2 to learn thoroughly: *I haven't really* **absorbed** *all the rules yet.*
absorbent *adjective* able to take in liquid
absorbing *adjective* very interesting: *an* **absorbing** *book*

7

absurd /əb'sɜːd/ *adjective*
very silly: *The story was so* **absurd** *that no one believed it.*
  absurdly *adverb*

abuse[1] /ə'bjuːz/ *verb* (*present participle* **abusing**, *past* **abused**)
1 to speak rudely to: *Don't* **abuse** *that old man, he can't help walking slowly.*
2 to treat badly or use wrongly: *The teacher* **abused** *his power: he made his students work in his garden after school.*

abuse[2] /ə'bjuːs/ *noun* (*no plural*)
1 rude things said to someone: *The taxi driver was shouting* **abuse** *at the slow cyclists.*
2 bad treatment or wrong use: *The pupil who tore the cover of his book was scolded for* **abuse** *of school property.*

accent[1] /'æksənt/ *noun*
1 the way a person from a certain place speaks: *Mr Singh speaks English with an Indian* **accent.**
2 greater weight given to one part of a word when it is said: *In "garden", the* **accent** *is on "gar".*

accent[2] /æk'sent/ *verb*
to give strength to a word or part of a word: *In the word "garden", "gar" is* **accented.**

° **accept** /ək'sept/ *verb*
1 to receive or take: *James* **accepted** *the apple I offered him.*
2 to agree to do something: *David asked three friends to his party, and they all* **accepted.**
  acceptable *adjective* of good enough quality: *Your work is not* **acceptable,** *please do it again.*

access /'ækses/ *noun* (*no plural*)
a way to get to a place, a person, or something: *There is no* **access** *to the street through that door. Students need* **access** *to books.*

° **accident**
/'æksɪdənt/ *noun*
something, often bad, that happens by chance: *John's had an* **accident:** *he's been knocked*

accident

down by a car. I'm sorry I broke the cup: it was an **accident.** *I met Jacob* **by accident** (=by chance) *in the market.*
  accidental /ˌæksɪ'dentl/ *adjective: I didn't mean to break it: it was* **accidental.**
  accidentally *adverb*

accommodate /ə'kɒmədeɪt/ *verb* (*present participle* **accommodating**, *past* **accommodated**)
1 to give someone a place to live or stay: *One flat can* **accommodate** *a family of five.*
2 to have space for: *You could* **accommodate** *another four children in your class.*
  ac,commo'dation *noun* (*no plural*) somewhere to live or stay: *to look for* **accommodation**

accompany /ə'kʌmpənɪ/ *verb* (*present participle* **accompanying**, *past* **accompanied**)
1 to go with someone: *He* **accompanied** *me to the doctor's.*
2 to play music while someone else is singing or playing another instrument: *Maria sang and I* **accompanied** *her on the piano.*

accomplish /ə'kʌmplɪʃ/ *verb*
to do or finish satisfactorily: *I* **accomplished** *two hours' work before dinner.*

° **according to** /ə'kɔːdɪŋ tə/ *preposition*
from what is said or written: **According to** *him, sugar is bad for you.*

account[1] /ə'kaʊnt/ *noun*
1 a story or description: *an exciting* **account** *of the match*
2 a list of payments owed to someone
3 an amount of money kept in a bank: *He paid the money into his* **bank account.**
   accountant *noun* a person whose job is to keep accounts for people or companies
   accounts *plural noun* lists of money spent and money earned

account[2] *verb*
to give the reason for: *I can't* **account for** *Peter's unhappiness.*

accurate /'ækjərət/ *adjective*
right; correct: *Is this watch* **accurate? accurately** *adverb*

accuse /ə'kjuːz/ *verb* (*present participle* **accusing,** *past* **accused**)
to say that someone has done something wrong: *The teacher* **accused** *Jacob of hiding the book.*
   accusation /ˌækjʊ'zeɪʃn/ *noun*

accustom /ə'kʌstəm/ *verb*
to make someone used to something: *She is* **accustomed** *to studying every day.*

° **ache**[1] /eɪk/ *verb* (*present participle* **aching,** *past* **ached**)
to be painful; hurt: *Her head* **ached** *all night.*

° **ache**[2] *noun*
a continuing pain: *a stomach* **ache**

achieve /ə'tʃiːv/ *verb* (*present participle* **achieving,** *past* **achieved**)
to do or get successfully by working: *He* **achieved** *top marks in the examination.*
   achievement *noun* something that you have worked hard for

acid /'æsɪd/ *noun*
a powerful liquid that can burn things

acknowledge /ək'nɒlɪdʒ/ *verb*
(*present participle* **acknowledging,** *past* **acknowledged**)
1 to agree that something is true: *Do you* **acknowledge** *that you've been wrong?*
2 to write that you have received something: *Please* **acknowledge** *my letter.* **acknowledgment** *noun*

acquaintance /ə'kweɪntəns/ *noun*
a person you know, but who isn't a friend

acquire /ə'kwaɪəʳ/ *verb* (*present participle* **acquiring,** *past* **acquired**)
to get or buy: *How did you* **acquire** *this money?*

acre /'eɪkəʳ/ *noun*
a measure of land; 4,047 square metres

° **across** /ə'krɒs/
adverb, preposition
from one side of a place to the other; on the other side of something: *They swam* **across** *the river. the house* **across** *the street*

° **act**[1] /ækt/ *verb*
1 to do or behave: *The children* **acted** *very badly at school.*
2 to pretend to be someone else, in a play or film
   action /'ækʃn/ *noun* something done: *The government's* **action** *will prevent war.*

° **act**[2] *noun*
1 an action; something done: *an* **act** *of bravery*
2 something pretended: *When Jane said she hated him, it was an* **act.** *She likes him really.*
3 a part of a play

° **active**[1] /'æktɪv/ *adjective*
always doing things: *He is an* **active** *member of the club, and loves arranging things for people to do.* **actively** *adverb*
   activity /æk'tɪvəti/ *noun* **1** (*plural* **activities**) something we

do, especially as an amusement: *Dancing is her favourite* **activity**.
2 (*no plural*) being active: *The classroom was full of* **activity**; *every child was busy.*

active[2] *adjective*
doing the action: *In the sentence "John kicked the ball", "kicked" is an* **active** *verb.*
The opposite of **active** is **passive**.

actor /'æktər/ *noun*
a man who acts in plays or films

actress /'æktrɪs/ *noun* (*plural* **actresses**)
a woman who acts in plays or films

actual /'æktʃʊəl/ *adjective*
real and clear: *We think he stole the money, but we have no* **actual** *proof.*
actually *adverb* really; in fact

A.D. /ˌeɪ 'diː/
after the birth of Christ (used in dates)

adapt /ə'dæpt/ *verb*
to change; make more suitable: *Have you* **adapted** *to living in a different country?*
adaptable *adjective* (of a person) able to adapt easily

° **add** /æd/ *verb*
1 to put together with something else: *James had seven eggs. I* **added** *three, so now they all* **add up to** *ten.* **Add** *these numbers* **up** *in your book.*
2 to say something more
addition /ə'dɪʃn/ *noun* **1** (*no plural*) adding **2** something added: *Our baby brother is an* **addition** *to our family.*

adder /'ædər/ *or* **viper** *noun*
a snake with a dangerous bite

° **address**[1] /ə'dres/ *noun* (*plural* **addresses**)
the name of the place where you live

° **address**[2] *verb*
1 to write an address on: *She* **addressed** *the letter.*
2 to speak to: *The football captain* **addressed** *his team.*

adequate /'ædɪkwət/ *adjective*
enough: *There is* **adequate** *food for everyone.*

° **adjective** /'ædʒɪktɪv/ *noun*
a word that describes something· *In the phrase "a beautiful song", "beautiful" is an* **adjective**.

adjust /ə'dʒʌst/ *verb*
to make a small change in something to make it better: *Joseph* **adjusted** *the bicycle seat so that his feet reached the ground.*

administer /əd'mɪnɪstər/ *verb*
to govern; look after the running of: *The government* **administers** *the country.*
administration /ədˌmɪnɪ'streɪʃn/ *noun* (*no plural*): *The headmistress's job is the* **administration** *of the school.*

admiral /'ædmərəl/ *noun*
the most important officer in the navy (see)

° **admire** /əd'maɪər/ *verb* (*present participle* **admiring**, *past* **admired**)
to think a person or thing is very good, nice to look at, etc.
admiration /ˌædmə'reɪʃn/ *noun* (*no plural*): *Maria looked at the skirt with* **admiration**.

° **admit** /əd'mɪt/ *verb*
(*present participle* **admitting**, *past* **admitted**)
1 to agree that something unpleasant about yourself is true: *She* **admitted** *she was lazy.*
2 to let in: *This ticket* **admits** *two people to the football match.*
admission /əd'mɪʃn/ *noun* **1** something, such as a crime, admitted **2** (*no plural*) permission

to go in: **Admission** *was free for children.*

adolescent /ˌædə'lesnt/ *noun*
someone between about 13 and 19 years old

adopt /ə'dɒpt/ *verb*
1 to take a child into your family and treat him or her as your own
2 to agree to use: *We* **adopted** *Paul's plan.*

adore /ə'dɔː^r/ *verb* (*present participle* **adoring**, *past* **adored**)
to like or love very much: *She* **adored** *her son. I* **adore** *chocolates.*

adult /'ædʌlt, ə'dʌlt/ *noun*
a grown-up person

advance /əd'vɑːns/ *verb* (*present participle* **advancing**, *past* **advanced**)
to move forward: *The army* **advanced** *towards the town.*
　advanced *adjective:* **advanced** (=more difficult) *lessons*

° **advantage** /əd'vɑːntɪdʒ/ *noun*
something that helps a person: *Anna speaks good English, but she has an* **advantage** *because her mother is English.*

° **adventure** /əd'ventʃə^r/ *noun*
an exciting thing that happens to someone: *He wrote a book about his* **adventures** *as a soldier.*
　adventurous *adjective* liking a life full of adventures

° **adverb** /'ædvɜːb/ *noun*
a word which tells us how, when, or where something is done: *In the sentence "She sang a song beautifully today", "beautifully" and "today" are both* **adverbs.**

° **advertise** /'ædvətaɪz/ *verb* (*present participle* **advertising**, *past* **advertised**)
to put notices where a lot of people will see them: *The company* **advertised** *for a new secretary.*

advertisement /əd'vɜːtɪsmənt/ *noun: The wall was covered with* **advertisements.**

° **advise** /əd'vaɪz/ *verb* (*present participle* **advising**, *past* **advised**)
to tell (someone) what you think they should do: *She* **advised** *me to wear my best clothes.*
　advice /əd'vaɪs/ *noun* (*no plural*): *He never* **takes my advice** (=does what I tell him).

aerial /'eərɪəl/
noun
a wire which
sends out or
receives radio
waves

aerials

aeroplane /'eərəpleɪn/
or **plane** *noun*
a large flying machine

affair /ə'feə^r/ *noun*
1 work or business: *He put his business* **affairs** *in order.*
2 an event: *The party was a very noisy* **affair.**

affect /ə'fekt/ *verb*
to make a difference to: *The great heat* **affected** *his health* (=he became ill).

affectionate /ə'fekʃnət/ *adjective*
feeling or showing love
　affectionately *adverb*

° **afford** /ə'fɔːd/ *verb*
to be able to pay for: *We can't* **afford** *a car.*

° **afraid** /ə'freɪd/ *adjective*
frightened: *James says he's not* **afraid** *of lions!*

° **after** /'ɑːftə^r/ *preposition*
1 later than: *Tomorrow is the day* **after** *today.*
2 behind: *The child ran* **after** *her dog. I wanted to go out, but I decided to stay at home and work* **after all** (=considering everything).

° **afternoon** /ˌɑːftəˈnuːn/ *noun*
the time between midday and
evening

° **afterwards** /ˈɑːftəwədz/ *adverb*
later: *We saw the film and*
afterwards *walked home together.*

° **again** /əˈgen, əˈgeɪn/ *adverb*
one more time; once more: *Come*
and see us **again** *soon. My aunt*
visits us **now and again**
(=sometimes).

° **against** /əˈgenst, əˈgeɪnst/
preposition
1 on the other side from; not
agreeing with: *We won our match*
against *that team. He is* **against**
hunting animals for their skins.
2 close to; touching: *The ladder is*
leaning **against** *the wall.*
3 to stop: *We have injections* (see)
against *serious illnesses.*

° **age** /eɪdʒ/ *noun*
1 the amount of time someone has
lived or something has been: *What*
is the **age** *of that church? Mary is*
eight years **of age.**
2 a period of time in history: *the*
Iron Age
 aged *adjective* being of the age
of: *He was* **aged** *ten.*

 agent /ˈeɪdʒənt/ *noun*
a person who looks after business
for someone else: *A travel* **agent**
arranges journeys and holidays.

° **ago** /əˈgəʊ/ *adverb*
in the past: *We came to live here*
six years **ago.**

 agony /ˈægəni/ *noun* (*no plural*)
very bad pain or trouble: *The*
wounded man was **in agony.**

° **agree** /əˈgriː/ *verb*
(*present participle* **agreeing,** *past*
agreed)
to think the same as someone else:
I **agree** *with you. He* **agreed to**
(=said yes to) *the plan.*

 agreement *noun: They have*
made an **agreement** *about the*
plan. They are all **in agreement.**

 agriculture /ˈægrɪkʌltʃəʳ/ *noun* (*no*
plural)
the science of growing crops and
raising animals; farming
 ˌ**agriˈcultural** *adjective*

° **ahead** /əˈhed/ *adverb*
in front; forward: *Walk straight*
ahead *until you reach the river.*

 aid[1] /eɪd/ *noun*
a help: *A dictionary is an* **aid** *to*
learning English.

 aid[2] *verb*
to help: *He* **aided** *the criminal.*

° **aim**[1] /eɪm/ *verb*
1 to point or get ready to throw
something towards something else:
He **aimed** (*the gun*) *at the lion.*
2 to want to be or do: *He* **aimed**
to swim a mile.

° **aim**[2] *noun*
1 pointing or getting ready to
throw something
2 something you want to do: *His*
aim *was to swim a mile.*

° **air**[1] /eəʳ/ *noun* (*no plural*)
1 what we breathe: *He came* **by air**
(=in an aircraft).
2 an appearance: *an* **air** *of*
excitement

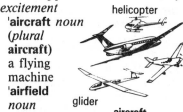
helicopter
glider
aircraft

 ˈ**aircraft** *noun*
(*plural*
aircraft)
a flying
machine
 ˈ**airfield**
noun
a place
where aeroplanes land
 ˈ**airforce** *noun* soldiers who use
aircraft for fighting
 ˈ**airline** *noun* a company which
carries people or goods by
aeroplane

'**airmail** *noun* (*no plural*) letters and parcels sent by aircraft

'**airport** *noun* a place where aircraft land and take off, and are kept

° **air**² *verb*
to make (a room or clothes) fresh by letting air into them

alarm¹ /ə'lɑːm/ *noun*
1 (*no plural*) a feeling of fear or danger
2 something that warns of danger: *They heard the fire* **alarm** (= bell).
3 a clock that rings a bell at the time you want to wake up

alarm² *verb*
to worry or frighten: *My mother was* **alarmed** *when I fell over.*

album /'ælbəm/ *noun*
a book with empty pages where you can put photographs, stamps, etc.

° **alcohol** /'ælkəhɒl/ *noun* (*no plural*)
a strong liquid, in beer and other drinks, which makes you feel drunk
,**alco'holic** *adjective: Beer is an* **alcoholic** *drink.*

alert¹ /ə'lɜːt/ *adjective*
awake and ready to act, study, etc.: *You must keep* **alert** *in class.*

alert² *noun*
a signal that someone is in danger

algebra /'ældʒɪbrə/ *noun* (*no plural*)
a kind of number work where you use letters instead of numbers you do not know

alight¹ /ə'laɪt/ *verb*
1 to step down from a train, bus, etc.
2 to land: *The bird* **alighted** *on the branch.*

alight² *adjective*
burning; on fire: *He set the dry leaves* **alight**.

° **alike** /ə'laɪk/ *adjective, adverb*
the same in some way: *They were all dressed* **alike** *in white dresses.*

° **alive** /ə'laɪv/ *adjective*
living; not dead: *Is his grandfather still* **alive?**

° **all** /ɔːl/ *adjective, adverb*
1 the whole amount of; every one of: *Don't eat* **all** *that bread!*
2 completely: *He was dressed* **all** *in black.*
3 at all (used to make "not" stronger): *I'm not* **at all** *sorry I came; I'm glad!*

alley /'ælɪ/ *noun*
a narrow road in a town

° **allow** /ə'laʊ/ *verb*
to let someone do something: *He* **allowed** *me to borrow his hammer.*

° **all right** /,ɔːl 'raɪt/ *or* **alright** *adjective, adverb*
1 well; unhurt: *The car turned over but the driver was* **all right**.
2 good enough; well enough: *Don't shut the door, it's* **all right** *as it is.*
3 yes; I agree: *Shall we go to town?* **All right**, *let's go now.*

ally¹ /'ælaɪ/ *noun* (*plural* **allies**)
someone who helps you against someone else: *France and England were* **allies** *in the war.*

ally² /ə'laɪ/ *verb* (*present participle* **allying**, *past* **allied**)
to be an ally of: *England* **allied** *with France.*
alliance *noun: The two countries made an* **alliance**.

° **almost** /'ɔːlməʊst/ *adverb*
nearly: *Hurry up — it's* **almost** *time for school.*

° **alone** /ə'ləʊn/ *adverb*
1 without others: *I was* **alone** *all day with no one to talk to.*
2 only: *This key* **alone** *will open the door.*

3 (used in some phrases): **Leave** *the dog* **alone!** (=don't touch it or trouble it)

○ **along** /ə'lɒŋ/ *preposition, adverb*
1 following the length of; from end to end of: *We walked* **along** *the road.*
2 on; forward: *Move* **along** *please!*
3 with (someone): *Can I bring my friend* **along**?

alongside /ə,lɒŋ'saɪd/ *preposition, adverb*
by the side of: *Put your chair* **alongside** *mine.*

○ **aloud** /ə'laʊd/ *adjective*
in a voice that is easy to hear: *She read the story* **aloud** *to her brother.*

○ **alphabet** /'ælfəbet/ *noun*
the letters of a language in a special order: *Our* **alphabet** *begins with A and ends with Z.*
,**alpha'betical** *adjective: These names are in* **alphabetical order:** *Joseph, Michael, Peter.*

○ **already** /ɔːl'redɪ/ *adverb*
1 before this or that time: *He has seen that film twice* **already.**
2 by now; by this or that time: *It was* **already** *raining when we started our journey.*

○ **also** /'ɔːlsəʊ/ *adverb*
as well; too: *Rose wasn't the only girl there; Sarah was there* **also.**

altar /'ɔːltəʳ/
noun
a raised table in a religious place

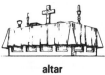

altar

where things are offered to a God

alter /'ɔːltəʳ/ *verb*
to change: *She* **altered** *her plans.*
,**alte'ration** *noun*

alternate /ɔːl'tɜːnət/ *adjective*
first one, then another: *He works on* **alternate** *Saturdays* (=he works

one Saturday, does not work the next, and so on).

alternative[1] /ɔːl'tɜːnətɪv/ *noun*
something you can do or use instead: *I wanted to go out, but I had no money; I had no* **alternative** *to staying at home.*

alternative[2] *adjective*
other; different: *The way was blocked, so we went by an* **alternative** *road.*

○ **although** /ɔːl'ðəʊ/
even if; in spite of something: **Although** *they are poor they are happy.*

altogether /ɔːltə'geðəʳ/ *adverb*
counting everyone or everything; completely: **Altogether** *there were 12 people in the bus. He's not* **altogether** *sure what to do.*

○ **always** /'ɔːlweɪz/ *adverb*
1 at all times: *The world is* **always** *turning.*
2 for ever: *I shall* **always** *remember my first day at school.*

am /əm; *strong* æm/ *verb*
the part of the verb **be** that we use with **I: Am I** *late for dinner?* **I'm** (=I am) *very late,* **aren't I?**

a.m. /,eɪ 'em/
in the morning: *I got up at 8* **a.m.**

amaze /ə'meɪz/ *verb* (*present participle* **amazing**, *past* **amazed**)
to surprise very much: *I was* **amazed** *when I found money in the old box.* **amazing** *adjective*
amazement *noun* (*no plural*): *I stopped in* **amazement** *at the strange sight.*

ambassador /æm'bæsədəʳ/ *noun*
an important person who represents his country in another country

ambition /æm'bɪʃn/ *noun*
1 (*no plural*) a strong wish to be successful

2 something wished for: *Her* **ambition** *was to be a famous singer.* **ambitious** *adjective*

ambulance /'æmbjʊləns/ *noun* a special car for carrying ill or wounded people

ammunition /ˌæmjʊ'nɪʃn/ *noun* (*no plural*) something that you can throw or shoot from a weapon to hurt someone or damage something

° **among** /ə'mʌŋ/ *preposition* in the middle of; between: *Share the fruit* **among** *your friends.* *houses* **among** *the trees* **amongst** is another word for **among**

° **amount** /ə'maʊnt/ *noun* a sum (of money) or a quantity: *a large* **amount** *of gold*

amp /æmp/ *noun* a measure of electricity

° **amuse** /ə'mjuːz/ *verb* (*present participle* **amusing**, *past* **amused**) to make someone laugh or smile: *The children* **amused** *the old man.* **amusement** *noun* **1** (*no plural*) enjoyment **2** an enjoyable thing to do: *There were* **amusements** *at the party.* **amusing** *adjective*

° **an** /ən; *strong* æn/ see **a**

analyse /'ænəlaɪz/ *verb* (*present participle* **analysing**, *past* **analysed**) to find out exactly what something is made of: *The scientist* **analysed** *the milk and found it contained too much water.* **analysis** /ə'næləsɪs/ *noun* (*plural* **analyses** /-siːz/): *an* **analysis** *of the milk*

ancestor /'ænsestər/ *noun* a person in your family who lived before you did

anchor /'æŋkər/ *noun* a heavy weight put down from a ship to the bottom of the sea

to stop it from moving

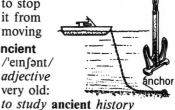
anchor

° **ancient** /'eɪnʃənt/ *adjective* very old: *to study* **ancient** *history*

° **and** /ənd; *strong* ænd/ a joining word: *James* **and** *Peter were singing* **and** *dancing.*

angel /'eɪndʒəl/ *noun* a messenger from God, usually imagined with wings **angelic** /æn'dʒelɪk/ *adjective*

° **anger** /'æŋgər/ *noun* (*no plural*) the fierce feeling of wanting to harm or fight other people.

° **angle** /'æŋgl/ *noun* the shape made when two lines meet each other; a corner

° **angry** /'æŋgrɪ/ *adjective* (**angrier, angriest**) feeling anger: *I came home late and my mother was* **angry** (*with me*). **angrily** *adverb*

° **animal** /'ænɪml/ *noun* something alive that is not a plant: *Dogs, goats, and lions are* **animals.**

° **ankle** /'æŋkl/ *noun* the part of the leg just above the foot, which can bend (picture on page 133)

anniversary /ˌænɪ'vɜːsərɪ/ *noun* (*plural* **anniversaries**) the same date each year that something important happened in the past: *We were married on 7 April 1973, so every year we have a party on our* **anniversary** (=7 April).

announce /ə'naʊns/ *verb* (*present participle* **announcing**, *past* **announced**) to say in public: *The captain*

announced *that the plane was going to land.*

announcement *noun: The headmaster read an* **announcement** *to the pupils.*

announcer *noun: The radio* **announcer** *read out the news.*

○ **annoy** /ə'nɔɪ/ *verb*
to make someone a little angry; trouble someone: *I was* **annoyed** *because I missed the bus and was late for school.*

annual /'ænjʊəl/ *adjective*
happening every year: *an annual event*

○ **another** /ə'nʌðəʳ/
1 one more: *Would you like* **another** *orange?*
2 a different one: *One boy was reading;* **another** *was writing.*

○ **answer**[1] /'ɑːnsəʳ/ *verb*
to say or write something after you have been asked a question: *"Did you do it?" "No, I didn't",* she **answered**.

○ **answer**[2] *noun*
1 what we say or write when we are asked a question: *I asked her the time but she gave no* **answer.**
2 the end of a sum; something we are asked to find out: *The* **answer's** *wrong.*

○ **ant** /ænt/
noun
a small insect that lives in large groups

ant

antelope /'æntɪləʊp/ *noun*
(*plural* **antelope** *or* **antelopes**)
any of the wild animals which run fast and usually have horns on their heads (picture opposite)

○ **anxious** /'æŋkʃəs/ *adjective*
worried

anxiety /æŋ'zaɪətɪ/ *noun: Her face was showing her* **anxiety.**

○ **any** /'enɪ/ *adjective*
1 no matter what or which: *You can buy sugar at* **any** *big store.*
2 (used in sentences like these to mean *some*): *Have you* **any** *coffee? There isn't* **any** *in the cupboard.*

○ **anybody** /'enɪˌbɒdɪ/ *or* **anyone**
any person: *Has* **anybody** *seen my pen?*

anyhow /'enɪhaʊ/ *adverb*
see **anyway**

anyone /'enɪwʌn/ see **anybody**

○ **anything** /'enɪθɪŋ/
some thing; no matter what thing: *Did you say* **anything**? *If you want* **anything** *to eat please tell me.*

anyway /'enɪweɪ/ *or* **anyhow** *adverb*
1 no matter what happens: *The dress cost a lot of money, but I bought it,* **anyway.**
2 in any way: *You can do the job* **anyway** *you like, but finish it.*

○ **anywhere** /'enɪweəʳ/ *adverb*
in, at, or to any place: *I can't find my key* **anywhere.**

apart /ə'pɑːt/ *adverb*
separately; away from another, or others: *The two villages are 6 miles* **apart.**

apart from except: *All the children like music* **apart from** *Joseph.*

apartment /ə'pɑːtmənt/ *or* **flat** *noun*
a part of a building, on one floor, where someone lives

ape /eɪp/ *noun*
a large animal like a monkey, but with a very short tail or no tail: *The gorilla (see) is an* **ape.**

apologize /ə'pɒlədʒaɪz/ *verb*
(*present participle* **apologizing**, *past* **apologized**)
to say you are sorry for something you have done: *You should*

elephants

animals

hump

tusk

trunk

camel

zebra

antelope

chimpanzee

monkey

tiger

gorilla

lion

bear

hippopotamus

giraffe

rhinoceros

17

apologize *to your mother.*
  apology /-dʒɪ/ *noun (plural*
  apologies): *I gave him an*
  apology.

apostrophe /əˈpɒstrəfɪ/ *noun*
the sign ' (used in writing to show
that letters have been left out, as
in *can't* for *cannot,* or with *s* to
show that someone owns
something, as in *Sarah's book* or
ladies' hats)

° **apparatus** /ˌæpəˈreɪtəs/ *noun (no*
plural)
tools or other things needed for a
special purpose: *There is sports*
apparatus in the gym.

apparent /əˈpærənt/ *adjective*
clearly seen or understood: *It was*
apparent *that he knew nothing*
about how to repair cars.
  apparently *adverb:* **Apparently,**
  you have done a lot of work.

appeal[1] /əˈpiːl/ *verb*
1 to ask for strongly; beg for: *The*
pupil **appealed** *for another day to*
finish his work.
2 to be pleasing: *The new toy*
appealed to *the child.*
  appealing *adjective* pleasing;
  sweet: *an* **appealing** *smile*

appeal[2] *noun*
asking for something: *The teacher*
listened to his **appeal.**

° **appear** /əˈpɪəʳ/ *verb*
1 to seem: *She* **appears** *to be*
unhappy.
2 to come into sight suddenly: *Her*
head **appeared** *round the door.*
  appearance *noun: His sudden*
  appearance *surprised her. She*
  had a sad **appearance** (=she
  seemed sad).

appetite /ˈæpɪtaɪt/ *noun*
the wish for food: *Anna has a*
good **appetite;** *she ate all her*
dinner.

applaud /əˈplɔːd/ *verb*
to strike the hands together or
shout, to show pleasure at
something: *Everyone* **applauded**
when the play ended.
  applause *noun (no plural)*

° **apple** /ˈæpl/ *noun*
a round hard juicy fruit

appliance /əˈplaɪəns/ *noun*
an instrument for doing something
useful: *kitchen* **appliances**
(=cooking tools)

apply /əˈplaɪ/ *verb (present*
participle **applying,** *past* **applied)**
1 to ask for: *I want to* **apply for**
the job.
2 to be about or important to: *The*
school rules **apply to** *us all.*
3 to put on: *The doctor* **applied**
some medicine to the wound.
  application /ˌæplɪˈkeɪʃn/ *noun*
  a written paper asking for
  something: *an* **application** *for a*
  job

appoint /əˈpɔɪnt/ *verb*
to give a job to: *I* **appointed** *her as*
my secretary.
  appointment *noun* **1** a time
  arranged for seeing someone: *I*
  made an **appointment** *to see the*
  doctor. **2** a job

appreciate /əˈpriːʃɪeɪt/ *verb*
(*present participle* **appreciating,**
past **appreciated)**
to be grateful for: *I* **appreciate**
your help.
  ap‚preci'ation *noun (no plural):*
  He gave me a present to show his
  appreciation.

apprentice /əˈprentɪs/ *noun*
someone who is learning a job

approach /əˈprəʊtʃ/ *verb*
to come near: *The soldier asked*
the boy to **approach** (*him*).

appropriate /əˈprəʊprɪət/ *adjective*
right; suitable: *A dirty face is not*

appropriate *for the school photograph.*

° **approve** /ə'pruːv/ *verb* (*present participle* **approving,** *past* **approved**)

to say that something is good: *My parents don't* **approve** *of me smoking cigarettes.*

approval *noun* (*no plural*): *He showed his* **approval** *by smiling.*

approximate /ə'prɒksɪmət/ *adjective*

not exact: *The* **approximate** *time is two o'clock* (=it might be just before or just after two)

approximately *adverb*

apricot /'eɪprɪkɒt/ *noun*
a round soft yellow fruit

° **April** /'eɪprəl/ *noun*
the fourth month of the year

apron /'eɪprən/ *noun*
a large piece of cloth you can put on top of your other clothes, to keep them clean

apt /æpt/ *adjective*
suitable: *an* **apt** *choice of words*

aquarium /ə'kweərɪəm/ *noun*
1 a large glass box where live fish are kept
2 a building where there are lots of these boxes, for people to look at

° **arch** /ɑːtʃ/ *noun* (*plural* **arches**)
a curved part of a roof, door, window or bridge

archaeology /ˌɑːkɪ'ɒlədʒɪ/ *noun* (*no plural*)
the study of very old things, especially things made by man
archaeologist *noun*

archbishop /ˌɑːtʃ'bɪʃəp/ *noun*
an important Christian leader; a chief bishop (see)

architect /'ɑːkɪtekt/ *noun*
someone who plans buildings
architecture /-tektʃər/ *noun* (*no*

plural): *He studies* **architecture.** *The* **architecture** *of this church is very fine.*

are /ər; *strong* ɑːr/ *verb*
the part of the verb **be** that we use with **we, you** and **they:** *Who* **are** *you?* **We're** (=we are) *Jane's friends. They* **aren't** *very tall,* **are** *they?*

° **area** /'eərɪə/ *noun*
1 a piece of land or sea: *We are going to build a school in this* **area.**
2 the measure of a surface: *The square has an* **area** *of nine square centimetres.*

° **argue** /'ɑːgjuː/ *verb* (*present participle* **arguing,** *past* **argued**)
to disagree in words

argument /'ɑːgjʊmənt/ *noun*
a disagreement; quarrel

arise /ə'raɪz/ *verb*
(*present participle* **arising,** *past tense* **arose** /ə'rəʊz/, *past participle* **arisen** /ə'rɪzn/)
1 to happen: *That question did not* **arise.**
2 to get up: *I* **arose** *early in the morning.*

arithmetic /ə'rɪθmətɪk/ *noun* (*no plural*)
number work, including addition, division, etc.

° **arm** /ɑːm/ *noun*
the part of the body between the shoulder and the hand (picture on page 133)
'armchair *noun* a comfortable chair with places to rest your arms on
arms *plural noun* weapons like guns and bombs: *The* **armed forces** *of a country are its army, navy* (see) *and airforce* (see).

armour /'ɑːmər/ *noun* (*no plural*)
a covering of metal worn by soldiers in old times to protect

them: *An* **armoured car** *is a special car protected by heavy metal.*

° **army** /ˈɑːmɪ/ *noun* (*plural* **armies**)
a large number of soldiers fighting together

° **around** /əˈraʊnd/ *or*
round *preposition, adverb*
1 on all sides of something: *There was a fence* **around** *the yard.*
2 in different places; about: *They walked* **around** (*the town*).

° **arrange** /əˈreɪndʒ/ *verb*
(*present participle* **arranging**, *past* **arranged**)
1 to put in order: *He* **arranged** *the books on the shelf.*
2 to make plans for: *I have* **arranged** *a party.*
   arrangement *noun: to make arrangements for a party*

arrest¹ /əˈrest/ *verb*
to make someone a prisoner: *The criminal was* **arrested** *yesterday.*

arrest² *noun*
an act of arresting: *The police made three* **arrests** *yesterday.*

° **arrive** /əˈraɪv/ *verb* (*present participle* **arriving**, *past* **arrived**)
to get to the place you were going to: *At last she* **arrived** (*at the village*).
   arrival *noun: The* **arrival** *of the train was delayed.*

° **arrow** /ˈærəʊ/
noun
1 a pointed stick that is shot from a bow (see)
2 a mark shaped like an arrow which shows you the way

arrows

° **art** /ɑːt/ *noun*
1 (*no plural*) drawing and painting: *He's very good at* **art.**
2 the ability to do certain things: *the* **art** *of cooking*

artery /ˈɑːtərɪ/ *noun*
(*plural* **arteries**)
one of the tubes in the body that carry blood from the heart around the body

° **article**¹ /ˈɑːtɪkl/ *noun*
1 a thing: **articles** *of clothing*
2 a piece of writing in a newspaper: *an* **article** *about ships*

article² *noun*
the words "a" or "an" (**indefinite article**) or "the" (**definite article**)

artificial /ˌɑːtɪˈfɪʃl/ *adjective*
not real: **artificial** *flowers*

artist /ˈɑːtɪst/ *noun*
someone who is good at dancing, painting, playing music, or something skilful like this
   ar'tistic *adjective*

° **as** /əz; *strong* æz/
1 when; while: *We sang* **as** *we walked along the road.*
2 in such a way; like: *Do* **as** *your mother says.*
3 because: *She did not hear us come in* **as** *she was asleep.*
4 (used in some phrases): *I am nearly* **as** *tall* **as** *my father. I'll cook the meal* **as long as** (=if) *you wash the pans afterwards. The man looked* **as if/as though** *he was lost.*

° **ash** /æʃ/ *noun* (*plural* **ashes**)
grey powder left after something has burnt

° **ashamed** /əˈʃeɪmd/ *adjective*
feeling bad about something you have done wrong: *I behaved badly yesterday and I am* **ashamed** (*of myself*) *now.*

ashore /əˈʃɔːr/ *adverb*
onto the land: *Pull the boat* **ashore!**

° **aside** /əˈsaɪd/ *adverb*
to or towards one side; away: *We had to move* **aside** *to let the car pass us.*

° **ask** /ɑːsk/ *verb*
1 to say a question: *"Who are you?" she* **asked.**
2 to try and get something from someone: *They* **asked** *me the time.*

° **asleep** /əˈsliːp/ *adjective*
sleeping: *Is the baby still* **asleep?**

aspirin /ˈæsprɪn/ *noun*
a medicine that makes pain go away

ass /æs/ *noun* (*plural* **asses**)
an animal like a small horse with long ears: **Ass** *is another word for* **donkey.**

assemble /əˈsembl/ *verb* (*present participle* **assembling,** *past* **assembled**)
to gather together: *All the people* **assembled** *at Mary's house.*
assembly *noun* (*plural* **assemblies**) a group of people gathered together for a special purpose or meeting

assist /əˈsɪst/ *verb*
to help: *We all* **assisted** *in mending the roof.*
assistance *noun* (*no plural*) help
assistant *noun* a person who helps

associate /əˈsəʊʃieɪt/ *verb* (*present participle* **associating,** *past* **associated**)
to think of something being with something else: *We* **associate** *blackboards and chalk with school.*
associ'ation *noun* a group of people joined together for one purpose

assume /əˈsjuːm/ *verb* (*present participle* **assuming,** *past* **assumed**)
to think something is true when no one has said so: *I* **assume** *you always get up at the same time.*

assure /əˈʃɔːr/ *verb* (*present participle* **assuring,** *past* **assured**)
to tell someone very firmly: *He* **assured** *me that he had finished.*

asterisk /ˈæstərɪsk/ *noun*
the sign *

astonish /əˈstɒnɪʃ/ *verb*
to surprise greatly: *I was* **astonished** *when I heard the school had burnt down.*
astonishment *noun* (*no plural*)

astronaut /ˈæstrənɔːt/ *noun*
a person who travels in space (picture on page 259)

astronomy /əˈstrɒnəmɪ/ *noun* (*no plural*)
the study of the sun, moon, and stars
astronomer *noun* a person who studies the stars

° **at** /ət; *strong* æt/ *preposition*
1 (showing where): *He left his bag* **at** *the station.*
2 (showing when): *It gets cold* **at** *night.*
3 (showing what people are doing or what is happening): *She is* **at** *work. The two armies are* **at** *war.*
4 (used in sentences like these): *I bought two pens* **at** *20 cents each. I am surprised* **at** *what you say. He is good* **at** *football.*

ate /et, eɪt/ see **eat**

athlete /ˈæθliːt/ *noun*
someone who is good at running, jumping and throwing: **Athletes** *are good at* **athletics.** /æθˈletɪks/

atlas /ˈætləs/ *noun* (*plural* **atlases**)
a book of maps

atmosphere /ˈætməsfɪər/ *noun* (*no plural*)
1 the air surrounding the Earth
2 a feeling that a place or group of people give you: *the exciting* **atmosphere** *of a football match*

atom /ˈætəm/ *noun*
the smallest part of a substance:

Atomic /əˈtɒmɪk/ **power** *uses the forces in an* **atom** *to make power.*

attach /əˈtætʃ/ *verb*
1 to fix something to something else
2 to like very much: *Mary was* **attached to** *her brother.*

○ **attack**[1] /əˈtæk/ *verb*
to go and fight against or harm someone: *The newspaper* **attacked** (=wrote things against) *the new tax.*

○ **attack**[2] *noun*
fighting; trying to harm someone: *an* **attack** *on the soldiers*

attempt[1] /əˈtempt/ *verb*
to try: *She* **attempted** *to cook the dinner.*

attempt[2] *noun*
a try: *She made an* **attempt** *to cook the dinner.*

○ **attend** /əˈtend/ *verb*
1 to be present at: *I* **attended** *his birthday party.*
2 to listen to: *Will you* **attend** *to what I'm saying?*
3 to look after: *The doctor* **attended** *me when I had a fever.*
attendance *noun* (*no plural*): *He sometimes comes to school, and sometimes stays at home: his* **attendance** *at school is not regular.*
attendant *noun*: *The car park* **attendant** *takes the money and tells people where to park.*

○ **attention** /əˈtenʃn/ *noun*
(*no plural*)
looking at and listening to someone or some event: *Margaret is not* **paying attention** (=listening) *to me.*

attitude /ˈætɪtjuːd/ *noun*
the way you think or feel about something: *What is your* **attitude** *to school?*

attract /əˈtrækt/ *verb*
to be pleasing to; make someone notice: *Does this job* **attract** *you?*
attractive *adjective* pleasing, especially to look at

aubergine /ˈəʊbəʒiːn/ *or* **egg plant** *noun*
a plant with large fruits with a yellow or purple skin, used as a vegetable

audience /ˈɔːdɪəns/ *noun*
all the people watching a play, listening to music, etc.

○ **August** /ˈɔːgəst/ *noun*
the eighth month of the year

○ **aunt** /ɑːnt/ *noun*
the sister of one of your parents, or the wife of the brother of one of your parents

author /ˈɔːθəʳ/ *noun*
a person who writes a book

authority /ɔːˈθɒrətɪ/ *noun*
1 (*no plural*) the power to make people do what you want: *The teacher has* **authority** *to punish any pupil.*
2 (*plural* **authorities**) a person or group who runs or governs something

automatic /ˌɔːtəˈmætɪk/ *adjective*
working by itself: *The* **automatic** *cooker never gets too hot. The heat is turned off* **automatically.**

autumn /ˈɔːtəm/ *noun, adjective*
the season before winter in cool countries, when the leaves fall off the trees

available /əˈveɪləbl/ *adjective*
able to be seen, used, etc.: *Is the manager* **available?**

avenue /ˈævənjuː/ *noun*
a road, especially with trees on both sides

○ **average** /ˈævrɪdʒ/ *adjective*
1 usual; ordinary: *The* **average**

child enjoys listening to stories.

2 a word used in number work: *Anne had three sweets, Richard had four and Maria had five; the* **average** *number of sweets was four* (3 + 4 + 5 = 12, *divided between 3 children* = 4 *each*).

° **avoid** /ə'vɔɪd/ *verb*
to get or keep away from: *Are you trying to* **avoid** *me?*

° **awake** /ə'weɪk/ *adjective*
not sleeping: *The baby is* **awake.**

° **award**[1] /ə'wɔːd/ *noun*
a prize, especially for work or courage

award[2] *verb*
to give as an award: *The school* **awarded** *Mercy a prize (for her good work).*

aware /ə'weə^r/ *adjective*
knowing: *I was not* **aware** *of the fire.*

° **away** /ə'weɪ/ *adverb*
1 at or to another place; not here: *Do you live* **far away?** — *No, quite near.*
2 all the time: *He hammered* **away** *until he made a hole in the wall.*

3 (used in some phrases): *Don't* **throw away** *those boxes; we can use them. Yes, I'll do that* **right a'way** (=now).

awful /'ɔːfəl/ *adjective*
1 very bad or frightening: *an* **awful** *accident*
2 not pleasing; not liked: *That's an* **awful** *book.*
awfully *adverb* very: *She's* **awfully** *clever.*

° **awkward** /'ɔːkwəd/ *adjective*
1 not skilful in handling things; not moving in an easy way: *He's very* **awkward,** *he keeps dropping things.*
2 not easy to handle: *The pan is an* **awkward** *shape.*
3 making you feel uncomfortable: *There was an* **awkward** *silence, when no one knew what to say.*
awkwardly *adverb*

° **axe** /æks/ *noun*
a metal blade fixed onto a handle, used for cutting down trees etc.

axe

Bb

° **baby** /'beɪbɪ/ *noun (plural* **babies)**
a very young child

bachelor /'bætʃələ^r/ *noun*
a man who is not married

° **back**[1] /bæk/ *noun*
1 the part of the body from the neck to the legs: *The* '**backbone** *runs down the* **back** *from the neck to the middle of the body. You*

shouldn't talk about Agnes **behind her back** (=when she's not here).
2 the part that is furthest from the front; at or near the end: *Write this exercise at the* **back** *of your book. There's a hut* **at the back of** (=behind) *the house. Peter's shirt is* ,**back to front** — *he's got the buttons down his* **back!**

°**back**[2] *adverb*

1 at or towards the back part; away from the front: *She tied her long hair* **back** *with a band. Stand* **back** *from the fire; it's very hot.*

2 to or in a place where something or someone was before: *Put the book* **back** *on the shelf when you've finished it.*

3 in return or in reply: *I wrote to her, and she wrote* **back** (*to me*) *the next day.*

backwards /'bækwədz/ *adverb* **1** towards the back: *He looked* **backwards** *to see who was following him.* **2** with the back part in front: *You've put your hat on* **backwards.** **3** starting at the end: *"Can you count* **backwards** *from 5?" "Yes; 5,4,3,2,1."*

back[3] *verb*

to move or make something move backwards: *She* **backed** *the car out of the narrow road.*

background /'bækgraʊnd/ *noun*

what is behind something: *This is a photo of Mary, with our house in the* **background.**

bacon /'beɪkən/ *noun* (*no plural*)

meat from the back or sides of a pig, with salt added

°**bad** /bæd/ *adjective*

(**worse** /wɜːs/, **worst** /wɜːst/)

1 not good: *I am* **bad** *at English, but Jo is* **worse** — *he got the* **worst** (=lowest) *marks in the class.*

2 severe: *a* **bad** *cut on his leg*

badly *adverb: His foot was* **badly** *hurt.*

badge /bædʒ/ *noun*

a small sign that we wear to show what we do or have done: *We wear the school* **badge** *on our coats.*

badminton /'bædmɪntən/ *noun* (*no plural*)

a game like tennis

°**bag** /bæg/ *noun*

a container made of soft material (cloth, paper, plastic, leather), which opens at the top

baggage /'bægɪdʒ/ *or* **luggage** *noun* (*no plural*)

the bags and other containers that a traveller takes with him

bait /beɪt/ *noun* (*no plural*)

food that is used for catching fish or animals

°**bake** /beɪk/ *verb* (*present participle* **baking,** *past* **baked**)

to cook in an oven

baker *noun* someone who owns or works in a bakery

bakery /'beɪkərɪ/ *noun* (*plural* **bakeries**) a place where bread and cakes are baked to be sold

°**balance**[1] /'bæləns/ *verb*

(*present participle* **balancing,** *past* **balanced**)

to keep oneself or something else steady, especially in a difficult position: *Can you* **balance** *a ball on your nose?*

°**balance**[2] *noun*

1 a machine for weighing

2 (*no plural*) steadiness: *The child couldn't* **keep his balance** (=stay steady) *on his new bicycle.*

balcony /'bælkənɪ/ *noun* (*plural* **balconies**) a place like a

balcony

shelf with sides, on the outside of a building above the ground

bald /bɔːld/ *adjective*

with no hair: *a* **bald** *old man*

bale /beɪl/ *noun*

a large quantity of goods or material tied tightly together: **bales** *of cotton on the factory floor*

○ **ball** /bɔːl/ *noun*
1 a round object used in games; anything of this shape: *a **ball** of wool*
2 a large party for dancing

ballet /'bæleɪ/ *noun*
a play without speech, where the story is told through dance

balloon /bə'luːn/ *noun*
a rubber bag that can be blown up with air or gas

ballot /'bælət/ *noun*
a way of marking a piece of paper to choose someone: *The club members held a secret **ballot** to choose the chairperson.*

ballpoint /'bɔːlpɔɪnt/ *or* **biro** /'baɪrəʊ/ *noun*
a pen with a metal ball at the point

ban[1] /bæn/ *verb* (*present participle* **banning**, *past* **banned**)
not to allow something: *Smoking is banned in school.*

ban[2] *noun*
an order not allowing something: *There is a **ban** on smoking.*

○ **banana** /bə'nɑːnə/ *noun*
a long yellow fruit

○ **band** /bænd/ *noun*
1 a narrow piece of material used for holding things together: *Put a **rubber band** round these books.*
2 a group of people collected for some purpose
3 a group of people who play music together

bandage[1] /'bændɪdʒ/ *noun*
a long piece of cloth used for covering a wound

bandage[2] *verb* (*present participle* **bandaging**, *past* **bandaged**)
to tie a bandage on

bandit /'bændɪt/ *noun*
a robber, usually armed and one of a group

○ **bang** /bæŋ/ *noun*
a loud noise: *There was a **bang** as the gun was fired.*
bang *verb*

bangle /'bæŋgl/ *noun*
a metal band or chain worn round the arm or ankle

banish /'bænɪʃ/ *verb*
to send away, usually out of the country, as a punishment

banister /'bænɪstə^r/ *noun*
a fence that guards the outer edge of stairs

○ **bank**[1] /bæŋk/ *noun*
1 land along the side of a river, lake, etc.
2 a long heap of earth raised above the ground

○ **bank**[2] *noun*
a place where money is kept and paid out when we want it
banker *noun* a person who owns or controls a bank
'banknote *or* **note** *noun* a piece of paper money

baptize /bæp'taɪz/ *verb* (*present participle* **baptizing**, *past* **baptized**)
to put holy water on someone and give him a Christian name: *The baby was **baptized** Maria.*
baptism /'bæptɪzəm/ *noun*

○ **bar**[1] /bɑː^r/ *noun*
1 a long piece of wood or metal
2 a piece of material such as soap or chocolate
3 a place where drinks and sometimes food can be bought

bars

a bar of soap

○ **bar**[2] *verb* (*present participle* **barring**, *past* **barred**)
1 to close firmly with a bar: *She **barred** the door.*
2 to block: *The soldiers **barred** the way to the airport.*

barbed wire /ˌbɑːbd 'waɪə^r/ *noun*
(*no plural*)
wire with short sharp points in it:
a **'barbed-wire** *fence*

barber /'bɑːbə^r/ *noun*
a person who cuts men's hair

○ **bare** /beə^r/ *adjective*
1 uncovered: *Don't walk on that broken glass with* **bare** *feet.*
2 empty: *a* **bare** *room* (=with no furniture)
  barely *adverb* almost not: *He had* **barely** *enough money to buy food.*

bargain[1] /'bɑːgɪn/ *verb*
to talk about the price of something with the buyer or seller: *She* **bargained** *with the trader till he sold her the fruit cheaply.*

bargain[2] *noun*
something bought for a little money but worth more

barge /bɑːdʒ/ *noun*
a large boat with a flat bottom, used for carrying things on rivers

bark[1] /bɑːk/ *verb*
to make the sound made by a dog
  bark *noun*

bark[2] *noun* (*no plural*)
the strong outer covering of a tree

barn /bɑːn/ *noun*
a building where farm animals and crops are kept

barometer /bə'rɒmɪtə^r/ *noun*
an instrument which helps us to know what the weather will be

barracks /'bærəks/ *plural noun*
buildings in which soldiers live

○ **barrel** /'bærəl/ *noun*
1 a large round container with flat ends
oil barrel
gun barrel
2 the long metal tube of a gun

barren /'bærən/ *adjective*
1 not able to have children or young ones, or having no fruit
2 so poor that crops cannot grow: *The desert is* **barren** *land.*

barrier /'bærɪə^r/ *noun*
a fence or wall: *The police put a* **barrier** *across the road.*

barrow /'bærəʊ/ *noun*
a small cart that is pushed or pulled by hand

○ **base** /beɪs/ *noun*
1 the bottom of something; the part something stands on: *A bottle has a flat* **base.**
2 the place where something starts: *That company has offices all over the world, but their* **base** *is in London.*

baseball /'beɪsbɔːl/ *noun*
(*no plural*)
a ball game played by two teams of nine players

○ **basin** /'beɪsn/ *noun*
1 a round wide open dish
2 a **washbasin**

basis /'beɪsɪs/ *noun* (*plural* **bases** /'beɪsiːz/)
the starting point or central idea of something: *What is the* **basis** *of your opinion?*

○ **basket** /'bɑːskɪt/ *noun*
a container made of thin bent wood used for carrying or holding things
baskets

○ **basketball** /'bɑːskɪtbɔːl/ *noun*
a game in which two teams try to throw a ball through a basket (=net)

ɔ **bat**[1] /bæt/ *noun*
a piece of wood used for hitting the ball in some games

bat[2] *verb* (*present participle* **batting,**
past **batted**)
to use or hit something with a bat

bat[3] *noun*
a small animal that flies at night

batch /bætʃ/ *noun*
a number of things together: *a*
batch *of cakes*

bath[1] /bɑːθ/ *noun* (*plural* **baths**
/bɑːðz, bɑːθs/)
a large water container in which
the whole body can be washed: *I*
have a bath (=wash in a bath)
every day.

bath[2] *verb* (*present participle*
bathing, /'bɑːθɪŋ/, *past* **bathed**
/bɑːθt/)
to wash oneself or someone else in
a bath: *I usually* **bath** *at night.*

○ **bathe** /beɪð/ *verb*
(*present participle* **bathing**
/'beɪðɪŋ/, *past* **bathed** /beɪðd/)
1 to put something in water; wash
in water: *to* **bathe** *a wound*
2 to swim in a river or the sea
'**bathing suit** *noun* what we
wear for bathing

bathroom /'bɑːθruːm/ *noun*
a room where people wash or have
a bath

batter /'bætər/ *verb*
to hit hard, again and again

battery
/'bætərɪ/
noun (*plural*
batteries)
a box that
produces or stores electricity: *Our*
car won't start because the **battery**
is flat (=worn out).

batteries

○ **battle**[1] /'bætl/ *noun*
a fight between people, ships or
aircraft

battle[2] *verb* (*present participle*
battling, *past* **battled**)
to fight

bay /beɪ/ *noun*
a part of
the shore
that curves
inwards

bay

bazaar /bə'zɑːr/
noun a market

B.C. /ˌbiː 'siː/
Before Christ, used in dates

○ **be** /bɪ; *strong* biː/ *verb*
present tense

singular	plural
I **am**	*We* **are**
You **are**	*You* **are**
He/She/It **is**	*They* **are**

past tense

singular	plural
I **was**	*We* **were**
You **were**	*You* **were**
He/She/It **was**	*They* **were**

present participle **being**
past participle **been**
1 (used to describe or give
information about people or
things and to join words for people
or things to the qualities or
position they have): *The sunflower*
is a beautiful flower. **Were** *you in*
the garden? My grandmother **was**
a cook. Please **be** *quick!*
2 (used to make some parts of
other verbs): *What* **are** *you* **doing?**
I **am painting** *a picture of a plane.*

beach /biːtʃ/ *noun* (*plural* **beaches**)
a shore covered in sand or stones
where people go to swim

bead /biːd/ *noun*
a small ball of glass or other
material, with a small hole for
string or wire to pass through: *She*
wore a string of **beads** *round her*
neck.

beak /biːk/ *noun*
the hard pointed mouth of a bird
(picture at **bird**)

beam

beam[1] /biːm/ *noun*
1 a large long heavy piece of wood etc., used in building
2 a line of light shining from some bright object

beam[2] *verb*
to smile brightly and happily

○ **bean** /biːn/ *noun*
the large seed, often used for food, of any **bean** plant: *We cook and eat* **green beans.** *We make coffee from* **coffee beans.**

bear[1] /beəʳ/ *noun*
a large and sometimes fierce animal with a thick coat (picture on page 17)

○ **bear**[2] /beəʳ/ *verb* (*past tense* **bore** /bɔːʳ/, *past participle* **borne** /bɔːn/)
1 to carry; support: *That won't* **bear** *your weight.*
2 to allow something to go on without complaining: *I can't* **bear** *that loud music!*
3 to have a child or young ones

beard /bɪəd/
noun
hair on a man's face below the mouth

moustache

beard

beast /biːst/ *noun*
1 an animal
2 an unkind or cruel person

○ **beat**[1] /biːt/ *verb* (*past tense* **beat**, *past participle* **beaten**)
1 to hit many times
2 to move regularly in time: *His heart* **beat** *fast after the race.*
3 to defeat; do better than: *We played the top class at football but we couldn't* **beat** *them.*

beat[2] *noun*
a single stroke or movement as part of a regular group: *a* **drumbeat**/*a* **heartbeat**

○ **beautiful** /ˈbjuːtɪfəl/ *adjective*
very good-looking; very pleasing: *What a* **beautiful** *day!*
beautifully /ˈbjuːtɪflɪ/ *adverb:* *The children danced* **beautifully.**

○ **beauty** /ˈbjuːtɪ/ *noun*
1 (*no plural*) being beautiful: *a flower of great* **beauty**
2 (*plural* **beauties**) something or someone beautiful

○ **because** /bɪˈkɒz/
for the reason that: *The roof is wet* **because** *it is raining.*

beckon /ˈbekən/ *verb*
to make a sign with a finger asking someone to come

○ **become** /bɪˈkʌm/ *verb* (*present participle* **becoming** /bɪˈkʌmɪŋ/, *past tense* **became** /bɪˈkeɪm/, *past participle* **become**)
1 to change or grow to be: *The prince* **became** *king when his father died.*
2 to happen to: *I haven't seen Simon for days; what's* **become of** *him?*

○ **bed** /bed/ *noun*
1 the thing we sleep on: *What time did you* **go to bed** *last night? You should* **make your bed** *before you go to school.*
2 the base or bottom of something: *There has been no rain for months, so the* **river bed** *is dry.*
bedclothes *plural noun* all the covers put on a bed
bedroom *noun* a room for sleeping in

○ **bee** /biː/ *noun*
a stinging, flying insect that makes **honey**

bee

beehive *or* **hive** *noun* a house, often a wooden box, made for bees to live in

beef /biːf/ *noun* (*no plural*)
the meat we get from cattle

been /biːn, bɪn/ see **be**

° **beer** /bɪəʳ/ *noun*
1 (*no plural*) an alcoholic drink
made from grain
2 a glass or bottle of this drink

beetle /'biːtl/ *noun*
an insect whose outside wings
make a hard cover for its body

° **before** /bɪ'fɔːʳ/
adverb, preposition
1 earlier than: *She was there* **before**
8 o'clock. I have seen you **before**
(=before this time), *but I can't
remember where.*
2 in front of
be'forehand *adverb* before
something happens: *She knew I
was coming because I telephoned
her* **beforehand.**

° **beg** /beg/ *verb* (*present participle*
begging, past begged)
1 to ask for money or food
2 to ask seriously: *I* **begged** *her not
to go.*
'beggar *noun* someone who
lives by begging

begin /bɪ'gɪn/ *verb*
(*present participle* **beginning,** *past
tense* **began** /bɪ'gæn/, *past
participle* **begun** /bɪ'gʌn/)
to start: *The film* **begins** *at two
o'clock. After running half a
kilometre, I* **began** *to feel tired.*
beginning *noun* the start

behalf /bɪ'hɑːf/ *noun*
instead of; for: *I have come* **on
behalf of** *my brother; he's ill. I
paid the money* **on your behalf**
(=for you).

° **behave** /bɪ'heɪv/ *noun*
to act in a good or bad way: *The
baby* **behaved** *very well last night;
he didn't cry at all. Please* **behave**
yourself (=behave properly)!

behaviour /bɪ'heɪvjəʳ/ *noun*
(*no plural*): *Everyone praises the
children's good* **behaviour.**

° **behind** /bɪ'haɪnd/
preposition, adverb
at the back (of): *He hangs his coat
on a nail* **behind** *the door. My
brother went in front and I walked*
behind (*him*).

being[1] /'biːɪŋ/ see **be**

° **being**[2] *noun*
a person: *Men, women, and
children are* **human beings.**

° **believe** /bɪ'liːv/ *verb*
(*present participle* **believing,** *past
believed)
1 to think someone is honest, right
or true: *Simon says he gave you
the money, and I* **believe** *him. The
soldiers all* **believe in** *their leader.*
2 to think something is true: *I*
believe *that he'll do what he said.*
belief /bɪ'liːf/ *noun* believing;
things we believe are right: *That
man has a strong* **belief** *in God.*

° **bell** /bel/ *noun*
a round,
hollow metal
object that
sounds when
it is struck

bells

bellow /'beləʊ/ *verb*
to make a loud, deep sound: *"Go
away!" he* **bellowed** *angrily.*

belly /'belɪ/ *noun* (*plural* **bellies**)
the stomach, especially of an
animal

° **belong** /bɪ'lɒŋ/ *verb*
1 to be one's own: *That book*
belongs *to me.*
2 to be a member of: *Do you*
belong *to the Scouts?*
belongings *plural noun* one's
own property

° **below** /bɪ'ləʊ/ *adverb, preposition*
at a lower place; lower than; under:

below

The children threw sticks from the bridge into the river **below**. *My brother is in the class* **below** *mine.*

○ **belt** /belt/ *noun*
a piece of cloth or leather, worn round the middle of the body: *I need a* **belt** *to keep up my trousers.*

bench /bentʃ/ *noun*
(*plural* **benches**)
1 a long wooden seat
2 a table at which someone works, in a factory or for woodwork

○ **bend**[1] /bend/ *verb*
(*past* **bent** /bent/)
1 to make into a curve: *He* **bent** *the wire.*
2 to bend

bend over

one's body: *She* **bent** (*over*) *to pick up a book from the floor.*

○ **bend**[2] *noun*
a curve: *a* **bend** *in the road*

○ **beneath** /bɪˈniːθ/ *preposition*
below; under: *Shall we rest in the shade* **beneath** *these trees?*

benefit[1] /ˈbenɪfɪt/ *noun*
help; advantage: *I did it for his* **benefit** (=to help him).

benefit[2] *verb*
to be useful or helpful to: *The plants* **benefited from** (=were helped by) *the rain.*

bent[1] /bent/ *adjective*
curved: *I can't draw a straight line; my ruler is* **bent.**

bent[2] see **bend**

○ **berry** /ˈberɪ/ *noun* (*plural* **berries**)
a small soft fruit

beside /bɪˈsaɪd/ *preposition*
at the side of: *"Come and sit* **beside** *me", he said.*

besides /bɪˈsaɪdz/ *adverb*
too; also: *I don't want to come out now, and* **besides**, *I must work.*

○ **best** /best/ *adjective, adverb, noun*
most good; most well; the most good thing: *This picture is* **the best** (*picture*) *you have painted.*

bet[1] /bet/ *verb* (*present participle* **betting,** *past* **bet** *or* **betted**)
to risk (money) on the result of a future event: *He* **bet** *me £1 that the school team would win.*

bet[2] *noun*
an agreement to bet or the money betted: *a* **bet** *of £1*

betray /bɪˈtreɪ/ *verb*
to be unfaithful; give away a secret or break a promise: *I asked you not to tell anyone, but you* **betrayed** *me. The expression on his face* **betrayed** *his feelings.*

○ **better** /ˈbetəʳ/ *adjective, adverb*
more good; in a way that is more good: *That song is* **better** *than the other one; I like it* **better**. *My father was ill, but he is* **better** (=not so ill) *now. You* **had better** (=ought to) *lock the door when you go out.*

○ **between** /bɪˈtwiːn/ *preposition*
1 (showing where): *There is a fence* **between** *his garden and our garden.*
2 (showing when): *Come* **between** *five and six o'clock.*
3 (showing how things are joined): *There is a railway* **between** *the two cities.*
4 (showing how things are divided): *She shared the oranges* **between** *the three children.*

beware /bɪˈweəʳ/ *verb*
(used to tell someone to be careful of something): **Beware of** *the dog!*

beyond /bɪˈjɒnd/
adverb, preposition
past; on the other side of; farther away: *My house is two kilometres* **beyond** *the school. From the top*

of that hill you can see the country **beyond**.

bib /bɪb/ *noun*
a piece of material that is tied under a child's chin to protect its clothes when it is eating

Bible /'baɪbl/ *noun*
the religious book of the Christian church
biblical /'bɪblɪkl/ *adjective: Joseph and Mary are* **biblical** *names.*

○ **bicycle** /'baɪsɪkl/ *or* **cycle** *or* **bike** /baɪk/ *noun*
a machine with two wheels for riding on

saddle handlebars
spokes
pedal
chain
bicycle

bid[1] /bɪd/ *noun*
an offer of an amount of money in order to buy something: *My uncle wants to sell his farm, and he has already had two large* **bids** *for it.*

bid[2] *verb (present participle* **bidding**, *past* **bid**)
to make an offer of money in order to buy something: *He* **bid** *ten pounds for the bicycle.*

○ **big** /bɪg/ *adjective (* **bigger, biggest**)
large in size, weight, number, importance, etc.: *How* **big** *is the school you go to? A cow is* **bigger** *than a goat.*

bill /bɪl/ *noun*
1 a piece of paper showing the amount you must pay for something: *How much was the* **bill** *for the electricity?*
2 a plan for a new law: *The government is considering the new education* **bill**.

billion /'bɪljən/ *noun, adjective*
the number 1,000,000,000,000 (=a million million), or especially in America 1,000,000,000 (=a thousand million)

billy goat /'bɪlɪ gəʊt/ *noun*
a male goat

bin /bɪn/ *noun*
a large container often with a lid, for bread, flour, coal, etc., or for waste: *Will you put these old newspapers in the* '**dustbin?**

bind /baɪnd/ *verb (past* **bound** /baʊnd/)
to tie with rope or string

binoculars /bɪ'nɒkjʊləz/ *plural noun*
a pair of special glasses to make things in the distance look bigger

binoculars

biography /baɪ'ɒgrəfɪ/ *noun (plural* **biographies**)
the story of a person's life

biology /baɪ'ɒlədʒɪ/ *noun (no plural)*
the scientific study of living things: *In* **biology** *we study plants and animals.* **biological** /ˌbaɪə'lɒdʒɪkl/ *adjective*
biologist /baɪ'ɒlədʒɪst/ *noun*
someone who studies biology

○ **bird** /bɜːd/ *noun*
an animal with wings and feathers (see) that lays eggs

wing
beak
bird tail
feathers

○ **birth** /bɜːθ/ *noun*
being born; being brought into the world: *My sister* **gave birth** *to a daughter yesterday.*

birthday /'bɜːθdeɪ/ *noun*
the day of the year on which a person was born

biscuit /'bɪskɪt/ *noun*
a dry thin cake, often sweet

bishop /'bɪʃəp/ *noun*
a Christian priest who looks after

churches in a large area

○ **bit** /bɪt/ *noun*

a small piece or amount: *He ate every* **bit** *of food. He dug the garden* **bit by bit** (=slowly, a little at a time).

○ **bite**[1] /baɪt/ *verb*

(*present participle* **biting** /'baɪtɪŋ/, *past tense* **bit** /bɪt/, *past participle* **bitten** /'bɪtn/)

to cut or wound with the teeth: *Jane's dog* **bit** *me. She was* **bitten** *by mosquitoes.*

○ **bite**[2] *noun*

1 an act of biting: *This apple's good; do you want a* **bite**?

2 a wound made by biting: *She was covered in insect* **bites**.

○ **bitter** /'bɪtəʳ/ *adjective*

1 having a sharp sour taste: **bitter** *fruit*

2 angry: *a* **bitter** *quarrel*

3 very cold: *a* **bitter** *wind*

○ **black**[1] /blæk/ *adjective*

1 (of) the darkest colour; of the colour of the words in this book: *At night the sky looks* **black**.

2 with dark-coloured skin: *Some of the children were* **black**, *the others were white.*

black[2] *noun*

1 (*no plural*) black colour: *He was dressed in* **black**.

2 a person with dark-coloured skin

blackboard /'blækbɔːd/ *noun*

the board that the teacher writes on

blacksmith /'blæk,smɪθ/ *noun*

a man who works with iron and makes shoes for horses

○ **blade** /bleɪd/
noun
1 the flat
cutting part
of anything
sharp

blades

2 a long flat leaf of grass or anything with such a shape

○ **blame**[1] /bleɪm/ *verb* (*present participle* **blaming**, *past* **blamed**)

to say that someone is the cause of something bad: *The policeman* **blamed** *the car driver for causing the accident.*

○ **blame**[2] *noun* (*no plural*)

the cause of something bad: *The car driver took the* **blame** *for the accident.*

blank /blæŋk/ *adjective*

1 without writing or other marks: *a* **blank** *piece of paper*

2 not showing any expression: *She looked at him with a* **blank** *face.*

blanket /'blæŋkɪt/ *noun*

a thick woollen cloth, used as a cover on a bed

blare /bleəʳ/ *verb* (*present participle* **blaring**, *past* **blared**)

to sound loudly and unpleasantly: *The radio was* **blaring**.

blast[1] /blɑːst/ *noun*

1 a sudden strong movement of wind or air: *There was a* **blast** *of wind as she opened the door.*

2 a sound made by instruments like a horn: *The driver gave a* **blast** *on his horn.*

blast[2] *verb*

1 to break something up by explosions: *They've* **blasted** *away the rock to build the new road.*

2 to begin a space flight: *The spaceship* **blasted off**.

blaze[1] /bleɪz/ *noun*

1 a very strong fire: *The fire burned slowly at first, but soon became a* **blaze**.

2 brightly shining light or colour: *The flowers were a* **blaze** *of colour.*

blaze[2] *verb* (*present participle* **blazing**, *past participle* **blazed**)

to burn strongly

bleach[1] /bliːtʃ/ *verb*
to make white: *Did you* **bleach** *this tablecloth? It looks very clean. Her hair was* **bleached** (=made lighter) *by the sun.*

bleach[2] *noun* (*no plural*)
something used for bleaching things, usually clothes

bleak /bliːk/ *adjective*
cold and unpleasant: *a* **bleak** *wind*

bleat /bliːt/ *verb*
to make the sound of a sheep, goat, etc. **bleat** *noun*

○ **bleed** /bliːd/ *verb*
(*past* **bled** /bled/)
to lose blood: *The cut on my arm* **bled** *for a long time.*

blend[1] /blend/ *verb*
1 to mix together: **Blend** *the sugar and eggs.*
2 to go well together: *When they sing, their voices* **blend** *nicely.*

blend[2] *noun*
a mixture produced by blending

bless /bles/ *verb* (*past tense* **blessed** /blest/)
to ask God's favour for something: *The holy man* **blessed** *the ship.*
blessing *noun* **1** asking or receiving God's help **2** something one is glad of: *His son is a great* **blessing** *to him.*

blew /bluː/ see **blow**

blind[1] /blaɪnd/
adjective
not able to see:
blind *in one eye*
blindness *noun*

blind

blind[2] *noun*
a piece of material which can be pulled down to cover a window

blindfold /ˈblaɪndfəʊld/ *verb*
to cover someone's eyes with material so that he or she cannot see

blink /blɪŋk/ *verb*
to shut and open the eyes quickly

blister /ˈblɪstər/ *noun*
a swelling under the skin, filled with liquid, usually caused by rubbing or burning

○ **block**[1] /blɒk/ *noun*
1 a solid mass or piece of wood, stone, etc.
2 a large building divided into separate parts: *an* **office block**
3 a building or group of buildings between two streets: *Turn left after two* **blocks.**
4 something that prevents movement: *The police put up a* **road block** *outside the city.*

○ **block**[2] *verb*
to prevent movement: *The police have* **blocked** *the road.*
blockage *noun: There's no water in the tap; perhaps there's a* **blockage** *in the pipe.*

blond *or* **blonde** /blɒnd/
noun, adjective
(a person) with light-coloured hair and skin

○ **blood** /blʌd/ *noun* (*no plural*)
the red liquid that flows round the body
blood vessel *noun* any of the tubes in the body that carry blood
bloody *adjective* (**bloodier, bloodiest**) covered with blood

bloom[1] /bluːm/ *noun*
a flower: *What beautiful* **blooms!**

bloom[2] *verb*
to have flowers: *These flowers* **bloom** *in the spring.*

blossom[1] /ˈblɒsəm/ *noun*
(*no plural*)
the flowers of a flowering tree

blossom[2] *verb*
to have flowers: *Those trees are* **blossoming.**

blot

blot[1] /blɒt/ *noun*
a dirty mark, such as that of ink on paper

blot[2] *verb* (*present participle* **blotting**, *past* **blotted**)
1 to make a blot on something: *He dropped his pen and* **blotted** *his book.*
2 to dry ink with special paper: *He* **blotted** *the page carefully with* **blotting paper.**

blouse /blaʊz/ *noun*
a loose garment for women, reaching from the neck to about the waist

blouse

○ **blow**[1] /bləʊ/ *verb* (*past tense* **blew** /bluː/, *past participle* **blown** /bləʊn/)
1 to move air; send air out quickly: *I* **blew** *the dust off the table.*
2 (of wind, air, etc.) to move: *The wind* **blew** *hard all night.*
3 to make air go into something: *He* **blew** *a whistle. She* **blew up** *the flat tyre of her bicycle with a pump.*
4 to break by exploding: *The soldiers* **blew up** *the bridge.*

○ **blow**[2] *noun*
1 a hard stroke with the hand or a weapon, etc.: *a* **blow** *on the head*
2 a shock: *It was a great* **blow** *to her when her mother died.*

○ **blue** /bluː/ *adjective, noun*
(of) the colour of the sky when there are no clouds: *The sea is* **blue.**

blunt /blʌnt/ *adjective*
not sharp: *a* **blunt** *knife*

blush /blʌʃ/ *verb*
to become red in the face, from shame or another cause

○ **board**[1] /bɔːd/ *noun*
1 a long thin flat piece of wood:

wooden **'floorboards**
2 a flat surface used for a special purpose: *Our teacher wrote on the* **'blackboard.** *Read the notices on the school* **'noticeboard.**
3 a group of people who have a special job, like running a company

on board *or* **aboard** *adverb* on or onto a ship or public vehicle: *We went* **on board** *the ship.*

board[2] *verb*
1 to cover with wooden boards: *He* **boarded up** *the broken window.*
2 to go on board: *He* **boarded** *the bus/plane/ship/train/taxi.*

'boarder *noun* a person who pays to live and eat in someone else's home

boast /bəʊst/ *verb*
to praise oneself: *He* **boasted** *that he could run very fast.*

○ **boat** /bəʊt/
noun
1 a small open ship: *a fishing* **boat**
2 any ship: *Are you going to America by* **boat** *or by plane?*

boats

bob /bɒb/ *verb* (*present participle* **bobbing**, *past* **bobbed**)
to move quickly up and down: *The small boat* **bobbed** *up and down on the lake.*

○ **body** /'bɒdɪ/ *noun* (*plural* **bodies**)
1 the whole of a person or animal, but not the mind
2 the central part, not the head, arms, or legs: *He had a cut on his leg and two more on his* **body.**
3 a dead person or animal
4 a group of people who do something together: *The town is controlled by a* **body** *called the Town Council.*

° **boil**¹ /bɔɪl/ *verb*

1 to become so hot, or make liquid so hot that it gives off steam

2 to cook food in boiling water: **Boil** *the eggs for five minutes.*

boil² *noun*

a painful swelling under the skin

bold /bəʊld/ *adjective*

brave; without fear: *By his* **bold** *actions, he saved the children from the fire.* **boldly** *adverb*

bolt¹ /bəʊlt/
noun

1 a piece of metal or wood used for keeping a door closed

2 a screw with no point

nut

bolts

bolt² *verb*

1 to fasten with a bolt: **Bolt** *the door, please.*

2 to run away suddenly: *The horse* **bolted** *and threw its rider to the ground.*

bomb¹ /bɒm/ *noun*

a container full of material that will explode

bomb² *verb*

to drop bombs on: *The airforce* **bombed** *two towns.*

  bomber /'bɒmər/ *noun* a plane built to carry and drop bombs

bond /bɒnd/ *noun*

1 a feeling, likeness, etc. that joins people together: *a* **bond** *of friendship*

2 a written promise, usually to pay money

° **bone** /bəʊn/ *noun*

one of the hard white parts in a person's or animal's body

bonfire /'bɒnfaɪər/ *noun*

a big fire made in the open air

bonnet /'bɒnɪt/ *noun*

1 a hat tied under the chin

2 the part of a car's body that covers the engine

° **book**¹ /bʊk/ *noun*

sheets of paper fastened together, for reading or writing: *You are reading a* **book** *now.*

  bookcase *noun* a piece of furniture for storing books

book² *verb*

to arrange something you want to do later: *We've* **booked** *seats for tomorrow's football match.*

boom /buːm/ *noun*

a loud hollow sound, like a big gun

boot /buːt/
noun

1 a shoe that covers the foot and ankle

2 the part of a car's body where bags, boxes, etc. can be carried

boot

boots

border /'bɔːdər/ *noun*

1 an edge: *a blue dress with a white* **border**

2 the dividing line between two countries

bore¹ /bɔːr/ *verb*
(*present participle* **boring**, *past* **bored**)

to make someone tired or uninterested, by something dull: *I'm* **bored** *with this job.*

  boredom *noun (no plural)* being bored

  boring *adjective: a* **boring** *job*

bore² *noun*

an uninteresting or dull person or thing

bore³ see **bear**

bore⁴ *verb (present participle* **boring**, *past* **bored**)

to make a round hole in something: *This machine can* **bore** *through solid rock.*

born

born /bɔːn/ *adjective*
given life: *The baby was born yesterday.*

borne /bɔːn/
see **bear**

borrow /ˈbɒrəʊ/ *verb*
to get the use of something which you are going to give back later: *I've left my pen at home; may I borrow yours?*

boss /bɒs/ *noun* (*plural* **bosses**)
someone who employs or controls people

bossy /ˈbɒsɪ/ *adjective*
(**bossier, bossiest**) liking to give orders: *a bossy little girl*

botany /ˈbɒtənɪ/ *noun (no plural)*
the scientific study of plants

botanical /bəˈtænɪkl/ *adjective*

'botanist *noun* a person who studies botany

both /bəʊθ/
this one and that one; the two: *Hold the dish with both hands. My brother and my sister both ran to help me.*

bother[1] /ˈbɒðər/ *verb*
to cause trouble to oneself or someone else: *He didn't bother to answer my letter. I'm sorry to bother you, but could you help me?*

bother[2] *noun* (*no plural*)
trouble or difficulty: *We had a little bother when the policeman stopped us.*

bottle[1] /ˈbɒtl/ *noun*
a tall round glass or plastic container, with a narrow neck: *a milk bottle*

bottle[2] *verb*
to put into a bottle: *This is where*

bottle   jar

they bottle the milk.

bottom /ˈbɒtəm/ *noun*
1 the lowest part or base of something: *The price is on the bottom of the box.*
2 the ground below the sea, etc.: *It sank to the bottom of the sea.*
3 the last part: *Go to the bottom of the street. My friend is at the bottom of* (=in the lowest position in) *the class.*
4 the part of the body that one sits on: *He fell on his bottom.*

bought /bɔːt/ see **buy**

boulder /ˈbəʊldər/ *noun*
a large rock

bounce /baʊns/ *verb* (*present participle* **bouncing,** *past* **bounced**)
1 to spring or jump back: *The baby was bouncing on the bed.*
2 to make something do this: *The children were bouncing a ball.*

bound[1] /baʊnd/ *adjective*
1 going towards: *This train is bound for the city.*
2 sure to: *If you work hard, you are bound to pass the exams.*

bound[2] see **bind**

bound[3] *verb*
to jump about: *The young animals were bounding about the field.*

bound[4] *noun*
a big jump

boundary /ˈbaʊndərɪ/ *noun* (*plural* **boundaries**)
the dividing line between two places: *Where is the boundary of the football field?*

bow[1] /baʊ/ *verb*
to bend the top part of the body forward to show respect: *Everyone bowed to the President.*

bow² /baʊ/ *noun*
an act of bowing: *a* **bow** *of respect*

bow³ /bəʊ/ *noun*
1 a piece of wood held in a curve by a string, used with an **arrow** as a weapon
2 a long thin piece of wood with tight strings fastened along it, used for playing musical instruments that have strings (picture at **violin**)
3 a knot used for ornament in the hair, for tying shoes, etc.: *She tied the ribbon* **in a bow.**

bowl /bəʊl/ *noun*
a deep round dish or container:

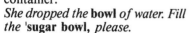
bowl

She dropped the **bowl** *of water. Fill the* '**sugar bowl,** *please.*

○ **box**¹ /bɒks/ *noun (plural* **boxes)**
a container with stiff straight sides, made from wood, cardboard, plastic, or metal: *a* **box** *of fruit*

box² *verb (past tense* **boxed)**
to fight with tightly closed hands: *Richard* **boxes** *well; he's the best* **boxer** *in our school.*
'**boxing** *noun (no plural)*

○ **boy** /bɔɪ/ *noun*
a male child: *They have five children: three* **boys** *and two girls.*

bracelet /'breɪslɪt/ *noun*
a band or chain worn

bracelets

round the wrist or arm

braces /'breɪsɪz/ *plural noun*
cloth bands worn over the shoulders to hold up trousers: *Have you* **a pair of braces,** *please?*

bracket¹ /'brækɪt/ *noun*
a piece of wood or metal put on a wall to support something: *We use* **brackets** *to hold up a shelf.*

bracket² *noun*
one of the signs ( ): *In the sentence "Do you want any (more) fruit?", (more) is* **in brackets.**

brag /bræg/ *verb*
(present participle **bragging,** *past* **bragged)**
to praise oneself: *He* **bragged** *that he had passed the exam easily.*

○ **brain** /breɪn/ *noun*
the part inside the head with which we think

brake¹ /breɪk/ *noun*
something for slowing down or stopping a bicycle, car, train, etc.

brake² *verb (present participle* **braking,** *past* **braked)**
to use brakes: *The driver* **braked** *quickly to avoid an accident.*

○ **branch**¹ /brɑːntʃ/ *noun*
(plural **branches)**
1 a part of a tree that grows from the main stem (picture at **tree**)
2 part of a business: *The company's head office is in the city, but it has* **branches** *all over the country.*

○ **branch**² *verb*
to divide into two parts: *Follow the road until it* **branches.**

brand¹ /brænd/ *noun*
1 the name of a particular kind of goods made by one company: *What* **brand** *of soap do you like?*
2 a mark, often made by burning, to show ownership: *These cattle have our* **brand** *on them.*
,**brand-**'**new** *adjective* unused: *His bike is* **brand-new.**

brand² *verb*
to put a brand on: *We've* **branded** *our cattle.*

○ **brass**¹ /brɑːs/ *noun (no plural)*
a very hard bright yellow metal, made by mixing copper (see) and zinc (see)

○ **brass**[2] *adjective*
made of brass: **brass** *ornaments*

○ **brave** /breɪv/ *adjective*
without fear, or not showing it: *a* **brave** *fireman* **bravely** *adverb* **bravery** /'breɪvərɪ/ *noun* (*no plural*): *The firemen showed great* **bravery.**

○ **bread** /bred/ *noun* (*no plural*)
a food made from flour, and baked: *a* **loaf of bread** (=a large baked piece of bread)

○ **breadth** /bretθ/ *noun* (*no plural*)
the distance from one side of something to the other; how broad something is: *What's the* **breadth** *of this river?*

○ **break**[1] /breɪk/ *verb* (*past tense* **broke** /brəʊk/, *past participle* **broken** /'brəʊkən/)
1 to cause to fall to pieces: *The stone* **broke** *the window.*
2 to fall to pieces: *The cup* **broke** *on the floor. Our lorry* **broke 'down** (=would not go further) *outside town. The thieves* **broke into** *the office* (= they broke something to get in) *and stole some money. Fire* **broke out** (=suddenly started) *in the kitchen. The police* **broke up** *the fighting crowd* (=they separated them and told them to go away).

break[2] *noun*
1 an opening made by breaking or being broken: *The sun shone through a* **break** *in the clouds.*
2 a short rest: *Let's have a* **break.**

○ **breakfast** /'brekfəst/ *noun*
the first meal of the day

breast /brest/ *noun*
1 one of the two parts on the front of a woman's body that can give milk
2 the top part of the front of the body

○ **breath** /breθ/ *noun*
air taken into and let out from the body: *He took a deep* **breath** *and jumped into the water. How long can you* **hold your breath** (=stop breathing)?
'breathless *adjective* breathing quickly, because of excitement or exercise

○ **breathe** /briːð/ *verb* (*present participle* **breathing**, *past* **breathed**)
to take air into the body and let it out

○ **breed**[1] /briːd/ *verb* (*past* **bred** /bred/)
1 to produce young: *Some animals will not* **breed** *in cages.*
2 to keep animals so that they will produce young ones: *He* **breeds** *cattle.*

breed[2] *noun*
a type of animal: *a* **breed** *of cattle*

breeze /briːz/ *noun*
a light wind

brew /bruː/ *verb*
1 to make drinks such as tea, coffee, or beer
2 to be going to happen: *I think a storm is* **brewing.**
brewery /'bruːərɪ/ *noun* (*plural* **breweries**) a place where beer is made

bribe[1] /braɪb/ *verb* (*present participle* **bribing**, *past* **bribed**)
to offer or give someone money or a present, so that he will do wrong to help you: *He tried to* **bribe** *the policeman to let him go.*

bribe[2] *noun*
something given in bribing: *A policeman should never* **take bribes. bribery** /'braɪbərɪ/ *noun* (*no plural*)

brick /brɪk/ *noun*
1 a block of baked clay, used in building

2 (*no plural*)
bricks as
material: *a*
house built
of **brick**

bricks

bride /braɪd/ *noun*
a woman who is going to be married, or who has just been married
    bridal /'braɪdl/ *adjective* of a bride or wedding
    bridesmaid /'braɪdz,meɪd/ *noun*
a girl or woman who helps a bride at her wedding

bridegroom /'braɪdgruːm/ *or* **groom** /gruːm/ *noun*
a man who is going to be married, or who has just been married

bridge /brɪdʒ/
noun
a thing that
carries a road,
railway, path,
etc. over
something: *a*
bridge *across*
the river

bridges

bridle /'braɪdl/ *noun*
leather bands put on a horse's head for controlling it

brief /briːf/ *adjective*
lasting a short time: *The meeting was very* **brief.**
    briefly *adverb*: *to explain* **briefly**

briefcase /'briːfkeɪs/ *noun*
a thin flat case for papers or books

○ **bright** /braɪt/ *adjective*
1 sending out light: *The sun was very* **bright.**
2 having a clear colour; not dull: *a* **bright** *yellow dress*
3 clever: *a* **bright** *pupil*

brilliant /'brɪljənt/ *adjective*
1 very bright; shining brightly: *a* **brilliant** *colour*
2 very clever: *a* **brilliant** *student*

brim /brɪm/ *noun*
1 the edge of a cup, glass, or bowl
2 the part of a hat that stands out sideways

○ **bring** /brɪŋ/ *verb* (*past* **brought** /brɔːt/)
to carry something, or go with someone, to the speaker: *Has anyone* **brought** *a ball to school today? If you take that book home,* **bring** *it* **back** *tomorrow.*
    bring up *verb* to care for and educate children until they are grown-up

brisk /brɪsk/ *adjective*
quick and active: *a* **brisk** *walk*

brittle /'brɪtl/ *adjective*
hard, but easily broken: *Glass is a* **brittle** *material.*

○ **broad** /brɔːd/ *adjective*
wide: **broad** *shoulders*

broadcast[1] /'brɔːdkɑːst/ *verb* (*past* **broadcast**)
to send out by radio or television to the public
    broadcaster *noun* someone who speaks on radio or television

broadcast[2] *noun, adjective*
something that is broadcast: *The news* **broadcast** *will be at 9.00.*

broke /brəʊk/ see **break**

broken /'brəʊkən/ *adjective*
1 in pieces: *a* **broken** *window*
2 not working: *a* **broken** *clock*

bronze /brɒnz/ *noun* (*no plural*)
a hard metal, made by mixing copper (see) and tin (see)

brooch /brəʊtʃ/ *noun* (*plural* **brooches**)
an ornament that is pinned on clothes

brood[1] /bruːd/ *noun*
a family of young birds

brood[2] *verb*
to think deeply and sadly about

brook /brʊk/
noun a small
stream

broom /bruːm/
noun
a brush with a
long handle

broom

○**brother** /ˈbrʌðəʳ/ *noun*
a boy or man with the same
parents as another person: *Peter is
Mary's* **brother.**

'**brother-in-ˌlaw** *noun* (*plural*
brothers-in-law) the brother of
your wife or husband, or the
husband of your sister

brought /brɔːt/ see **bring**

brow /braʊ/ *noun*
the part of the face between the
eyes and the hair

○**brown** /braʊn/ *adjective, noun*
(of) a dark colour like coffee or
earth: **brown** *eyes*

bruise[1] /bruːz/ *noun*
a mark left on the skin when it has
been hit

bruise[2] *verb* (*present participle*
bruising, *past* **bruised**)
to mark with a bruise: *She fell and*
bruised *her knee.*

○**brush**[1] /brʌʃ/
noun (*plural*
brushes)
an instrument
with a handle
made of
sticks, stiff hair, etc. for cleaning
or painting or tidying

brushes

○**brush**[2] *verb*
to clean or tidy with a brush: *Have
you* **brushed** *your hair?*

brute /bruːt/ *noun*
an animal; a cruel person who acts
like an animal

brutal /ˈbruːtl/ *adjective: a*
brutal *criminal* **brutally** *adverb*

bubble[1] /ˈbʌbl/ *noun*
a hollow ball of liquid containing
air or gas: *You can see* **bubbles** *in
soapy water.*

bubble[2] *verb* (*present participle*
bubbling /ˈbʌblɪŋ/ *past* **bubbled**
/ˈbʌbld/)
to make bubbles: *The water was*
bubbling *gently in the pan.*

buck /bʌk/ *noun*
a male deer (see) or rabbit (see)

○**bucket** /ˈbʌkɪt/ *or* **pail** /peɪl/ *noun*
a container made of metal or
plastic, with a handle, for holding
or carrying water etc.

buckle /ˈbʌkl/ *noun*
a fastener, used for joining the
ends of a belt

bud /bʌd/ *noun*
a young leaf or flower before it
opens (picture at **flower**)

budge /bʌdʒ/ *verb* (*present
participle* **budging**, *past* **budged**)
to make something heavy move a
little: *I can't* **budge** *this rock.*

budget /ˈbʌdʒɪt/ *noun*
a plan of how to spend money: *a
government's* **budget**

bug /bʌg/ *noun*
an insect that drinks juices from
plants or animals

bugle /ˈbjuːgl/ *noun*
a musical instrument like a horn

○**build** /bɪld/ *verb* (*past* **built** /bɪlt/)
to make something by putting
pieces together: *That house is* **built**
of brick.

'**building** *noun* something with a
roof and walls that has been built
to stay in one place: *The new
hospital is a
big* **building.**

bulb /bʌlb/ *noun*
1 a round part
of some

bulbs

plants, from which they grow

2 any object of this shape, especially the part of an electric lamp that gives out the light

bulge[1] /bʌldʒ/ verb (*present participle* **bulging,** *past* **bulged**)
to swell outwards: *His pocket was* **bulging** *with sweets.*

bulge[2] *noun*
a swelling shape

bull /bʊl/ *noun*
the male form of cattle and some other animals
bullock *noun: A* **bullock** *is a young bull which is unable to be the father of young ones.*

bulldozer /ˈbʊldəʊzəʳ/ *noun*
a powerful machine that moves earth to make land flat

bullet /ˈbʊlɪt/ *noun*
a piece of metal that is fired from a gun

bully[1] /ˈbʊlɪ/ *noun* (*plural* **bullies**)
a person who likes to hurt weaker people or make them afraid

bully[2] *verb* (*present participle* **bullying,** *past* **bullied**)
to act like a bully to someone: *He's always* **bullying** *smaller boys.*

bump[1] /bʌmp/ *verb*
to knock (against): *I* **bumped** *my head on a low branch.*

bump[2] *noun*
1 a sudden blow: *a* **bump** *on the head*
2 a raised round swelling on the body where it has been hit

bumper *noun*
a metal bar at the front or back of a car etc. to protect the body if it bumps something

bumper

bun /bʌn/ *noun*
a small round sweet cake

bunch /bʌntʃ/ *noun*
(*plural* **bunches**)
several things of the same kind fastened together: *a* **bunch** *of flowers*

bundle /ˈbʌndl/ *noun*
a number of things tied or held together: *a* **bundle** *of clothes*

bungalow /ˈbʌŋɡələʊ/ *noun*
a house that has only a ground floor

bunk /bʌŋk/ *noun*
a narrow bed which is sometimes fixed to the wall, often put one on top of another, to save space

buoy /bɔɪ/
noun
a floating object used to show ships where there are rocks

buoy

burden /ˈbɜːdn/ *noun*
something heavy that is carried: *He could not carry the* **burden** *alone.*

burglar /ˈbɜːɡləʳ/ *noun*
a person who breaks into buildings to steal things
burglary *noun*
(*plural* **burglaries**): *The police were asking questions about the* **burglaries** *in our village.*

°**burn**[1] /bɜːn/ *verb* (*past* **burned** /bɜːnd/ *or* **burnt** /bɜːnt/)
1 to be on fire: *The house is* **burning** — *help!*
2 to set on fire: *We* **burnt** *the old furniture.*
3 to harm or destroy by fire: *How did you* **burn** *your fingers? The building* **burned down** (= nothing was left).

°**burn**[2] *noun*
a wound or mark caused by burning: *a* **burn** *on his arm*

burrow /'bʌrəʊ/ *noun*
a hole in the ground made as a
home by some small animals

° **burst**[1] /bɜːst/ *verb* (*past* **burst**)
1 to break because of force inside:
*You'll **burst** that bag if you put any
more things in it.*
2 to do something suddenly: *He
burst into the room. She **burst** into
tears* (=began to cry suddenly).

° **burst**[2] *noun*
something which happens
suddenly: *a **burst** of laughter*

bury /'berɪ/ *verb*
(*present participle* **burying**, *past*
buried /'berɪd/)
1 to put a dead person into the
ground
2 to put or hide something in the
ground: *The dog **buried** the bone.*
burial /'berɪəl/ *noun* the
ceremony of burying a dead
person

° **bus** /bʌs/
noun (*plural*
buses)
a large car
that carries
people for a small payment

bus

'**bus stop** *noun*
a place where buses stop for people
to get on and off

° **bush** /bʊʃ/ *noun*
1 (*plural* **bushes**) a small tree
2 (*no plural*) wild country that has
not been cleared

° **business** /'bɪznɪs/ *noun*
1 (*no plural*) trading: **Business** *has
been bad this year.*
2 (*plural* **businesses**) an activity
that earns money; a place for
trade: *He has a **business** in the
town.*
3 (*no plural*) what is important to
you: *Please leave me alone and
mind your own business* (=look

after your own things). *It's **none of
your business*** (=nothing to do
with you).
businessman *noun* (*plural*
businessmen) someone whose
work is trading

° **busy** /'bɪzɪ/ *adjective* (**busier,
busiest**)
working; not free; having a lot to
do: *He is **busy** now. He's **busy**
writing letters.* **busily** *adverb*

° **but** /bət; *strong* bʌt/
and yet; although it is true, it is
also true that: *On the mountain it
was sunny **but** it was cold.*

butcher /'bʊtʃər/ *noun*
a person who kills animals for
food and sells meat

butter /'bʌtər/ *noun* (*no plural*)
yellow fat made from milk: *Do
you want some **butter** on your
bread?*

butterfly
/'bʌtəflaɪ/ *noun*
(*plural* **butterflies**)
an insect that
has four wings with bright colours
and patterns on them

butterfly

° **button** /'bʌtn/ *noun*
1 a small round object which is
pushed through a hole to fasten
clothes
2 a round object which is pushed
to start or stop something
'**buttonhole** *noun* the hole that a
button goes through

° **buy** /baɪ/ *verb*
(*past* **bought** /bɔːt/)
to get something by giving money
for it: *I **bought** a new radio.*

buzz /bʌz/ *verb*
to make a low steady noise like a
bee (see) makes
buzzer *noun* an electric
instrument that makes a buzzing
noise

by /baɪ/ *preposition, adverb*
  1 near; beside: *a table* **by** *the bed*
  2 through; by way of: *Did you come* **by** *train?*
  3 before: *Please do it* **by** *tomorrow.*
  4 past: *He walked* **by** *me without seeing me.*
  5 (to show who or what does something): *We were woken* **by** *a loud noise. This story is* **by** *a famous writer.*
  6 (to show how or with what): *I mended the door* **by** *putting a nail in it. He took me* **by** *the hand.*

Cc

cab /kæb/ *noun*
  1 a taxi
  2 the part of a lorry where the driver sits

cabbage /ˈkæbɪdʒ/ *noun*
  a vegetable with many large green leaves

cabin /ˈkæbɪn/ *noun*
  1 a room on a ship or aeroplane
  2 a small wooden house

cabinet /ˈkæbɪnɪt/ *noun*
  1 a cupboard: *a medicine* **cabinet**
  2 the people in a government who have the most power

cable /ˈkeɪbl/ *noun*
  1 a thick rope
  2 wires that carry electricity or telephone calls
  3 a message sent by cable

cackle /ˈkækl/ *verb* (*present participle* **cackling**, *past* **cackled**)
  to make a noise like a hen

cactus /ˈkæktəs/ *noun* (*plural* **cacti** *or* **cactuses**) a prickly plant with thick stems that grows in hot dry places

cacti

cafe /ˈkæfeɪ/ *noun*
  a place where you can buy drinks and simple meals

cage /keɪdʒ/ *noun*
  a box with metal bars where birds or animals are kept

cake /keɪk/ *noun*
  a sweet cooked food made of flour, fat, and eggs: *to bake a* **cake**

calculate /ˈkælkjʊleɪt/ *verb* (*present participle* **calculating**, *past* **calculated**)
  to use numbers to find the answer to a sum: *Have you* **calculated** *the cost of the journey?*
  calculation *noun*

calendar /ˈkæləndəʳ/ *noun*
  a list of days, weeks, and months of the year

calf[1] /kɑːf/ *noun* (*plural* **calves** /kɑːvz/)
  the young form of cattle and some other animals

calf[2] *noun*
  the part of the leg between the knee and the ankle (picture on page 133)

call[1] /kɔːl/ *verb*
  1 to name: *They* **called** *him John.*
  2 to shout: *to* **call** *for help*

3 to visit: *He* **called on** *me last Tuesday.*

4 to telephone: *I* **called** *my sister today.*

5 to ask to come: *Mother* **called** *the doctor.*

○ **call²** *noun*

1 a shout: *a* **call** *for help*

2 a visit: *a* **call** *from the doctor*

3 the act of talking to someone on the telephone: *There's a* **call** *for you, Mr Brown.*

○ **calm** /kɑːm/ *adjective*

quiet; peaceful: *The sea was* **calm** *after the storm. He was* **calm** *when I told him the bad news.*

calmly *adverb*

came /keɪm/ see **come**

camel /'kæml/ *noun*

a large animal with one or two humps (see) on its back used to carry things and people in deserts (picture on page 17)

○ **camera** /'kæmrə/ *noun*

cameras

an instrument for taking photographs

camouflage¹ /'kæməflɑːʒ/ *noun* (*no plural*)

special clothes or colours which make a person or animal seem to be part of the surroundings: *The soldier fixed leaves to his green clothes as* **camouflage** *in the forest.*

camouflage² *verb*

(*present participle* **camouflaging**, *past* **camouflaged**)

to hide by using camouflage

camp¹ /kæmp/ *noun*

a place with tents or huts where people live for a time

camp² *verb*

to live in a camp

camping *noun* (*no plural*): *The children liked* **camping.**

campaign /kæm'peɪn/ *noun*

1 battles and movements of soldiers in a war

2 a plan to get a result: *a* **campaign** *to stop people smoking*

○ **can¹** /kən; *strong* kæn/ *verb*

to know how to; be able to: **Can** *she swim? No, she* **can't** (= can not). *She* **cannot** (= can not) *swim.*

can² /kæn/ *or* **tin** *noun*

a container made of metal: *Food in* **cans** *is called* **canned** *food.*

canal /kə'næl/ *noun*

a man-made river: *The* **canals** *take water to the rice fields.*

canary /kə'neərɪ/ *noun* (*plural* **canaries**)

a small yellow bird with a sweet song

cancel /'kænsl/ *verb*

(*present participle* **cancelling**, *past* **cancelled**)

to stop some planned event: *We had to* **cancel** *the match, because so many people were ill.*

cancer /'kænsəʳ/ *noun*

a serious illness in which a growth (see) spreads in the body

candidate /'kændɪdət/ *noun*

1 a person who hopes to be chosen for something

2 a person who takes an examination

candle /'kændl/ *noun*

a long piece of wax (see) with a string in the middle which burns to give light

cane¹ /keɪn/ *noun*

a hollow stick from some plants like sugar

cane² *verb* (*present participle* **caning**, *past* **caned**)

to hit with a cane

cannon /'kænən/ *noun*
a large gun

cannot /'kænət, 'kænɒt/ see **can**

canoe /kə'nuː/
noun
a narrow,
light
boat

canoes

can't
/kɑːnt/ see **can**

canteen /kæn'tiːn/ *noun*
a place where people in a factory,
school, or office can eat meals

canvas /'kænvəs/ *noun (no plural)*
strong cloth used to make tents,
bags, etc.

cap /kæp/ *noun*
1 a soft hat
2 the covering for the end of a
bottle or tube

capable /'keɪpəbl/ *adjective*
able to do something: *Are you*
capable of *climbing that tree? She*
is my most **capable** (= cleverest)
student.

capacity /kə'pæsəti/ *noun*
1 the amount something can
contain: *That bowl has a* **capacity**
of two pints.
2 ability: *Paul has a great* **capacity**
for working hard.

cape /keɪp/ *noun*
1 a high piece of land which goes
out into the sea
2 a covering for the shoulders and
arms

° **capital** /'kæpɪtl/ *noun*
1 the chief city of a country, where
the government is
2 a large letter: *A, D, H are* **capital**
letters; *a, d, h are small letters.*
Write your name in **capitals.**

° **captain** /'kæptɪn/ *noun*
1 the person who controls a ship
or aircraft

2 an officer in the army or the navy
(see)

3 the leader of a team or group

captive /'kæptɪv/ *noun*
a prisoner
cap'tivity *noun (no plural)*:
They were in **captivity**
(=prisoners) *for a week.*

capture /'kæptʃəʳ/ *verb*
(*present participle* **capturing,**
past **captured**)
to take as a prisoner

° **car** /kɑːʳ/
noun
a vehicle on
wheels,
driven by an
engine, that you can travel in

car

'**car park** *noun* a place where
cars can be left

caravan /'kærəvæn/ *noun*
a little house on wheels that can be
pulled by a car

carbon /'kɑːbən/ *noun (no plural)*
a chemical found in coal, and in
all living things

carcass /'kɑːkəs/ *noun*
(*plural* **carcasses**)
the dead body of an animal or bird

° **card** /kɑːd/ *noun*
a piece of stiff thick paper: *A*
'**playing card** *has signs and*
numbers on it and is used with
others in games. A '**Christmas**
card *has a picture and a message*
on it, and is sent at Christmas.

° **cardboard** /'kɑːdbɔːd/ *noun (no*
plural)
stiff thick paper used for making
boxes, book covers, etc.

cardigan
/'kɑːdɪgən/
noun
a short
woollen coat usually
worn over a shirt

cardigan

cardinal /'kɑːdɪnl/ *noun*
an important priest of the Roman Catholic (see) church

° **care**[1] /keə^r/ *verb* (*present participle* **caring**, *past* **cared**)
1 to feel interest or worry: *Does she* **care about** *her work?*
2 to look after: *His son* **cared for** *him when he was ill.*
3 to like or love: *She* **cares for** *him very much.*

° **care**[2] *noun*
1 (*no plural*) the act of looking after a person or thing: **Take care of** *your brother while I am away.*
2 (*no plural*) thought: *When you are crossing the road,* **take care!**
3 something that makes you sad: *He was worried by all the* **cares** *of the family.*
'**careful** *adjective*: *Be* **careful** *when you cross the road.*
'**careless** *adjective*: **Careless** *driving causes accidents.*

cargo /'kɑːgəʊ/ *noun*
(*plural* **cargoes**)
something carried on a ship or in an aeroplane: *a* **cargo** *of cotton/of oil*

carpentry /'kɑːpəntrɪ/ *noun* (*no plural*)
the art of making things out of wood
carpenter /'kɑːpəntə^r/ *noun* a person who does carpentry as a job

carpet /'kɑːpɪt/ *noun*
a large mat used to cover the floor

carriage /'kærɪdʒ/ *noun*
1 one of the parts of a train, where people sit
2 a vehicle pulled by horses instead of a motor

carrot /'kærət/ *noun*
a vegetable with a long orange or red root

° **carry** /'kærɪ/ *verb* (*present participle* **carrying**, *past* **carried**)
1 to take something somewhere: *He* **carried** *the food to the table.*
2 (used in sentences like these): **Carry on** (= go on) *reading! I have* **carried out** (= done) *my work.*
carrier /'kærɪə^r/ *or* **carrier bag** *noun* a large paper or plastic bag with handles

° **cart** /kɑːt/ *noun*
a wooden vehicle, pulled by horses or oxen, and used for carrying goods

carton /'kɑːtn/ *noun*
a cardboard box for holding goods: *a* **carton** *of eggs*

carve /kɑːv/ *verb* (*present participle* **carving**, *past* **carved**)
1 to cut wood or stone into shapes: *He* **carved** *the figure of a woman from a piece of wood.*
2 to cut meat into pieces: *She* **carved** *the chicken.*

° **case**[1] /keɪs/ *noun*
1 something that is true or has happened: *It's raining!* **In that case,** *put on your coat before you go. Take a hat with you* **in case** (= because it might happen that) *the sun is very hot.*
2 (the facts about) a question that is decided in a court (see) of law: *a difficult* **case** *to prove*
3 one example of an illness: *There are three* **cases** *of fever in school.*

case[2] *noun*
a box or bag for carrying or covering things: *He took a* **case** *full of clothes with him.*

cash[1] /kæʃ/ *noun* (*no plural*)
coins and paper money: *Have you any* **cash?**

cash[2] *verb*
to get cash in return for a cheque

(see): I **cashed** *a cheque at the bank.*

cashier /kæ'ʃɪəʳ/ *noun: A* **cashier** *takes and gives out money in a bank or shop.*

cassette /kə'set/ *noun* a small plastic container cassette recorder holding tape (see) that plays music when fitted into a **cassette recorder** or tape recorder (see)

cast /kɑːst/ *noun* the people acting in a play: *He was in the* **cast** *of the school play.*

castle /'kɑːsl/ *noun* a large strong building made so that no one can attack the people inside

casual /'kæʒʊəl/ *adjective* 1 not planned or arranged: *a* **casual** *meeting* 2 not used for a special time or place: *He was wearing* **casual** *clothes, not his school ones.* **casually** *adverb*

○ **cat** /kæt/ *noun* 1 a small animal often kept in houses to catch mice (see) cat 2 any of the larger wild animals that are like the house cat: *Lions and leopards are some of the big cats.*

catalogue /'kætəlɒg/ *noun* a list of something in a special order: *a* **catalogue** *of all the books in the library*

○ **catch**[1] /kætʃ/ *verb* (*past* **caught** /kɔːt/) 1 to get in the hand and hold: *She threw the ball and I* **caught** *it.* 2 to run after and take hold of: *We ran after the dog and* **caught** *it.* 3 to get: *I* **caught** *the train. She* **caught** *a cold. I walked fast but I couldn't* **catch up** *with you* (= couldn't get to where you were).

catch[2] *noun* (*plural* **catches**) 1 a metal fastener for a window or door 2 something that is caught

category /'kætɪgərɪ/ *noun* (*plural* **categories**) a sort: *There are different* **categories** *of books in a library.*

caterpillar /'kætə,pɪləʳ/ *noun* the young form of a caterpillar butterfly (see) or moth (see), which is like a worm with short legs

cathedral /kə'θiːdrəl/ *noun* the chief church in a city

Catholic /'kæθəlɪk/ *or* **Roman Catholic** /'rəʊmən ~ / *noun, adjective* (a Christian) belonging to the church whose head is the Pope

○ **cattle** /'kætl/ *plural noun* large animals kept for meat, milk, and skins

cauliflower /'kɒlɪ,flaʊəʳ/ *noun* a vegetable with a hard white flower

○ **cause**[1] /kɔːz/ *verb* (*present participle* **causing**, *past* **caused**) to make something happen; be the reason: *The heavy rain* **caused** *the flood.*

○ **cause**[2] *noun* 1 a person or thing that makes something happen; a reason: *The heavy rain was the* **cause** *of the flood.* 2 something you believe in or care about: *They were all fighting for the same* **cause**.

caution /'kɔːʃn/ *noun* (*no plural*)
great care: *Drive with* **caution.**
cautious /'kɔːʃəs/ *adjective: He
was* **cautious** *when he was riding
the bicycle.* **cautiously** *adverb*

cave /keɪv/ *noun*
a hollow place under the ground or
in the side of a mountain or rock

cease /siːs/ *verb* (*present
participle* **ceasing,** *past* **ceased**)
to stop: *Her mother never* **ceases**
telling you about her troubles.
'ceaseless *adjective: The*
ceaseless *rain was bad for the
crops.* **ceaselessly** *adverb*

ceiling /'siːlɪŋ/ *noun*
the inside of the roof of a room

celebrate /'selɪbreɪt/ *verb* (*present
participle* **celebrating,** *past*
celebrated)
to show you are happy about a
special event, especially by having
a party or feast
ˌcele'bration *noun: There was a
great* **celebration** *when the baby
was born.*

cell /sel/ *noun*
1 a small room in which a prisoner
lives
2 a very small piece of living
substance: *We lose a few skin* **cells**
every time we wash our hands.

cellar /'selər/ *noun*
a room under the ground in a
house

cement /sɪ'ment/ *noun* (*no plural*)
a powder which becomes hard like
stone when mixed with water; it is
used in building

cemetery /'semɪtrɪ/ *noun*
(*plural* **cemeteries**)
an area of ground where dead
bodies are put under the earth

census /'sensəs/ *noun*
(*plural* **censuses**)
a count of the people in a country

cent /sent/ *noun*
a small coin used in some
countries

centigrade /'sentɪgreɪd/ *noun*
(*no plural*)
a way of measuring temperature
(= how hot something is): *In the
summer, the temperature is
sometimes forty* **degrees centigrade
(40°C).**

centimetre /'sentɪˌmiːtər/ *noun*
a measure of length: *There are a
hundred* **centimetres** *in a metre.*
cm *is a short way of writing*
centimetre.

° **centre** /'sentər/ *noun*
1 the middle: *We went into the
town* **centre.**
2 a place where a lot of people
come with a special purpose: *The
doctors worked at the Health*
Centre. *Have you seen the new
shopping* **centre?**
central /'sentrəl/ *adjective* in
the middle

century /'sentʃərɪ/ *noun*
(*plural* **centuries**)
(a period of) one hundred years: *It
was built in the 19th* **century.**

cereal /'sɪərɪəl/ *noun*
a crop such as wheat, rice, and
maize, used as a food

° **ceremony** /'serɪmənɪ/ *noun*
(*plural* **ceremonies**)
a number of things done at a
special happening: *The marriage*
ceremony *took place in the church.*

certain¹ /'sɜːtn/ *adjective*
sure: *I am* **certain** *he told me to
come at two o'clock.*
certainly *adverb: Will you help
me please?* **Certainly!** (= Of
course!)

certain² *adjective*
some: *People who smoke cannot
travel in* **certain** *parts of the train.*

certificate /sə'tɪfɪkət/ *noun*
a written paper saying something
important: *Your* 'birth certificate
tells people when you were born.

chain[1] /tʃeɪn/ *noun*
a number of metal rings joined
together: *She wore a gold* **chain**
around her neck.

chain[2] *verb*
to tie with a
chain: *The
dog was*
chained (up)
to the wall.

chain

○ **chair** /tʃeəʳ/ *noun*
a piece of furniture you sit on, with
four legs and a back

chairman /'tʃeəmən/ (*plural* **chair-
men** /-mən/) *or* 'chair,woman
(*plural* 'chair,women) *or*
'chair,person (*plural*
'chair,persons) *noun*
a person who controls a meeting

○ **chalk** /tʃɔːk/ *noun*
1 (*no plural*) a soft white substance
2 a piece of this substance used for
writing on a blackboard

challenge[1] /'tʃælɪndʒ/ *verb*
(*present participle* **challenging,**
past **challenged**)
1 to offer to fight or play a game
against: *Their school* **challenged**
ours to a football match.
2 to test or question: *I did not
think he was right, so I* **challenged**
him.

challenge[2] *noun*
1 an offer to fight or play against
someone
2 a test of ability: *This
examination is a real* **challenge.**

champion /'tʃæmpɪən/ *noun*
someone who is the best at
something
championship *noun* a competition to find who is the best at

something: *Our team won the
swimming* **championships.**

○ **chance** /tʃɑːns/ *noun*
1 something unexpected: *I met him*
by chance.
2 something which may happen:
There is a **chance** *that I will be
chosen for the team.*
3 a time when something may be
done: *I haven't had a* **chance** *to
read my letter.*
4 a risk: *He is* **taking a chance** *by
driving his car so fast.*

○ **change**[1] /tʃeɪndʒ/ *verb* (*present
participle* **changing,** *past* **changed**)
1 to become or make different:
This town has **changed** *since I was
a child. You said you were going
to the supermarket; won't you
change your mind and stay here?*
2 to take or put something in the
place of something else: *She took
the dress back to the shop and
changed it (for another).*
3 to put on different clothes: *He
changed when he arrived home
from school.*

○ **change**[2] *noun*
1 something that has become
different: *You will see many
changes in the village since last
year.*
2 (*no plural*) money you get back
when you give too much for
something: *I gave him a pound,
and he gave me 20 pence* **change.**

channel[1] /'tʃænl/ *noun*
a narrow piece of flowing water:
The English **Channel** *is between
France and England. They cut a*
channel *from the river to bring
water to the field.*

channel[2] *verb* (*present participle*
channelling, *past* **channelled**)
to make flow in one direction:
They **channelled** *the water towards
the field.*

chant[1] /tʃɑːnt/ *verb*
to say in a singing way: *He chanted a prayer. The crowd chanted "We want jobs!"*

chant[2] *noun*
words said in this way

chapel /'tʃæpl/ *noun*
a small church, or part of a church

chapter /'tʃæptər/ *noun*
part of a book: *Open your books at* **Chapter 3.**

° **character** /'kærəktər/ *noun*
1 what a person or thing is like: *He has a strong but gentle* **character.** *The new buildings have changed the* **character** *of the village.*
2 a person in a book, film, or play
,**characte'ristic** *noun* something that is typical of someone or something: *Kindness is one of his* **characteristics.**

charcoal /'tʃɑːkəul/ *noun* (*no plural*)
wood made black by slow heating under earth and used for burning

charge[1] /tʃɑːdʒ/ *verb* (*present participle* **charging,** *past* **charged**)
1 to ask money for: *The fruit seller* **charged** *me too much money.*
2 to say that a person has done something wrong: *He was* **charged with** *stealing a car.*
3 to run or hurry: *The little boy* **charged** *into the room.*

charge[2] *noun*
1 a price asked for something: *a* **charge** *for the use of the telephone*
2 a statement that a person has done wrong: *a* **charge** *of stealing*
3 a hurried attack
4 care: *I was in* **charge of** *my sister* (= I looked after her).

charity /'tʃærətɪ/ *noun*
1 (*no plural*) goodness and kindness: *She helped him out of* **charity.**

2 (*plural* **charities**) a group of people who give money, food, etc. to those who need it

charm[1] /tʃɑːm/ *verb*
to please greatly
charming *adjective* beautiful; pleasing

charm[2] *noun*
1 (*no plural*) pleasing behaviour: *He had great* **charm:** *everyone liked him.*
2 a thing or words that are said to be magic (see): *He has a stone which he says is a lucky* **charm.**

chart /tʃɑːt/ *noun*
1 a map, especially of an area of sea
2 a large piece of paper with information on it in pictures and writing

° **chase**[1] /tʃeɪs/ *verb* (*present participle* **chasing,** *part* **chased**)
to run after: *The boy* **chased** *the dog.*

chase[2] *noun*
an act of chasing: *He caught it after a long* **chase.**

chat[1] /tʃæt/ *verb* (*present participle* **chatting,** *past* **chatted**)
to talk in a friendly way

chat[2] *noun*
a friendly talk: *to have a* **chat**

chatter /'tʃætər/ *verb*
to talk quickly, especially about unimportant things: *They just sat and* **chattered.**

° **cheap** /tʃiːp/ *adjective*
costing only a little money: *A bicycle is much* **cheaper** *than a car.*

° **cheat**[1] /tʃiːt/ *verb*
to deceive; do something which is not honest: *He didn't play the game fairly — he* **cheated.**

° **cheat**[2] *noun*
a person who is not fair or honest

check[1] /tʃek/ *verb*
to make sure that something has been done well or is in good order: *You should* **check** *your bicycle before you ride it.*

check[2] *noun*
1 an act of checking: *a police* **check** *on cars and lorries*
2 a pattern of squares: *The material had* **checks** *on it. It was* **checked** *material.*

○ **cheek** /tʃiːk/ *noun*
one of the two parts on each side of the face under the eyes (picture on page 133)

cheeky /'tʃiːkɪ/ *adjective*
(cheekier, cheekiest)
not polite or respectful: *He is* **cheeky** *to his teacher.*

○ **cheer**[1] /tʃɪəʳ/ *verb*
1 to make happy: *The children's laughter* **cheered (up)** *the old woman.*
2 to shout because you are pleased

○ **cheer**[2] *noun*
a shout of happiness or to support someone or something: *Let's give three* **cheers** *for our team — they've won!*
cheerful *adjective* smiling and happy **cheerfully** *adverb*

cheese /tʃiːz/ *noun*
a food made from thickened milk

○ **chemical**[1] /'kemɪkl/ *noun*
a substance, especially one made by or used in chemistry (see)

○ **chemical**[2] *adjective*
of or made by chemistry (see)

chemist /'kemɪst/ *noun*
1 a person who makes and sells medicines
2 a person who studies chemistry
○ **chemistry** *noun (no plural)* the science which studies substances like gas, metals, liquids, etc.,

what they are made of, and what they do

cheque /tʃek/ *noun*
a printed piece of paper which you write on, and which can be exchanged for money at the bank

○ **chest** /tʃest/ *noun*
1 the front of the body between the shoulders and the stomach (picture on page 133)
2 a large box: *a tool* **chest**

chew /tʃuː/ *verb*
to break up food with the teeth

○ **chick** /tʃɪk/ *noun*
a young bird, especially a young chicken

○ **chicken** /'tʃɪkɪn/ *noun*
a bird kept by people for its eggs and meat

○ **chief**[1] /tʃiːf/ *adjective*
the most important
chiefly *adverb* mostly: *He kept animals —* **chiefly** *cattle, with some pigs.*

○ **chief**[2] *noun*
a leader; ruler; head of a group or tribe: *the* **chief** *of police*

chieftain /'tʃiːftən/ *noun*
a chief, especially of a tribe or large family group

○ **child** /tʃaɪld/ *noun*
(*plural* **children** /'tʃɪldrən/)
1 a young person older than a baby
2 a son or daughter: *They have three* **children.**
'**childhood** *noun* the time when you are a child
'**childish** *adjective* like or for a child: *a* **childish** *game* '**childishly** *adverb*

chime /tʃaɪm/ *verb* (*present participle* **chiming**, *past* **chimed**)
to make a sound like a bell: *The*

clock **chimed** *three o'clock.*
chime *noun*

chimney /'tʃɪmnɪ/ *noun*
a pipe which takes smoke away
from a fire

chimpanzee /ˌtʃɪmpæn'ziː/ *noun*
an African animal like a monkey
but without a tail: **Chimpanzees**
are apes (see). (picture on page 17)

° **chin** /tʃɪn/ *noun*
the part of the face below the
mouth (picture on page 133)

china /'tʃaɪnə/ *noun (no plural)*
things like cups and plates, or the
special kind of white earth from
which they are made

chip[1] /tʃɪp/ *noun*
1 a small piece of something
broken off: *a cup with a* **chip** *out
of it*
2 a small piece of fried potato
3 a very small piece of metal or
plastic used in computers to store
information or make the computer
work. Sometimes called a
microchip.

chip[2] *verb (present participle*
chipping, *past* **chipped)**
to break a small piece off
something hard: *He* **chipped** *the
cup when he dropped it.*

chirp /tʃɜːp/ *noun*
a short high sound made by some
birds and insects

° **chocolate** /'tʃɒklət/
noun, adjective
(a sweet or food) made from cocoa
(see): **chocolate** *cake*

° **choice** /tʃɔɪs/ *noun*
the act of choosing or something
chosen: *She had to* **make a choice**
between the two dresses. Her
choice *was the blue one.*

choir /'kwaɪəʳ/ *noun*
a number of people who sing

together: *the school* **choir**

choke /tʃəʊk/ *verb (present
participle* **choking,** *past* **choked)**
to be unable to breathe because of
something in the throat: *to* **choke
on** *a fish-bone*

° **choose** /tʃuːz/ *verb*
(present participle **choosing,** *past
tense* **chose** /tʃəʊz/, *past
participle* **chosen** /'tʃəʊzn/)
to pick out from a number of
things or people the one you want:
She **chose** *to study chemistry.*

chop[1] /tʃɒp/ *verb*
(present participle **chopping,** *past*
chopped)
to cut with an axe or sharp knife

chop[2] *noun*
a piece of meat with a bone cut
from the side of an animal's body

chorus /'kɔːrəs/ *noun*
(plural **choruses)**
1 a group of singers
2 a part of a song which is repeated

christen /'krɪsn/ *verb*
to give a Christian name to: *They*
christened *the baby John.*
christening *noun* the ceremony
when a baby is given its Christian
name

° **Christian** /'krɪstʃən, -tɪən/
noun, adjective
(a person) following the teachings
of Jesus Christ

° **Christmas** /'krɪsməs/ *noun*
the day of the year when Jesus
Christ is said to have been born

chuckle /'tʃʌkl/ *verb*
(present participle **chuckling,** *past*
chuckled)
to laugh quietly: *He* **chuckled** *at
the funny story.* **chuckle** *noun*

° **church** /tʃɜːtʃ/ *noun*
(plural **churches)**
a building that Christians meet
and pray in

cigar /sɪˈɡɑːʳ/ *noun*
tobacco (see) leaves rolled together for smoking

° **cigarette** /ˌsɪɡəˈret/ *noun*
tobacco (see) cut into small pieces and rolled in paper for smoking

cinema /ˈsɪnəmə/ *noun*
a building where you see films

° **circle** /ˈsɜːkl/ *noun*
1 something round; a ring: *They sat in a* **circle** *round the fire.* (picture on page 185)
2 a group of people
circular /ˈsɜːkjʊləʳ/ *adjective*

circulate /ˈsɜːkjʊleɪt/ *verb*
(*present participle* **circulating**, *past* **circulated**)
to go round: *Blood* **circulates** *round your body.* ˌcircuˈlation *noun*

circumference /sɜːkʌmfrəns/ *noun* (see picture on page 185)

circumstances /ˈsɜːkəmstənsɪz/ *plural noun*
the facts about what happens: **In/under the circumstances** (= considering what has happened), *I won't come.*

circus /ˈsɜːkəs/ *noun*
a show given by people and trained animals, often in a large tent (see)

citizen /ˈsɪtɪzn/ *noun*
a person who lives and has special rights in a country or town

city /ˈsɪtɪ/ *noun* (*plural* **cities**)
a large town

civil /ˈsɪvl/ *adjective*
1 polite: *Be* **civil** *to the headmaster.*
2 not part of the armed forces (see)
ˌcivil ˈservice *noun*: *The* **civil service** *is all the people who work for a government except the armed forces.*

civilian /sɪˈvɪljən/ *noun*
a person who is not in the armed forces (see)

civilize /ˈsɪvɪlaɪz/ *verb* (*present participle* **civilizing**, *past* **civilized**)
to change the way that people live together, by making laws and having government and education
ˌciviliˈzation *noun* people sharing their way of life and living in one place at one time

claim[1] /kleɪm/ *verb*
1 to ask for something that you say is yours: *I* **claimed** *the coat that the teacher found.*
2 to say that something is true: *He* **claimed** *that he hadn't done it, but I didn't believe him.*

claim[2] *noun*
something that is claimed: *They made a* **claim** *for higher pay.*

clang /klæŋ/ *noun*
the sound of one piece of metal hitting another: *There was a* **clang** *as he dropped the tools.* **clang** *verb*

clap[1] /klæp/ *verb* (*present participle* **clapping**, *past* **clapped**)
to make a sound by hitting your hands together, often to show that we like something: *When the singer finished, we* **clapped.**

clap[2] *noun*
1 the sound of clapping
2 **a clap of thunder** the sudden sound of thunder

clash[1] /klæʃ/ *verb*
1 to hit or fight: *The police* **clashed** *with the angry crowd.*
2 (of colours) to look wrong together: *His shirt* **clashed** *with his coat.*

clash[2] *noun*
1 an act of clashing: *a* **clash** *with the police*
2 a loud noise of metal on metal: *the* **clash** *of weapons*

clasp[1] /klɑːsp/ *verb*
to hold tightly: *He* **clasped** *my arm with fear.*

clasp

clasp² *noun*
something that fastens two things together: *He had a gold* **clasp** *on his belt.*

○ **class** /klɑːs/ *noun (plural* **classes**)
1 a group of people who learn together: *She was in a* **class** *of thirty students.*
2 a group of people or things of the same kind: *Cats belong to one* **class** *of animals, fish to another.*
'classroom *noun: There are fourteen pupils in the* **classroom**.

clatter /'klætə'/ *noun*
the loud noise of things being knocked together: *The pans fell with a* **clatter**. **clatter** *verb*

clause /klɔːz/ *noun*
a group of words in a sentence that contains a verb: *The sentence "As I was walking home, I met my friend" contains two* **clauses**. *"As I was walking home" is one* **clause**, *and "I met my friend" is another.* Look at **phrase**.

claw¹ /klɔː/ *noun*
one of the sharp, hard points on the foot of a bird or animal

claw² *verb*
to tear with the claws: *The cat* **clawed** *the chair.*

○ **clay** /kleɪ/ *noun (no plural)*
soft, sticky earth from which pots and bricks are made

○ **clean**¹ /kliːn/ *adjective*
not dirty: *That shirt is dirty, here is a* **clean** *one.*

○ **clean**² *verb*
to make something clean; take dirt from something: *Have you* **cleaned** *the kitchen?*
cleaner *noun* a person who cleans

○ **clear**¹ /klɪə'/ *adjective*
1 easy to understand: *It was* **clear** *that he wanted to be alone.*
2 easy to see or hear: *a* **clear** *voice*
3 easy to see through: **clear** *water*
clearly *adverb* **1** in a clear way: *Please speak more* **clearly**, *we can't hear you.* **2** without any doubt: **Clearly**, *he's very clever!*

○ **clear**² *verb*
1 to take away: *to* **clear** *plates from a table*
2 to clean; tidy; put away: *They* **cleared up** *the kitchen.*

clergyman /'klɜːdʒɪmən/ *noun (plural* **clergymen** /-mən/)
a Christian priest

clerk /klɑːk/ *noun*
a person who works in an office and writes letters

○ **clever** /'klevə'/ *adjective*
quick at learning and understanding things
cleverly *adverb*

click /klɪk/ *noun*
a single light sound like a door shutting **click** *verb*

cliff /klɪf/ *noun*
an area of high, steep rock, often close to the sea

climate /'klaɪmɪt/ *noun (no plural)*
the weather that a place has

○ **climb**¹ /klaɪm/ *verb*
to go up: *The two boys* **climbed** *(up) the tree.*

climb² *noun*
an act of climbing; the distance climbed: *a long* **climb** *up the hill*

cling /klɪŋ/ *verb*
(*past* **clung** /klʌŋ/)
to hold on tightly: *The baby monkey* **clung to** *its mother.*

clinic /'klınık/ *noun*
a place where people go to see a doctor

clip[1] /klıp/ *noun*
a small metal object used for fastening something: *The letters were held together with a paper clip.*

clip[2] *verb* (*present participle* **clipping,** *past* **clipped**)
1 to hold with a clip: *The letters were clipped together.*
2 to cut with a sharp instrument: *He clipped his finger nails.*

cloak /kləʊk/ *noun*
a loose piece of clothing, worn on top of everything else

cloak

° **clock** /klɒk/ *noun*
a machine that tells you what time it is
clockwise /'klɒkwaız/ *adverb*
in the same direction as the hands of a clock. '**Anti,clockwise** is the opposite way.

° **close**[1] /kləʊz/ *verb* (*present participle* **closing,** *past* **closed**)
to shut: *The shop is closed today.* (=not open for business)

° **close**[2] /kləʊs/ *adjective*
1 near: *I live close to the shops. They were standing close together* (= very near each other).
2 liking or loving: *Peter and John are close friends.*

° **cloth** /klɒθ/ *noun*
1 (*no plural*) a soft substance made of wool, cotton, etc.; material: *She bought some cloth to make some new dresses.*
2 a piece of cloth: *A red 'tablecloth covered the table. He dried the dishes with a dishcloth.*

° **clothes** /kləʊðz/ *plural noun*
things we wear
clothing /'kləʊðıŋ/ *noun* (*no plural*) things that are used as clothes

clothes

° **cloud** /klaʊd/ *noun*
a mass of very small drops of water floating in the sky
cloudy *adjective* (**cloudier, cloudiest**) having lots of cloud

clown /klaʊn/ *noun*
a person whose job is to make people laugh

° **club**[1] /klʌb/ *noun*
a group of people who meet for some purpose: *a football club*

club[2] *noun*
a large heavy stick

clue /kluː/ *noun*
something which helps you find the answer to a difficult question: *The police found a clue which will help them catch the robber.*

clumsy /'klʌmzı/ *adjective* (**clumsier, clumsiest**)
likely to drop things or move in an awkward way: *You are clumsy! You've knocked over my cup of coffee! clumsily adverb*

clung /klʌŋ/ see **cling**

clutch /klʌtʃ/ *verb*
to take hold of something tightly: *The falling man clutched the rope.*

coach[1] /kəʊtʃ/ *noun* (*plural* **coaches**)
1 a bus, or part of a train, that can carry many people
2 a four-wheeled covered vehicle drawn by horses

coach[2] *verb*
to give special lessons: *He coached her for the English examination.*

coach[3] *noun (plural* **coaches)**
a person who gives special lessons:
Our football **coach** *trains the team.*

coal /kəʊl/ *noun (no plural)*
black hard material dug out of the
ground and burnt to give heat

coarse /kɔːs/ *adjective*
rough; not smooth or fine

° **coast** /kəʊst/ *noun*
the land next to the sea: *a town on
the* **coast**

   coastline *noun: From the ship,
they saw the rocky* **coastline.**

° **coat** /kəʊt/ *noun*
a piece of clothing with coverings
for the arms worn over everything
else

coax /kəʊks/ *verb*
to persuade by kindness: *She*
coaxed *him to take the medicine.*

cobweb
/'kɒbweb/
noun
the thin net
spun by a   cobweb
spider (see), in which flies and
insects are caught

cock /kɒk/ *noun*
a male bird, especially a male
chicken

cocoa /'kəʊkəʊ/ *noun (no plural)*
1 a brown powder made from the
seeds of a tree, from which
chocolate is made
2 a hot drink made from this
powder

° **coconut**
/'kəʊkənʌt/
noun
a large
brown nut   **coconut**
with a hard shell and a hollow
centre filled with juice

cod /kɒd/ *noun (plural* **cod)**
a sea fish used for food

code /kəʊd/ *noun*
a way of using words, letters,
numbers, etc. to keep messages
secret: *The letter was written* **in
code** *and I could not understand it.*

° **coffee** /'kɒfɪ/ *noun*
1 (*no plural*) (a drink made from)
a brown powder from the seeds of
the coffee tree
2 a cup of this drink: *Two* **coffees,**
please!

coffin /'kɒfɪn/ *noun*
a box in which a dead body is put

coil[1] /kɔɪl/ *verb*
1 to gather a rope, wire, or pipe in
rings one above the other
2 to go round in a ring: *The snake*
coiled *round the tree.*

coil[2] *noun*
a set of rings joined to each other;
a continuous circling shape: *a* **coil**
of rope

° **coin** /kɔɪn/ *noun*
a piece of money made of metal

° **cold**[1] /kəʊld/ *adjective*
having very little heat; not hot: *a*
cold *drink*

° **cold**[2] *noun*
1 an illness of the nose and throat:
I've got a **cold.**
2 (*no plural*) cold weather; absence
of heat: *I don't like the* **cold.**

collapse /kə'læps/ *verb (present
participle* **collapsing,** *past*
collapsed)
to break into pieces; fall down: *The
roof of the old house* **collapsed.**
The old man **collapsed** *in the
street.*

collar /'kɒlə{r}/
noun
1 the part of   collars
your clothes
worn round
the neck: *The* **collar** *of his shirt
was dirty.*

2 a leather or metal band put round the neck of an animal

○ **collect** /kə'lekt/ *verb*
to gather together in the same place: *A crowd had* **collected** *to watch the ceremony. I* **collect** *stamps from all over the world.*
collection *noun: a large* **collection** *of stamps*

○ **college** /'kɒlɪdʒ/ *noun*
a place where people study after they have left school

collide /kə'laɪd/ *verb* (*present participle* **colliding**, *past* **collided**)
to come together with great force: *The two trains* **collided**.
collision /kə'lɪʒn/ *noun: a* **collision** *between two trains*

colon /'kəʊlɒn/ *noun*
the sign : which in this book comes before an example

colonel /'kɜːnl/ *noun*
an officer in the army

colony /'kɒlənɪ/ *noun*
(*plural* **colonies**)
a country that is under the control of another country
colonial /kə'ləʊnɪəl/ *adjective*
of or about a colony

○ **colour**[1] /'kʌlər/ *noun*
the quality that makes things look green, red, yellow, etc.: *The* **colour** *of leaves is green in summer.*
colourful *adjective* bright; having a lot of colours: **colourful** *clothes*

○ **colour**[2] *verb*
to put colour onto something: *Sarah is* **colouring** *the picture in her book.*

column /'kɒləm/ *noun*
1 a large post used to support a part of a building
2 a long narrow piece of printing in a newspaper or book
3 a row: *Can you add up this* **column** *of figures?*

○ **comb**[1]
/kəʊm/ *noun*
a thin piece of plastic, metal, etc.

teeth   comb

with teeth, used to make tidy hair

○ **comb**[2] *verb*
to arrange with a comb: *Have you* **combed** *your hair?*

combine /kəm'baɪn/ *verb* (*present participle* **combining**, *past* **combined**)
to join or mix together: *The two small shops* **combined** *to make one large one.*
combination /kɒmbɪ'neɪʃn/ *noun: His character is a* **combination** *of strength and kindness.*

○ **come** /kʌm/ (*present participle* **coming** /'kʌmɪŋ/, *past tense* **came** /keɪm/, *past participle* **come**)
to move towards the person speaking: *"***Come** *here Mary, I want to speak to you!" "I'm going out. Are you* **coming** *with me?" My shoe has* **come off** (= it is not on my foot any more). *We were walking to town when we* **came across** (= found) *a cat in the road. I* **come from** *London* (= I was born there, my home is there).

comedy /'kɒmədɪ/ *noun*
(*plural* **comedies**)
a funny play, film, etc.; something that makes us laugh

comet /'kɒmɪt/ *noun*
(see picture on page 259)

○ **comfort**[1] /'kʌmfət/ *noun*
being free from pain, trouble, etc.: *He lived* **in comfort** (= he had enough money to live well)

○ **comfort**[2] *verb*
to give help or show kindness to someone in pain or trouble: *She* **comforted** *the ill child.*
comfortable /'kʌmftəbl/

adjective: This is a very **comfortable** *chair* (= it is nice to sit in).
comfortably *adverb*

comic[1] /'kɒmɪk/ *adjective*
that makes us laugh; funny

comic[2] *noun*
a small book for children, with pictures that tell the story

comma /'kɒmə/ *noun*
the sign , used in writing to divide up a sentence

command[1] /kə'mɑːnd/ *verb*
1 to order: *I command you to go!*
2 to be in charge of: *A general is a man who* **commands** *a large number of soldiers.*

command[2] *noun*
1 an order
2 (*no plural*) power: *The officer is* **in command** *of his men.*

comment[1] /'kɒment/ *verb*
to say something about a special thing: *He* **commented** *on the bad road.*

comment[2] *noun*
something said: *He made a* **comment** *about the bad road.*

commentary /'kɒməntrɪ/ *noun*
a description spoken during a special event, match, etc.

commentator /'kɒmənteɪtəʳ/ *noun: A* **commentator** *is a person who gives a commentary on the radio or television.*

commerce /'kɒmɜːs/ *noun* (*no plural*)
business; buying and selling

commercial /kə'mɜːʃl/ *adjective: A* **commercial** *college teaches things that would be useful in business.*

commit /kə'mɪt/ *verb*
(*present participle* **committing**, *past* **committed**)
to do something wrong: *A robbery was* **committed** *last night.*

committee /kə'mɪtɪ/ *noun*
a group of people chosen to do a job: *The football club* **committee** *arranges all the matches.*

° **common** /'kɒmən/ *adjective*
1 found everywhere; usual: *Palms are* **common** *trees in Africa. If you have* **common sense,** *you don't do silly or careless things.*
2 shared by several people; belonging to or used by several people: *The park is* **common** *property: everyone can use it.*

Commonwealth /'kɒmənwelθ/ *noun*
a group of independent countries which used to be part of the British empire (= under the control of Britain)

communicate /kə'mjuːnɪkeɪt/ *verb* (*present participle* **communicating,** *past* **communicated**)
to speak or write to; be understood by: *If you know English, you can* **communicate** *with people everywhere. We* **communicate** *by letter.*

com,muni'cation *noun* (*no plural*): **Communication** *between people who speak different languages is difficult.*

communications *plural noun*
roads, railways, radio, telephones, and all other ways of moving or sending information between places

community /kə'mjuːnətɪ/ *noun* (plural **communities**)
the people living in one place, who share some things: *All the children in our* **community** *go to the same school.*

° **companion** /kəm'pænjən/ *noun*
a person you are with, often a friend: *He was my travelling* **companion** *for many months.*

○ **company** /'kʌmpənɪ/ *noun*
1 (*no plural*) people to be with: *I had no* **company** *on the journey.*
2 (*plural* **companies**) a group of people doing business; firm: *I work for a mining* **company.**

comparative /kəm'pærətɪv/ *noun, adjective*
a word or a form of a word that shows that something is bigger, smaller, better, worse, etc. than something else: *This pen is quite good, but that one is* **better.** "Better" is a **comparative.** Look at **superlative.**

○ **compare** /kəm'peə'/ *verb* (*present participle* **comparing,** *past* **compared**)
to decide in what way things are alike or different: *I* **compared** *my shoes* **with** *my sister's.*
comparison /kəm'pærɪsn/ *noun: My shoes are small* **in comparison with** *my sister's.*

compass
/'kʌmpəs/
noun
an
instrument
with a metal needle that always points north and south

○ needle

compass

compel /kəm'pel/ *verb* (*present participle* **compelling,** *past* **compelled**)
to force: *The floods* **compelled** *us to turn back.*

○ **compete** /kəm'piːt/ *verb* (*present participle* **competing,** *past* **competed**)
to try to win a race, prize, etc.: *Five children* **competed in** *the race.*
competition /kɑmpə'tɪʃn/ *noun* a test of who is best at something: *She came first in a drawing* **competition.**
competitor /kəm'petɪtə'/ *noun* a person who competes

○ **complain** /kəm'pleɪn/ *verb*
to say that something is not good, or that you are unhappy or angry with something: *We* **complained about** *the bad food.*
complaint *noun: We made a* **complaint** *about the food.*

○ **complete**[1] /kəm'pliːt/ *adjective*
1 whole; with nothing left out: *a* **complete** *set of stamps*
2 total: *a* **complete** *waste of time*
completely *adverb: Have you* **completely** *finished your work?*

complete[2] *verb* (*present participle* **completing,** *past* **completed**)
to finish: *to* **complete** *a piece of work*

complicated /'kɑmplɪkeɪtɪd/ *adjective*
difficult to understand; not simple: *A car engine is a* **complicated** *machine.*

compliment[1] /'kɑmplɪmənt/ *noun*
something nice said about someone

compliment[2] /'kɑmplɪment/ *verb*
to say something nice to someone: *He* **complimented** *my mother* **on** *her driving.*

compose /kəm'pəʊz/ *verb* (*present participle* **composing,** *past* **composed**)
1 to form out of parts: *Cakes are* **composed** *of flour, fat, eggs, and sugar.*
2 to write or make up: *to* **compose** *songs and music*
composer *noun* a person who composes music
composition /kɑmpə'zɪʃn/ *noun* something composed, often a story: *to write a* **composition**

○ **compound** /'kɑmpaʊnd/ *noun*
a building or group of buildings and the land around: *You must stay on the school* **compound.**

compulsory /kəm'pʌlsərɪ/ *adjective*
that must be done: *Learning science is* **compulsory** *at our school — we have no choice.*

computer /kəm'pjuːtəʳ/ *noun*
a machine that can store information and work out answers quickly: *A small computer is called a* **micro-computer.**

conceal /kən'siːl/ *verb*
to hide: *He* **concealed** *the sweets in his pocket.*

concentrate /'kɒnsəntreɪt/ *verb*
to keep your thoughts or attention on one thing: *Are you* **concentrating on** *your work?*

concern[1] /kən'sɜːn/ *noun*
worry: *He shows no* **concern** *for his children.*
concerned *adjective* worried

concern[2] *verb*
to be about: *This letter* **concerns** *you.*
concerning *preposition* about: *I spoke to him* **concerning** *his behaviour.*

concert /'kɒnsət/ *noun*
music played for a lot of people

conclude /kən'kluːd/ *verb*
(*present participle* **concluding,** *past* **concluded**)
1 to finish: *The headmistress* **concluded** *her speech quickly.*
2 to decide: *When I had heard his story, I* **concluded** *that he had told me the truth.*
conclusion /kən'kluːʒn/ *noun:* *My* **conclusion** *was that the boy had told me the truth.*

concrete /'kɒŋkriːt/ *noun* (*no plural*)
a grey powder (**cement**), mixed with sand and water, which becomes very hard and is used for building

condemn /kən'dem/ *verb*
to send someone to prison for a crime

condition /kən'dɪʃn/ *noun*
1 the state of someone or something: *The car is in very good* **condition.** *Weather* **conditions** *are bad today.*
2 something that must happen before something else happens: *One of the* **conditions** *of having the job was that I had to learn English. I was given the job* **on condition that** *I learnt English.*

conduct[1] /kən'dʌkt/ *verb*
to lead or guide: *The headmaster* **conducted** *us round the school.*
conductor *noun* **1** a person who controls a group of people playing music **2** a person who sells tickets on a bus or train

conduct[2] /'kɒndʌkt/ *noun* (*no plural*)
behaviour

cone /kəʊn/ *noun*
a round shape that is pointed at one end, like the end of a sharp pencil (picture on page 185)

conference /'kɒnfərəns/ *noun*
a meeting of people to find out what they think about a special thing: *a doctors'* **conference**

confess /kən'fes/ *verb*
to tell about the things you have done wrong: *When the police questioned the man, he* **confessed.**
confession /kən'feʃn/ *noun:* *He made a* **confession.**

confident /'kɒnfɪdənt/ *adjective*
feeling sure or safe: *I was* **confident that** *I had passed the examination.*
confidence *noun* (*no plural*): *She has a lot of* **confidence**; *she doesn't mind giving a speech to the whole school.*

confirm /kən'fɜːm/ *verb*
to give proof (of): *Please **confirm** your telephone message by writing to me.*
  confirmation /ˌkɒnfə'meɪʃn/ *noun (no plural)* proof

conflict¹ /'kɒnflɪkt/ *noun*
a fight or argument: *a **conflict** between two groups of children*

conflict² /kən'flɪkt/ *verb*
to disagree: *The two stories **conflicted**, so I did not know what to believe.*

confuse /kən'fjuːz/ *verb (present participle* **confusing**, *past* **confused**)
to mix up in your mind: *I **confused** the two boys, because they looked so alike.*
  confusion /kən'fjuːʒn/ *noun (no plural)* mixing up; disorder: *The room was in complete **confusion**.*

congratulate /kən'grætʃʊleɪt/ *verb*
to say you are pleased about a happy event: *I **congratulated** them on the birth of their baby.*
  congratulations /kənˌgrætʃə'leɪʃnz/ *plural noun:* **Congratulations** on the birth of your baby!

conjunction /kən'dʒʌŋkʃn/ *noun*
a word that joins two parts of a sentence: *I walked to the shop **and** I bought some fruit. "**And**" is a conjunction.*

° **connect** /kə'nekt/ *verb*
to join: *Will you **connect** this wire to the television?*
  con'nection *noun:* *The television isn't working; is there a loose **connection**?*

conquer /'kɒŋkəʳ/ *verb*
to defeat in war: *to **conquer** the enemy*
  conquest /'kɒŋkwest/ *noun:* *the **conquest** of the enemy*

conscience /'kɒnʃəns/ *noun*
the feeling inside you which tells you whether something is right or wrong: *His **conscience** troubled him after he took the money.*

conscious /'kɒnʃəs/ *adjective*
awake and knowing what is happening around you: *He became **conscious** a few minutes after the accident.* **consciously** *adverb*

consent¹ /kən'sent/ *verb*
to agree: *I asked my mother if I could go out, and she **consented**.*

consent² *noun (no plural)*
agreement: *I had to get my mother's **consent** before I went.*

consequence /'kɒnsɪkwəns/ *noun*
something that happens as a result: *As a **consequence** of being in hospital, Jane decided that she wanted to become a nurse.*
  consequently *adverb*

conservation /ˌkɒnsə'veɪʃn/ *noun*
saving and protecting: *There is a need for the **conservation** of trees, or there will soon be no forests.*

° **consider** /kən'sɪdəʳ/ *verb*
to think about: *I'm **considering** changing my job.*
  con,side'ration *noun (no plural)* *They gave the plan careful **consideration** (= thought). She shows great **consideration** to (=cares about the wishes of) her parents.*

consist /kən'sɪst/ *verb*
to be made (of): *A knife **consists** of a blade and a handle.*

consonant /'kɒnsənənt/ *noun*
a written letter, or the sound of a letter, which is not *a, e, i, o,* or *u.* Look at **vowel**.

constant /'kɒnstənt/ *adjective*
happening all the time: **constant** *rain* **constantly** *adverb*

constituency /kən'stɪtjʊənsɪ/ *noun*
(*plural* **constituencies**)
an area that chooses one member
of parliament (see)

constitution /kɒnstɪ'tjuːʃn/ *noun*
a set of laws governing a country,
club, etc. **constitutional** *adjective*

construct /kən'strʌkt/ *verb*
to build or make: *to* **construct** *a
bridge*
  con'struction *noun* **1** (*no plural*)
  building: *a* **construction**
  company **2** something that is
  built

consul /'kɒnsl/ *noun*
a person who represents his
country in a foreign town: *The*
consul *gave us information about
colleges in his country.*

consult /kən'sʌlt/ *verb*
to ask or look at for information:
I **consulted** *George about buying
a car.*

consume /kən'sjuːm/ *verb*
(*present participle* **consuming**, *past*
consumed)
to eat or use up: *The big car*
consumed *a lot of petrol.*
  consumption /kən'sʌmpʃn/
  noun (*no plural*): *The petrol*
  consumption *of the big car was
  very high.*

contact[1] /'kɒntækt/ *verb*
to talk or write to: *She* **contacted**
me as soon as she arrived.

○ **contact**[2] *noun*
touching or coming together: *The
two wires were in* **contact**. *She*
comes into contact with (= meets)
many people.

○ **contain** /kən'teɪn/ *verb*
to have inside; hold: *The speech*
contained *some interesting ideas.*
  container *noun*: *A* **container** *is a
  box, pot, or anything you can put
  something into.*

content /kən'tent/ *adjective*
happy; pleased: *Is he* **content** *with
his work?* **contented** *adjective*

contents /'kɒntents/ *plural noun*
what is in something: *The* **contents**
of the box fell onto the floor.

contest /'kɒntest/ *noun*
a fight or competition

continent /'kɒntɪnənt/ *noun*
one of the seven large masses of
land on the Earth: *Europe is a*
continent. (see picture on page
185) **continental** /ˌkɒntɪ'nentl/
adjective

○ **continue** /kən'tɪnjuː/ *verb*
(*present participle* **continuing**, *past*
continued)
to go on: *Please* **continue** *reading.*
  continual *adjective* happening
  often: **continual** *arguments*
  continuous *adjective* never
  stopping: *a* **continuous** *noise*

contract /'kɒntrækt/ *noun*
a written agreement to do work or
sell goods at an agreed price

contrary[1] /'kɒntrərɪ/ *noun*
the opposite: *"You must be tired."*
"On the **contrary**, *I feel wide
awake."*

contrary[2] *adjective*
opposite: *He passed the
examination,* **contrary** *to what I
expected.*

contrast[1] /kən'trɑːst/ *verb*
to compare two things and find the
differences between them: *The hot
sunny day* **contrasted** *greatly with
the cold rainy night.*

contrast[2] /'kɒntrɑːst/ *noun* (*no
plural*)
difference: *There is a great* **contrast**
between good and evil.

contribute /kən'trɪbjuːt/ *verb*
(*present participle* **contributing**,
past **contributed**)
to give with other people: *We all*

contributed *money to buy Richard's present.*
contribution /ˌkɒntrɪˈbjuːʃn/ *noun: Peter collected all the* **contributions.**

control[1] /kənˈtrəʊl/ *verb* (*present participle* **controlling,** *past* **controlled**)
to have power over someone or something; decide or guide the way something or someone works: *That woman* **controls** *the newspaper. This handle* **controls** *the flow of electricity* (= makes it more or less strong).

control[2] *noun*
power; guidance: *He was* **in control** *of the car. The horse got* **out of control,** *and the rider fell to the ground.*

convenient /kənˈviːnjənt/ *adjective*
useful or suitable: *The school is in a* **convenient** *place, near my home.*
convenience *noun: My mother likes the* **convenience** *of living close to the shops.*

convent /ˈkɒnvənt/ *noun*
a place where nuns (= women who lead a religious life) live; a school or college run by nuns

° **conversation** /ˌkɒnvəˈseɪʃn/ *noun*
a talk: *I had a long* **conversation** *with your teacher.*

convert /kənˈvɜːt/ *verb*
to change into something else: *That building has been* **converted into** *a school.*
conversion /kənˈvɜːʃn/ *noun*

convey /kənˈveɪ/ *verb*
to take or carry (usually over a long distance): *The lorry* **conveyed** *machinery across the country.*

convict[1] /kənˈvɪkt/ *verb*
to decide in a law court (see) that somebody is guilty of a crime: *He*

was **convicted** *of stealing.*

convict[2] /ˈkɒnvɪkt/ *noun*
a person who has been convicted of a crime

convince /kənˈvɪns/ *verb* (*present participle* **convincing,** *past* **convinced**)
to make a person believe something: *He* **convinced** *me that I should study law.*

° **cook**[1] /kʊk/ *verb*
to make food ready to eat by heating it: *I haven't* **cooked** *the dinner. Does he* **cook** *well?*

° **cook**[2] *noun*
a person who cooks: *Sarah is a very good* **cook** (= she cooks well).
cooker *noun* an apparatus for cooking food: *a gas* **cooker**

° **cool**[1] /kuːl/ *adjective*
1 not warm, but not very cold: *The room was* **cool** *after the sun had gone down.*
2 calm: *Don't get excited about the examination; keep* **cool.**

cool[2] *verb*
to make or become cool: *We* **cooled down** *by swimming in the river.*

cooperate /kəʊˈɒpəreɪt/ *verb* (*present participle* **cooperating,** *past* **cooperated**)
to work with (one another): *If we all* **cooperate,** *we'll soon finish.*
co,ope'ration *noun* (*no plural*): *Thank you for your* **cooperation.**
cooperative /kəʊˈɒprətɪv/ *adjective* willing to help other people

copper /ˈkɒpər/ *noun* (*no plural*)
a red-gold metal

° **copy**[1] /ˈkɒpɪ/ *verb* (*present participle* **copying,** *past* **copied**)
to make or do something exactly the same as something else: *I* **copied** *the letters into my book.*

○ **copy²** *noun (plural* **copies)**
something that is the same as something else: *Please send a* **copy** *of this letter to Mr Brown.*

cord /kɔːd/ *noun*
thin rope

cork /kɔːk/ *noun*
1 (*no plural*) a light substance that comes from the bark (= outside part of the stem) of a tree
2 a piece of this, used to fill the holes in the tops of bottles

○ **corn** /kɔːn/ *noun (no plural)*
the seed of grain plants, including wheat and maize

○ **corner** /ˈkɔːnəʳ/ *noun*
an angle; the place where two lines, streets, etc. meet each other: *The table stood in the* **corner** *of the room. His house is on the* **corner** *of School Road and Green Street.*

corporation /ˌkɔːpəˈreɪʃn/ *noun*
a group of people who run a town, business, etc.

corpse /kɔːps/ *noun*
a dead body, usually of a person

○ **correct¹** /kəˈrekt/ *adjective*
right; not wrong: *a* **correct** *answer*

correct² *verb*
to make right: *Please* **correct** *this mistake.* **correctly** *adverb*
corˈrection *noun: He made several* **corrections** *to the letter.*

correspond /ˌkɒrɪˈspɒnd/ *verb*
to write and receive letters from: *to* **correspond** *with a friend*
correspondence *noun* (*no plural*) letters

corridor /ˈkɒrɪdɔːʳ/ *noun*
a long narrow part of a building, with rooms on each side of it: *Go down the* **corridor,** *to the third room on the left.*

cosmetics /kɒzˈmetɪks/ *plural noun*
substances put on the skin, especially of the face, and on the hair to make them look prettier

○ **cost¹** /kɒst/ *noun*
the price you pay when you buy something: *The* **cost** *of the house was too high for me.*

○ **cost²** *verb (past* **cost)**
to have as a price: *How much did that bag* **cost**? *It* **cost** *five pounds!*
ˈcostly *adjective* costing a lot of money: *The ring was very* **costly.**

costume /ˈkɒstjuːm/ *noun*
clothes worn for a special reason, or to represent a country or time in history: *Her* **national costume** *showed which country she came from.*

cot /kɒt/ *noun*
a small bed with high sides, for a baby

cottage /ˈkɒtɪdʒ/ *noun*
a small house in the country: *a thatched* (see) **cottage**

○ **cotton** /ˈkɒtən/ *noun (no plural)*
a plant grown in hot countries for the fine white threads (**cotton**) which cover its seeds and which are made into thread or material: *She sewed the* **cotton** *dress with* **cotton** *(thread).*
ˌcotton-ˈwool *noun* (*no plural*) soft feathery white material from cotton used for treating wounds, etc.

couch /kaʊtʃ/ *noun* (*plural* **couches)**
a long seat on which you can sit or lie

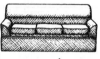
couch

○ **cough¹** /kɒf/ *noun*
a sharp noise made by sending air out of the lungs (see) suddenly: *The child had a bad* **cough,** *so his mother took him to the doctor.*

° **cough**[2] *verb*
to make the noise of a cough: *The child was* **coughing** *all night.*

° **could** /kəd; *strong* kʊd/ *verb*
1 (the word for can in the past): *Before I had a bicycle, I* **couldn't** (= could not) *visit my friend.*
2 (used in sentences like these): *She would help us if she* **could,** *but she can't.*
3 (used as a polite way of asking someone something): **Could** *you help me, please?*

council /'kaʊnsl/ *noun*
a group of people who are chosen to make laws or decisions or to advise people: *The town* **council** *will decide where to plant the trees.*
councillor *noun* a member of a council

° **count**[1] /kaʊnt/ *verb*
1 to say numbers in the right order: *to* **count** *from 1 to 100*
2 to name one by one to find out how many there are; add up: *She* **counted** *the books — there were fourteen of them.*

count[2] *noun (no plural)*
an act of counting: *There were so many cars that I* **lost count** (= could not remember how many).

counter
/'kaʊntəʳ/ *noun*
1 a long table between buyers and sellers in a shop

counter

2 a small round piece of plastic or wood used in playing games

° **country** /'kʌntrɪ/ *noun*
1 (*plural* **countries**) an area ruled by one government: *France and Germany are European* **countries.**
2 (*no plural*) the land that is not a town: *He lives in the* **country.**
countryside *noun* (*no plural*) land outside towns and cities

couple /'kʌpl/ *noun (no plural)*
two people or things usually thought of together: *I waited a* **couple** *of hours. My brother and his wife are a happy* **couple.**

coupon /'kuːpɒn/ *noun*
a piece of paper that can be exchanged for goods or money: *I've kept the special* **coupon** *from the box of washing powder, so that I can get my next box cheaper.*

° **courage** /'kʌrɪdʒ/ *noun (no plural)*
not being afraid; bravery: *The soldier had shown great* **courage** *in the battle.* **courageous** /kə'reɪdʒəs/ *adjective*

course /kɔːs/ *noun*
1 the way that something happens or the time when something is happening: *During the* **course** *of the journey, we saw a lot of new places.* **Of course** (= you can be sure) *I'll write to you when I am away.*
2 the path or direction of something: *The* **course** *of the river was marked on the map. The plane had to* **change course** *and go another way.*
3 part of a meal: *We had three* **courses:** *soup, meat and vegetables, and fruit.*
4 a set of lessons: *What* **course** *are you taking at college?*

court /kɔːt/ *noun*
1 a place where someone is questioned about a crime, and where people decide whether he is guilty or not
2 an open space where games are played: *a* **'tennis-court**
3 a king or queen (see) and all the people who live with them

cousin

cousin /ˈkʌzn/ *noun*
the child of an aunt or uncle

° **cover**[1] /ˈkʌvəʳ/ *verb*
to put something over something else: *She* **covered** *the table with a cloth.*

° **cover**[2] *noun*
something that is put over something else: *The book had a blue* **cover.**

° **cow** /kaʊ/ *noun*
the full grown female form of cattle: *I have ten* **cows** *and one bull* (see).

coward /ˈkaʊəd/ *noun*
a person who avoids pain or danger because he has no courage: *I never go to the dentist; I'm really a* **coward.**
   cowardly *adjective:* **cowardly** *behaviour*

cowboy /ˈkaʊbɔɪ/ *noun*
a man who rides a horse and looks after cattle in America

crab /kræb/ *noun*
a sea-animal with ten legs and a hard shell

shell

crab

° **crack**[1] /kræk/ *verb*
1 to break, but not into separate parts: *One of these cups is* **cracked.**
2 to make a sharp noise, like thunder or a gun

° **crack**[2] *noun*
1 a thin line where something is broken: *There's a* **crack** *in this cup!*
2 a sharp noise: *a* **crack** *of thunder*

cradle /ˈkreɪdl/ *noun*
a bed for a baby which can be swung from side to side

craft /krɑːft/ *noun*
1 a job or trade needing skill, especially with your hands: *He*

knew the **craft** *of making furniture. He was a* **craftsman.**
2 (*no plural*) a boat or plane

cram /kræm/ *verb* (*present participle* **cramming,** *past* **crammed**)
to fill or force in: *Lots of people were* **crammed** *into the bus.*

crane /kreɪn/ *noun*
a tall machine for lifting heavy things from one place to another

crane

° **crash**[1] /kræʃ/ *noun* (*plural* **crashes**)
1 a loud noise, like something large falling over: *The car hit the tree with a* **crash.**
2 an accident when vehicles hit each other: *a car* **crash**

° **crash**[2] *verb*
to make the noise of a crash: *The cars* **crashed** *into each other.*

crate /kreɪt/ *noun*
a big wooden box: *a* **crate** *of fruit*

crawl /krɔːl/ *verb*
to go along slowly, often on hands and knees: *The baby* **crawled** *towards his father. The insects were* **crawling** *across the wall.*

crayon /ˈkreɪən/ *noun*
a soft coloured pencil

crazy /ˈkreɪzɪ/ *adjective*
mad; foolish: *He's* **crazy** *to drive his car so fast.*

creak /kriːk/ *verb*
to make the sound of a door which has not been oiled: *The door* **creaked** *as she opened it.* **creak** *noun*

cream[1] /kriːm/ *noun* (*no plural*)
the fatty part of the milk that rises to the top

cream[2] *adjective, noun*
(of) the colour of this milk, yellowish-white

create /krɪ'eɪt/ *verb* (*present participle* **creating,** *past* **created**)
to make something new: *He* **created** *his house from stone and his own ideas.*
   creation /krɪ'eɪʃn/ *noun*

creature /'kriːtʃəʳ/ *noun*
an animal or insect

credit /'kredɪt/ *noun* (*no plural*)
1 attention and approval: *We both made the machine, but James was given the* **credit** *for it.*
2 buying things and paying for them later: *We bought the furniture* **on credit.**

° **creep** /kriːp/ *verb* (*past* **crept** /krept/)
to move quietly, often with the body close to the ground

crest /krest/ *noun*
1 feathers that stick up on top of a bird's head
2 the top of something: *the* **crest** *of a hill*

crew /kruː/ *noun*
the people who work on a ship

cricket[1] /'krɪkɪt/ *noun*
a ball game played by two teams of eleven players each

cricket[2] *noun*
a small brown insect that makes a noise which seems to go on all the time

cried /kraɪd/ see **cry**[1]

cries /kraɪz/ see **cry**[2]

° **crime** /kraɪm/ *noun*
something that is wrong and can be punished by the law: *Killing people is a* **crime.**
   criminal /'krɪmɪnl/ *noun*: *The person who carries out a crime is a* **criminal. criminal** *adjective*

crimson /'krɪmzn/
adjective, noun
(of) a deep red colour, like blood

cripple[1] /'krɪpl/ *noun*
a person who has an arm or leg that he cannot use, or who cannot walk

cripple[2] *verb* (*present participle* **crippling,** *past* **crippled**)
to hurt someone so that he cannot use his arms and legs: *She was* **crippled** *in the car accident.*

crisis /'kraɪsɪs/ *noun*
(*plural* **crises** /'kraɪsiːz/)
a time when something serious or dangerous happens: *We had a* **crisis** *at work today — Jane fell down the stairs.*

crisp[1] /krɪsp/ *adjective*
1 firm and dry; easily broken: *The outside of fresh bread is* **crisp.**
2 firm and fresh: **crisp** *apples*

crisp[2] *or* po'tato crisp *noun*
a thin piece of potato (see) cooked in very hot oil: *a packet of* **crisps**

criticize /'krɪtɪsaɪz/ *verb* (*present participle* **criticizing,** *past* **criticized**)
to say what is wrong with something; find faults in something: *The teacher* **criticized** *my work — he said it was very badly written.*
   critic /'krɪtɪk/ *noun* a person who criticizes
   critical /'krɪtɪkl/ *adjective*: *She was very* **critical** *of my work.*
   criticism /'krɪtɪsɪzəm/ *noun*: *I listened to all her* **criticisms.**

croak /krəʊk/ *verb*
to make a low hard sound in the throat, like a frog (see)

crockery /'krɒkərɪ/ *noun* (*no plural*)
plates, cups, and other things which we use for eating

crocodile

crocodile
/'krɒkədaɪl/
noun
a large
animal (**reptile**)
of hot places, which can swim

crocodile

crooked /'krʊkɪd/ *adjective*
bent or curved: *a crooked road*

° **crop** /krɒp/ *noun*
1 food that is grown: *Which crops does he grow?*
2 vegetables, grain, etc. that are cut or gathered at one time: *a crop of apples*

° **cross**[1] /krɒs/ *noun* (*plural* **crosses**)
a shape with four arms (×)

° **cross**[2] *verb*
to go over: *They crossed the road.*
'**crossing** *noun* a special place where you may cross a road

cross[3] *adjective*
feeling angry: *Why are you cross with me?*

crossroads /'krɒsrəʊdz/ *plural noun*
a place where several roads meet each other

crossword /'krɒsˌwɜːd/ *noun*
a game in which words have to be guessed so that the letters will fit empty places in a picture

crouch /kraʊtʃ/ *verb*
to make the body come close to the ground by bending the knees: *She crouched by the fire to get warm.*

crow /krəʊ/ *noun*
a large black bird with a hard low cry

crowd[1] /kraʊd/ *noun*
a large mass of people: *a crowd (of people) at the football match*

crowd[2] *verb*
to come together in a large group: *They all crowded round the teacher.*

crowded *adjective* full of people: *I don't like the market; it is too crowded.*

crown[1] /kraʊn/ *noun*
a special hat made of metal, beautiful stones, etc., worn by a king or queen for ceremonies

crown[2] *verb*
to make someone king or queen

crude /kruːd/ *adjective* (**cruder, crudest**)
1 raw; in a natural state: **Crude** *oil has to be made pure before it can be used by man.*
2 rude: *a crude joke*

° **cruel** /'kruːəl/ *adjective*
liking to hurt other people or animals: *He is cruel to animals.*
cruelly *adverb*
cruelty *noun* (*no plural*): **cruelty** *to animals*

crumb /krʌm/ *noun*
a little piece of something you can eat, like bread: *He dropped crumbs of cake all over the table.*

crumble /'krʌmbl/ *verb*
(*present participle* **crumbling**, *past* **crumbled**)
to break up into little pieces: *The walls of that old house are crumbling.*

° **crush** /krʌʃ/ *verb*
to hurt or damage by pressing heavily: *Her hand was crushed under the bricks.*

crust /krʌst/ *noun*
the hard part on the outside of bread or some other things: *He ate a crust (of bread).*

crutch /krʌtʃ/ *noun*
(*plural* **crutches**)
a piece of wood or metal that supports a person who cannot walk well:
to walk on crutches

crutches

° **cry**[1] /kraɪ/ *verb* (*past* **cried**/kraɪd/)
1 to call out loudly: *The boy* **cried** *for help.*
2 to have water running from the eyes: *She started to* **cry** *when she heard the sad news.*

° **cry**[2] *noun* (*plural* **cries**)
a shout; a call: *They heard a* **cry** *for help.*

cub /kʌb/ *noun*
a young one of any of the big cats or of a fox (see)

cube /kjuːb/ *noun*
a solid shape that has a square on every side (picture on page 185)
cubic /'kjuːbɪk/ *adjective*

cucumber /'kjuːkʌmbəʳ/ *noun*
a long thin green vegetable which can be eaten without cooking

cuddle /'kʌdl/ *verb*
(*present participle* **cuddling**, *past* **cuddled**)
to hold someone close to your body, in a loving way: *She* **cuddled** *her little boy.*

cuff /kʌf/ *noun*
the end of a sleeve (= arm of a shirt, dress, etc.)

° **cultivate** /'kʌltɪveɪt/ *verb* (*present participle* **cultivating**, *past* **cultivated**)
to grow plants on land that has been specially prepared: *The land by the river was* **cultivated.**
culti'vation *noun* (*no plural*)

culture /'kʌltʃəʳ/ *noun*
the way of life of a group of people: *These two countries have different* **cultures.**

cunning /'kʌnɪŋ/ *adjective*
clever at deceiving people: *For a long time nobody knew he told lies, because he is so* **cunning.**

° **cup** /kʌp/ *noun*
1 a container that you can drink from, usually having a handle: *a* **cup** *of tea*
2 a prize, shaped like a bowl, usually made of metal

° **cupboard** /'kʌbəd/ *noun*
a piece of furniture with space inside for storing things

° **cure**[1] /kjʊəʳ/ *verb*
(*present participle* **curing**, *past* **cured**)
to make someone better when they have been ill: *I hope the doctor can* **cure** *the pain in my shoulder.*

° **cure**[2] *noun*
a way of making better: *a* **cure** *for an illness*

curious /'kjʊərɪəs/ *adjective*
wanting to know about things or people: *It is good to be* **curious** *about the world around you.*
curiously *adverb*
curiosity /ˌkjʊərɪ'ɒsətɪ/ *noun* (*no plural*): *He is full of* **curiosity.**

curl[1] /kɜːl/ *verb*
to roll or bend in a round or curved shape: *The snake* **curled** *round the branch. She* **curled** *her hair.*

curl[2] *noun*
a roll or round shape: *Her hair was in* **curls.**
'curly *adjective* (**curlier**, **curliest**): **curly** *hair*

currency /'kʌrənsɪ/ *noun* (*plural* **currencies**)
the money used in a country: *"Have you any British* **currency?"** *Yes, I have £10.*

current /'kʌrənt/ *noun*
a flow of water, electricity, etc.: *Don't swim in the river, the* **current** *is very fast.*

curry /'kʌrɪ/ *noun* (*plural* **curries**)
food cooked with special plants

that make it taste hot: *chicken* **curry** *and rice*

    curried *adjective:* **curried** *chicken*

curse[1] /kɜːs/ *verb*

(*present participle* **cursing**, *past* **cursed**)

1 to wish harm to come to someone: *He* **cursed** *the person who had stolen his money.*

2 to speak angry words: *He* **cursed** *when he hit his head on the shelf.*

curse[2] *noun*

1 something you say asking for harm to come to someone

2 angry words

curtain /'kɜːtn/ *noun*

a piece of cloth hung up to cover a window, door, or part of a room

curtains

○ **curve**[1] /kɜːv/ *noun*

a smooth round shape; a bend: *a* **curve** *in the road*

○ **curve**[2] *verb* (*present participle* **curving**, *past* **curved**)

to make a curve; bend: *The river* **curved** *round the hill.*

cushion /'kʊʃn/ *noun*

a bag filled with soft material to sit on or rest against

○ **custom** /'kʌstəm/ *noun*

a special way of doing something that a person or group of people has: *In England it is the* **custom** *to say "How do you do?" when you meet someone.*

    customary /'kʌstəmrɪ/ *adjective* usual: *He talked to us with his* **customary** *kindness.*

○ **customer** /'kʌstəməʳ/ *noun*

a person who buys from a shop or market

customs /'kʌstəmz/ *plural noun*

a department of the government that controls what is brought into a country: *At the airport, the* **customs** *officers searched his case.*

○ **cut**[1] /kʌt/ *verb* (*present participle* **cutting**, *past* **cut**)

to break with a knife or blade: *He* **cut** *the apple in half. He has* **cut** *his leg, and it is bleeding. She* **cut** *her hair* (= made it shorter). **Cut down** *the tree* (= cut it so that it falls down). *He was* **cutting up** *the chicken* (= cutting it into pieces). *The girl* **cut out** *a picture from the newspaper* (= took it out by cutting the paper round the edge).

○ **cut**[2] *noun*

1 an opening or wound made by cutting: *a* **cut** *on the leg*

2 something made shorter or stopped: *I need a* '**hair cut**. *There was a* '**power cut** *yesterday when all the electricity went off.*

cutlery /'kʌtlərɪ/ *noun* (*no plural*) metal things used in eating: *Knives and forks are* **cutlery**.

cycle[1] /'saɪkl/ *noun*

a bicycle

    cyclist /'saɪklɪst/ *noun* a person who rides a bicycle

○ **cycle**[2] *verb* (*present participle* **cycling**, *past* **cycled**)

to ride a bicycle: *He* **cycles** *to school every day.*

cylinder /'sɪlɪndəʳ/ *noun*

a long round shape like a tube or a pencil (picture on page 185)

    cylindrical /sɪ'lɪndrɪkl/ *adjective*

Dd

daddy /'dædɪ/ (*plural* **daddies**) *or* **dad** *noun*
father

dagger /'dægəʳ/ *noun*
a short knife used as a weapon

daily /'deɪlɪ/ *adjective, adverb*
every day: *I catch the bus* **daily.**

dairy /'deərɪ/ *noun* (*plural* **dairies**)
a place where milk is kept and foods from milk are made; a shop where these things are sold

dam¹ /dæm/ *noun*
a wall built to keep water at a high level

dam² *verb* (*present participle* **damming**, *past* **dammed**)
to put a dam across something: *The river was* **dammed** (**up**) *to make a lake.*

dam

°**damage**¹ /'dæmɪdʒ/ *noun* (*no plural*)
harm, especially to things

°**damage**² *verb* (*present participle* **damaging**, *past* **damaged**)
to hurt; cause damage to: *The cars are badly* **damaged** *in the accident.*

damp /dæmp/ *adjective*
rather wet: *These clothes aren't dry yet; they're still* **damp.**

°**dance**¹ /dɑːns/ *verb* (*present participle* **dancing**, *past* **danced**)
to move to music, or as if to music
dancer *noun*

°**dance**² *noun*
1 a set of movements you do to music: *to learn a new* **dance**

2 a party where there is dancing: *Are you going to the* **dance?**

°**danger** /'deɪndʒəʳ/ *noun*
1 (*no plural*) the possibility of loss or harm: *There is always* **danger** (*of floods*) *in a storm. He put his life* **in danger** *when he ran across the busy street.*
2 something that causes danger: *the* **dangers** *of smoking*
dangerous *adjective*: *a* **dangerous** *bend in the road*

°**dare** /deəʳ/ *verb* (*present participle* **daring**, *past* **dared**)
to be brave enough to: *David* **dared** (**to**) *climb the tree. She* **daren't** (= dare not) *tell her sister that she has lost her money.*

°**dark**¹ /dɑːk/ *adjective*
1 like night; not light or bright: *It was getting* **dark**, *so we hurried home.*
2 of a deep colour, nearer black than white: *He wore a* **dark** *suit.*
darkness *noun* (*no plural*): *We couldn't see the houses in the* **darkness.**

dark² *noun* (*no plural*)
the lack of light: *We could not see in the* **dark.**

darling /'dɑːlɪŋ/ *noun, adjective*
a name for someone who is loved: **Darling**, *go now, or you will be late.*

dart¹ /dɑːt/ *noun*
a sharp-pointed metal weapon thrown by the hand, also used in the game of darts

dart² *verb*
to go quickly: *The bird* **darted** *across the river.*

dash[1] /dæʃ/ *verb*
to go quickly: *She* **dashed** *home from school.*

dash[2] *noun (plural* **dashes***)*
the sign — used in writing to show a short space, or to separate two parts of a sentence

○ **date**[1] /deɪt/ *noun*
the day, month and year: *What is the* **date** *today? The* **date** *of this battle was 1857.*

date[2] *noun*
a small sweet brown fruit

○ **daughter** /'dɔːtəʳ/ *noun*
a female child: *They have three* **daughters** *and one son.*

dawn /dɔːn/ *noun*
the time when the sun rises: *I woke up at* **dawn.**

○ **day** /deɪ/ *noun*
1 the time when it is light; the opposite of night: *In the* **day,** *we work and go out, but at night we sleep.*
2 twenty-four hours: *It hasn't stopped raining for* **days.**
'**daylight** *noun (no plural)*: *How many hours of* **daylight** *do we have in a day?*
'**daytime** *noun (no plural)*: *In the* **daytime,** *we go to school, but in the evenings we play.*

○ **dead**[1] /ded/ *adjective*
not living: *My grandfather has been* **dead** *for ten years.*
deadly *adjective (* **deadlier, deadliest***)* causing death: *This seed is* **deadly** *if you eat it.*

dead[2] *noun (no plural)*
dead people: *After the battle, they counted* **the dead.**

deaf /def/ *adjective*
not able to hear: *I've called you three times, are you* **deaf?**

deal[1] /diːl/ *noun*
1 a business arrangement: *Let's*

72

make a deal — *I'll clean you, bicycle if you let me ride it today.*
2 a lot: *He has* **a great deal** *of work to do.*

deal[2] *verb (past* **dealt** /delt/*)*
1 to do business with; buy and sell: *I have* **dealt with** *this farmer for years.*
2 to do what is necessary: *I can't* **deal with** *all this work, I need someone to help me.*
3 to give: I **dealt (out)** *the pieces of cake, one to each child.*
dealer *noun* a person who buys and sells something

dear[1] /dɪəʳ/ *adjective*
loved: *He is my* **dearest** *friend. She began the letter with "***Dear** *James". ***dearly** *adverb*

dear[2] *adjective*
costing a lot of money: *Fruit is* **dear** *at this time of year.*

○ **death** /deθ/ *noun*
being dead, or dying: *The* **death** *of his father was sudden.*

debate[1] /dɪ'beɪt/ *noun*
a public talk about something important: *a* **debate** *about the punishment for criminals*

debate[2] *verb (present participle* **debating,** *past* **debated***)*
to talk about something important: *The government is* **debating** *the education laws.*

debt /det/ *noun*
money owed: *He has a* **debt** *of £30 which he must pay me. He is* **in debt** *to me* (= he owes me money).

decay[1] /dɪ'keɪ/ *verb*
to go bad: *His teeth had* **decayed,** *because he never cleaned them.*

decay[2] *noun (no plural)*
the state of being bad: *tooth* **decay**

○ **deceive** /dɪ'siːv/ *verb (present participle* **deceiving,** *past* **deceived***)*
to make someone believe what is

not true: *He* **deceived** *her into thinking he could drive a car.*
  deceit *noun* (*no plural*): *He got the money* **by deceit.**

○ **December** /dɪ'sembə^r/ *noun*
  the 12th month of the year

decent /'diːsnt/ *adjective*
  good enough: *a* **decent** *house*

○ **decide** /dɪ'saɪd/ *verb*
  (*present participle* **deciding,** *past* **decided**)
  to think that you will do one thing; choose what to do: *I* **decided** *to go home, although they asked me to stay at the party. She could not* **decide** *which dress to buy.*
  decision /dɪ'sɪʒn/ *noun*: *She could not* **make a decision** *about the dresses.*

deck /dek/
noun
a part of a ship, bus, etc. where passengers sit or stand

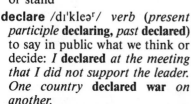

deck

declare /dɪ'kleə^r/ *verb* (*present participle* **declaring,** *past* **declared**)
  to say in public what we think or decide: *I* **declared** *at the meeting that I did not support the leader. One country* **declared war** *on another.*
  declaration /ˌdeklə'reɪʃn/ *noun*

decorate /'dekəreɪt/ *verb*
  to make prettier with ornaments, colour, etc.: *She* **decorated** *the room with flowers.*
  ˌ**deco'ration** *noun*: **decorations** *in the room*

decrease[1] /dɪ'kriːs/ *verb* (*present participle* **decreasing,** *past* **decreased**)
  to get less or fewer: *The number of children in the school has* **decreased** *this year.*

decrease[2] /'diːkriːs/ *noun* (*no plural*)
  getting less or fewer: *There was a* **decrease** *in the number of children in school.*

deed /diːd/ *noun*
  something that you do: *He was punished for his bad* **deeds.**

○ **deep** /diːp/ *adjective*
  1 going down a long way: *This is a* **deep** *river; it is 50 feet* **deep.** *He has a* **deep** *voice.*
  2 strong or dark in colour: *He has* **deep** *brown eyes.*
  3 felt strongly: *Her love for the child was very* **deep.**
  depth /depθ/ *noun*: *What is the* **depth** *of the river? Nobody knew the* **depth** *of her love for the child.*

deer /dɪə^r/ *noun* (*plural* **deer**)
  an animal which has horns and which runs fast

○ **defeat**[1] /dɪ'fiːt/ *verb*
  to beat; win over: *They were* **defeated** *in the football match.*

○ **defeat**[2] *noun*
  loss; being beaten: *The football team suffered a* **defeat.**

defend /dɪ'fend/ *verb*
  to fight for in order to protect: *She had to* **defend** *herself against the guard dog.* **defence** *noun*

definite /'defɪnət/ *adjective*
  clear; sure: *Let's fix a* **definite** *date for the next meeting.*
  definitely *adverb*: *I can't tell you* **definitely** *when I will come.*

defy /dɪ'faɪ/ *verb*
  (*present participle* **defying,** *past* **defied** /dɪ'faɪd/)
  to be ready to fight against; show no respect for: *The child* **defied** *his mother and didn't go to school.*
  defiant /dɪ'faɪənt/ *adjective*: *The* **defiant** *child was punished.*

degree

degree /dɪˈgriː/ *noun*

1 a measurement of heat or angle (°): *The temperature* (= heat) *today is two* **degrees** *hotter than yesterday.*

2 a piece of paper saying that you have completed training at a university (see): *He passed his examinations and now has a* **degree** *in English.*

○ **delay**[1] /dɪˈleɪ/ *noun*
a time of waiting: *There was a* **delay** *while Father went back to the house to get his money.*

○ **delay**[2] *verb*
to make something take a longer time; wait: *The letter was* **delayed** *three days by the train accident.*

deliberate /dɪˈlɪbrət/ *adjective*
planned or done on purpose: *She knew she had written the wrong word, it was a* **deliberate** *mistake.*
deliberately *adverb: I didn't knock it over* **deliberately**, *it was an accident.*

delicate /ˈdelɪkət/ *adjective*
fine; easily harmed or broken: *a* **delicate** *glass/a* **delicate** *child who is often ill*

delicious /dɪˈlɪʃəs/ *adjective*
good to eat: *The soup is* **delicious.**

delight[1] /dɪˈlaɪt/ *noun* (*no plural*)
joy: *to laugh with* **delight**

delight[2] *verb*
to give joy to: *I was* **delighted** *to be invited to her party.*

deliver /dɪˈlɪvər/ *verb*
1 to bring goods to a special place: *Some new books have been* **delivered** *to the school.*
2 to help a mother have a baby: *Which doctor* **delivered** *the baby?*
delivery *noun* (*plural* **deliveries**): *a* **delivery** *of books*

demand[1] /dɪˈmɑːnd/ *verb*
to ask strongly for: *"Give me my book at once!" she* **demanded** *rudely.*

demand[2] *noun*
something asked for: *He listened to the workers'* **demand** *for more money. Teachers are* **in demand** (= needed) *in this area.*

democracy /dɪˈmɒkrəsɪ/ *noun*
a government or country where everyone has an equal right to choose their leaders, by voting (see)

demolish /dɪˈmɒlɪʃ/ *verb*
to knock down; destroy: *All these old houses are going to be* **demolished.**
demolition /deməˈlɪʃn/ *noun* (*no plural*)

demonstrate /ˈdemənstreɪt/ *verb* (*present participle* **demonstrating**, *past* **demonstrated**)
to show clearly: *He* **demonstrated** *how to use the new machine.*
demonˈstration *noun: to give a* **demonstration**

den /den/ *noun*
a place in which a wild animal lives

dense /dens/ *adjective*
thick: **dense** *forest*

dentist /ˈdentɪst/ *noun*
a doctor who looks after your teeth

deny /dɪˈnaɪ/ *verb* (*present participle* **denying**, *past* **denied** /dɪˈnaɪd/)
to say something is not true: *He said that I had stolen his bicycle, but I* **denied** *it.*

depart /dɪˈpɑːt/ *verb*
to leave; go away: *When does the next train* **depart**?
departure /dɪˈpɑːtʃər/ *noun: The* **departure** *of the train was delayed.*

○ **department** /dɪˈpɑːtmənt/ *noun*
a part of a business, company,

government, etc.: *He teaches in the History* **department** *of the college. A* **department store** *is a big shop which sells many kinds of goods.*

○ **depend** /dɪ'pend/ *verb*

1 to be a result of: *"Are you going for a walk?" "That* **depends on** *the weather." "Are you coming with us?" "It* **depends** (= I have some doubts about it)."*

2 to need; trust: *She* **depends on** *him to take her to school every day. Can I* **depend** *on your help?*

dependent *adjective: She is completely* **dependent on** *her daughter for money.*

deposit[1] /dɪ'pɒzɪt/ *verb*

1 to put down: *He* **deposited** *his books on the kitchen table.*

2 to put into a bank: *She* **deposited** *her money in the bank.*

deposit[2] *noun*

money you pay to show that you want something and will pay the rest later: *He put a* **deposit** *on a house.*

depot /'depəʊ/ *noun*

a place where goods or vehicles are stored

depress /dɪ'pres/ *verb*

to make someone feel sad: *He was* **depressed** *because he had not passed his examinations.*

depression /dɪ'preʃn/ *noun* (*no plural*) feeling sad: *A holiday will help his* **depression.**

depth /depθ/ *noun* see **deep**

deputy /'depjʊtɪ/ *noun* (*plural* **deputies**)

someone who is second in importance to the head of something: *When the headmaster was away, the* **deputy** *head did his job.*

descend /dɪ'send/ *verb*

to go down: *to* **descend** *the steps*

descendant *noun* a person in your family who lives after you

○ **describe** /dɪ'skraɪb/ *verb* (*present participle* **describing**, *past* **described**)

to tell about; say what something is like: *I will* **describe** *you: you are 5 feet tall, quite strong, you laugh a lot, and you like reading.*

description /dɪ'skrɪpʃn/ *noun: That is a* **description** *of you.*

○ **desert**[1] /'dezət/ *noun*

a large empty, usually very dry, place where almost nothing grows: *the Sahara* **desert**

desert[2] /dɪ'zɜːt/ *verb*

to leave completely: *He* **deserted** *his family and went to the city.*

○ **deserve** /dɪ'zɜːv/ *verb* (*present participle* **deserving**, *past* **deserved**)

to be worth: *He has worked very hard; he* **deserves** *more money.*

design[1] /dɪzaɪn/ *noun*

1 a pattern: *a* **design** *on material*

2 a plan: *designs for a new house*

design[2] *verb*

to make a plan for something: *Who* **designed** *the new house?*

desire[1] /dɪ'zaɪər/ *noun*

a strong wish: *I had a* **desire** *to go swimming.*

desire[2] *verb* (*present participle* **desiring**, *past* **desired**)

to want very much: *She* **desires** *money, and she will do everything she can to get it.*

○ **desk** /desk/

noun

a work-table, often with space inside it for keeping books, pens, etc.

desk

despair[1] /dɪ'speər/ *noun*

a feeling of not being able to hope:

I was in despair *when my daughter went to live in New York — I knew she would never come back.*

despair[2] *verb*
to have no hope: *I* despair of *ever seeing my daughter again.*

desperate /'desprət/ *adjective*
ready to do anything to get what you want: *The man lost in the desert was* desperate *for water.*
    desperately *adverb*

despise /dɪ'spaɪz/ *verb* (*present participle* **despising**, *past* **despised**)
to hate a person or thing because you think it is not worth anything: *She* despises *cheap clothes and will only wear the best.*

despite /dɪ'spaɪt/ *preposition*
in spite of: Despite *the bad weather we enjoyed our holiday.*

dessert /dɪ'zɜːt/ *noun*
a sweet dish or fruit that you eat at the end of a meal

destination /destɪ'neɪʃn/ *noun*
the place you are going to: *It took us all day to reach our* destination.

○ **destroy** /dɪ'strɔɪ/ *verb*
to break up or get rid of completely: *The fire* destroyed *all my books.*
    destruction /dɪ'strʌkʃn/ *noun* (*no plural*): *The fire caused the* destruction *of my books.*

detail /'diːteɪl/ *noun*
one of the small points which make up the whole of something: *Give me all the* details *of the accident — tell me what happened* in detail.

detect /dɪ'tekt/ *verb*
to discover: *I* detected *a smell of gas. A policeman* detects *criminals.*
    detective *noun* a special policeman who finds out who has done a crime

detergent /dɪ'tɜːdʒənt/ *noun*
a sort of soap for washing clothes, dishes, etc.

deteriorate /dɪ'tɪərɪəreɪt/ *verb* (*present participle* **deteriorating**, *past* **deteriorated**)
to get worse: *Your work has* deteriorated *in the last month.*

determine /dɪ'tɜːmɪn/ *verb* (*present participle* **determining**, *past* **determined**)
to make up your mind firmly; decide: *I am* determined to *do better than Anne.*
    de,termi'nation *noun: That girl has great* determination; *I am sure she will do well.*

detest /dɪ'test/ *verb*
to hate: *I* detest *cheese; I can't eat it.*

○ **develop** /dɪ'veləp/ *verb*
to grow: *Several industries are* developing *in this area. Some children* develop *more slowly than others. When a photograph is* developed, *the film is treated with special liquids so that the picture can be seen.*
    development *noun* **1** something new in the growth of something: *an exciting* development *in the story of the robbery* **2** (*no plural*) growing: *The* development *of this industry will take several years.*

device /dɪ'vaɪs/ *noun*
a useful thing or trick: *a* device *for opening bottles*

devil /'devl/ *noun*
a bad being, thought to cause all the bad things in people's lives

devote /dɪ'vəʊt/ *verb* (*present participle* **devoting**, *past* **devoted**)
to give your time, thoughts, etc. completely to: *She* devoted *all her time to her job.*

dew /djuː/ *noun* (*no plural*)
water which forms on the ground, on plants, etc. when the sun has set

diagonal /daɪˈægənl/ *noun*
(see picture on page 185)

diagram /ˈdaɪəgræm/ *noun*
a plan drawn to explain an idea, or how something works

dial[1] /ˈdaɪəl/ *noun*
a round part of a machine or instrument, often with numbers on it

dials

dial[2] *verb* (*present participle* **dialling**, *past* **dialled**)
to make a telephone call by moving the dial to get the right numbers

diameter /daɪˈæmɪtəʳ/ *noun*
(see picture on page 185)

diamond /ˈdaɪəmənd/ *noun*
a very hard, clear stone that is worth a lot of money: *a ring with a* **diamond** *in the centre*

diary /ˈdaɪərɪ/ *noun* (*plural* **diaries**)
a book in which you can write down things that have happened or things to remember each day

dice /daɪs/ *noun* (*plural* **dice**)
a small square block with a different number of spots on each side (from 1 to 6), used in games

dictate /dɪkˈteɪt/ *verb* (*present participle* **dictating**, *past* **dictated**)
to say something for someone else to write: *I* **dictated** *a letter to my secretary.* **dic'tation** *noun*

○ **dictionary** /ˈdɪkʃənrɪ/ *noun* (*plural* **dictionaries**)
a book which tells you what words mean and how to spell them

did /dɪd/ *verb*
(past tense of the verb **do**): *I did*

all my homework, but my sister **didn't** (= did not) *do hers.*

○ **die** /daɪ/ *verb* (*present participle* **dying**, *past* **died** /daɪd/)
to stop living: *to* **die** *of an illness*

diesel /ˈdiːzl/ *or* ˈ**diesel oil** *noun* (*no plural*)
oil used to make buses and trains go

diet /ˈdaɪət/ *noun*
1 what you eat
2 special food eaten by people who want to get thinner, or people who are ill: *She is* **on a diet.**

differ /ˈdɪfəʳ/ *verb*
to be different: *My sister and I* **differ** *in many ways. She* **differs from** *me in many ways.*

○ **different** /ˈdɪfrənt/ *adjective*
not the same: *I don't like that dress, I want a* **different** *one.*
difference *noun*

○ **difficult** /ˈdɪfɪkəlt/ *adjective*
hard to do or understand; not easy: *a* **difficult** *question*
difficulty *noun* (*plural* **difficulties**): *This question is full of* **difficulties.** *Do you have any* **difficulty** *with English?*

○ **dig** /dɪg/ *verb* (*present participle* **digging**, *past* **dug** /dʌg/)
to cut downwards into

spade

dig

something; make a hole by cutting and taking material from: *He is* **digging** *in his garden. He has* **dug up** *some vegetables. She* **dug** *a fork into the vegetable. The old miner was* **digging** *for gold.*

digest /daɪˈdʒest/ *verb*
to take food into the body from

the stomach: *Some foods are easier to digest than others.*
digestion /dɪ'dʒestʃən/ *noun*

dignity /'dɪgnɪtɪ/ *noun (no plural)*
1 a person's feeling of their own worth: *Although she is very poor, she has not lost her dignity.*
2 serious and calm behaviour: *It is difficult to act with dignity when you are angry about something.*

dim /dɪm/ *adjective*
not very bright: *a dim light*
dimly *adverb*

din /dɪn/ *noun (no plural)*
loud noise: *What a din the children are making!*

○ **dinner** /'dɪnər/ *noun*
the largest meal of the day

○ **dip** /dɪp/ *verb (present participle* **dipping,** *past* **dipped)**
to put something into a liquid and then take it out again: *She dipped her hand in the sea to find out how cold it was.*

○ **direct¹** /daɪ'rekt, dɪ-/ *adjective*
straight: *Which is the most direct way to the station?*
directly *adverb* straight: *We live directly opposite the school. You must go to bed directly after tea.*

direct² *verb*
to tell someone the way to go or what to do: *I directed the traveller to the hotel.*

○ **di'rection** *noun* where someone or something is going or pointing; the way: *In which direction are you going, north or south?*
director *noun* a person who controls a business: *He is one of the directors of the company.*
directory *noun*
(*plural* **directories**) a book to tell you where people live or what their telephone numbers are

○ **dirt** /dɜːt/ *noun (no plural)*
anything which stops something being clean; something that has to be washed off: *There is some dirt on your coat.*
dirty *adjective* (**dirtier, dirtiest**) having dirt on it; not clean: *My shoes were dirty.*

disabled /dɪs'eɪbəld/ *adjective*
not being able to move your body easily because of some illness or wound: *The disabled man could not use the stairs. Blind people and deaf people are disabled too.*

disadvantage /ˌdɪsəd'vɑːntɪdʒ/ *noun*
something that makes things more difficult for you: *This child is at a disadvantage in school because she cannot hear well. One of the disadvantages of this house is that it is very far from the city.*

disagree /ˌdɪsə'griː/ *verb* (*past* **disagreed**)
not to agree: *He said it would rain, but I disagreed with him — I was sure it wouldn't rain.*
disagreement *noun: a small disagreement about the weather*

disappear /ˌdɪsə'pɪər/ *verb*
to go away; be no longer seen: *The boy disappeared round the corner.*

○ **disappoint** /ˌdɪsə'pɔɪnt/ *verb*
to be less interesting, nice, etc. than you expected, and so make you sad: *Don't be disappointed if you lose, next time you might win!*
disappointment *noun: He could not hide his disappointment when his team lost the game.*

disaster /dɪ'zɑːstər/ *noun*
something very bad, especially something that happens to a lot of people: *The floods were a disaster, hundreds of people were killed and crops destroyed.*

disc /dɪsk/
noun
any round
flat thing:
The dog had

discs

a **disc** *on a band round its neck,
with the name of its owner on it.
A record* (see) *can also be called a*
disc.

discipline /'dɪsɪplɪn/ *noun* (*no
plural*)
teaching you to obey and control
yourself: *Soldiers have to learn*
discipline *in the army.*

discount /'dɪskaʊnt/ *noun*
some money taken off the price of
something: *We will give you a*
discount *if you pay now.*

discourage /dɪs'kʌrɪdʒ/ *verb*
(*present participle* **discouraging,**
past **discouraged**)
to take away or try to take away the
wish to do something from
someone: *The school teachers*
discourage *smoking.*

○ **discover** /dɪ'skʌvər/ *verb*
to find or find out: *Scientists*
discovered *that there was no water
on the moon.*
discovery *noun* (*plural* **discover-
ies**) something discovered: *a new*
discovery *in medical science*

discriminate /dɪ'skrɪmɪneɪt/ *verb*
(*present participle* **discriminating,**
past **discriminated**)
to treat a person or people in a
different way from others, because
of race or religion or another
reason: *In Europe, employers are
not allowed to* **discriminate against**
women.
di,scrimi'nation *noun* (*no
plural*): **Discrimination** *against
women is not allowed.*

discuss /dɪ'skʌs/ *verb*
to talk about: *I want to* **discuss**

your work with you.
di'scussion *noun: a* **discussion**
about his work

disease /dɪ'ziːz/ *noun*
illness: *a* **disease** *of the eyes*

disgrace /dɪs'greɪs/ *noun* (*no
plural*)
the loss of other people's good
opinion of you: *He was in* **disgrace**
because he had lied.

disguise¹ /dɪs'gaɪz/ *verb*
(*present participle* **disguising,** *past*
disguised)
to try to look like someone else, as
a trick: *The policeman* **disguised**
*himself as a farmer, so the
criminals would not notice him.*

disguise² *noun*
something that you wear to make
you look like someone else

disgust¹ /dɪs'gʌst/ *verb*
to give someone a strong feeling of
not liking to see, taste, or smell
something unpleasant
disgusting *adjective: The bad
fish had a* **disgusting** *smell.*

disgust² *noun* (*no plural*)
a strong feeling of dislike: *The
smell filled me with* **disgust.**

○ **dish** /dɪʃ/ *noun* (*plural* **dishes**)
1 a container for food: *a* **dish** *of
rice*
2 part of a meal: *We had a fish*
dish *and a meat* **dish.**

dishonest /dɪs'ɒnɪst/ *adjective*
not honest

disinfect /ˌdɪsɪn'fekt/ *verb*
to clean thoroughly with special
chemicals: *The ill man's room was*
disinfected *when he got better.*
disinfectant *noun* (*no plural*) a
chemical used to disinfect

dislike¹ /dɪs'laɪk/ *verb* (*present
participle* **disliking,** *past* **disliked**)

not to like: *He likes cats but* **dislikes** *dogs. He* **dislikes** *reading.*

dislike² *noun*

not liking; something that is not liked: *I felt a strong* **dislike** *of the new teacher.*

disloyal /dɪs'lɔɪəl/ *adjective*

not faithful or true to someone: *She is* **disloyal** *to her family; she says bad things about them.*

dismal /'dɪzməl/ *adjective*

dull or sad; not bright or happy: *a* **dismal** *rainy day*

dismay /dɪ'smeɪ/ *noun (no plural)*

a feeling of loss and fear: *"Someone's robbed my house!" she said* **in dismay.**

dismiss /dɪs'mɪs/ *verb*

to send away: *The children were* **dismissed** *and sent home. He was* **dismissed** *from his job.*

disobey /ˌdɪsə'beɪ/ *verb*

not to do what you are told; not to obey: *Jane's mother told her to stay inside, but she* **disobeyed** (*her*) *and went out.*

disobedience /ˌdɪsə'biːdɪəns/ *noun (no plural)*: *She was punished for her* **disobedience.**
disobedient *adjective*

disorganized /dɪs'ɔːgənaɪzd/ *adjective*

untidy; not in order: *Her desk is very* **disorganized.**

display¹ /dɪ'spleɪ/ *verb*

to show something so that many people can see it: *The children's work was* **displayed** *on the wall.*

display² *noun*

a show: *All the parents were looking at the* **display** *of children's work. The work was* **on display.**

dispose /dɪ'spəʊz/ *verb (present*

participle **disposing,** *past* **disposed)**

to get rid of: *I have* **disposed of** *my old clothes.*

dispute /dɪ'spjuːt/ *noun*

a quarrel: *We had a* **dispute** *about how much money he owes me.*

dissatisfied /dɪ'sætɪsfaɪd/ *adjective*

not pleased enough: *I have tried to write this story four times but I am still* **dissatisfied** *with it.*

dissolve /dɪ'zɒlv/ *verb (present participle* **dissolving,** *past* **dissolved)**

to mix completely with a liquid: *Sugar* **dissolves** *in hot tea.*

distant /'dɪstənt/ *adjective*

far: *The foreign visitors came from a* **distant** *country.*

○ **distance** *noun: What* **distance** *do you have to walk to school? I could see the bus coming* **in the distance** (= far away).

distinct /dɪ'stɪŋkt/ *adjective*

1 clear; easily seen or heard: *The hills were* **distinct** *against the sky.*
2 separate; different: *There are several* **distinct** *languages in every African country.*

distinctly *adverb: I told you* **distinctly** *not to go to the park, so why did you go?*

distinguish /dɪ'stɪŋgwɪʃ/ *verb*

to see or hear clearly; notice: *Can you* **distinguish** *the different musical instruments playing now?*

distinguished *adjective* famous

distress¹ /dɪ'stres/ *noun (no plural)*

a feeling of sadness or difficulty: *The mother was* **in great distress** *when her baby became ill.*

distress² *verb*

to make someone sad: *The mother was* **distressed** *by her baby's illness.*

distribute /dɪ'strɪbjuːt/ *verb*
(*present participle* **distributing,**
past **distributed**)
to give or send to different people
or places: *We* **distributed** *the books
to the schoolchildren.*

ˌdistri'bution *noun* (*no plural*):
the **distribution** *of the books*

district /'dɪstrɪkt/ *noun*
a part of a country, city, etc.: *He
doesn't live in this* **district.**

disturb /dɪ'stɜːb/ *verb*
(*present participle* **disturbing,** *past*
disturbed)
1 to break the calm state of a
person; make someone feel
worried: *Please don't* **disturb** *me
while I'm working. I have heard
some bad news which has*
disturbed *me very much.*
2 to move something out of order:
Please don't **disturb** *the papers on
my desk.*

disturbance *noun* a breaking of
the calm state; trouble: *There has
been a* **disturbance** *in the street:
someone has been hurt.*

ditch /dɪtʃ/ *noun*
(*plural* **ditches**)
a deep narrow
place for water
to run,
especially by a
road or field

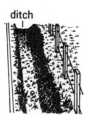

ditch

dive /daɪv/ *verb*
(*present participle* **diving,** *past*
dived)
to go head first into water: *He*
dived *into the swimming pool. She*
dived *to the bottom of the river.*

diver *noun* a person who works
under water and wears special
instruments to help him breathe

○ **divide** /dɪ'vaɪd/ *verb* (*present
participle* **dividing,** *past* **divided**)

1 to split into pieces: *The road*
divided *into three, and I took the
middle road.*
2 to share: *We* **divided** *the apple
between us.*
3 to find out how many times a
number will go into another: *I*
divided *39 by 3. The answer was 13.*

division /dɪ'vɪʒn/ *noun* **1** (*no
plural*) dividing sums: *I haven't
learnt how to do* **division** *yet.*
2 part of something: *Which*
division *of the company do you
work in?*

divine /dɪ'vaɪn/ *adjective*
of or like a god or God

divorce[1] /dɪ'vɔːs/ *verb*
(*present participle* **divorcing,** *past*
divorced)
to arrange by law for a husband
and wife to separate, so that either
may marry again: *"When did she*
divorce *her husband?" "They got*
divorced *last year."*

divorce[2] *noun*
an act of divorcing: *She got a*
divorce *from him last year.*

dizzy /'dɪzɪ/ *adjective*
(**dizzier, dizziest**)
feeling as if things are turning
round you, and you are going to
fall: *I feel* **dizzy** *when I look out
of a high window.*

○ **do**[1] /duː/ *verb*
present tense

singular	plural
I **do**	*We* **do**
You **do**	*You* **do**
He/She/It **does**	*They* **do**

past tense **did**
past participle **done**
present participle **doing**
to act; carry out: *When you have*
done *your school work, you can*
do *something else.* **Do up**
(= fasten) *your shirt, it is not* **done**

up *properly. What have you* **done with** *your bicycle? I put it in the yard. I can't* **do without** (= live comfortably without) *my books.*

○ **do²** *verb*

1 (used with **not** before another verb, to say that something is not so): *I do not like apples — I don't* (= do not) *like oranges either.*

2 (used with another verb, to ask a question): **Don't** *you want to come to see the film?*

3 (used with **not,** to tell someone not to do something): **Do not** *leave your bag in the bus.*

4 (used to make another verb stronger): *You're wrong if you think I don't like school; I* **do** *like it!*

dock¹ /dɒk/ *noun*

a place where ships are loaded and unloaded

dock² *verb*

(of a ship) to come into a dock

○ **doctor** /'dɒktər/ *noun*

a person who looks after people's health

dodge /dɒdʒ/ *verb* (*present participle* **dodging,** *past* **dodged**) to move quickly to one side to avoid something: *He* **dodged** *the book that I threw at him.*

does /dəz; *strong* dʌz/ *verb*

(the part of the verb **do** that we use with **he, she,** and **it**): *Anna* **does** *a lot of jobs in the house, but her sister* **doesn't** (= does not).

○ **dog** /dɒg/ *noun*

an animal with four legs and a tail, that eats meat: *Some people keep* **dogs** *in their houses.*

doll /dɒl/ *noun*

a toy made to look like a person

dollar /'dɒlər/ *noun*

the money used in America and some other countries

dome /dəʊm/ *noun*
a high rounded roof

dome

domestic /də'mestɪk/ *adjective*

1 found in or to do with the home: **domestic** *jobs like cleaning and cooking*

2 not wild: *Cattle are* **domestic** *animals.*

dominate /'dɒmɪneɪt/ *verb* (*present participle* **dominating,** *past* **dominated**)

to have power over: *That child* **dominates** *all the smaller children.*

donate /dəʊ'neɪt/ *verb* (*present participle* **donating,** *past* **donated**)

to give: *The businessman* **donated** *a lot of money to the hospital.*

donation /dəʊ'neɪʃn/ *noun: a* **donation** *of money to the hospital*

donor /'dəʊnər/ *noun* someone who gives: *She is a* **'blood donor** (= she gives her blood to be used in the hospital).

done /dʌn/ see **do**

donkey
/'dɒŋkɪ/
noun
an animal
like a small
horse with long ears

donkey

don't /dəʊnt/ see **do**

○ **door** /dɔːr/ *noun*

the entrance to a building or room; the flat piece of wood, metal, etc. which shuts the entrance: *Will you wait at the* **door**? *Please open the* **door** *for me.*

doorway *noun* the opening for an entrance to a room or a building: *He stood in the* **doorway** *and watched me.*

dormitory /'dɔːmɪtrɪ/ *noun*
(*plural* **dormitories**)
a room for several people to sleep in: *Children sleep in* **dormitories** *when they live at school.*

dose /dəʊs/ *noun*
an amount of medicine that you should take at one time: *Here is your medicine — the* **dose** *is two spoonfuls every four hours.*

° **dot** /dɒt/ *noun*
a small round mark: *On·the map towns were marked by a red* **dot**. *A small "i" has a* **dot** *on it.*

double[1] 'dʌbl/
adjective, adverb, noun
1 twice as much: *He took a* **double** *share of the sweets, two bags instead of one.*
2 with two parts: *a* **double** *door*
3 made for two: *a* **double** *bed*

° **double**[2] *verb* (*present participle* **doubling**, *past* **doubled**)
to become or make twice as big or twice as much: *He worked so well that I* **doubled** *his wages.*

° **doubt**[1] /daʊt/ *verb*
to be unsure of something: *I* **doubt** *if he will pass the examinations.*

° **doubt**[2] *noun*
reason for being unsure about: *I have (my)* **doubts** *about whether he is the best man for the job. There is no* **doubt** *that he is guilty.*
doubtful *adjective* unsure: *It is* **doubtful** *that he will come.*
doubtless *adverb* surely: *He will* **doubtless** *arrive by the next train.*

dough /dəʊ/ *noun* (*no plural*)
a soft mixture of flour and water: *We use* **dough** *to make bread.*

° **down** /daʊn/
adverb, preposition, adjective
in or to a lower place: *Sit* **down**, *please, and put your bags* **down** *on the floor. The children ran* **down**

(= along) *the road. The men are* **down** *by the river.*

'**downwards** *adverb* from a higher to a lower place; towards the ground or floor: *She climbed* **downwards** *to a lower branch of the tree. He fell face* **downwards** *in the sand.*

,**upside-'down** *adverb*
with the top part downwards: *If you hold the bottle* **upside-down**, *all the liquid will run out.*

upside-down

downhill /daʊn'hɪl/ see **hill**

downstairs /daʊn'steəz/ see **stairs**

doze[1] /dəʊz/ *verb* (*present participle* **dozing**, *past* **dozed**)
to sleep lightly for a short time: *I* **dozed (off)** *for about an hour.*

doze[2] *noun*
a short sleep: *to have a* **doze**

dozen /'dʌzən/ *noun*
twelve: *I want a* **dozen** *eggs, please. There were* **dozens of** (= a lot of) *people there.*

Dr /'dɒktər/
the short way of writing **doctor** in a name: **Dr** *Brown*

drag /dræg/ *verb* (*present participle* **dragging**, *past* **dragged**)
to pull along behind you: *The bag was too heavy to carry, so he had to* **drag** *it into the house.*

dragon /'drægən/ *noun*
an imaginary animal in stories that is said to breathe fire

drain[1] /dreɪn/ *noun*
a pipe or hollow which takes dirty water away: *Your kitchen* **drain** *has become blocked by tea leaves.*

drain[2] *verb*
1 to flow away; make water flow

drama

away: *Some farmers have to* **drain**
water off their fields. The water
drained away *slowly.*
2 to become drier as water flows
away: *After I washed the plates, I*
left them to **drain.**

drama /ˈdrɑːmə/ *noun* (*no plural*)
1 stories that can be acted; plays
2 excitement: *I like the* **drama** *of*
a big storm.
   dramatic /drəˈmætɪk/ *adjective*
exciting: *a* **dramatic** *scene*

drank /dræŋk/ see **drink**

draught /drɑːft/ *noun*
air blowing into a room: *a cold*
draught *under the door*

draughts /drɑːfts/ *plural noun*
a game played with 24 round
pieces on a board of black and
white squares

○ **draw** /drɔː/ *verb* (*past tense*
drew /druː/, *past participle*
drawn / drɔːn/)
1 to make a picture, especially with
a pencil or pen: *I* **drew** (*a picture*
of) *my cat. I like* **drawing** (*cats*).
2 to pull or pull up: *The cart was*
drawn *by oxen.*
3 to come: *The day of the party*
drew *nearer.*
   drawing *noun* **1** (*no plural*)
making pictures: **Drawing** *is my*
favourite lesson. **2** a picture done
by pen or pencil: *She had done*
a **drawing** *of her mother.*

○ **drawer** /drɔːʳ/
noun
a box that fits
into a piece of
furniture, with
handles so
that it can be
pulled out and
pushed in

chest of drawers

chest of ˈdrawers *noun* a piece
of furniture with several drawers

dreadful /ˈdredfəl/ *adjective*
very bad or unpleasant: *There's*
been a **dreadful** *accident — two*
people have died. I've had a
dreadful *day — everything seems*
to have gone wrong.

○ **dream**[1] /driːm/ *verb* (*present*
participle **dreaming**, *past* **dreamt**
/dremt/ *or* **dreamed** /driːmd/)
1 to imagine things while you are
asleep: *I* **dreamt about** *my teacher*
last night.
2 to imagine something nice: *I*
dream of *being the best footballer*
in the town.

○ **dream**[2] *noun*
1 something that you imagine
while you are asleep: *a frightening*
dream
2 something nice that you imagine,
or that you want to do: *It is my*
dream *to come first in the race.*

drench /drentʃ/ *verb*
to make completely wet: *I was*
drenched *in the storm.*

○ **dress**[1] /dres/ *verb*
1 to put on and wear clothes: *He*
is **dressed** *very well. She like to*
dress up (= put on nice, special
clothes) *for a party.* **Dress yourself**
quickly.
2 to clean and put cloth round a
wound: *I* **dressed** *his cut hand.*

○ **dress**[2] *noun*
1 (*plural* **dresses**) a piece of
clothing with a top and a skirt,
worn by women and girls
2 (*no plural*) clothes: *He was in*
special **dress** *for the ceremony.*

drift /drɪft/ *verb*
to float along:
The piece of
wood was **drifting**
down the river.

drill[1] /drɪl/ *verb*
to make a

drills

hole in something with a special machine: *to* **drill** *a hole in the wall*

drill[2] *noun*

a machine for making holes

○ **drink**[1] /drɪŋk/ *verb* (*present participle* **drinking**, *past tense* **drank** /dræŋk/, *past participle* **drunk** /drʌŋk/)

to take liquid into the mouth and swallow it: *He* **drank** *some beer. Would you like something to* **drink**?

○ **drink**[2] *noun*

some liquid taken and swallowed: *Can I have a* **drink**? *Would you like a* **drink** *of water?*

drip[1] /drɪp/ *verb* (*present participle* **dripping**, *past* **dripped**)

to fall or let fall in drops: *The rain* **dripped** *through the trees. The trees* **dripped**.

drip[2] *noun*

a small drop: **Drips** *of water fell down her neck.*

○ **drive**[1] /draɪv/ *verb* (*present participle* **driving**, *past tense* **drove** /drəʊv/, *past participle* **driven** /'drɪvn/)

to make a vehicle move in the direction you want: *Can you* **drive** *(a car)? I* **drove** *to town yesterday.* **driver** *noun: a bus* **driver**

drive[2] *noun*

1 a journey by road vehicle: *It is a short* **drive** *to the village.*
2 a road going to a house only: *He left his car in the* **drive**.

droop /druːp/ *verb*

to hang down: *The flowers* **drooped** *soon after we picked them.*

○ **drop**[1] /drɒp/ *verb* (*present participle* **dropping**, *past* **dropped**)

to fall or let fall: *The plate* **dropped** *from her hands. She* **dropped** *the*

plate. *Why don't you* **drop in** (= visit us) *tomorrow?*

○ **drop**[2] *noun*

a small amount of liquid: *A few* **drops** *of rain landed on the roof.*

drought /draʊt/ *noun*

a time when no rain falls and the land becomes very dry

drove see **drive**

drown /draʊn/ *verb*

to die by not being able to breathe under water: *Don't play by the river in case you fall in and* **drown**!

drug /drʌg/ *noun*

medicine: *This drug will get rid of the pain in your back.*

○ **drum**[1] /drʌm/ *noun*

drums

1 a musical instrument made of a round hollow box with skin stretched tightly over it, which is beaten
2 a metal container for oil, water etc.

○ **drum**[2] *verb* (*present participle* **drumming**, *past* **drummed**)

to beat or make music on a drum **drummer** *noun*

drunk[1] /drʌŋk/ *adjective*

having had too much alcohol: *The man who started singing outside our house was* **drunk**.

Drunken means the same as drunk, but can only be used with a noun: *a* **drunken** *man*

drunk[2] see **drink**

○ **dry**[1] /draɪ/ *adjective* (**drier** /'draɪər/ **driest** /'draɪ-ɪst/)

not containing water; not wet: *This coat will keep you* **dry** *in the rain.*

○ **dry**[2] *verb* (*present participle* **drying**, *past* **dried** /draɪd/)

to make or become dry: *The*

clothes **dried** *quickly outside. She* **dried** *her hair in the sun.*

duchess /'dʌtʃɪs/ *noun*
the wife of a duke (see)

duck /dʌk/ *noun*
a bird that swims on water and can be kept by people for its eggs and meat

duckling /'dʌklɪŋ/ *noun*
a young duck

due /djuː/ *adjective*
1 owed; that should be paid or given: *Our thanks are* **due** *to him.*
2 expected: *The train is* **due** *at five. I am* **due** *for* (= it is time for me to have) *a rise in pay.*

    due to *preposition* because of; caused by: *His illness was* **due to** *bad food.*

duet /djuː'et/ *noun*
a song or piece of music for two people

dug /dʌg/ see **dig**

duke /djuːk/ *noun*
the title of a man from a very important family in Britain

○ **dull** /dʌl/ *adjective*
1 not bright or light: *a* **dull**, *cloudy day/a* **dull** *brown colour*
2 not interesting or clever: *a* **dull** *speech*

dumb /dʌm/ *adjective*
not able to speak

○ **dump**[1] /dʌmp/ *verb*
to leave, drop, or throw away: *We* **dumped** *our bags on the floor. There are special places where you can* **dump** *things you don't want.*

dump[2] *noun*
a place where things can be thrown away: *They dumped their old car in the town* **dump.**

○ **during** /'djʊərɪŋ/ *preposition*
1 all the time that something is going on: *They swim every day* **during** *the holidays.*
2 at some time while something else is happening: *He fell asleep* **during** *the lesson.*

dusk /dʌsk/ *noun* (no plural)
the time when the sun has just set: *It is difficult to see clearly at* **dusk.**

○ **dust**[1] /dʌst/ *noun* (no plural)
fine powder carried in the air or lying on dry ground: *There is a lot of* **dust** *on this table.*

dust[2] *verb*
to clean dust from: *She* **dusted** *the table.*

    '**dustbin** *noun* a large metal or plastic container for unwanted waste
    dusty *adjective* (**dustier, dustiest**): *a* **dusty** *road*

○ **duty** /'djuːtɪ/ *noun* (plural **duties**)
1 what you ought to do: *It is your* **duty** *to look after your children.*
2 a time when you are looking after things: *Only one doctor is* **on duty** *today — the other doctor is* **off duty.**

dwarf /dwɔːf/ *noun*
a person, plant, or animal that is much smaller than usual

dye[1] /daɪ/ *verb* (*present participle* **dyeing**, *past* **dyed** /daɪd/)
to give a colour to: *She* **dyed** *her hair black.*

dye[2] *noun*
something that gives a lasting colour: **Dyes** *come from plants or from chemicals.*

Ee

° **each** /iːtʃ/
every one separately: **Each** *child has an exercise book for his own work. The two brothers help* **each 'other** (= each brother helps the other).

° **eager** /'iːgəʳ/ *adjective*
very anxious to do something: *The boy was* **eager** *to show me his stamps.* **eagerly** *adverb*

eagle /'iːgl/
noun
a large bird
that kills other
creatures for
food

eagle

° **ear** /ɪəʳ/ *noun*
1 one of the parts on each side of the head with which you hear (picture on page 133)
2 the part of a plant where the seed is: *an* **ear** *of corn*
earring /'ɪəˌrɪŋ/ *noun:*
Ornaments worn in or on the ears are called **earrings**.

° **early** /'ɜːlɪ/ *adjective, adverb*
(**earlier, earliest**)
1 before the usual or agreed time: *We agreed to meet at seven o'clock but I was* **early**; *I arrived at half past six. The bus arrived* **early**.
2 near the beginning (of a day, year, etc.): *It often rains in the* **early** *morning. Do you get up* **early**?

° **earn** /ɜːn/ *adjective*
to get money in return for work you do: *He has* **earned** *a lot of money by working in the evenings.*

° **earth** /ɜːθ/ *noun*
1 the world on which we live: *The* **Earth** *goes round the sun once a year.* (picture on page 259)
2 (*no plural*) the substance on the ground in which plants can grow: *She put the seeds in the* **earth**.
earthquake /'ɜːθˌkweɪk/ *noun* a strong and sudden shaking of the ground

° **ease**[1] /iːz/ *noun* (*no plural*)
the ability to do something without difficulty: *He passed the examination* **with ease**.
ease[2] *verb* (*present participle* **easing,** *past* **eased**)
to make better: *The medicine* **eased** *the pain.*

° **east** /iːst/ *noun, adjective, adverb*
the direction from which the sun comes up in the morning: *Our house faces* **east**. *There is a strong* **east** *wind* (= from the east).
eastern /'iːstən/ *adjective* in or of the east
eastwards *adverb* towards the east: *to travel* **eastwards**

° **easy** /'iːzɪ/ *adjective*
(**easier, easiest**)
not difficult; done with no trouble: *It was an* **easy** *job and we did it quickly.*
easily /'iːzəlɪ/ *adverb: He did the job* **easily**.

° **eat** /iːt/ *verb* (*present participle* **eating,** *past tense* **ate** /et, eɪt/, *past participle* **eaten** /'iːtn/)
to put food into the mouth and swallow it: *Have you* **eaten** *your breakfast yet?*

echo[1] /'ekəʊ/ *verb*
(of a sound) to come back again: *Our voices* **echoed** *in the empty room.*

echo[2] *noun (plural* **echoes***)*
a sound that comes back to you·
the **echoes** *of our voices*

eclipse /ɪ'klɪps/ *noun*
a time when the light from the sun
(or moon) is blocked by the moon
(or Earth) (picture on page 259)

economy /ɪ'kɒnəmɪ/ *noun (no
plural)*
the management of money: *The
country's* **economy** *depends on the
amount of goods it sells abroad. It
is good* **economy** *to buy well-made
shoes, as they will last longer.*
  economic /,iːkə'nɒmik, ,ekə-/
  adjective: What is the **economic**
  state of the country?
  economical *adjective* cheap:
  Going by train is more
  economical *than going by plane.*

∘ **edge** /edʒ/ *noun*
  1 the outside end of something; the
  part which is furthest from the
  middle: *The* **edge** *of the plate was
  blue.*
  2 the cutting part of a knife, axe,
  etc.: *That knife has a sharp* **edge***.*

editor /'edɪtəʳ/ *noun*
a person who prepares books or
newspapers before they are printed
  edition /ɪ'dɪʃn/ *noun* a book or
  newspaper brought out at a
  special time

∘ **educate** /'edjʊkeɪt/ *verb*
  (*present participle* **educating***, past*
  educated*)*
  to teach people: *School teachers
  educate children.*
  edu'cation *noun (no plural)*
  teaching and learning: **Education**
  *is given to children by the
  government in many countries.*
  edu'cational *adjective* helping
  you to learn: *an* **educational** *toy*

eel /iːl/ *noun*
a long fish shaped like a snake

effect /ɪ'fekt/ *noun*
a result: *Alcoholic drink can have
a bad* **effect** *on your body.*
  effective *adjective* getting the
  result you want: *The medicine is
  an* **effective** *cure for a headache.*

efficient /ɪ'fɪʃnt/ *adjective*
working well and getting a lot of
things done: *an* **efficient** *secretary*
  efficiently *adverb*

effort /'efət/ *noun*
the use of strength in trying to do
something: *With a great* **effort** *he
pushed open the door. Please put
more* **effort** *into your school work.*

e.g. /,iː 'dʒiː/
for example: *They keep animals,*
e.g. *goats and cattle.*

∘ **egg** /eg/ *noun*
a rounded
thing from
which baby
birds, snakes,
fish, or insects come: *We eat hens'*
eggs*.*

white   yolk
eggs

eight /eɪt/ *noun, adjective*
the number 8
  eighth /eɪtθ/ *noun, adjective*
  number 8 in order; 8th

eighteen /eɪ'tiːn/ *noun, adjective*
the number 18
  eighteenth *noun, adjective*
  number 18 in order; 18th

eighty /'eɪtɪ/ *noun, adjective*
the number 80
  eightieth /'eɪtɪ-əθ/
  noun, adjective number 80 in
  order; 80th

either /'aɪðəʳ, 'iːðəʳ/
  1 one or the other of two: *Both
  skirts are too small, so I can't wear
  either (of them). **Either** the father
  or his sons drive the truck.*
  2 (used in sentences with **not***): I
  haven't been to America, or to
  England,* **either***.*

elaborate /ɪˈlæbrət/ *adjective*
having many different parts or needing a lot of different sorts of work done on it

elastic[1] /ɪˌlæstɪk/ *adjective*
which goes back to its first shape after being stretched or pulled: *Rubber is an* **elastic** *substance.*

elastic[2] *noun*
a material which is elastic: *a belt made of* **elastic**

○ **elbow** /ˈelbəʊ/ *noun*
the part of your arm which bends it in the middle (picture on p.133)

○ **elder** /ˈeldər/ *adjective*
the older of two: *Which brother did you see, the* **elder** *or the younger?*

○ **eldest** /ˈeldɪst/ *adjective*
the oldest of three or more: *My* **eldest** *brother lives abroad.*

elect /ɪˈlekt/ *verb*
to choose, usually by vote (see): *The government is made up of men and women* **elected** *by the people of the country.*

  election *noun* a time when we choose people for special positions: *The government* **elections** *will be next month. Who won the* **election**?

○ **electricity** /ˌɪləkˈtrɪsətɪ/ *noun*
(*no plural*)
power for lighting, heating, machinery, etc. that is sent through wires: *Do you use* **electricity** *for cooking?*

  electric /ɪˈlektrɪk/ *adjective*
working by electricity: *an* **electric** *cooker*

  electrical *adjective* about electricity: *The cooker isn't working because of an* **electrical** *fault.*

  electrician /ˌɪləkˈtrɪʃn/ *noun*: *An* **electrician** *repaired the cooker*

elegant /ˈelɪgənt/ *adjective*
graceful and beautiful: **elegant** *clothes* **elegantly** *adverb*

element /ˈelɪmənt/ *noun*
one of the very simple substances from which everything is made: *Gold and iron are* **elements** *but brass is not, because it is made by mixing two other metals.*

elementary /ˌelɪˈmentrɪ/ *adjective*
having to do with the beginning of something: *an* **elementary** *reading book for a child who is learning to read*

elephant /ˈelɪfənt/ *noun*
a very large animal which has two long curved teeth (**tusks**) and a long nose (**trunk**), and lives in hot places (picture on page 17)

eleven /ɪˈlevn/ *noun, adjective*
the number 11: **Eleven** *minus one is ten* (11−1 = 10).

  eleventh *noun, adjective* number 11 in order; 11th

eliminate /ɪˈlɪmɪneɪt/ *verb* (*present participle* **eliminating**, *past* **eliminated**)
to take out; get rid of: *She has been* **eliminated** *from the swimming race because she did not win any of the practice races.*

○ **else** /els/ *adverb*
1 other; different; instead: *If you don't like eggs I can cook something* **else.**
2 more; as well: *Would you like something* **else** *to eat?*
3 (used in some questions and phrases): *It's not here; where* **else** *can we look? If the train has gone, how* **else** *can we get home. Hold the bottle in both hands* **or else** (= if not) *you may drop it.*

  else'where *adverb* in or to some other place: *They left the village and went* **elsewhere.**

embarrass

embarrass /ɪmˈbærəs/ *verb*
to make someone feel nervous or silly in front of other people: *When I began to sing, he laughed and made me **embarrassed**.*
embarrassment *noun* (*no plural*)

embassy /ˈembəsɪ/ *noun* (*plural **embassies***)
a place where people work to represent their own country in another country

embrace[1] /ɪmˈbreɪs/ *verb* (*present participle **embracing**, past **embraced***)
to hold in the arms to show love: *The child **embraced** his parents.*

embrace[2] *noun*
holding in the arms: *a loving **embrace***

embroider /ɪmˈbrɔɪdəʳ/ *verb*
to sew with ornamental patterns: *to **embroider** a dress*

embroidery

embroidery *noun* (*no plural*): *The dress was covered with beautiful **embroidery**.*

emerge /ɪˈmɜːdʒ/ *verb* (*present participle **emerging**, past **emerged***)
to come out: *The baby birds **emerged from** their eggs.*

emergency /ɪˈmɜːdʒənsɪ/ *noun* (*plural **emergencies***)
a sudden happening that needs something done about it all at once: *The hospital has to treat **emergencies** such as car accidents. In an **emergency**, telephone the police.*

emir /ˈemɪəʳ/ *noun*
a Muslim ruler, especially in Asia and parts of Africa

emotion /ɪˈməʊʃn/ *noun*
a feeling: *Anger and love are strong **emotions**.*

emperor /ˈemprəʳ/ *noun*
a ruler of a country or several countries
empire /ˈempaɪəʳ/ *noun* a group of countries ruled by an emperor
empress /ˈemprɪs/ *noun* a female ruler of a country or several countries; the wife of an emperor

emphasize /ˈemfəsaɪz/ *verb* (*present participle **emphasizing**, past **emphasized***)
to show that something is important: *He **emphasized** the need for hard work.*

○ **employ** /ɪmˈplɔɪ/ *verb*
to give work to: *I am **employed** by the National Bank, which **employs** hundreds of people.*
employee /ɪmˈplɔɪ-iː/ *noun* a person who is employed by someone else: *There are ten **employees** in his firm.*
employer *noun* a person who employs others
employment *noun* (*no plural*): *He left his home to look for **employment**.*

○ **empty**[1] /ˈemptɪ/ *adjective* (**emptier**, **emptiest**)
having nothing inside: *The house is **empty**, no one is living there.*

○ **empty**[2] *verb* (*present participle **emptying**, past **emptied***)
to take everything out of: *He **emptied** the box of books (onto the floor).*

enable /ɪˈneɪbl/ *verb* (*present participle **enabling**, past **enabled***)
to make possible: *The new machine **enables** us to cut and tie up our wheat quickly.*

Roland Ayotte

enamel /ɪˈnæml/ *noun*
a kind of paint for metal: *The iron pan was covered with white enamel.*

enclose /ɪnˈkləʊz/ *verb* (*present participle* **enclosing**, *past* **enclosed**)
to shut something in: *The football field is enclosed by a wall. When I wrote to my parents, I enclosed a photograph of the baby (in the letter).*

    enclosure /ɪnˈkləʊʒəʳ/ *noun*: *They put the cattle into an enclosure.*

° **encourage** /ɪnˈkʌrɪdʒ/ *verb* (*present participle* **encouraging**, *past* **encouraged**)
to give praise or hope to someone so that he will do something: *I encouraged her to work hard and to try for the examinations.*

encyclopaedia /ɪnˌsaɪkləˈpiːdɪə/ *noun*
a book that gives you knowledge about a lot of things; it is usually arranged in alphabetical order

° **end**[1] /end/ *noun*
the furthest point or edge of anything: *When you get to the end of this road, turn right. At the end of the lesson, we went home.* **In the end** (= at last) *we found the house.*

° **end**[2] *verb*
to finish: *When the lesson ended, we went home.*

    ending *noun* the end of a story, film, play, or word: *The story had a happy ending.*

    endless *adjective*: *There is endless work to do when you have children in the house.*

endure /ɪnˈdjʊəʳ/ *verb* (*present participle* **enduring**, *past* **endured**)
to bear: *I can't endure loud music.*

    endurance *noun* (*no plural*) the power to bear something or to keep doing something for a long time: *Long-distance races are a test of a runner's endurance.*

enemy /ˈenəmɪ/ *noun*
(*plural* **enemies**)
a person or country that is not friendly to you or that wants to harm you: *The two countries are enemies.*

energy /ˈenədʒɪ/ *noun* (*no plural*)
power to do things or to make things work: *I have no energy left after playing football. Coal and oil give us energy for heating, lighting, moving things, etc.*

    energetic /enəˈdʒetɪk/ *adjective*: *He is an energetic boy; he enjoys sports.* **energetically** *adverb*

engaged /ɪŋˈɡeɪdʒd/ *adjective*
1 busy or being used: *The headmaster is engaged — can you come back later? The telephone number you want is engaged; try again in a few minutes.*
2 having promised to marry someone: *My brother is engaged to Anne, they will be married next year.*

    engagement *noun*: *My brother has just told me about his engagement to Anne. I have three engagements* (= things to do which will make me busy) *today — so can I see you tomorrow?*

° **engine** /ˈendʒɪn/ *noun*
a machine which uses petrol, oil, gas, electricity, or steam and which makes things work or move: *a car engine*

    engine driver *noun* someone who drives a train

engineer /ˌendʒɪˈnɪəʳ/ *noun*
a person who plans and makes machines, roads, bridges, etc.

    engineering *noun* (*no plural*) the science or job of an engineer: *He is studying engineering at college.*

enjoy

° **enjoy** /ɪn'dʒɔɪ/ *verb*
to get pleasure from: *I enjoy my job.* **enjoyable** *adjective*
enjoyment *noun* (*no plural*): *I get a lot of enjoyment from my job.*

enlarge /ɪn'lɑːdʒ/ *verb* (*present participle* **enlarging,** *past* **enlarged**)
to make bigger: *to enlarge a photograph*

enormous /ɪ'nɔːməs/ *adjective*
very large: *an enormous plate of food*

° **enough** /ɪ'nʌf/
adjective, adverb, noun
as much as is needed: *There is* **enough** *paper here. Are you sure there is* **enough** (*of it*)? *That seat is not big* **enough** *for 5 people.*

enquire /ɪn'kwaɪə'/ see **inquire**

° **enter** /'entə'/ *verb*
to go or come in: *He entered the room quietly.*

entertain /,entə'teɪn/ *verb*
to do something to amuse or interest people: *He entertained us with stories about life abroad.*
entertainment *noun*: *If you want* **entertainment** *in the city, you can go to a film or play.*

enthusiasm /ɪn'θjuːzɪæzm/ *noun* (*no plural*)
an eager feeling of wanting to do something: *He plays football with* **enthusiasm.**
enthusiastic /ɪn,θjuːzɪ'æstɪk/ *adjective*

entire /ɪn'taɪə'/ *adjective*
whole; complete: *The entire class will be there.*
entirely *adverb*: *I agree with you* **entirely.**

° **entrance** /'entrəns/ *noun*
1 a place where you go in: *He stood in the entrance of the hospital.*
2 going or coming in: *The music* played for the **entrance** of the dancers.

entry /'entrɪ/ *noun* (*plural* **entries**)
entrance: *That road sign says "No* **entry",** *which means that cars cannot go into the road.*

envelope
/'envələʊp, 'ɒnvələʊp/
noun
a folded
paper cover for a letter  envelope

environment /ɪn'vaɪərənmənt/ *noun*
the conditions surrounding something: *The children have a happy* **environment** *at school.*

envy[1] /'envɪ/ *noun* (*no plural*)
the feeling of anger or bitterness because someone has more of something or a better life than you have: *He was filled with* **envy** *because Richard passed the examination and he did not.*
envious /'envɪəs/ *adjective*: *He was* **envious** *of my new car.*

envy[2] *verb* (*present participle* **envying,** *past* **envied**)
to feel envy: *He envied his friend.*

epidemic /epɪ'demɪk/ *noun*
an illness that spreads quickly to a lot of people

° **equal**[1] /'iːkwəl/ *adjective*
the same as: *I gave the three children* **equal** *sums of money.*
equality /ɪ'kwɒlətɪ/ *noun* (*no plural*) being equal: *All three children have* **equality** *in our family — they are all treated in the same way.*
equally *adverb*: *They are both* **equally** *good at reading.*

equal[2] *noun*
someone who is as good as someone else: *All people should be treated as* **equals** *by the law.*

equal³ *verb* (*present participle* **equalling**, *past* **equalled**)
1 to be the same as: *Three and five equals eight* (3 + 5 = 8).
2 to be as good, clever, etc. as: *None of us can* **equal** *Sarah — she's always top of the class.*

equator /ɪˈkweɪtəʳ/ *noun*
an imaginary line that runs round the middle of the Earth (picture on page 185)

equip /ɪˈkwɪp/ *verb* (*present participle* **equipping**, *past* **equipped**)
to give things that are useful for doing something: *Our school is* **equipped with** *a radio and a television.*
   equipment *noun* (*no plural*): *Our school has been given some new* **equipment** *— a radio and a television.*

erect¹ /ɪˈrekt/ *adjective*
standing straight: *to stand* **erect**

erect² *verb*
to put up: *They* **erected** *the hut in two hours.*

errand /ˈerənd/ *noun*
a short journey made to do something useful or necessary: *My mother asked me to go* **on an errand** *— she wanted me to buy some food.*

error /ˈerəʳ/ *noun*
a mistake: *This work is full of* **errors!**

erupt /ɪˈrʌpt/ *verb*
to burst out: *Volcanoes are mountains from which melted rock* **erupts.**

escalator /ˈeskəleɪtəʳ/ *noun*
moving stairs which can take

escalator

you up or down without you walking

° **escape¹** /ɪˈskeɪp/ *verb* (*present participle* **escaping**, *past* **escaped**)
to get free from: *to* **escape** *from prison*

° **escape²** *noun*
the act of escaping: *The prisoner* **made his escape** *at night.*

escort /ɪˈskɔːt/ *verb*
to go with someone: *A group of soldiers* **escorted** *the President.*
   escort /ˈeskɔːt/ *noun*: *an* **escort** *of soldiers*

° **especially** /ɪˈspeʃlɪ/ *adverb*
1 very; more than usual: *She is* **especially** *good at science.*
2 most of all: *I would like a bicycle,* **especially** *a blue one.*

essay /ˈeseɪ/ *noun*
a piece of writing on a special thing: *She wrote an* **essay** *on "My Family".*

essential /ɪˈsenʃl/ *adjective*
necessary; very important: *If you travel abroad, it is* **essential** *that you have the right papers.*

estate /ɪˈsteɪt/ *noun*
a large piece of land, usually with a house on it: *A* **housing estate** *is a piece of land on which a group of houses has been built. An* **estate agent** *is a person who arranges the buying and selling of houses.*

estimate¹ /ˈestɪmeɪt/ *verb* (*present participle* **estimating**, *past* **estimated**)
to make a reasonable guess: *I* **estimate** *that the journey will take three hours.*

estimate² /ˈestɪmət/ *noun*
a guess

etc. /etˈsetrə/
and so on: *There are lots of things to buy — tea, sugar, bread,* **etc.**

° **even**[1] /'iːvn/ *adjective*

1 flat and smooth: *an even surface*
2 equal: *He won the first game and I won the second, so we're* **even.**
3 (of a number) that can be divided exactly by two: *2 and 4 are* **even** *numbers, but 3 and 5 are odd numbers.*
  evenly *adverb: Divide the sweets* **evenly** *among the three boys* (= give the same number to each boy).

° **even**[2] *adverb*

1 more than we usually expect: *He let me use his bicycle and he* **even** *said I could keep it all day.*
2 still; yet: *Yesterday it rained hard, and today it's raining* **even** *harder.*

° **evening** /'iːvnɪŋ/ *noun*

the time between the end of the afternoon and when you go to bed

° **event** /ɪ'vent/ *noun*

a happening, often an important one: *What* **events** *do you remember from your schooldays?*

  eventually /ɪ'ventʃəlɪ/ *adverb*
  at last; in the end: *I looked everywhere for my glass and* **eventually** *found it under my chair.*

° **ever** /'evəʳ/ *adverb*

1 at any time: *Have you* **ever** *been abroad? She used to sing well, but now she sings better* **than ever.**
2 always: *I have lived here* **ever since** *I was a child. I would like to stay here* **for ever.**

° **every** /'evrɪ/

each one; not missing out one: *I have read* **every** *book in the cupboard.*

  everybody /'evrɪbɒdɪ/ *or*
  everyone /'evrɪwʌn/
  every person: **Everybody** *wanted to watch the match.*

  everyday /ˌevrɪ'deɪ/ *adjective*
  usual; not special: *This is an* **everyday** *dress; I shall wear something better to the party.*

everything /'evrɪθɪŋ/
every thing; all things: *I got* **everything** *I needed in the market.*

everywhere /'evrɪweəʳ/ *adverb*
in or to every place: *I looked* **everywhere** *for my watch, but I couldn't find it.*

evidence /'evɪdəns/ *noun*
(*no plural*)
words or things which prove something: *You say that John took your book, but have you any* **evidence** *of that?*
  evident *adjective* clear: *It is* **evident** *that you have done the job well.* **evidently** *adverb*

evil /'iːvl/ *adjective*
very bad: *It was* **evil** *to kill the old woman and steal all her money.*

ex- /eks/
used of someone who used to be what is said, but no longer is: *She is his* **ex-***wife.*

° **exact** /ɪg'zækt/ *adjective*
completely correct: *Can you tell me the* **exact** *time?*
  exactly *adverb: It is* **exactly** *four o'clock, not one minute more nor one minute less.*

exaggerate /ɪg'zædʒəreɪt/ *verb*
(*present participle* **exaggerating,** *past* **exaggerated**)
to make something seem bigger, better, worse, etc. than it really is: *When he had been ill, he* **exaggerated** *and said he had nearly died.* **ex,agge'ration** *noun*

° **examination** /ɪgˌzæmɪ'neɪʃn/ *noun*
a test of knowledge: *Have you* **passed the examination** *you took last month? No, I* **failed that examination** *but I'm taking it again next year.*

ex'am *noun:* **Exam** *is short for examination and is nearly always used in spoken English.*

examine /ɪg'zæmɪn/ *verb* (*present participle* **examining,** *past* **examined**)
1 to look at closely: *The doctor examined my throat.*
2 to give someone an examination

○ **example** /ɪg'zɑːmpl/ *noun*
one thing taken from a number of things of the same kind to show what the other things are like: *I showed my new employer some examples of my work. You can use any two colours* — **for example,** *red and yellow.*

exceed /ɪk'siːd/ *verb*
to be more than: *If your lorry exceeds this weight, you cannot cross the bridge.*

excellent /'eksələnt/ *adjective*
very good: *This is excellent work, Paul.* **excellently** *adverb*

○ **except** /ɪk'sept/
apart from; not including: *I have washed all the clothes except your shirt.*

exception /ɪk'sepʃn/ *noun*
something which is different from what is usually expected: *Most children like sweets, but she is the exception* — *she will not eat them!*
exceptional *adjective* unusual, especially unusually good: *an exceptional pupil*
exceptionally *adverb*

excess /'ekses/ *noun, adjective*
more than is usual or allowed: *You have to pay for excess luggage* (see) *on a plane.*

○ **exchange**[1] /ɪks'tʃeɪndʒ/ *verb* (*present participle* **exchanging,** *past* **exchanged**)
to change something for something else

○ **exchange**[2] *noun*
an act of exchanging: *We made an exchange* — *she had my dress and I had hers.*

○ **excite** /ɪk'saɪt/ *verb* (*present participle* **exciting,** *past* **excited**)
to give strong and pleasant feelings; cause to lose calmness: *The games excited the children and they all started to shout.*
excited *adjective* having strong and pleasant feelings; not calm
excitement *noun:* *The excitement of the games has made them tired.*
exciting *adjective* able to make someone excited: **exciting** *news*

exclaim /ɪk'skleɪm/ *verb*
to shout out or say loudly in surprise: *"Look there's James on the television!"* **exclaimed** *Peter.*
exclamation /ˌeksklə'meɪʃn/ *noun*

exclamation mark *noun*
the sign ! used in writing to show surprise, shock, etc., or when calling someone: *Come here!*

exclude /ɪk'skluːd/ *verb* (*present participle* **excluding,** *past* **excluded**)
to keep someone or something out: *We had to exclude John from the team because he hurt his leg.*

excursion /ɪk'skɜːʃn/ *noun*
a short journey, for pleasure: *We went on an excursion to the city.*

○ **excuse**[1] /ɪk'skjuːz/ *verb* (*present participle* **excusing,** *past* **excused**)
to forgive: *I excused James's bad work, as I knew he had been ill.* **Excuse me** (*troubling you*), *could you tell me the way to the station?*

○ **excuse**[2] /ɪk'skjuːs/ *noun*
a reason given when you ask someone to forgive you: *I haven't done the work well; my excuse is that I have been ill.*

execute /'eksɪkjuːt/ *verb* (*present participle* **executing**, *past* **executed**)
to kill as a punishment decided by law **exe'cution** *noun*

° **exercise**[1] /'eksəsaɪz/ *noun*
1 using your body to make it stronger or more healthy: *Running is good* **exercise**.
2 a piece of work given in school: *I wrote in my* **exercise book**.

° **exercise**[2] *verb* (*present participle* **exercising**, *past* **exercised**)
to use part of the body: *He was* **exercising** *his arms by swinging from a rope.*

exhaust[1] /ɪgˈzɔːst/ *verb*
to make very tired: *We are all* **exhausted** *after the journey.*

exhaust[2] *noun* (*no plural*)
burnt gas which comes out from the back of a car

exhibit /ɪgˈzɪbɪt/ *verb*
to show in public: *She* **exhibited** *her paintings at our school.*
exhibition /ˌeksɪˈbɪʃn/ *noun:* *an* **exhibition** *of paintings*

exile /'eksaɪl/ *noun*
someone who is not allowed to live in his own country as a punishment: *He had been five years* **in exile** (= made to live abroad).

exist /ɪgˈzɪst/ *verb*
to be: *The elephant* (see) *is the largest land animal that* **exists**.
existence *noun* (*no plural*): *The elephant is the largest land animal in* **existence**.

exit /'eksɪt/ *noun*
the way out of a place: *Where is the* **exit**?

expand /ɪkˈspænd/ *verb*
to grow or make larger: *The business has* **expanded** *from having one office to having twelve.*
expansion /ɪkˈspænʃn/ *noun*

° **expect** /ɪkˈspekt/ *verb*
to think that something will happen: *Do you* **expect** *to win the race? Yes, I* **expect** *I will win.*

expedition /ˌekspəˈdɪʃn/ *noun*
a journey, usually a long one to find out something: *an* **expedition** *to find the beginning of the River Nile*

expel /ɪkˈspel/ *verb* (*present participle* **expelling**, *past* **expelled**)
to send away, especially from a school: *The pupils were* **expelled** *for stealing.*
expulsion /ɪkˈspʌlʃn/ *noun*

expensive /ɪkˈspensɪv/ *adjective*
costing a lot of money: *It is* **expensive** *to travel by plane.*
expense *noun* cost; money spent: *What are the* **expenses** *of moving house?*

experience[1] /ɪkˈspɪərɪəns/ *noun*
1 something that happens to you: *The accident was an* **experience** *she will never forget.*
2 (*no plural*) work you have done before of the same sort: *Have you any* **experience** *of teaching?*

experience[2] *verb* (*present participle* **experiencing**, *past* **experienced**)
to have something happen to you: *to* **experience** *fear*
experienced *adjective* having done something before: *an* **experienced** *teacher*

experiment[1] /ɪkˈsperɪmənt/ *noun*
a careful test done to see whether something is true: *We can learn by* **experiment** *that oil and water will not mix.*

experiment[2] /ɪkˈsperɪment/ *verb*
to make a careful test to see if something is true: *We* **experimented** *by putting oil and water together, and we saw that they did not mix.*

expert /'eksp3:t/ *noun*
a person who is very good at something special: *an* **expert** *in cookery/a cookery* **expert**

○ **explain** /ɪk'spleɪn/ *verb*
to make clear: *Can you* **explain** *why you were late?*
explanation /ˌeksplə'neɪʃn/ *noun: What is your* **explanation** *for being late?*

○ **explode** /ɪk'spləʊd/ *verb* (*present participle* **exploding**, *past* **exploded**)
to burst with a loud noise: *When you blow air into a paper bag, and then hit the bag, it* **explodes.**
explosion /ɪk'spləʊʒn/ *noun: The* **explosion** *was caused by a burst gas pipe.*
explosive /-sɪv/ *noun*
something that makes things explode: *The miners put some* **explosives** *in the mine, to loosen the coal.*

explore /ɪk'splɔːr/ *verb*
(*present participle* **exploring**, *past* **explored**)
to find out about a place by going and looking: *Have you really* **explored** *your nearest town?*
exploration /ˌeksplə'reɪʃn/ *noun*
ex'plorer *noun* a person who travels into an unknown area to find out about it

export[1] /ɪk'spɔːt/ *verb*
to send something out of the country to be sold abroad: *South Africa* **exports** *fruit.*

export[2] /'ekspɔːt/ *noun*
something that is exported: *Fruit is one of South Africa's* **exports.**

expose /ɪk'spəʊz/ *verb* (*present participle* **exposing**, *past* **exposed**)
to uncover: *He* **exposed** *the wound on his arm.*

○ **express**[1] /ɪk'spres/ *verb*
to say clearly: *He wanted to* **express** *his thanks but he could not think of the best words.*
expression /ɪk'spreʃn/ *noun* **1**
something that is said: *You should not use that* **expression** — *it's not polite.* **2** the look on someone's face: *a sad* **expression**

express[2] *noun*
a fast train which makes only a few stops on its journey

extend /ɪk'stend/ *verb*
to stretch out; make larger or longer: *The headmaster* **extended** *our holiday by four days.*
extension /ɪk'stenʃn/ *noun*
something that extends: *We built an* **extension** *onto the school, so now we have two more classrooms.*
extensive /-sɪv/ *adjective*
spreading over a large area: *The school has* **extensive** *playing fields.*
extent /ɪk'stent/ *noun* the area that something spreads over: *What is the* **extent** *of your garden?*

external /ɪk'stɜːnl/ *adjective*
of or on the outside: *the* **external** *walls of a house*

extinguish /ɪk'stɪŋgwɪʃ/ *verb*
to put out: *to* **extinguish** *a fire*
extinguisher *noun* a container of chemicals which will put out a fire quickly

extra /'ekstrə/
adjective, adverb, noun
more than usual; more than is expected: *Can I have* **extra** *time to finish my work? This hotel charges* **extra** *for a room with a bath.*

extract /ɪk'strækt/ *verb*
to take out: *The dentist* (see) **extracted** *my tooth.*

extraordinary /ɪkˈstrɔːdnrɪ/
adjective
very unusual or strange: *I heard an* **extraordinary** *story the other day.*

extravagant /ɪkˈstrævəgənt/
adjective
spending too much money: *She's very* **extravagant** *— she spends all her money on clothes.*
extravagance *noun*

extreme /ɪkˈstriːm/ *adjective*
the furthest possible: *She lives at the* **extreme** *edge of the forest.*
extremely *adverb* very: *I am* **extremely** *hot.*

°**eye** /aɪ/ *noun*
1 the part of the head with which you see (picture on p. 133) **2** a small hole at one end of a needle

'**eyebrow** *noun* the hairy line above the eye (picture on p. 133)
'**eyelash** *noun* one of the hairs growing on the part of the eye which shuts
'**eyelid** *noun* either of the pieces of skin which shut over the eye
'**eyesight** *noun* (*no plural*): *Her* **eyesight** *is very good, she can see a ship far out in the sea.*

Ff

fable /ˈfeɪbl/ *noun*
a story which teaches something about good behaviour

fabric /ˈfæbrɪk/ *noun*
woven material; cloth: *She bought some* **fabric** *to make shirts from.*

°**face**¹ /feɪs/ *noun*
1 the front part of the head, with the eyes, nose, and mouth
2 the front of other things, such as a **clock face**

°**face**² *verb* (*present participle* **facing**, *past* **faced**)
to have the front towards; look at: *Our house* **faces** *the school. I knew he was angry and I could not* **face** *him* (= I wasn't brave enough to meet him).

facilities /fəˈsɪlətɪz/ *plural noun*
something for you to use, especially in a public place: *Are there washing* **facilities** *in the school?* (= is there somewhere you can wash, with soap, running water etc.?)

°**fact** /fækt/ *noun*
something that is true; something that has happened: *It is a* **fact** *that you are reading this sentence. I said it was Tuesday, but* **in fact** (=really) *it was Monday.*

°**factory** /ˈfæktrɪ/ *noun* (*plural* **factories**)
a place where things are made, often by machines

fade /feɪd/ *verb* (*present participle* **fading**, *past* **faded**)
to lose colour or brightness: *If you leave that blue dress in the sun, it will* **fade.**

Fahrenheit /ˈfærənhaɪt/ *noun* (*no plural*)
a way of measuring temperature (= how hot something is): *Water freezes at* **32 degrees Fahrenheit (32°F).**

°**fail** /feɪl/ *verb*
1 not to do well, or not to do what you intend: *He tried to jump the wall, but he* **failed.** *Our crops*

failed *because there was no rain.*
2 not to pass (an examination): *He*
failed *his English examination.*
   failure /ˈfeɪljəʳ/ *noun: The*
   failure *of the crops meant that*
   there was no food.

faint[1] /feɪnt/ *verb*
to lose the feeling of being awake
suddenly and fall down: *She*
fainted *because of the heat.*

° **faint**[2] *adjective*
not strong; not clear: *a* **faint** *sound*
of music/a **faint** *light*

° **fair**[1] /feəʳ/ *adjective*
1 equally good to everyone; just:
It is not **fair** *that my brother has*
a bicycle and I haven't.
2 good, but not very good: *His*
writing is good, but his reading is
only **fair.**
3 pale: *English people usually have*
fair *skin.*
   fairly *adjective* a bit but not very:
   This bed is **fairly** *soft.*

fair[2] *noun*
a gathering of people to buy and
sell things and to amuse themselves

fairy /ˈfeərɪ/ *noun* (*plural* **fairies**)
a small imaginary person who can
do things that ordinary people
cannot do

faith /feɪθ/ *noun*
belief in something: *I have* **faith** *in*
you; I am sure you will do well.
   faithful *adjective* able to be
   trusted: *a* **faithful** *friend*
   faithfully *adverb: You must end*
   a letter starting "Dear Sir" with
   "Yours **faithfully"**, *and then put*
   your name.

° **fall**[1] /fɔːl/ *verb*
(*past tense* **fell** /fel/, *past*
participle **fallen** /ˈfɔːlən/)
to drop to a lower place: *The price*
of food has **fallen.** *Rain was*
falling *steadily. The apples* **fell off**
the tree. The pile of books **fell over**
(= fell to the ground).

° **fall**[2] *noun*
an act of falling: *The child had a*
bad **fall** *and hurt himself. There*
has been a **fall** *in the price of food.*

false /fɔːls/ *adjective*
1 not true: *Is this statement true or*
false?
2 not real: **false** *teeth*
   falsely *adverb*

fame /feɪm/ *noun* (*no plural*)
being well-known
   ° **famous** /ˈfeɪməs/ *adjective*
   well-known: *This town is* **famous**
   for its beautiful buildings.

familiar /fəˈmɪlɪəʳ/ *adjective*
known; often seen or heard; usual:
This song sounds **familiar.** *Are you*
familiar with (= do you know) *this*
type of car?

° **family** /ˈfæməlɪ/ *noun*
(*plural* **families**)
a group of relatives

famine /ˈfæmɪn/ *noun*
a time when there is no food

fan[1] /fæn/
noun
an
instrument
for moving

fans
the air to make us cooler: *The*
electric **fan** *made his office cool.*

fan[2] *verb* (*present participle*
fanning, *past* **fanned**)
to make the air move: *She* **fanned**
herself with the newspaper to cool
her face.

fancy[1] /ˈfænsɪ/ *adjective* (**fancier,**
fanciest)
not usual or plain: **fancy** *clothes*

fancy[2] *verb* (*present participle*
fancying, *past* **fancied** /ˈfænsɪd/)
1 to imagine: **Fancy** *James winning*
the competition! (= Isn't it
surprising?)

2 to want or like: *I don't* **fancy** *fish today.*

° **far** /fɑːʳ/ *adverb, adjective*
(**farther** /'fɑːðəʳ/, **farthest** *or* **further** /'fɜːðəʳ/, **furthest**)
1 not near; a long distance away: *How* **far** *is it to town? It isn't* **far** *away. As* **far** *as I know* (= what I know), *he has gone to town.*
2 very much: *She is* **far** *better than me at writing.*

fare /feəʳ/ *noun*
an amount of money that you pay for travelling somewhere: *a bus* **fare**/*a taxi* **fare**

° **farm** /fɑːm/ *noun*
buildings and land where people grow food or keep animals
'**farmer** *noun* a person who owns or works on a farm
'**farming** *noun* (*no plural*) the job of farmers: **Farming** *is difficult when the weather is bad.*
'**farmyard** *noun: Outside the farmhouse is the* **farmyard**, *where the chickens and dogs live.*

fascinate /'fæsɪneɪt/ *verb* (*present participle* **fascinating**, *past* **fascinated**)
to make someone feel very strong interest: *The city* **fascinates** *him.*
fasci'nation *noun* very strong interest: *The city has a* **fascination** *for him.*

fashion /'fæʃn/ *noun*
the way of dressing or doing something that is considered best at one time: *Is it the* **fashion** *to wear short skirts? Yes, short skirts are* **in fashion.**
fashionable /'fæʃnəbl/ *adjective: Short skirts are* **fashionable** *now.*
fashionably *adverb*

° **fast**[1] /fɑːst/ *adjective*
1 quick; not slow: *He is a* **fast**

runner. The clock is (*a minute*) **fast** (= it shows a time which is later than the real time).
2 firmly fixed

› **fast**[2] *adverb*
1 quickly: *to run* **fast**
2 firmly; tightly: *The boat stuck* **fast** *in the mud.*

fast[3] *verb*
to eat no food, usually for religious reasons

° **fasten** /'fɑːsn/ *verb*
to fix firmly; join or tie together: *She* **fastened** *her coat.*
fastener /'fɑːsnəʳ/ *noun: The* **fastener** *on her skirt broke.*

° **fat**[1] /fæt/ *adjective* (**fatter, fattest**)
having a wide, rounded body; not thin: *I think he's too* **fat.**
fatten /'fætn/ *verb* to make a person or animal fat

° **fat**[2] *noun* (*no plural*)
an oily substance, especially the oil that comes from meat when it is cooked: *Cakes are made of* **fat** *and flour.*

fatal /'feɪtl/ *adjective*
causing death: *a* **fatal** *car accident*
fatally *adverb*

fate /feɪt/ *noun* (*no plural*)
the power which seems to cause everything to happen: *When they met again after ten years, they felt that* **fate** *brought them together.*

° **father** /'fɑːðəʳ/ *noun*
a male parent
'**father-in-,law** *noun* (*plural* **fathers-in-law**) the father of your wife or husband

° **fault** /fɔːlt/ *noun*
something that is wrong; a mistake or weak point: *His greatest* **fault** *is that he talks too much. Who broke the cup? It's my* **fault**, *I dropped it.*
faultless *adjective* having no faults; perfect: **faultless** *work*

○ **favour** /'feɪvə^r/ *noun*
something kind done for somebody: *May I* **ask you a favour?** *Will you* **do me a favour** *and lend me some money? I am* **in favour of** (= I like the idea of) *stopping work now.*
favourable /'feɪvrəbl/ *adjective* good and suitable: **favourable** *weather for working outside*
favourite /'feɪvrɪt/ *adjective* that is liked best of all: *Oranges are my* **favourite** *fruit.*

○ **fear**[1] /fɪə^r/ *verb*
to be afraid of: *He did not* **fear** *the snake. I* **fear** (= I am worried) *that you'll be late if you don't go now.*

○ **fear**[2] *noun*
the feeling of being afraid: *He was shaking with* **fear.**
fearful *adjective* causing fear; very bad: *a* **fearful** *sound*
fearless *adjective* without fear; never afraid: *a* **fearless** *soldier*

○ **feast**[1] /fiːst/ *noun*
a large meal of good food for a special reason

○ **feast**[2] *verb*
to eat a feast

○ **feather** /'feðə^r/ *noun*
one of the things which cover birds,
like a thin stick with soft hairs

feature

feature /'fiːtʃə^r/ *noun*
1 any part of the face, especially eyes, nose, and mouth: *Her eyes were her best* **feature.**
2 a part of something that you notice specially: *The unusual chair was a* **feature** *of the room.*

February /'februəri/ *noun*
the second month of the year

federal /'fedrəl/ *adjective*
having several states or countries joined under one government, but able to look after certain things themselves: *Nigeria is a* **federal** *country.*
federation /ˌfedə'reɪʃn/ *noun*: *The small countries joined together into a* **federation.**

fee /fiː/ *noun*
money charged by a doctor, school, etc.

feeble /'fiːbl/ *adjective*
weak: *I felt* **feeble** *when I was ill.*

feed /fiːd/ *verb (present participle* **feeding,** *past* **fed** /fed/)
to give food to: *Have you* **fed** *the animals?*

feel /fiːl/ *verb (present participle* **feeling,** *past* **felt** /felt/)
1 to touch; know through your senses: *I* **feel** *cold. I* **felt** *the branch touch my face. I* **feel** *afraid.*
2 to think: *I* **feel** *that he doesn't like me.*
feeling *noun* something that is felt: *Her words gave me a* **feeling** *of pleasure. I* **have a feeling** (= I think) *he'll come.*

feet /fiːt/ see **foot**

fell /fel/ see **fall**

fellow /'feləʊ/ *noun*
a man: *Who's that old* **fellow?**

female[1] /'fiːmeɪl/ *adjective*
belonging to the sex of women: **Female** *animals give birth to young ones.*

female[2] *noun*
a female person or animal: *We've got three cats — two* **females** *and a male.*

feminine /'femɪnɪn/ *adjective*
like or of a woman

○ **fence**[1] /fens/ *noun*
a wooden or wire wall round something: *The* **fence** *kept the dog in the yard.*

fence[2] verb (*present participle* **fencing,** *past* **fenced**)
to put a fence around something

fern /fɜːn/ *noun*

fern
a green plant that has no flowers and grows in wet or shady places

ferry /ˈferɪ/ *noun* (*plural* **ferries**)
a boat that takes people or things across water: *A* **ferry** *crosses the river every hour.*

fertile /ˈfɜːtaɪl/ *adjective*
having good earth for things to grow: *His farm is on* **fertile** *land.*

fertilize /ˈfɜːtɪlaɪz/ *verb* (*present participle* **fertilizing,** *past* **fertilized**)
to make fertile: **Fertilizer** *is a substance put on land to* **fertilize** *it.*

festival /ˈfestɪvl/ *noun*
a time when people get together to amuse themselves, dance, sing, etc.

fetch /fetʃ/ *verb*
to go somewhere and bring something back: *Will you* **fetch** *some water?*

° **fever** /ˈfiːvəʳ/ *noun*
an illness when you feel hot, have a headache, etc.
feverish *adjective: I felt* **feverish** *all night.*

° **few** /fjuː/
not many: **Few** *people like snakes. Are your friends here? Yes,* **a few** (= some, but not many) *are here.*

fibre /ˈfaɪbəʳ/ *noun*
a thin thread of plant or animal substance, especially when used to make something: *Coconut* **fibre** *can be made into mats.*

° **field** /fiːld/ *noun*
a piece of ground, usually with a fence or wall round it, usually used for farming: *a* **field** *of maize*

° **fierce** /fɪəs/ *adjective*
wild; angry; cruel: *a* **fierce** *dog/a* **fierce** *storm* **fiercely** *adverb*

fifteen /fɪfˈtiːn/ *adjective, noun*
the number 15
fifteenth *adjective, noun*
number 15 in order; 15th

fifty /ˈfɪftɪ/ *adjective, noun*
the number 50
fiftieth /ˈfɪftɪ-ɪθ/ *adjective, noun* number 50 in order; 50th

fig /fɪg/ *noun*
a fruit which is full of small seeds

° **fight**[1] /faɪt/ (*present participle* **fighting,** *past* **fought** /fɔːt/)
to use your body or weapons against someone or something: *What are the boys* **fighting** *about?*

° **fight**[2] *noun*
an act of fighting: *The two boys had a* **fight.**

° **figure** /ˈfɪgəʳ/ *noun*
1 a written number like *3* or *8*
2 a shape, especially the shape of a human body: *I could see a tall* **figure** *near the door.*

file[1] /faɪl/ *noun*
1 a cardboard cover for papers
2 a metal instrument with a rough edge for making things smooth
files
3 a line of people: *They went into the school* **in single 'file.**

file[2] *verb* (*present participle* **filing,** *past* **filed**)
1 to put papers into a file: *to* **file** *letters*
2 to make something smooth with a file
3 to walk in a line one behind the other: *The children* **filed** *into the classroom.*

°**fill** /fɪl/ *verb*
to put as much as possible or needed into something: *He* **filled** (**up**) *the bucket with water. Will you* **fill in** (= put answers in the spaces in) *this printed paper?*
filling *noun: I have a* **filling** (= something put into a hollow part) *in my tooth.*

°**film**[1] /fɪlm/ *noun*
1 a story shown in a cinema or on television
2 a band put into a camera on which photographs are made
3 a thin covering: *a* **film** *of oil on water*

°**film**[2] *verb*
to photograph something on film; make a film: *The* **television** *company is* **filming** *in our town.*

filthy /ˈfɪlθɪ/ *adjective* (**filthier, filthiest**)
very dirty

fin /fɪn/ *noun*
a part of a fish which helps it to swim (picture at **fish**)

final /ˈfaɪnl/ *adjective*
coming at the end; last: *The* **final** *thing she did before she left the house was to lock the door.*
finally *adverb: She* **finally** *agreed with me.*

finance[1] /ˈfaɪnæns/ *noun*
(*no plural*)
controlling large sums of money: *People who work in banks know about* **finance.**
financial /faɪˈnænʃl/ *adjective: The bank gave him* **financial** *advice.* **financially** *adverb*

finance[2] *verb* (*present participle* **financing,** *past* **financed**)
to give the money for something: *The government will* **finance** *the building of the new roads with the taxes it collects.*

°**find** /faɪnd/ *verb*
(*present participle* **finding,** *past* **found** /faʊnd/)
to see or get something after you have been looking for it: *After looking in every room for my glasses, I* **found** *them in the kitchen, but I* **found** *that* (= I saw that it was true that) *they were broken. I* **found out** (= discovered) *later who had broken them.*

°**fine**[1] /faɪn/ *adjective*
1 nice; pleasant; very good: *a* **fine** *piece of work/* **fine** *weather*
2 very thin: **fine** *lines*

fine[2] *noun*
money paid as a punishment: *to pay a* **fine** *of £100*

fine[3] *verb* (*present participle* **fining,** *past* **fined**)
to make someone pay a fine: *The man was* **fined** *£100.*

°**finger** /ˈfɪŋgəʳ/ *noun*
one of the five long parts of your hand (picture on page 133)

°**finish** /ˈfɪnɪʃ/ *verb*
to end: *The game* **finished** *at four o'clock. Have you* **finished** (**doing**) *your work? You can use the scissors when I've* **finished with** *them* (= finished using them).

°**fire** /faɪəʳ/ *noun*
things that are burning: *He* **set fire to** (= made burn) *the dry grass. The grass* **caught fire.** *The grass was* **on fire** *for a short time. A* **fire-place** *is an area in a house where you can light fires.*
ˈ**fire-bri͵gade** *noun: The men who fight fires are called* ˈ**firemen,** *and a group of them who work together is called the* **fire-brigade.**
ˈ**firework** *noun* a cardboard tube filled with powder, which burns with bright lights or a loud noise

firm¹ /fɜːm/ *adjective*
fixed and steady: *You must always build on* **firm** *ground. The teacher was* **firm** *and did not change her mind.*

firmly *adverb: She told him* **firmly** *that he must sit down and wait his turn*(= in a way he could not argue with).

firm² *noun*
a group of people running a business; company

first /fɜːst/
1 coming before all others; earliest: *The* **first** *boy who came in was James.* **First** *we'll have breakfast, then we'll walk to school.*
2 (used in some phrases): **At first** *it was very hot, but then it got cooler.* ˌ**First of 'all** (= before everything else) *tell us your name.*

first aid /ˌfɜːst 'eɪd/ *noun*
(*no plural*)
simple help that anyone can learn to give an ill or wounded person

fish¹ /fɪʃ/
noun (*plural* **fish** *or* **fishes**)
a cold-

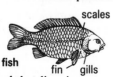

fish

scales

fin   gills

blooded animal that lives in water: *A person who catches* **fish** *is a* **fisherman** /'fɪʃəmən/.

fish² *verb*
to try to catch fish: *They are* **fishing** *in the river.*

fishing *noun* (*no plural*) catching fish: *They went* **fishing** *yesterday.*

fist /fɪst/ *noun*
the hand with the fingers closed tightly together: *He hit me with his* **fist.**

fit¹ /fɪt/ *adjective*
1 not ill; well: *Do you feel* **fit**?
2 good enough: *This food is not* **fit** *for your visitors.*

fit² *verb* (*present participle* **fitting,** *past* **fitted**)
1 to be the right size for: *The trousers don't* **fit** *him, they are too small.*
2 to fix something in place: *He* **fitted** *a telephone in my office.*

five /faɪv/ *adjective, noun*
the number 5
fifth /fɪθ/ *adjective, noun*
number 5 in order: 5th

fix /fɪks/ *verb*
1 to put in place firmly: *He* **fixed** *a picture to the wall.*
2 to mend: *I asked the boy to* **fix** *the bicycle.*
3 to arrange: *We have* **fixed** *a date for the school dance.*

fizzy /'fɪzɪ/ *adjective*
(**fizzier, fizziest**)
(of a drink) having gas in it

flag /flæg/ *noun*
a piece of cloth with a special pattern on it, used as the sign of a country, club, etc.

flag

flagpole

flagpole *noun* a tall pole at the top of which a flag is hung

flake /fleɪk/ *noun*
a small thin piece: *We wash clothes with* 'soap-**flakes.**

flame /fleɪm/ *noun*
a bright piece of burning gas that you see in a fire: *The house was* **in flames** (= burning).

flap¹ /flæp/ *verb* (*present participle* **flapping,** *past* **flapped**)
to wave up and down: *The bird* **flapped** *its wings.*

flap² *noun*
a piece of something which hangs down over an opening: *a* **flap** *on a pocket*

○ **flash**¹ /flæʃ/ *noun*
a sharp sudden light: *a* **flash** *of lightning*

○ **flash**² *verb*
to shine for a moment; move quickly: *He* **flashed** *the light in my eyes. The cars* **flashed past** (= went past quickly).

flask /flɑːsk/ *noun*
a sort of bottle: *A* **'vacuum flask** *keeps cool drinks cool and hot drinks hot.*

○ **flat**¹ /flæt/ *adjective*
not hilly or sloping; with no pieces sticking out: *That building has a* **flat** *roof. The car tyres were* **flat** (= had no air in them).
flatten /'flætn/ *verb* to make something flat: *The rain* **flattened** *the corn.*

○ **flat**² *or* **apartment** *noun*
a number of rooms on one floor of a building where a person or family lives

flatter /'flætər/ *verb*
to say that someone is better, nicer, etc. than they really are: *She only* **flatters** *you so you will help her.*
flattery /'flætərɪ/ *noun* (*no plural*)

flavour /'fleɪvər/ *noun*
a taste: *This cake has an unusual* **flavour.**

flea /fliː/ *noun*
a very small jumping insect that drinks blood from animals and people

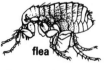
flea

flee /fliː/ *verb* (*present participle* **fleeing,** *past* **fled**)
to run away: *The cat* **fled** *from the dog.*

fleece /fliːs/ *noun*
the wool of a sheep or goat

fleet /fliːt/ *noun*
a lot of ships together, especially warships: *a* **fleet** *of fishing boats*

flesh /fleʃ/ *noun* (*no plural*)
the soft part of the body; meat: *The knife cut the* **flesh** *of his arm.*

flew /fluː/ see **fly**¹

flight /flaɪt/ *noun*
flying: *The (aeroplane)* **flight** *took three hours. They saw the birds* **in flight.**

○ **float** /fləʊt/ *verb*
to stay on the surface of a liquid; not to sink: *A boat* **floats** *on water.*

flock /flɒk/ *noun*
a number of sheep, goats, birds, etc. together: *a* **flock** *of sheep*

○ **flood**¹ /flʌd/ *noun*
a great quantity of water staying in places that are usually dry: *The* **floods** *swept away many homes.*

○ **flood**² *verb*
to cover with water: *The river rose and* **flooded** *the fields.*

○ **floor** /flɔːr/ *noun*
1 the part of a room you walk on: *a wooden* **floor**
2 all the rooms on one level: *We live on the third* **floor** (or *three* **floors** *above the ground*).

○ **flour** /flaʊər/ *noun* (*no plural*)
fine powder made from wheat, or sometimes from other grain: *Bread is made from* **flour.**

flourish /'flʌrɪʃ/ *verb*
1 to grow well: *Plants* **flourish** *in this earth.*
2 to wave about

○ **flow**¹ /fləʊ/ *verb*
(of liquids or gases) to move: *The water* **flowed** *down the hill.*

○ **flow**² *noun* (*no plural*)
a flowing movement: *The* **flow** *of air was stopped when she closed the window.*

○ **flower**¹ /ˈflaʊəʳ/
  noun
  the part of a
  plant which
  holds the
  seeds and
  which is usually
  brightly coloured

petal, stem, leaf, roots, **flower**

ˈflower-bed *noun*
  an area of earth
  with flowers planted in it

flown /fləʊn/ see **fly**¹

flu /fluː/ see **influenza**

fluent /ˈfluːənt/ *adjective*
  speaking a language smoothly and
  easily: *He speaks* **fluent** *English.*
  fluently *adverb*

fluff /flʌf/ *noun* (*no plural*)
  soft fine bits that come off
  animals, wool, etc.

fluid¹ /ˈfluːɪd/ *noun*
  something that flows; a liquid

fluid² *adjective*
  liquid; not solid; able to flow

flute /fluːt/
  noun
  a musical
  instrument
  which you
  blow

flute

○ **fly**¹ /flaɪ/ *verb* (*present participle*
  flying, *past tense* **flew** /fluː/, *past
  participle* **flown** /fləʊn/)
  1 to move through the air: *Birds
  were* **flying** *above the houses. The
  plane* **flew** *from Paris to Rome.*
  2 to go quickly: *She* **flew** (= ran)
  out of the house.

fly² *noun* (*plural* **flies**)
  a small flying insect

foal /fəʊl/ *noun*
  a baby horse

foam /fəʊm/ *noun* (*no plural*)
  the white substance which we
  sometimes see on top of water: *We*

see **foam** *on water with a lot of
soap in it.*

fog /fɒg/ *noun* (*no plural*)
  thick cloud that forms close to the
  ground: *The* **fog** *was so thick that
  I could not see my way.*
  foggy *adjective* (**foggier,
  foggiest**): *a* **foggy** *night*

○ **fold**¹ /fəʊld/ *verb*
  to turn part of something over the
  other part: *She* **folded** *the letter so
  that it would fit into her bag.*
  folder *noun* a cardboard cover
  for papers etc.

○ **fold**² *noun*
  a part of something which has
  been folded over another part

folk /fəʊk/ *noun* (*no plural*)
  people: *The old* **folk** *sat and talked.*

○ **follow** /ˈfɒləʊ/ *verb*
  to go after: *The children* **followed**
  their mother into the room. We
  followed (= went along) *the road
  to the top of the hill. He didn't*
  follow (= understand) *what the
  teacher was saying.*

fond /fɒnd/ *adjective*
  loving: *She has* **fond** *parents. I am
  not* **fond of** (= I do not like)
  eating meat.

○ **food** /fuːd/ *noun* (*no plural*)
  what you eat: *Is there enough* **food**
  for everyone?

fool¹ /fuːl/ *noun*
  someone silly: *I'm a* **fool,** *I left my
  coat on the train.*
  foolish *adjective* not reasonable;
  silly **foolishly** *adverb*

fool² *verb*
  to trick or deceive: *He* **fooled** *me
  into giving him money. Don't* **fool
  about** (= behave like a fool).

○ **foot** /fʊt/ *noun* (*plural* **feet** /fiːt/)
  1 the part of your leg that you
  stand on: *We decided to go* **on foot**
  (= walking). (picture on p. 133)

2 the bottom of something: *the* **foot** *of a hill*

3 a measure of length equal to twelve inches: *The man was six* **foot/feet** *two* (*inches*).

'**football** *noun* a game in which two teams try to kick the ball into a special space

'**footpath** *noun*: *This is a* **footpath**; *cars are not allowed.*

'**footprint** *noun* the mark of a foot: *He left* **footprints** *behind him on the sand.*

'**footstep** *noun* the sound of someone walking: *I heard* **footsteps** *in the room behind me.*

° **for** /fə^r; *strong* fɔː^r/ *preposition*

1 meant to be used in this way: *This knife is* **for** *cutting bread.*

2 meant to be given to or used by: *This book is* **for** *you — you can keep it.*

3 (showing how far or how long): *She has lived in this town* **for** *many years. I waited* **for** *three hours.*

4 going to: *the train* **for** *London*

5 at a price of: *She bought the dress* **for** *£5.*

6 as a sign of; with the meaning of: *What is the word* **for** *"tree" in your language?*

7 (used in sentences like these): *He worked* **for** *peace when he was in the government. It is hard* **for** *me to understand this work.*

for ex'ample, for 'instance showing an example of what is meant: *You can buy fruit here — oranges and bananas,* **for example.**

forbid /fə'bɪd/ *verb*
(*present participle* **forbidding**, *past tense* **forbade** /fə'bæd/, *past participle* **forbidden**)
to say no to something that someone wants to do: *I* **forbid** *you to go swimming.*

° **force**[1] /fɔːs/ *verb* (*present participle* **forcing**, *past* **forced**)
to make happen, using strength: *She* **forced** *her daughter to go to school. Don't* **force** *the door* (= make it open using strength).

° **force**[2] *noun*

1 (*no plural*) strength: *You must use* **force** *to open that bottle.*

2 a group of specially trained people like the army, etc.: *He joined the* **police force.**

ford /fɔːd/ *noun*
a place where you can walk across a river

forecast /'fɔːkɑːst/ *noun*
saying what you think will happen: *a weather* **forecast**

° **forehead** /'fɔːhed, 'fɒrəd/ *noun*
the front of the head above the eyes, where no hair grows (picture on page 133)

° **foreign** /'fɒrən/ *adjective*
of or from another country: *a* **foreign** *language*

foreigner *noun*: *He is not from this country, he is a* **foreigner.**

foreman /'fɔːmən/ *noun*
a man who controls a group of workmen

° **forest** /'fɒrɪst/ *noun*
an area where a lot of trees grow thickly together

forever /fə'revə^r/ *adverb*
always; for all time; continually: *I shall remember that happy day* **forever.**

forge /fɔːdʒ/ *verb* (*present participle* **forging**, *past* **forged**)
to make a copy of something in order to deceive: *He was sent to prison for* **forging** *money.*

forgery /'fɔːdʒərɪ/ *noun* (*plural* **forgeries**) making copies in order to deceive; a copy made like this: *This letter is a* **forgery!**

forget

° **forget** /fə'get/ *verb*
(*present participle* **forgetting**, *past tense* **forgot** /fə'gɒt/, *past participle* **forgotten** /fə'gɒtn/)
not to have a memory of; not to remember: *She* **forgot** *to post the letter.*

° **forgive** /fə'gɪv/ *verb*
(*present participle* **forgiving**, *past tense* **forgave** /fə'geɪv/, *past participle* **forgiven**)
to stop being angry with someone: *Please* **forgive** *me — I didn't mean to be rude.*

° **fork**[1] /fɔːk/
noun
1 an instrument with a

forks

handle and two or more points at the end: *We use a* **fork** *to eat food. A big* **fork** *is used to dig the earth.*
2 the place where something divides into two: *When you get to the* **fork** *in the road, go right.*

fork[2] *verb*
to divide into two: *The road* **forks** *soon after the bridge.*

° **form**[1] /fɔːm/ *noun*
1 a school class: *He is in* **Form** *2.*
2 a shape: *a sweet in the* **form** *of an egg*
3 a piece of printed paper on which you have to write things: *If you fill in this* **form**, *you can take books out of the library.*

° **form**[2] *verb*
to make: *We* **formed** *a club for people who liked cars.*
for'mation *noun* making: *the* **formation** *of a club*

formal /'fɔːml/ *adjective*
obeying the firm laws and customs of your people in every way: *a* **formal** *meeting with the leader of the government* **formally** *adverb*

former /'fɔːmə'/ *adjective*
1 the first of two: *There are Jane and Anne; the* **former** (Jane) *is wearing a green dress.*
2 earlier in time: *The owner of that shop is Mr Johnson — the* **former** *owner was Mrs Brown.*
formerly *adverb*: *The shop was* **formerly** *owned by a woman.*

formula /'fɔːmjʊlə/ *noun* (*plural* **formulas** or **formulae** /-liː/)
a list of substances used to make something: *This plastic is made from a new* **formula**.

fort /fɔːt/ *noun*
a strong place which can protect the people inside from attack
fortress /'fɔːtrɪs/ *noun* a large fort

fortnight /'fɔːtnaɪt/ *noun*
two weeks: *In a* **fortnight's** *time I will be home.*

fortune /'fɔːtʃuːn/ *noun*
1 (*no plural*) luck or chance: *It was his good* **fortune** *to be chosen to play for the school.*
2 a very large amount of money: *He made a* **fortune** *by selling houses.*
fortunate /'fɔːtʃənət/ *adjective* lucky: *You are very* **fortunate** *to have so many kind relatives.*
fortunately *adverb*: *You have a headache? Well,* **fortunately** *I have some medicine with me.*

forty /'fɔːtɪ/ *adjective, noun*
the number 40
fortieth /'fɔːtɪ-ɪθ/ *adjective, noun* number 40 in order; 40th

° **forward** /'fɔːwəd/ *or* **forwards** /'fɔːwədz/ *adverb*
towards the front; away from the back: *When the lights were green the cars moved* **forwards**. *She is* **looking forward to** (= thinking about with pleasure) *seeing you.*

108

fought /fɔːt/ see **fight**

foul /faʊl/ *adjective*
unpleasant or dirty: *a* **foul** *smell/***foul** *weather*

found¹ /faʊnd/ see **find**

found² *verb*
to start: *He* **founded** *the school in 1954.*
foun'dation *noun*
foun'dations *plural noun* the parts of a building under the ground

fountain
/'faʊntən/
noun
water thrown
high into the
air from a
pipe

fountain

four /fɔːʳ/ *adjective, noun*
the number 4: *I have* **four** *brothers.*
fourth *adjective, noun* number 4 in order; 4th

fourteen /fɔː'tiːn/ *adjective, noun*
the number 14
four'teenth *adjective, noun* number 14 in order; 14th

fowl /faʊl/ *noun*
a bird, usually one that is kept for food: *Chicken and ducks are two types of* **fowl.**

fox /fɒks/ *noun (plural* **foxes**)
a wild animal like a dog, with a thick tail

fraction /'frækʃn/ *noun*
a part, especially a small part: *A half* (½) *is a* **fraction** *of one* (1). *Only a* **fraction** *of my friends have television.*

fracture¹ /'fræktʃəʳ/ *verb (present participle* **fracturing,** *past* **fractured**)
to break: *His leg was* **fractured** *in an accident.*

fracture² *noun*
a break

fragment /'frægmənt/ *noun*
a piece broken off from something: *a* **fragment** *of glass*

frail /freɪl/ *adjective*
weak: *He is* **frail** *after his illness.*

○ **frame¹** /freɪm/
noun

picture frame

door frame

1 the bars
around which
a building,
car, etc. is
made: *a
building with
a steel* **frame**
2 a piece of wood or metal round a picture

frame² *verb (present participle* **framing,** *past* **framed**)
to put a frame around

○ **free¹** /friː/ *adjective*
1 able to do what you like; not shut up or in prison: *You are* **free** *to go where you want.*
2 not working: *Are you* **free** *this evening?*
3 not costing any money
'freedom *noun (no plural)*: *The children enjoyed the* **freedom** *of the school holidays.*
'freely *adverb*: *You can speak* **freely** (= say what you want to say) *here.*

○ **free²** *verb (past* **freed**)
to make someone or something free: *They* **freed** *the birds from the cages.*

freeze /friːz/ *verb (present participle* **freezing,** *past tense* **froze** /frəʊz/, *past participle* **frozen**)
to change from a liquid into a solid: *When water* **freezes** *it becomes ice.*
'freezer *noun* a machine that keeps food very cold, so that it keeps fresh for a long time: *We keep* **frozen** *food in a* **freezer.**

○ **frequent** /ˈfriːkwənt/ *adjective*
happening often: *I enjoyed his* **frequent** *visits.*
   'frequently *adverb*

○ **fresh** /freʃ/ *adjective*
1 picked, killed, etc. a short time ago: *These vegetables are* **fresh**, *I picked them this morning.*
2 new: *Use a* **fresh** *page.*
3 pleasantly cool: *The air smelt* **fresh** *after the rain.*

○ **Friday** /ˈfraɪdeɪ, -dɪ/ *noun*
the sixth day of the week

fridge /frɪdʒ/ *noun*
the usual word for a **refrigerator**; a machine for keeping food cold and fresh

○ **friend** /frend/ *noun*
a person you like and feel you can trust: *He is my* **friend**. *We are* **friends**. *Peter is Jane's* **boyfriend** (= special male friend) — *Jane is Peter's* **girlfriend**.
   'friendly *adjective: He is* **friendly** (= kind and helpful) *to us all.*
   'friendship *noun* being friends: *The boys have had a long* **friendship**.

fright /fraɪt/ *noun*
being frightened: *The loud thunder* **gave me a fright**.

frighten /ˈfraɪtn/ *verb*
to make someone afraid: *He was* **frightened** *of the fierce dog.*

fringe /frɪndʒ/ *noun*
1 threads, hair, etc. hanging down in a straight line: *a* **fringe** *round the edge*

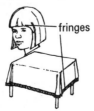

of a bed cover
2 edge: *on the* **fringe** *of the*

fro /frəʊ/ see **to**

frock /frɒk/ *noun*
a dress for a girl or woman

frog /frɒg/ *noun*
a small jumping animal that can live in water or on land

○ **from** /frəm; *strong* frɒm/ *preposition*
1 starting at: *The train goes* **from** *Paris to Rome.*
2 given or sent by: *This letter is* **from** *my uncle.*
3 out of; away: *books* **from** *the cupboard*
4 using: *Bread is made* **from** *flour.*
5 because of: *She was nearly crying* **from** *the pain of her cut leg.*

○ **front** /frʌnt/ *noun, adjective*
the side opposite the back; the forward part: *My sister is waiting* **in front of** *the school. I went out by the* **front** *door.*

frontier /ˈfrʌntɪəʳ/ *noun*
the dividing line between two countries

frost /frɒst/ *noun* (*no plural*)
frozen water that stays on every outdoor surface in cold weather: *The trees were white with* **frost**.

frown[1] /fraʊn/ *verb*
to draw the eyebrows (= hairy lines above the eyes) down over the nose, as you do when you are angry or thinking: *He* **frowned** *as he tried to work out the sum.*

frown[2] *noun*
a frowning expression

froze /frəʊz/, **frozen** see **freeze**

○ **fruit** /fruːt/ *noun* (*plural* **fruit**)
the part of a plant which carries the seeds; it is often sweet and good to eat: *Would you like some* **fruit** — *an apple or an orange?*

fry /fraɪ/ *verb* (*present participle* **frying**, *past* **fried**)
to cook in hot oil over a fire: *She* **fried** *the eggs in a* **frying-pan.**

fuel /'fjuːəl/ *noun*
a substance that burns to give heat, light, etc.: *Gas and coal are* **fuels.**

fulfil /fʊl'fɪl/ *verb* (*present participle* **fulfilling**, *past* **fulfilled**)
to do what you have promised or are expected to do: *He has* **fulfilled** *the orders that I gave him.*

○ **full** /fʊl/ *adjective*
having as much as it will hold: *The cup is* **full** — *it is* **full of** *milk.*
'**fully** *adverb*

full stop /ˌfʊl 'stɒp/ *noun*
the sign . used in writing to show the end of a sentence, or after a short form of a word

○ **fun** /fʌn/ *noun* (*no plural*)
amusement: *The children had great* **fun** *playing by the river.*

function[1] /'fʌŋkʃn/ *noun*
how something works; what something does: *The* **function** *of a clock is to show you the time.*

function[2] *verb*
to work: *This machine isn't* **functioning** *well.*

fund /fʌnd/ *noun*
an amount of money collected for something special: *a* **fund** *to help poor children*

funeral /'fjuːnərəl/ *noun*
the ceremony held when someone dies

fungus /'fʌŋɡəs/ *noun*
(*plural* **fungi** /'fʌŋɡaɪ, -dʒaɪ/ *or* **funguses**)
a plant which has no leaves or flowers

funnel /'fʌnl/ *noun*
1 a tube wide at the top and narrow at the bottom, used for pouring things into a narrow opening: *He poured the petrol into the car through a* **funnel.**
2 a pipe to take smoke from a ship or engine

○ **funny** /'fʌnɪ/ *adjective* (**funnier**, **funniest**)
1 making you laugh; amusing: *a* **funny** *joke*
2 strange; unusual: *I had a* **funny** *feeling that you would come. What's that* **funny** *smell?*

fur /fɜːʳ/ *noun* (*no plural*)
the soft hair on some animals: *Cats have* **fur.**

furious /'fjʊərɪəs/ *adjective*
very angry: *I was* **furious** *when he crashed my car.*

furnace /'fɜːnɪs/ *noun*
a large covered fire in which metals are melted, or which makes heat for an engine

furnish /'fɜːnɪʃ/ *verb*
to put furniture in: *She rents a* **furnished** *flat* (= with furniture in it). *to* **furnish** *a house*

○ **furniture** /'fɜːnɪtʃəʳ/ *noun* (*no plural*)
things used in a house, like beds, tables, and chairs

○ **further** /'fɜːðəʳ/, **furthest** see **far**

fuss[1] /fʌs/ *noun*
a worried and excited state: *My parents always* **make a fuss** *if I stay out late.*

fuss[2] *verb*
to behave in an unnecessary, worried or excited way: *Don't* **fuss** *over the children, they can take care of themselves.*
fussy *adjective* (**fussier, fussiest**): *I am not* **fussy** *about what I eat* (= I don't mind what I eat).

○ **future**[1] /'fjuːtʃəʳ/ *noun* (*no plural*)
time that will come; things that have not happened yet: *He has a*

good **future** *with that company,*
they will do well. **In future,** *please*
write your name clearly.

° **future**[2] *noun, adjective*
talking about an action that will
happen later: *The sentence "We*
will see them tomorrow" has the
verb in the **future.** Look at **tense.**

Gg

° **gain** /geɪn/ *verb*
to win or get: *She* **gained** *first prize*
in the race.

gale /geɪl/ *noun*
a very strong wind

gallery /ˈgælərɪ/ *noun*
(*plural* **galleries**)
a building or a large long room
where you can see pictures on the
walls, or other artistic things: *Let's*
visit the art **gallery.**

gallon /ˈgælən/ *noun*
a measure of liquid equal to 8 pints

gallop[1] /ˈgæləp/ *verb*
to run very fast: *The horse*
galloped *across the plains.*

gallop[2] *noun*
galloping: *He set off at a* **gallop.**

gamble /ˈgæmbl/ *verb* (*present*
participle **gambling,** *past* **gambled**)
to try and win money on games,
races, etc.: *He is a* **gambler.** *He*
spends all his money on **gambling.**

° **game**[1] /geɪm/ *noun*
something you play, with laws that
tell you what to do: *Football is a*
team **game.** *a* **game** *of cards*

game[2] *noun* (*no plural*)
wild animals or birds which people
hunt: *Animals like lions are called*
big '**game.**

gang[1] /gæŋ/ *noun*
a group of people: *a* **gang** *of young*
men (= a group of friends)/*a* **gang**
of criminals

gang[2] *verb*
to form a gang: *The older children*
ganged up *against the younger*
ones.

gaol *or* **jail** /dʒeɪl/ *noun*
prison: *The man was sent to* **gaol**
for stealing.

garage /ˈgærɑːʒ/ *noun*
a place where cars, buses, etc. are
kept or repaired

garden[1] /ˈgɑːdn/ *noun*
a place where trees, flowers, or
vegetables are grown, round a
house or in a public place

garden[2] *verb*
to work in a garden: *He* **enjoys**
gardening.
gardener *noun*

° **garment** /ˈgɑːmənt/ *noun*
a piece of clothing: *Why did you*
leave these **garments** *on the floor?*

° **gas** /gæs/ *noun*
1 any substance like air; not liquid
or solid: *The air we breathe is*
made chiefly of two **gases.**
2 (*no plural*) a gas got by burning
coal and used to give heat: *a* **gas**
cooker

gasp[1] /gɑːsp/ *verb*
to take in a breath quickly: *I*
gasped *as I jumped into the cold*
river.

gasp[2] *noun*
the sound of gasping: *a* **gasp** *of*
surprise

°**gate** /geɪt/ *noun*
a sort of door
which closes
an opening in
a wall or
fence: *The
school has
iron* **gates**

gates

between the yard and the road.

°**gather** /'gæðər/ *verb*
1 to bring together: *She* **gathered
up** *her books and left.*
2 to know from something that has
been said: *I* **gather** *that you like
football.*
'**gathering** *noun* a lot of people
together in one place: *There was
a large* **gathering** (*of people*) *at
the ceremony.*

gauge[1] /geɪdʒ/ *verb* (*present
participle* **gauging**, *past* **gauged**)
to measure: *I tried to* **gauge** *how
many people were there.*

gauge[2] *noun*
something that measures: *A* **petrol
gauge** *shows the amount of petrol
left in a car.*

gave /geɪv/ see **give**

gay /geɪ/ *adjective*
happy and cheerful: *It was a* **gay**
picture, with lots of colour in it.

gaze /geɪz/ *verb* (*present participle*
gazing, *past* **gazed**)
to look steadily: *The child* **gazed**
at the toys in the shop window.

gear /gɪər/ *noun*
a set of wheels with teeth in an
engine. They work together to
make the wheels of a car go faster
or more slowly: *The lorry driver*
changed gear *to go up the hill.*

geese /giːs/ see **goose**

gem /dʒem/ *noun*
any sort of stone which is worth a
lot of money and is used as an
ornament

°**general**[1] /'dʒenrəl/ *adjective*
about, for, or by everyone or
everything: *Today is a* **general**
holiday. I like games **in general**
(= most or all games), *and
especially football.*
generally *adverb*: *It is* **generally**
(= usually) *hot in summer.*

general[2] *noun*
a very important officer in the
army

generate /'dʒenəreɪt/ *verb* (*present
participle* **generating**, *past*
generated)
to make: *When coal burns, it*
generates *heat.*
generator *noun* a machine that
makes electricity

generation /ˌdʒenə'reɪʃn/ *noun*
the people born at a certain time:
*My parents and I belong to
different* **generations.**

°**generous** /'dʒenrəs/ *adjective*
giving what you can: *He is very*
generous — *he often buys things
for other people.*
generosity /ˌdʒenə'rɒsətɪ/ *noun*
(*no plural*): *He was famous for
his* **generosity.**

genius /'dʒiːnɪəs/ *noun*
someone who is much cleverer
than anyone else

°**gentle** /'dʒentl/ *adjective*
not rough; quiet and kind: *a* **gentle**
kiss/a **gentle** *wind*
gently *adverb*: *You must hold
the baby* **gently.**

gentleman /'dʒentlmən/ *noun*
(*plural* **gentlemen** /-mən/)
1 a kind, polite man
2 a polite word for a man: *When
he made a speech, he began by
saying "Ladies and* **gentlemen".**

genuine /'dʒenjʊɪn/ *adjective*
real and true: *This ring is* **genuine**
gold.

genuinely *adverb* truly: *She was* **genuinely** *frightened by the storm.*

geography /dʒɪˈɒɡrəfɪ/ *noun (no plural)*
the study of the Earth and the people who live on it: *In our* **geography** *class, we are learning about rivers.*

geology /dʒɪˈɒlədʒɪ/ *noun (no plural)*
the study of rocks, and how they were made

geometry /dʒɪˈɒmətrɪ/ *noun (no plural)*
the study of measuring shapes, lines, etc.

germ /dʒɜːm/ *noun*
a very small piece of living substance that can grow in animals or people, often giving them an illness

germinate
/ˈdʒɜːmɪneɪt/ *verb (present participle* **germinating,** *past* **germinated)**

germination

(of plants) to start to grow: *Seeds will not* **germinate** *without water.*
germi'nation *noun (no plural)*

gesture[1] /ˈdʒestʃər/ *noun*
a movement of the hands, head, etc. made to express something

gesture[2] *verb (present participle* **gesturing,** *past* **gestured)**
to make a gesture: *He* **gestured** *angrily at me.*

° **get** /get/ *verb (present participle* **getting,** *past* **got** /gɒt/)
1 to take, have, or buy: *I got a letter from Maria this morning. I must* **get** *some fruit in the market. I have got a dog.*
2 to become: *I* **got** *angry with him.*
3 to make be or happen: *He* **got**

the shirt clean in hot water. He is still asleep, he hasn't **got up** (= got out of bed) *yet.*
4 to arrive: *When we* **got to** *the station, the train was waiting.*
5 must: *I* **have got to** *see him today.*

ghost /ɡəʊst/ *noun*
the form of a dead person which a living person thinks he sees
'ghostly *adjective* frightening, as if there were ghosts

giant[1] /ˈdʒaɪənt/ *noun*
a very very large person, usually only talked about in stories

giant[2] *adjective*
very large: *a* **giant** *snake*

giddy /ˈɡɪdɪ/ *adjective* (**giddier, giddiest)**
having a turning feeling in the head: *She felt* **giddy** *when she looked down from the high bridge.*

gift /ɡɪft/ *noun*
something given; a present

gigantic /dʒaɪˈɡæntɪk/ *adjective*
very very big: *The new aeroplane looked like a* **gigantic** *bird.*

giggle /ˈɡɪɡl/ *verb (present participle* **giggling,** *past* **giggled)**
to laugh in a silly way: *The girls were* **giggling** *in class.*

gills /ɡɪlz/ *plural noun*
part of a fish, near its head, through which it breathes (picture at **fish**)

ginger /ˈdʒɪndʒər/ *noun*
1 a plant with stems under the ground
2 a powder made from these stems which gives food a hot taste

giraffe /dʒɪˈræf, dʒɪˈrɑːf/ *noun (plural* **giraffe** *or* **giraffes)**
a tall African animal with a very long neck and very long legs and large brown spots on its coat (picture on page 17)

° **girl** /gɜːl/ *noun*
a female child: *She has two children, a girl and a boy.*

° **give** /gɪv/ *verb* (*present participle* **giving**, *past tense* **gave** /geɪv/, *past participle* **given** /'gɪvn/)
1 to let someone have: *Have you* **given** *him your telephone number? The supermarket is* **giving away** (= letting people have for no money) *a box of sugar to everyone who comes today.*
2 to bring a feeling to: *The child* **gave** *his parents much worry.*
3 to stop: *I have* **given up** *smoking cigarettes. I can't guess the answer to your question, I* **give in** (= I have stopped trying to guess). *The criminal* **gave himself up** (= stopped trying to run away from the police).

° **glad** /glæd/ *adjective*
happy: *I am* **glad** *to see you.*
gladly *adverb* willingly: *He* **gladly** *lent me the money.*

glance[1] /glɑːns/ *verb* (*present participle* **glancing**, *past* **glanced**)
to look quickly: *She* **glanced** *along the road to see if he was coming.*

glance[2] *noun*
looking quickly: *She saw* **at a glance** *that he was coming.*

glare[1] /gleəʳ/ *verb* (*present participle* **glaring**, *past* **glared**)
1 to shine with an unpleasantly bright light: *The sun* **glared** *down.*
2 to look hard and unpleasantly: *She* **glared** *at me.*

glare[2] *noun*
unpleasant brightness: *The* **glare** *of the sun made her eyes hurt.*

° **glass** /glɑːs/ *noun*
1 (*no plural*) a clear hard substance used for windows
2 (*plural* **glasses**) a cup made of glass, without a handle

glasses /'glɑːsɪz/ *plural noun* specially shaped pieces of glass or plastic which help people to see better, held on the nose by a frame

glasses

gleam /gliːm/ *verb*
to shine faintly: *The moonlight* **gleamed** *on the river.* **gleam** *noun*

glide /glaɪd/ *verb* (*present participle* **gliding**, *past* **glided**)
to move very smoothly
'glider *noun* an aeroplane without an engine (picture at **aircraft**)

glimpse[1] /glɪmps/ *noun*
a very quick sight: *I just* **caught a glimpse** *of the plane as it flew over.*

glimpse[2] *verb* (*present participle* **glimpsing**, *past* **glimpsed**)
to see very quickly: *He* **glimpsed** *his friend in the crowd.*

glitter /'glɪtəʳ/ *verb*
to shine with a light that flashes: *The sea* **glittered** *in the sun.*
glitter *noun*

globe /gləʊb/ *noun*
1 a ball representing the Earth, with all the countries, seas, etc., marked on it
2 anything round like a ball

gloom /gluːm/ *noun*
1 darkness: *In the* **gloom** *of the thick forest, he nearly lost his way.*
2 a feeling of sadness: *He was deep in* **gloom** *because his girlfriend had gone away.*
'gloomy *adjective* (**gloomier**, **gloomiest**): *a* **gloomy** *day/a* **gloomy** *expression on his face*

glory /'glɔːrɪ/ *noun* (*no plural*)
fame and respect that is given to someone who has done something great

glorious /'glɔːrɪəs/ *adjective:*
Isn't it a **glorious** (= very
beautiful) *day?*

glove /glʌv/
noun
one of a pair
of coverings
for the hands

a pair
of gloves

glow[1] /gləʊ/ *verb*
to shine with a warm-looking light:
The dying fire **glowed** *in the dark.*

glow[2] *noun*
a warm shine: *the* **glow** *of a sunset*

glue[1] /gluː/ *noun* (*no plural*)
a substance used for sticking
things together: *She stuck the
handle onto the cup with* **glue.**

glue[2] *verb* (*present participle*
glueing or **gluing,** *past* **glued**)
to stick with glue: *She* **glued** *the
handle onto the cup.*

gnaw /nɔː/ *verb*
to bite something until it is worn
away: *The rat* **gnawed** *a hole in the
wooden box.*

○**go**[1] /gəʊ/ *verb* (*present participle*
going /'gəʊɪŋ/, *past tense* **went**
/went/, *past participle* **gone**
/gɒn/)
to move: *Are you* **going** *to school
today? The food* **goes** (= has a
special place) *in the cupboard.
Please* **go on** (= continue) *reading.
They* **went out** *to a party. When a
light or a fire* **goes out,** *it stops
shining or burning. I* **am going to**
wear (= will wear) *the blue dress
tomorrow. Will you* **go through**
this work (= look at it) *and make
sure there are no mistakes?*

go[2] *noun*
a try: *Can I* **have a go** *at mending
the bicycle?*

goal /gəʊl/ *noun*
1 a place to which you try to hit
or kick the ball in games like
football: *The* **goalkeeper** *is the
player who guards the* **goal.**
2 a point won when the ball goes
to that place: *to score a* **goal**

○**goat** /gəʊt/
noun
an animal
like a sheep
that is kept
for milk and for its hairy coat

goat

god /gɒd/ *noun*
a being to whom people pray, and
who is believed to control the
world

goddess /'gɒdes/ *noun* a
female god

○**gold** /gəʊld/ *noun* (*no plural*)
1 a yellow metal that costs a lot of
money: *She wore a* **gold** *ring.*
2 the colour of this metal

golden *adjective* like or made of
gold: *a* **golden** *sky*

golf /gɒlf/ *noun* (*no plural*)
a game in which a small ball is hit
into a number of holes arranged
on a large piece of land called a
'golf-course

gong /gɒŋ/ *noun*
a flat piece of metal that is hung
up and hit with a stick to make a
noise

○**good**[1] /gʊd/ *adjective* (**better**
/'betə'/, **best** /best/)
1 not wrong or bad; right: *He is a*
good *man — he always tries to do
what is right.*
2 suitable; useful: *This material is
quite* **good,** *but that one is* **better.**
Fruit is **good** *for you.*
3 well behaved: *Children, be* **good!**
4 nice; pleasant: *We had a* **good**
time at the party.
5 (used in greeting people): **Good**
morning, *doctor!* **Good night,**
children, sleep well! I must go now
— **goodbye!**

° **good**[2] *noun* (*no plural*)
what is right or useful: *We should try to do* **good** *to other people* (= help them).

'**goodness** *noun* (*no plural*) **1** being good, especially for the health: *There is a lot of* **goodness** *in milk.* **2** (to show surprise): **Goodness!** *It's late. I must go!*

goods *plural noun* things which are bought, sold, or owned: *What* **goods** *does your shop sell?*

goose /guːs/ *noun*
(*plural* **geese** /giːs/)
a large strong bird that can swim on water

gorgeous /'gɔːdʒəs/ *adjective*
very nice or beautiful: *a* **gorgeous** *meal*

gorilla /gə'rɪlə/ *noun*
a very large strong animal like a monkey, which is the largest ape (see) (picture on page 17)

gossip[1] /'gɒsɪp/ *noun*
1 (*no plural*) talk about people, often unkind: *You shouldn't listen to* **gossip.**
2 a person who talks like this

gossip[2] *verb*
to talk gossip: *They sat and* **gossiped** *all evening.*

got /gɒt/ see **get**

gourd /gʊəd/ *noun*
a large fruit or its hard shell which is used as a container

° **govern** /'gʌvn/ *verb*
to be in control of: *A lot of people help to* **govern** *a country.*

government /'gʌvəmənt/ *noun* the people who control what happens in a country

governor *noun* a person who controls a country or state

gown /gaʊn/ *noun*
1 a long dress for a woman: *a beautiful silk* **gown**

2 a loose long piece of clothing worn by special people: *The doctor in the hospital wore a* **gown** *over his ordinary clothes.*

grab /græb/ *verb* (*present participle* **grabbing,** *past* **grabbed**)
to take hold of quickly and roughly: *He* **grabbed** *the book and ran away.*

grace /greɪs/ *noun* (*no plural*)
1 a nice way of moving: *She walks with* **grace.**
2 a short prayer before or after a meal: *Who is going to say* **grace?**

'**graceful** *adjective* with grace
'**gracefully** *adverb*

gracious /'greɪʃəs/ *adjective* showing kindness: *a* **gracious** *smile*

grade[1] /greɪd/ *noun*
a level, size, or quality: *We sell three* **grades** *of eggs.*

grade[2] *verb* (*present participle* **grading,** *past* **graded**)
to put into groups according to size, quality, etc.: *We have* **graded** *the eggs into several sizes.*

gradual /'grædʒʊəl/ *adjective* happening slowly: *a* **gradual** *improvement in his work*

° **gradually** /'grædʒəlɪ/ *adverb*

graduate[1] /'grædʒʊeɪt/ *verb*
(*present participle* **graduating,** *past* **graduated**)
to take and pass the last examination at a college: *She* **graduated** *from an American college. She* **graduated** *in history.*

graduate[2] /'grædʒʊət/ *noun*
a person who has graduated: *a* **graduate** *of a college*

° **grain** /greɪn/
noun
1 (*no plural*) a

grain

gram

crop like wheat, maize, or rice that has seeds which we eat: **Grain** *is used for making flour.*
2 a seed or small piece of something: *a few* **grains** *of salt*

gram *or* **gramme** /græm/ *noun*
a measure of weight: *There are 1,000* **grams** *in a kilogram.*
g. is a short way of writing **gram(s)**

grammar /'græmə^r/ *noun* (*no plural*)
the laws of a language: *English* **grammar** *is quite difficult to learn.*

gramophone /'græməfəʊn/ *noun*
a machine on which records (= round flat things with music or words on them) can be played, so that you can hear the music or words

grand /grænd/ *adjective*
very large and fine: *He lives in a* **grand** *house.*
'**grandchild** *noun* the child of your child
'**granddaughter** *noun* the daughter of your child
'**grandfather** *noun* the father of one of your parents
'**grandmother** *noun* the mother of one of your parents
'**grandson** *noun* the son of your child

grant¹ /grɑːnt/ *verb*
to give; allow: *The children were* **granted** *a holiday from school.*

grant² *noun*
an allowed sum of money: *The government gave us a* **grant** *to build another classroom.*

grape
/greɪp/ *noun*
a small round juicy fruit that grows in bunches (see) on a grape vine in warm places

a bunch of grapes

grapefruit /'greɪpfruːt/ *noun*
a large yellow or green fruit that is like an orange but not as sweet

graph /grɑːf/ *noun*
a picture or line that shows how something changes: *They made a* **graph** *of how hot the weather was every day for a month.*
'**graph-paper** *noun: Paper with squares on it for making graphs is called* **graph-paper.**

grasp /grɑːsp/ *verb*
1 to take hold of firmly: *I* **grasped** *the cat by the back of its neck.*
2 to understand or learn: *I could not* **grasp** *what the teacher said.*

°**grass** /grɑːs/ *noun* (*no plural*)
a low plant with thin leaves that cattle eat: *We sat on the* **grass** *to have our picnic* (see).
'**grassy** *adjective* (**grassier, grassiest**): *a* **grassy** *river bank*

grasshopper /'grɑːsˌhɒpə^r/ *noun*
an insect with strong back legs for jumping

grate¹ /greɪt/ *noun*
a metal frame where a fire is lit

grate² *verb* (*present participle* **grating**, *past* **grated**)
to cut into small thin pieces with a special instrument (a **grater**): *to* **grate** *cheese*

°**grateful** /'greɪtfəl/ *adjective*
feeling that you want to thank someone: *I am* **grateful** *to you for helping me.* '**gratefully** *adverb*
gratitude /'grætɪtjuːd/ *noun* (*no plural*): *I am full of* **gratitude** *to you for helping me.*

grave¹ /greɪv/ *noun*
a hole in the ground where a dead body is placed, and then covered with earth

grave² *adjective*
serious: *a* **grave** *accident*
gravely *adverb:* **gravely** *ill*

gravel /'grævl/ *noun* (*no plural*)
a mixture of small stones and sand used for roads

gravity /'grævətɪ/ *noun* (*no plural*)
the force which brings things down to Earth: *When you let go of something,* **gravity** *makes it fall to the floor.*

graze[1] /greɪz/ *verb* (*present participle* **grazing,** *past* **grazed**)
1 to eat grass: *Cattle were* **grazing** *in the field.*
2 to hurt the skin by rubbing it against something: *He* **grazed** *his knee when he fell.*

graze[2] *noun*
a small wound on the surface of the skin

grease[1] /griːs/ *noun* (*no plural*)
oil or fat: *You put* **grease** *on a wheel to make it turn more easily.*

grease[2] (*present participle* **greasing,** *past* **greased**)
to put grease on something
greasy *adjective* (**greasier, greasiest**) covered with grease

° **great** /greɪt/ *adjective*
very large, important, etc.: *We learn about* **great** *people in history. He is my* **greatest** (= best) *friend. It gives me* **great** (= a lot of) *pleasure to see you all tonight. The party was* **great** (= very enjoyable)!
ˌgreat-'grandchild *noun* the son (ˌgreat-'grandson) or daughter (ˌgreat-'granddaughter) of a grandchild
ˌgreat-'grandparent *noun* the father (**great-grandfather**) or mother (**great-grandmother**) of a grandparent

greed /griːd/ *noun* (*no plural*)
the feeling that you want more than enough: *He can't stop eating sweets — it's just* **greed**!

greedy *adjective* (**greedier, greediest**): *He's so* **greedy** *he ate all our sweets.*

° **green** /griːn/ *adjective, noun*
(of) the colour of growing leaves and grass: *She wore a* **green** *dress. She was dressed in* **green**.
'greenhouse *noun* a little house made of glass for growing plants

° **greet** /griːt/ *verb*
to welcome with words or actions: *He* **greeted** *her by saying "Good morning".*
'greeting *noun*: *She sent* **greetings** (= good wishes) *to my mother on her birthday.*

grew /gruː/ see **grow**

° **grey** /greɪ/ *adjective, noun*
(of) the colour of rain clouds; a mixture of black and white: *She wore a* **grey** *dress. She was dressed in* **grey**.

grief /griːf/ *noun* (*no plural*)
great sadness: *She did not show her* **grief** *when her son died.*

grin[1] /grɪn/ *verb* (*present participle* **grinning,** *past* **grinned**)
to smile widely, showing the teeth: *He* **grinned** *with pleasure when he was given the money.*

grin[2] *noun*
a wide smile: *"I've been given some money!" he said with a* **grin**.

grind /graɪnd/ *verb* (*present participle* **grinding,** *past* **ground** /graʊnd/)
to crush something so that it becomes powder: *We* **grind** *grain to make flour.*

grip[1] /grɪp/ *verb* (*present participle* **gripping,** *past* **gripped**)
to hold onto: *She* **gripped** *her mother's hand.*

grip[2] *noun*
a hold: *She took a firm* **grip** *on the heavy case.*

groan /grəʊn/ *verb*
to make a low, sad noise: *He* **groaned** *with pain.* **groan** *noun*

grocer /'grəʊsəʳ/ *noun*
a person who sells dry foods like sugar, tea, and rice: *Have you been to the* **grocer's?**

  '**groceries** *plural noun* the goods you can buy in a grocery
  '**grocery** *noun* a grocer's shop

groove /gruːv/ *noun*
a narrow line cut into something: *When we play a record* (see), *the needle moves along very small* **grooves** *to make the sound.*

° **ground**[1] /graʊnd/ *noun* (*no plural*)
the surface of the Earth: *Trees grow in the* **ground.** *The* **ground** '**floor** *of a building is on the same level as the ground.*

  grounds *plural noun* garden or land around a building

ground[2] see **grind**

groundnut
/'graʊndnʌt/
or **peanut**
noun
a kind of
bean plant that is an important food crop in hot dry places

groundnut

° **group** /gruːp/ *noun*
a number of people or things together; quantity: *A* **group** *of girls was waiting by the school.*

° **grow** /grəʊ/ *verb* (*present participle* **growing,** *past tense* **grew** /gruː/, *past participle* **grown** /grəʊn/)
1 to get bigger: *Children* **grow** (**up**) *fast. I am* **growing** *an orange-tree* (= I have planted the seed and I am waiting for it to get bigger).
2 to become: *The weather* **grew** *colder.*

  '**grown-up** *adjective, noun* a full-grown person: *The* **grown-**ups *talked while the children played.*

  growth /grəʊθ/ *noun* (*no plural*)
an act or amount of growing; something which grows: *The child's* **growth** *was fast.*

growl /graʊl/ *verb*
to make a low angry noise in the throat: *The dog* **growled** *at the visitors.* **growl** *noun*

grubby /'grʌbɪ/ *adjective* (**grubbier, grubbiest**)
dirty: **grubby** *hands*

grumble /'grʌmbl/ *verb* (*present participle* **grumbling,** *past* **grumbled**)
to complain: *She was* **grumbling** *about the cost of food.*

grumpy /'grʌmpɪ/ *adjective* (**grumpier, grumpiest**)
bad-tempered: *a tired and* **grumpy** *child* '**grumpily** *adverb*

grunt /grʌnt/ *verb*
to make a short low noise like a pig **grunt** *noun*

guarantee[1] /ˌgærən'tiː/ *noun*
a promise: *He gave me a* **guarantee** *that he would repair the car today. The new radio had a* **guarantee** *with it* (= a written paper saying that if anything was wrong with it, it would be mended free).

guarantee[2] *verb* (*past* **guaranteed**)
to promise: *He* **guaranteed** *that he would do it today.*

° **guard**[1] /gɑːd/ *verb*
to look after and make sure no one touches, takes, etc.: *The dog* **guards** *the house when we go out.*

° **guard**[2] *noun*
1 a person who guards
2 (*no plural*) guarding: *The soldiers were* **on guard** *all night.*

guardian /'gɑːdɪən/ *noun*
a person who looks after a child if his parents are dead or away

guava /ˈgwɑːvə/ *noun*
a pink fruit with a yellow skin

guerilla /gəˈrɪlə/ *noun*
a person who fights secretly against the government or against an army

° **guess**[1] /ges/ *verb*
to give an answer that you feel may be right: *I don't know how old David is — I* **guess** *he's five.*

° **guess**[2] *noun*
something you think is right, but do not know: *If you don't know the answer, make a* **guess**.

guest /gest/ *noun*
a visitor to someone's house: *We have three* **guests** *to dinner. This hotel has ninety* **guests**.

° **guide**[1] /gaɪd/ *verb* (*present participle* **guiding**, *past* **guided**)
to lead or show the way to: *He* **guided** *the old woman across the busy street.*

° **guide**[2] *noun*
a person or thing that guides: *He is a* **guide** *and shows visitors around the town. We have bought a* **guide** (**book**) *to the town, with maps in it.*

'**guidance** *noun* (*no plural*) help: *I did the work with my teacher's* **guidance**.

° **guilt** /gɪlt/ *noun* (*no plural*)
knowing you have done wrong: *The* **guilt** *of the criminal* (= the fact that he had done wrong) *was proved.*

'**guilty** *adjective* (**guiltier**, **guiltiest**): *I felt* **guilty** *when I spent all his money.*

guitar /gɪˈtɑːʳ/ *noun*
a musical instrument with six

guitar

strings that you pluck (= pull and let go quickly)

gulf /gʌlf/ *noun*
a narrow piece of sea with land on three sides of it: *the Persian* **Gulf**

gulp[1] /gʌlp/ *verb*
to swallow quickly: *He* **gulped** (**down**) *the water.*

gulp[2] *noun*
a swallow: *He drank it* **in one gulp**.

gum /gʌm/ *noun*
1 (*no plural*) a sticky substance used for joining things together: *There is* **gum** *on the back of a stamp.*
2 the pink part of your mouth where the teeth grow

° **gun** /gʌn/ *noun*
an instrument which sends out bullets (= small pieces of metal) very fast, used for hurting or killing animals or people: *Soldiers carry* **guns**.

gust /gʌst/ *noun*
a sudden strong wind: *A* **gust** *of wind blew the leaves along.*

gutter /ˈgʌtəʳ/ *noun*
an open pipe for water along the edge of a roof or the side of a road: *The*

gutter

gutter

gutter *took away the rain-water from the roof.*

gymnastics /dʒɪmˈnæstɪks/ *plural noun*
exercises for the body: *We do* **gymnastics** *in a* **gymnasium** /dʒɪmˈneɪzɪəm/.

gym /dʒɪm/ *noun:* **Gym** *is short for gymnastics and for gymnasium.*

Hh

° **habit** /'hæbɪt/ *noun*
something you always do: *I have a **habit** of getting up late every day.*

had /hæd/ *verb*
past tense of the verb **have**: *He **had** lots of cloth last week, but he **hadn't** any today.*

hail[1] /heɪl/ *noun (no plural)*
drops of rain that are so cold they have become hard: *There was a **hail** storm yesterday.*
    'hailstone *noun* a hard cold drop of rain

hail[2] *verb*
to rain in hard drops: *It's **hailing**.*

° **hair** /heə'/ *noun*
1 (*no plural*) fine threads which grow on the skin of men and animals: *His **hair** (= the hair on his head) is black.* (picture on p. 133)
2 one of these threads: *This hair brush is full of **hairs**!*
    'hairdresser *noun: A person who cuts and shapes your hair as a job is a **hairdresser**.*

° **half** /hɑːf/ *noun*
(*plural* **halves** /hɑːvz/)
one of the two equal parts of anything: *I had **half** the apple and my brother had the other **half**. We had **half** each. It's **half** past ten* (= 30 minutes after ten o'clock). **Half'way** (= when I had gone half the distance) *to school, I met my teacher.*

hall /hɔːl/ *noun*
1 a large room or building: *The children were in the school **hall**.*
2 the room just inside the front door of a house: *Hang your coat in the **hall**.*

halt[1] /hɔːlt/ *verb*
to stop: *The policeman **halted** us. The car **halted** by the house.*

halt[2] *noun (no plural)*
a stop: *The car came to a **halt**.*

halve /hɑːv/ *verb*
(*present participle*) **halving**, *past* **halved**)
to divide in half: *James and I **halved** the apple* (= we each had half of it).

ham /hæm/ *noun (no plural)*
meat from a pig's leg that is kept from going bad by salt or by smoke

° **hammer**[1]
/'hæmə'/
noun
a tool with a

hammer

metal head and a wooden handle, used for knocking nails into things or for breaking things

° **hammer**[2] *verb*
to hit with a hammer: *She **hammered** the nail in the wood.*

° **hand**[1] /hænd/ *noun*
1 the end part of your arm, with which you hold things: *This toy was made **by hand** (= not by machine). I **shook hands** (= took hold of the right hand firmly with my right hand) with the teacher.* (picture on page 133)
2 the part of a clock which moves to show the time: *When the **minute hand** points to twelve and the **hour hand** points to three, it's three o'clock.*
    'handbag *noun* a woman's bag for small things, held in the hand
    'handful *noun* the amount that

can be held in the hand: *a* **handful** *of rice*

'**handwriting** *noun* writing done by hand: *Your* **handwriting** *is very good.*

'**handy** *adjective* (**handier, handiest**) suitable or near: *This house is* **handy** *for the market.*

○ **hand**[2] *verb*

to give with the hands: **Hand** *me that plate, please.* **Hand in** *your books to the teacher at the end of the lesson. The teacher* **handed out** *the books* (= gave one to each person).

handicap[1] /'hændɪkæp/ *noun* something that makes it difficult to do well: *His sore leg will be a* **handicap** *in the race.*

handicap[2] *verb* (*present participle* **handicapping,** *past* **handicapped**) to make it difficult for someone to do well: *I expected her to do well in the examination, but she has been* **handicapped** *by her illness.*

○ **handkerchief** /'hæŋkətʃiːf/ *noun* a square piece of cloth for cleaning the nose

○ **handle**[1] /hændl/ *noun*

part of a tool or instrument that you hold in the hand

handles
door handle

○ **handle**[2] *verb* (*present participle* **handling,** *past* **handled**)

1 to use: *He learnt how to* **handle** *an axe.*

2 to control: *I can't* **handle** *children.*

handlebars /'hændl,bɑːz/ *plural noun* the part of a bicycle that you hold when you ride it (picture at **bicycle**)

handsome /'hænsəm/ *adjective* nice to look at (usually used of men)

○ **hang** /hæŋ/ *verb*

1 (*past* **hung** /hʌŋ/) to fasten something at the top so that the lower part is free: *I* **hung** *my coat* (**up**) *on a hook.*

2 (*past* **hanged**) to kill, usually as a punishment, by holding someone above the ground with a rope around his neck

3 (*past* **hung**) to wait: *He* **hung about** *outside my house.*

'**hanger** *noun* a specially shaped piece of wire or wood for hanging clothes on: *a* **coat hanger**

○ **happen** /'hæpən/ *verb*

1 to take place; be: *The accident* **happened** *outside my house.*

2 to do by chance: *I* **happened** *to be in the market yesterday when a fire started.*

'**happening** *noun* an event: *There were some unusual* **happenings** *at school last week.*

○ **happy** /'hæpɪ/ *adjective* (**happier, happiest**)

feeling very pleased: *I am* **happy** *to see you again.*

'**happily** *adverb:* *They were laughing* **happily.**

'**happiness** *noun* (*no plural*) pleasure; being happy: *After they got married, they had many years of* **happiness.**

○ **harbour** /'hɑːbəʳ/ *noun*

a place where ships may shelter safely: *The boats in the* **harbour** *were safe during the storm.*

○ **hard**[1] /hɑːd/ *adjective*

1 not moving or soft when touched; firm like rock or metal: *This ground is too* **hard** *to dig.*

2 difficult to do or understand: *Is science* **harder** *than English?*

hard

hard[2] *adverb*
a lot; very much: *It's raining* **hard**. *Are you working* **hard**?

harden /'hɑːdn/ *verb*
to become hard: *The earth* **hardens** *under the hot sun.*

hardly /'hɑːdlɪ/ *adverb*
almost not at all; only just: *It was so dark that I could* **hardly** *see. He* **hardly ever** (= almost never) *eats meat.*

hare /heəʳ/ *noun*

hare

an animal like a rabbit (see), that has long ears and long back legs

harm[1] /hɑːm/ *noun* (*no plural*)
hurt: *The child fell over but* **came to no harm** (= was not hurt). **There is no harm in** *asking him for a job* (= Nothing bad will happen if you ask).
'**harmful** *adjective* bad; hurtful: *Smoking can be* **harmful** *to your health.*
'**harmless** *adjective* which cannot do harm: *a* **harmless** *snake*

harm[2] *verb*
to do harm; hurt: *Our dog won't* **harm** *you.*

harsh /hɑːʃ/ *adjective*
hard to bear; cruel: **harsh** *weather/a* **harsh** *punishment*
'**harshly** *adverb*: *He spoke to the child* **harshly**.

harvest[1] /'hɑːvɪst/ *noun*
1 the time when the crops are gathered: *We all helped with the* **harvest**.
2 the amount gathered: *a good fruit* **harvest**

harvest[2] *verb*
to gather a crop: *Have you* **harvested** *your crops?*

has /z, əz, s, həz; *strong* hæz/ *verb*
the part of the verb **have** that we use with **he, she** and **it**: *She* **has** *three children, but she* **hasn't** *any sons.*

haste /heɪst/ *noun*
hurry; quick movement or action: *In my* **haste** *I forgot my coat.*
'**hasty** *adjective* (**hastier, hastiest**) done in a hurry: *He ate a* **hasty** *lunch.* '**hastily** *adverb*

hat /hæt/ *noun*
something worn on the head

hats

hatch[1] /hætʃ/ *verb*
to come out of an egg: *The chickens* **hatched** *this morning.*

hatch[2] *noun* (*plural* **hatches**)
an opening in a wall or in the floor: *She passed food through the* **hatch** *from the kitchen.*

hate /heɪt/ *verb* (*present participle* **hating**, *past* **hated**)
not to like: *I* **hate** *snakes.*
hatred /'heɪtrɪd/ *or* **hate** *noun* (*no plural*): *She looked at me with an expression of* **hatred**.

haul /hɔːl/ *verb*
to pull (something heavy): *They* **hauled** *the boat up onto the shore.*

haunt /hɔːnt/ *verb*
(of ghosts (see) or spirits) to visit or be in a place: *People say that old house is* **haunted**.

have[1] /v, əv, həv; *strong* hæv/ *present tense*

singular	plural
I **have**	We **have**
You **have**	You **have**
He/She/It **has**	They **have**

past **had**
present participle **having**
a word that helps another word to

say that something happened in the past: *We* **have given** *some food to the goat. When I arrived, she* **had** *already* **gone** *away. The teacher* **hasn't** (= has not) **locked** *the door.* **I've** (= I have) *told you this story before.*

have to *or* **have got to** *verb*
must: *We* **have to** *leave now, so that we can catch the bus.* **We've got to** *go straight away.*

○ **have**[2] *verb*

1 to own; hold; keep: *Do you* **have** *any fruit? I* **haven't** *any today.*

2 (used with some other things): *I* **have** *an idea! My father* **has** *no time to play with us.*

Have got is often used instead of **have**: **Have** *you* **got** *any fruit? No, I* **haven't got** *any fruit.*

hawk /hɔːk/ *noun*
a large bird that kills small animals and birds for food

hay /heɪ/ *noun* (*no plural*)
dry grass fed to cattle

hazard /'hæzəd/ *noun*
a danger: *There are many* **hazards** *in a journey across Africa.*
hazardous *adjective*

haze /heɪz/ *noun* (*no plural*)
fine cloud which stops you seeing clearly: *mountains covered in* **haze**
'hazy *adjective* (**hazier, haziest**)
not clear: *Since it was* **hazy***, we couldn't see the mountains.*

○ **he** /hɪ; *strong* hiː/
(*plural* **they** /ðeɪ/)
the male person or animal that the sentence is about: **He** *is my brother:* **he's** (= he is) *twelve and* **he's** (= he has) *got brown eyes. Be careful of that dog,* **he** *bites.*

○ **head**[1] /hed/ *noun*

1 the top part of your body, where eyes, ears, and mouth are (picture on page 133)

2 what we think with: **Use your head** (= Think!) *Sarah! Don't* **lose your head** (= get excited), *just* **keep your head** (= stay calm).

3 the top of something: *The* **head** *of the hammer fell off the handle.*

4 a chief person: *the* **head** *of the government*

5 the front: **At the head of** *the line of cars was a bus.*

'headache *noun: My head hurts inside, I've got a* **headache.**

'heading *noun* something written at the top of a piece of writing

'headlight *noun*
one of the big lights at the front of a car

headlight

'headline *noun*
words printed in large letters at the top of a newspaper story

head'master, head'mistress *noun* the man or woman who is the chief person in a school

○ **head**[2] *verb*

1 to be at the front or the top of something: *The bus* **headed** *the line of cars.*

2 to go towards something: *The thirsty animals* **headed for** *the water.*

3 to hit a ball with the head

headquarters /hed'kwɔːtəz/ *plural noun*
the chief office of a business or other group

heal /hiːl/ *verb*
to make or get better: *The wound on my arm has* **healed.**

○ **health** /helθ/ *noun* (*no plural*)
the state of your body; how you are: *His* **health** *is not good* (= he is often ill).

'healthy *adjective* (**healthier,**

healthiest): *You look very* **healthy** (= well in body). *It is* **healthy** (= good for the health) *to eat fruit.*

○ **heap**[1] /hi:p/ *noun*
a number of things put untidily on top of each other: *A* **heap** *of old clothes was lying in the corner.*

heap[2] *verb*
to put into a large heap: *He* **heaped** *his plate with food.*

○ **hear** /hɪəʳ/ *verb* (*present participle* **hearing,** *past* **heard** /hɜːd/)
1 to get sounds through the ears: *I* **heard** *the rain on the roof.*
2 to get news of: *Have you* **heard** **from** *John since he has been abroad? I have* **never heard of** *her* (= I don't know her).
'**hearing** *noun* (*no plural*): *My* **hearing** *is very good; I can hear the bell two miles away.*

○ **heart** /hɑːt/ *noun*
1 the part of your body in your chest that pumps the blood round the body (picture on page 133)
2 what we feel with: *He has a kind* **heart** (= he is kind by nature).
3 the middle: *in the* **heart** *of the forest*
'**heartbeat** *noun* the movement or sound the heart makes as it pumps the blood around the body
'**heartless** *adjective* without kind feelings; cruel

○ **heat**[1] /hi:t/ *noun*
1 (*no plural*) the feeling of something hot: *The* **heat** *of the sun made her feel ill.*
2 a race run earlier than the chief race, to decide who will run in it: *The winners of the* **heats** *run in the chief race.*

○ **heat**[2] *verb*
to make something hot: *We* **heated** *the soup on the cooker.*
'**heater** *noun* a machine that heats: *She used an electric* **heater** *to warm the room.*

heave /hi:v/ *verb* (*present particle* **heaving,** *past* **heaved**)
to lift or pull with difficulty: *I* **heaved** *the heavy box up the steps.*

heaven /'hevn/ *noun*
a place where God or the gods are said to live, and where good people are believed to go after they die: *Will you go to* **heaven** *or hell?*
'**heavenly** *adjective* **1** of or from heaven: *God is our* **heavenly** *father.* **2** very pleasant: *What a* **heavenly** *day!*

○ **heavy** /'hevɪ/ *adjective* (**heavier, heaviest**)
weighing a lot: *How* **heavy** *was the baby when he was born? We had* **heavy** (= a large amount of) *rain today.* **Heavy** *lorries can damage roads and buildings.*

hectare /'hektɑːʳ/ *noun*
a measure of land, equal to 10,000 square metres

hedge /hedʒ/ *noun*
small trees planted between fields or along roads to make a wall

○ **heel** /hi:l/ *noun*
1 the back part of the foot below the ankle (picture on page 133)
2 the back part of the bottom of a shoe: *shoes with high* **heels**

○ **height** /haɪt/ *noun*
how tall or far from the ground something is: *He measured the* **height** *of the bridge.* (picture on page 185)

heir /eəʳ/ *noun*
a person who gets money or goods when someone dies: *Richard was his father's only* **heir,** *as he had no brothers or sisters.*

held /held/ see **hold**

helicopter
/'helikɒptə^r/
noun
a sort of
aeroplane

helicopter

with blades which go round on its top, which can go straight up from the ground and stay still in the air

hell /hel/ *noun*
a place where the devil (see) is said to live, and where bad people are believed to go after they die

hello /he'ləʊ/
a greeting said when you meet someone you know: **Hello,** *Jane!*

helmet /'helmɪt/ *noun*
a covering which protects the head from being hit: *The man on the motorcycle wore a* **helmet.**

○ **help**¹ /help/ *verb*
to do something or part of something for someone: *I can't lift this box — will you* **help** *me please?* **Help yourself** *to the food* (= Take what you want). *I* **can't help** (= I can't stop) *crying, I'm so sad.*

'**helpful** *adjective: The* **helpful** *boy carried my bags for me.*
'**helping** *noun* the amount of food on a plate: *Would you like a second* **helping** *of soup?*
'**helpless** *adjective: The rain is coming into my house and I am* **helpless** (= I can do nothing about it).

○ **help**² *noun*
someone or something that helps: *It will be a* **help** *if you carry the basket.*

hem¹ /hem/ *noun*
the sewn bottom edge of a skirt, shirt, etc.: *Are you going to* **let down** *or* **take up the hem** *of that dress* (= make the dress longer or shorter)?

hem² *verb* (*present participle* **hemming,** *past* **hemmed**)
to sew the hem of something

hemisphere /'hemɪsfɪə^r/ *noun*
1 one half of a sphere (see): *If you cut a round fruit into two, each half is a* **hemisphere.**
2 one of two parts of the world: *The* **Northern Hemisphere** *is the part of the world north of the equator* (see), *and the* **Southern Hemisphere** *is south of the equator.*

○ **hen** /hen/ *noun*
a female chicken

○ **her** /ə^r, hə^r; *strong* hɜː^r/
1 a woman or girl, (used in sentences like this): *Give* **her** *the book. I had a letter from* **her.**
2 belonging to a woman or girl: **Her** *baby is sleeping in* **her** *arms.*

herb /hɜːb/ *noun*
any plant used for medicine or for giving a special taste to food

herd¹ /hɜːd/ *noun*
a group of animals of the same kind: *a* **herd** *of cattle*

herd² *verb*
to drive animals as a herd: *He* **herded** *his cattle into the yard.*

○ **here** /hɪə^r/ *adverb*
at or to this place: *Come* **here** *and sit by me.*

hero /'hɪərəʊ/ *noun*
(*plural* **heroes**)
a man who does something great or brave: *The football player was Paul's* **hero** *when he was at school.*
heroic /hɪ'rəʊɪk/ *adjective*
heroine /'herəʊɪn/ *noun* a woman who does something great or brave

hers /hɜːz/
something belonging to a woman or girl: *Is the pen* **hers**? *Yes, it's* **her** *pen.*

herself /hə'self/
(*plural* **themselves**)
1 the same female person as the one the sentence is about: *The woman dressed* **herself** *in her best clothes. She went for a walk by* **herself** (= alone). *She lifted that heavy box by* **herself** (= without help).
2 (used to give **she** a stronger meaning): *She gave me some money, although she* **herself** *didn't have much money.*

hesitate /'heziteit/ *verb* (*present participle* **hesitating**, *past* **hesitated**)
to stop what you are doing for a short time: *He* **hesitated** *before he answered because he didn't know what to say.* **hesi'tation** *noun*

○ **hide**[1] /haid/ *verb* (*present participle* **hiding**, *past tense* **hid** /hid/, *past participle* **hidden**)
to put in a place not known to other people: *Where did you* **hide** *the money? I* **hid** *behind the door, so that no one would see me. She* **hid** *her feelings* (= no one knew what she felt).

hide[2] *noun*
the skin of an animal

○ **high** /hai/ *adjective*
1 tall, or far from the ground: *The* **highest** *mountain in Africa is Mount Kilimanjaro. It is nearly 20,000 feet* **high**.
2 great: *high prices/a* **high** *wind*
3 not low in sound: *a* **high** *voice*
highlands /'hailəndz/ *plural noun* land which has a lot of hills, or is high up in the hills
highness *noun* a title of a prince (see) or princess (see)
'**highway** *noun* a chief road

hijack /'haidʒæk/ *verb*
to force the driver of a plane, train, etc. to take you somewhere or give you something
'**hijacker** *noun*

○ **hill** /hil/ *noun*
a piece of ground higher than usual: small mountain: *I climbed up the* **hill** *and ran down the other side; I had to go slowly* **uphill**, *but I could run* **downhill**.

○ **him** /im; *strong* him/
a man or boy, (used in sentences like this): *Give* **him** *the book. I had a letter from* **him**.

himself /him'self/
(*plural* **themselves** /ðəm'selvz/)
1 the same male person as the one the sentence is about: *The man dressed* **himself** *in his best clothes. He stayed at home by* **himself** (= alone). *He lifted that heavy box by* **himself** (= without help).
2 (used to give **he** a stronger meaning): *He gave me some money, although he* **himself** *didn't have much money.*

hinder /'hində^r/ *verb*
to prevent or make it more difficult for someone to do something: *I haven't cooked the dinner because the children* **hindered** *me.*

Hindu /'hindu:/ *noun*
a person who follows the main religion of India (**Hinduism**)

hinge /hindʒ/ *noun*
an instrument which joins two pieces of metal, wood, etc. and allows one piece to swing away from the other: *The lid of the suitcase had a broken* **hinge**, *so it wouldn't open easily.*

hinge

hint[1] /hint/ *verb*
to say something in a way that is not direct: *He* **hinted** *that he was looking for another job.*

hint[2] *noun*

something said in a way that is not direct: *When she said she was tired, it was a* **hint** *that she wanted us to go.*

hip /hɪp/ *noun*

the part of your body where it joins your legs (picture on p. 133)

hippopotamus /hɪpə'pɒtəməs/ *noun* (*plural* **hippopotamuses**)

a large African animal that lives in rivers (picture on page 17)

hire /haɪəʳ/ *verb* (*present participle* **hiring**, *past* **hired**)

to pay for the use of something or for someone's help: *He* **hired** *a car for two days.*

his /ɪz; *strong* hɪz/

1 belonging to a man or boy: *My uncle took* **his** *children to school.* **2** something belonging to a man or boy: *That pen is my brother's; I know it is* **his**. *It is* **his**, *not hers.*

hiss /hɪs/ *verb*

to make a sound by forcing air out through the teeth: *Snakes* **hiss**.

hiss *noun*

○ **history** /'hɪstrɪ/ *noun* (*no plural*)

learning about the past: *a* **history** *lesson at school*

historic /hɪ'stɒrɪk/ *adjective* causing important changes: *a* **historic** *meeting between the two leaders*

historical /hɪ'stɒrɪkl/ *adjective* of history; in or about the past: *a* **historical** *play*

○ **hit**[1] /hɪt/ *verb* (*present participle* **hitting**, *past* **hit**)

to bring down (something) hard on something else: *He* **hit** *me with his hand. The falling tree* **hit** *a car.*

○ **hit**[2] *noun*

1 a blow or stroke, especially a good one: *He aimed at the mark on the wall and hit it exactly — it*

was a good **hit**. **2** a song or film which everybody likes: *That song was a* **hit** *last year.*

hoard[1] /hɔːd/ *verb*

to collect and store, but not use: *She* **hoards** *her money — she never spends it.*

hoard[2] *noun*

a lot of something which has been stored: *a* **hoard** *of money*

hoarse /hɔːs/ *adjective*

(of the voice) rough, as when your throat is sore or dry: *His voice was* **hoarse** *after talking for an hour.*

hobby /'hɒbɪ/ *noun* (*plural* **hobbies**)

something you do to amuse yourself: *He works in a bank, but his* **hobby** *is building model boats.*

hockey /'hɒkɪ/ *noun* (*no plural*)

a game played by two teams who use curved sticks to hit a ball into a net

hoe /həʊ/ *noun*

a tool used to loosen the ground

hoes

hoist /hɔɪst/ *verb*

to pull up: *You* **hoist** *a flag when you pull it to the top of its pole.*

○ **hold**[1] /həʊld/ *verb* (*present participle* **holding**, *past* **held** /held/)

1 to have in the hand: *She was* **holding** *a book (in her hand).* **2** to have inside: *This bottle* **holds** *one litre.* **3** to arrange and give (an event): *We're* **holding** *a party next week.* **4** to have: *He* **holds** *an important position at the bank. The policemen* **held up** (= stopped) *all the traffic.*

○ **hold**[2] *noun*

1 holding in the hand: *Can you* **get**

hole

hold of *that rope?*
2 the place on a ship where goods are stored

° **hole** /həʊl/ *noun*
an empty space or opening in something: *I fell into a* **hole** *in the road.*

° **holiday** /'hɒlɪdeɪ/ *noun*
a time when you do not work or go to school: *When I was* **on holiday,** *I visited my uncle.*

° **hollow** /'hɒləʊ/ *adjective*
having an empty space inside: *A water pipe is* **hollow.**

° **holy** /'həʊlɪ/ *adjective*
(holier, holiest)
of God or of the gods: *The Bible is the* **holy** *book of Christians.*

° **home** /həʊm/
noun, adjective, adverb
the place where someone lives: *Her* **home** *is far away, so we don't often see her. We ran* **home** *to have our dinner. I stayed* **at home** *to read.*

'**homework** *noun* work given to you at school to be done at home

° **honest** /'ɒnɪst/ *adjective*
not lying or deceiving people; truthful: *I gave James too much money by mistake, but he was* **honest** *— he gave me some back.*
'**honestly** *adverb*
honesty *noun* (*no plural*): *He was praised for his* **honesty** *when he returned the money.*

honey /'hʌnɪ/ *noun* (*no plural*)
sweet, sticky liquid that bees collect from flowers, and that people can eat
honeymoon /'hʌnɪmuːn/ *noun*
a holiday taken by people who have just got married

honour[1] /'ɒnəʳ/ *noun* (*no plural*)
great respect: *The things that he has done have brought* **honour** *to*

our country. I have cooked a special meal **in honour of** (= to show our respect for) *our visitors.*

honour[2] *verb*
to respect: *He was* **honoured** *for his courage in battle.*

hood /hʊd/ *noun*
1 a piece of clothing that covers the head and neck
2 the covering of an open car: *It's raining. Put the* **hood** *up.*

hoof /huːf/
noun
(*plural*
hooves
/huːvz/)

hooves

the foot of a horse, cow, sheep, or goat

° **hook**[1] /hʊk/ *noun*
a bent piece of metal or hard plastic: *He hung his coat on the* **hook** *behind the door. She caught a fish on her* **hook.**

° **hook**[2] *verb*
to fasten with hooks or onto a hook: *My dress* **hooks** *at the back.*

hoop /huːp/ *noun*
a round band; a ring: *The barrel had two metal* **hoops** *round it.*

hoot /huːt/ *verb*
to make or cause to make a low whistle on one note: *The bus driver* **hooted** *at the man who stepped onto the road.*
hoot *noun*

hop /hɒp/ *verb* (*present participle* **hopping,** *past* **hopped**)
1 to move on one foot: *She* **hopped** *across the room because she had hurt her foot.*
2 to jump with both legs together, like some birds and animals

° **hope**[1] /həʊp/ *verb*
to wish for and expect: *I* **hope** *to go to college.*

° **hope**[2] *noun*
wishing and expecting: *I* **gave up**
hope *of going to college when I*
failed my examinations.
'**hopeful** *adjective: I am* **hopeful**
that she will come tomorrow.
'**hopefully** *adverb: The dog*
waited **hopefully** *beside the table*
for some food.
'**hopeless** *adjective: It is*
hopeless *to go on learning science*
— I shall never understand it! I
am **hopeless** (= very bad) *at*
science.
'**hopelessly** *adverb:* **hopelessly**
lost

horizon /həˈraɪzn/ *noun*
the line between the land or sea
and the sky: *I could see a ship on*
the **horizon.**
horizontal /ˌhɒrɪˈzɒntl/
adjective going from side to side:
On a map there are **horizontal**
lines and **vertical** (= going up
and down) *lines.*

° **horn** /hɔːn/ *noun*
1 one of the two hard pieces
sticking out from the heads of
some animals
2 the instrument on a car, bus, etc.
which makes a noise to warn
people
3 a musical instrument that you
blow into

horrify /ˈhɒrɪfaɪ/ *verb*
(*present participle* **horrifying,** *past*
horrified)
to shock or make someone feel
fear: *I was* **horrified** *by the news.*

horror /ˈhɒrəʳ/ *noun*
great fear and shock: *The man saw*
with **horror** *that there had been a*
bad accident.
horrible /ˈhɒrəbl/ *adjective* very
unpleasant: *There was a* **horrible**
accident here yesterday.
horrid /ˈhɒrɪd/ *adjective*

unpleasant: **horrid** *food*

° **horse** /hɔːs/
noun
an animal
with long legs
that eats grass
and can pull a
cart or carry
people

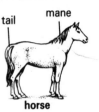

tail   mane

horse

'**horseback** *noun: There were*
two soldiers **on horseback**
(= riding horses).
'**horse-shoe** *noun* a piece of
iron shaped like a half circle
which is nailed to a horse's foot
to protect it

hose[1] /həʊz/ *noun*
a long piece of tube which bends
easily, used for getting water from
one place to another

hose[2] *verb* (*present participle*
hosing, *past* **hosed**)
to put water onto something from
a hose: *Will you* **hose down** *my car*
— it's very dirty.

° **hospital** /ˈhɒspɪtl/ *noun*
a building where ill people are
taken to be looked after and given
medicine

hospitality /ˌhɒspɪˈtælətɪ/ *noun*
(*no plural*)
welcome and kindness to visitors:
The people of your village showed
me great **hospitality.**

host /həʊst/ *noun*
the person whose house a visitor
is in, or who is paying for a meal
for someone: *Mr Brown was our*
host *at the party.*
hostess /həʊˈstes/ *noun: They*
thanked their **hostess,** *Mrs*
Brown. An '**air-hostess** *on an*
aeroplane looks after the
passengers.

hostage /ˈhɒstɪdʒ/ *noun*
a person taken and kept by

someone so that someone else will do what he wants

hostel /'hɒstl/ *noun*
a building where students, people away from their families, etc. can live

hostile /'hɒstaɪl/ *adjective*
not friendly: *Ever since I got better marks than Richard, he has been* **hostile** *to me.*

◦ **hot** /hɒt/ *adjective* (**hotter, hottest**)
1 having a lot of heat; not cold: *The sun is very* **hot**. *Here is some* **hot** *tea for you.*
2 having a strong, burning taste: *Pepper makes food taste* **hot**.

◦ **hotel** /həʊ'tel/ *noun*
a building where visitors can sleep and eat meals if they pay

hound /haʊnd/ *noun*
a dog used for hunting or racing

◦ **hour** /aʊə'/ *noun*
a measure of time; sixty minutes: *He went away for* **half an hour.** *Our business* **hours** (= the time when we are open for business) *are 9.30 to 5.30.*

◦ **house** /haʊs/ *noun*
a building that people live in
household /'haʊs,həʊld/ *noun*
all the people who live in a house together
'housewife *noun* (*plural* **housewives**) a woman who works in the house for her family

hover /'hɒvə'/ *verb*
to stay in the air without moving: *Some birds* **hover** *when they look for animals to kill on the ground.*

'hovercraft *noun* a sort of boat that travels over land or water by floating on air pushed out by its engines

hovercraft

◦ **how** /haʊ/ *adverb*
1 (used in questions to ask in what way): **How** *do you open this box?*
2 (used in questions about time, amount, or size): **How much** *money did you pay?* **How many** *children are there in the school?*
3 (used to ask about health): **How** *are you? I'm very well, thank you.* **How do you do?** *is a greeting we use when we first meet people.*
4 (used to show surprise or pleasure): **How** *beautiful those flowers are!*

however /haʊ'evə'/
1 in whatever way; it does not matter how: *He can answer the question* **however** *hard it is.*
2 but: *I don't think we can do it* — **however,** *we'll try.*

howl /haʊl/ *verb*
to cry loudly and with a long breath: *The dog* **howled** *when it was shut in the house. Wind* **howled** *round the house.*
howl *noun*

hug[1] /hʌg/ *verb* (*present participle* **hugging,** *past* **hugged**)
to put the arms round someone and hold them: *He* **hugged** *his daughter.*

hug[2] *noun*
hugging: *He gave her a* **hug**.

huge /hju:dʒ/ *adjective*
very large: *a* **huge** *amount of food*

hum /hʌm/ *verb* (*present participle* **humming,** *past* **hummed**)
1 to make a low steady noise like a bee
2 to sing with the lips closed: *She* **hummed** (*a song*).

◦ **human** /'hju:mən/ *adjective*
of or like a person: *We are all* **human beings.**

humble /'hʌmbl/ *adjective*
1 having a simple opinion of

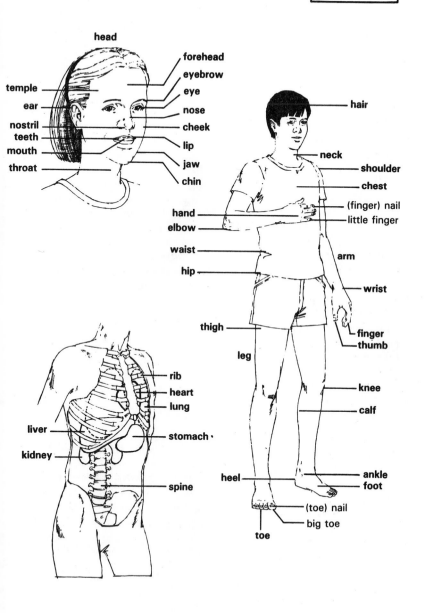

head

forehead
eyebrow
eye
nose
cheek
lip
jaw
chin

temple
ear
nostril
teeth
mouth
throat

hair

neck
shoulder
chest
(finger) nail
little finger

hand
elbow

waist

hip

arm

wrist

thigh

leg

finger
thumb

rib
heart
lung

knee

calf

liver

stomach

kidney

spine

heel

ankle
foot

(toe) nail
big toe

toe

yourself; not proud: *The doctor was* **humble** *about his work, although he cured many people.*
2 simple or poor: **humble** *people*

humour /'hjuːmə^r/ *noun* (*no plural*)
being able to laugh at things or to make others laugh: *He has no* **sense of humour** — *he never laughs at anything.*
'**humorous** *adjective* funny

hump /hʌmp/ *noun*
a round lump: *A camel* (see) *has a* **hump** *on its back.*

hundred /'hʌndrəd/
noun, adjective
the number 100: *That farmer has* **a hundred** *cows, and this one has* **two hundred.**
hundredth *noun, adjective*
number 100 in order; 100th

hung /hʌŋ/ see **hang**

◦ **hunger** /'hʌŋgə^r/ *noun* (*no plural*)
the feeling of wanting to eat: *If you have nothing to eat for a day, you feel great* **hunger.**
hungry /'hʌŋgrɪ/ *adjective*
(**hungrier, hungriest**): *Can I have an apple? I'm* **hungry.**

◦ **hunt** /hʌnt/ *verb*
1 to chase and kill animals or birds for food or sport
2 to look for: *I* **hunted for** *my book everywhere.*
'**hunter** *noun* a person who hunts animals or birds

hurl /hɜːl/ *verb*
to throw hard: *He* **hurled** *the brick through the window.*

hurray /hʊ'reɪ/
a word you shout when you are pleased about something: *Our team has won!* **Hurray!**

hurricane /'hʌrɪkən/ *noun*
a great storm with a strong wind

◦ **hurry**^{1} /'hʌrɪ/ *verb* (*present participle* **hurrying,** *past* **hurried**)
to move or do something quickly: *I'm late — I must* **hurry** (**up**)!

hurry^2 *noun*
hurrying: *You always seem to be* **in a hurry.**

◦ **hurt** /hɜːt/ *verb* (*past* **hurt**)
to give pain or cause damage: *My leg* **hurts.** *I* **hurt** *it playing football. It won't* **hurt** *your bicycle if you leave it outside. She's* **hurt** (= sad) *because you haven't visited her.*

◦ **husband** /'hʌzbənd/ *noun*
the man to whom a woman is married

◦ **hut** /hʌt/ *noun*
a small, usually wooden, building

hydrogen /'haɪdrədʒən/ *noun*
(*no plural*)
a very light colourless gas

hyena /haɪ'iːnə/ *noun*
a wild animal like a large dog

hygiene /'haɪdʒiːn/ *noun*
(*no plural*)
keeping yourself and your home clean
hy'gienic *adjective* clean

hymn /hɪm/ *noun*
a religious song

hyphen /'haɪfn/ *noun*
the sign - used between two parts of a word or two words joined together, as in *half-price*

Ii

° **I** /aɪ/ (*plural* **we** /wɪ; *strong* wiː/)
the person who is speaking: *He wants bananas, but* **I** *want oranges.* **I'm** (= I am) *very glad to see you.* **I've** (= I have) *been waiting a long time.* **I'll** (= I will or I shall) *wait a little longer. When* **I'd** (= I had) *written the story, I read it to my friend. I thought that* **I'd** (= I would or I should) *miss the bus, but I didn't.*

° **ice** /aɪs/ *noun* (*no plural*)
water which is so cold that it has become hard: *He put some* **ice** *in his drink to make it cold.*

    ice-'cream *noun* a sweet food made from very cold milk fat with different tastes added
    icy /'aɪsɪ/ *adjective* very cold (**icier, iciest**)

iceberg /'aɪsbɜːg/ *noun*
a very large mass of ice floating in the sea

iceberg

icing /'aɪsɪŋ/ *noun* (*no plural*)
a mixture of sugar and water put on top of cakes

° **idea** /aɪ'dɪə/ *noun*
a thought; something formed in the mind: *I've had an* **idea.** *We could play football! What time is it? I* **have no idea** (= I do not know).

ideal /aɪ'dɪəl/ *adjective*
the best possible: *This book is* **ideal** — *it's exactly what I needed.*

identical /aɪ'dentɪkl/ *adjective*
exactly the same: *The two bowls are* **identical,** *they are the same size, shape, and colour.*

identify /aɪ'dentɪfaɪ/ *verb*
(*present participle* **identifying,** *past* **identified**)
to say who someone is or what something is: *Can you* **identify** *the three plants in the picture?*
    i,dentifi'cation *noun* (*no plural*) saying or showing who someone is or what something is: *Have you any* **identification** (= something that shows who you are)?
    i'dentity *noun* (*plural* **identities**) who someone is or what something is: *Can you prove your* **identity?**

idiom /'ɪdɪəm/ *noun*
a group of words which when used together have a special meaning: *"I've got cold feet" is an* **idiom** — *it doesn't only mean that my feet feel cold, it means that I am afraid.*

idle /'aɪdl/ *adjective*
1 doing no work: **idle** *machines in a factory*
2 lazy: *He never does any work* — *he's* **idle.**

idol /'aɪdl/ *noun*
a figure that people respect and honour: *They prayed to an* **idol.**

i.e. /ˌaɪ 'iː/
this is what is meant: *The best pupil in the class,* **i.e.** *Peter, won the prize.*

° **if** /ɪf/
1 on condition that: *You can catch the bus* **if** *you go now.*
2 whether: *I don't know* **if** *he will play or not.*
3 (used in phrases like this): *Do you like coffee?* **If so** (= if you do like it), *have a cup of coffee.* **If not**

ignorant

(= if you do not like it) *I'll make you a cup of tea.*

ignorant /'ɪgnərənt/ *adjective*
not knowing much: *She is very* **ignorant** *about her own country.*
'**ignorance** *noun* (*no plural*): *Her* **ignorance** *is surprising.*

ignore /ɪg'nɔːʳ/ *verb* (*present participle* **ignoring**, *past* **ignored**)
to take no notice of; pretend someone or something is not there: *I tried to tell her but she* **ignored** *me.*

○ **ill**[1] /ɪl/ *adjective* (**worse** /wɜːs/, **worst** /wɜːst/)
not feeling healthy; unwell: *She can't go to school because she is* **ill**.
'**illness** *noun* (*plural* **illnesses**): *He has had a bad* **illness**, *but he is better now.*

ill[2] *adverb*
(often joined to other words) badly: *The cruel man* **ill-'treated** *his children.*

illegal /ɪ'liːgl/ *adjective*
not allowed by law: *It is* **illegal** *to steal things.*

illegible /ɪ'ledʒəbl/ *adjective*
not able to be read: **illegible** *writing*

illuminate /ɪ'luːmɪneɪt/ *verb* (*present participle* **illuminating**, *past* **illuminated**)
to light up: *The river was* **illuminated** *by the setting sun.*

illustrate /'ɪləstreɪt/ *verb* (*present participle* **illustrating**, *past* **illustrated**)
to add pictures to: *The book was* **illustrated** *with colour photographs.*

‚**illu'stration** *noun*: *Who drew these* **illustrations**?

illustration

image /'ɪmɪdʒ/ *noun*
1 a picture in the mind, or in a mirror: *He saw the* **image** *of his face in the mirror.*
2 a figure made of stone, wood, etc.

○ **imagine** /ɪ'mædʒən/ *verb* (*present participle* **imagining**, *past* **imagined**)
1 to have a picture in the mind of: *When he talked about the city, I tried to* **imagine** *it.*
2 to think: *John* **imagines** *that we don't like him.*
i'**maginary** *adjective*: *He told a story about an* **imaginary** (= not real) *land.*
‚**magi'nation** *noun*: *You didn't really see it — it was just your* **imagination**.

imitate /'ɪmɪteɪt/ *verb* (*present participle* **imitating**, *past* **imitated**)
to copy: *She* **imitated** *the way her teacher talked.*
‚**imi'tation** *noun*: *This isn't a real gun — it's only an* **imitation**.

immediate /ɪ'miːdɪət/ *adjective*
happening at once: *I need an* **immediate** *answer.*
i'**mmediately** *adverb*: *She came* **immediately**.

immense /ɪ'mens/ *adjective*
very large: *He made an* **immense** *amount of money in business.*
i'**mmensely** *adverb*: *I am* **immensely** *pleased to have this job.*

immunize /'ɪmjʊnaɪz/ *verb* (*present participle* **immunizing**, *past* **immunized**)
to put a special substance into the body, usually by an injection, to prevent an illness (see **inject**)
‚**immuni'zation** *noun* (*no plural*)

impatient /ɪm'peɪʃnt/ *adjective*
not able to wait for something to

happen: *It is no use getting* **impatient** *when you are waiting for a train.*

im'patience *noun* (*no plural*)
im'patiently *adverb*

imperative /ɪmˈperətɪv/
noun, adjective
the form of a verb we use when we are telling someone to do something: *In the sentence "Come over here!", "come" is in the* **imperative.**

impertinent /ɪmˈpɜːtɪnənt/
adjective
rude, especially to older people: *She scolded her son for being* **impertinent.**

im'pertinence *noun* (*no plural*)

impolite /ˌɪmpəˈlaɪt/ *adjective*
not polite; rather rude: *I think I was* **impolite** *when I asked the woman how old she was.*

import[1] /ɪmˈpɔːt/ *verb*
to bring into a country for use there: *We* **import** *machinery that we cannot make in our country.*

import[2] /ˈɪmpɔːt/ *noun*
something that is imported: *Machinery is one of our* **imports.**

○**important** /ɪmˈpɔːtnt/ *adjective*
having power; of great value: *The headmaster is the most* **important** *person in the school. It is* **important** *that we tell the truth.*
○**im'portance** *noun* (*no plural*): *The* **importance** *of telling the truth cannot be doubted.*

impossible /ɪmˈpɒsəbl/ *adjective*
not possible; not able to happen: *I can't come today; it's* **impossible.**
im'possibly *adverb*: *That piece of work looks* **impossibly** *difficult.*

impress /ɪmˈpres/ *verb*
to cause strong good feelings or thought: *His teacher was so*

impressed *by his work, that she showed it to the headmaster.*

im'pression *noun*: *His work made a great* **impression** *on his teacher.*

im'pressive *adjective*: *His work was very* **impressive.**

imprison /ɪmˈprɪzn/ *verb*
to put in prison: *He was* **imprisoned** *for two years.*

im'prisonment *noun*: *He was given two years'* **imprisonment.**

○**improve** /ɪmˈpruːv/ *verb* (*present participle* **improving,** *past* **improved**)
to make or get better: *Your reading has* **improved** *this year, but you must try to* **improve** *your writing.*

im'provement *noun*: *There have been great* **improvements** *in your reading, but your writing still needs* **improvement.**

impulse /ˈɪmpʌls/ *noun*
a sudden wish to do something: *She had an* **impulse** *to buy a new dress. She bought the dress* **on impulse.**

im'pulsive *adjective*: *An* **impulsive** *person does things without thinking carefully about them first.*

○**in** /ɪn/ *preposition, adverb*
1 (showing where): *Don't stand* **in** *the sun, sit* **in** *the shade.*
2 at or to the inside of a place: *We ran to the water and jumped* **in.**
3 during; before the end of: *The house was built* **in** *1978. He woke up* **in** *the middle of the night.*
4 at home or in an office: *My brother is out now but he will be* **in** *this evening.*
5 using: *She spoke* **in** *a quiet voice. The words were written* **in** *pencil.*
6 wearing: *The guard was* **in uniform.**
7 (used in phrases like this): *Emily*

was **in tears** (= crying). *Are all your family* **in good health** (= well)? *Those kind of trousers are* **in** (= liked and worn by a lot of people) *this year.*

○ **inadequate** /ɪn'ædɪkwət/ *adjective*
not enough: *The food was* **inadequate** *for ten people — there was only enough for five.*

incapable /ɪn'keɪpəbl/ *adjective*
not able to do something: *Since her accident, she has been* **incapable of** *walking.*

○ **inch** /ɪntʃ/ *noun* (*plural* **inches**)
a measure of length, equal to 2.5 centimetres: *There are twelve* **inches** *in a foot* (see).
ins is a short way of writing **inches.**

incident /'ɪnsɪdnt/ *noun*
an event; something that happens: *Were there any exciting* **incidents** *during your journey?*

incline /ɪn'klaɪn/ *verb* (*present participle* **inclining**, *past* **inclined**)
to be inclined to to want to or be likely to: *I am* **inclined to** *be ill after eating fish.*

○ **include** /ɪn'kluːd/ *verb* (*present participle* **including**, *past* **included**)
1 to have as part of: *His class* **includes** *the two cleverest students in the school.*
2 to count or think of someone or something as part of: *I* **included** *my uncle in my list of people to thank.*

income /'ɪŋkʌm/ *noun*
all the money you receive: *What is your* **income** *from your job?*
'Income tax *is taken by the government from what you earn, to be spent on schools, roads, hospitals, etc.*

incomplete /ˌɪnkəm'pliːt/ *adjective*
not finished: *This list of names is* **incomplete:** *you have left out Paul.*

inconvenient /ˌɪnkən'viːnjənt/ *adjective*
not suitable; causing difficulty: *This shelf is at an* **inconvenient** *height. It's too high for me to reach.*
ˌincon'venience *noun* (*no plural*)

incorrect /ˌɪnkə'rekt/ *adjective*
not right; wrong: *The answer to the sum is* **incorrect.**
incorrectly *adverb*

○ **increase**[1] /ɪn'kriːs/ *verb*
(*present participle* **increasing**, *past* **increased**)
to make or grow larger: *My wages have* **increased** *this year. My employer has* **increased** *my wages.*

○ **increase**[2] /'ɪŋkriːs/ *noun*
getting larger: *an* **increase** *in wages*

indeed /ɪn'diːd/ *adverb*
1 really: *Did he say that? He did* **indeed.**
2 (used to make **very** even stronger): *He runs very fast* **indeed.**

indefinite /ɪn'defɪnət/ *adjective*
not clear or fixed: *He gave an* **indefinite** *answer. I am staying for an* **indefinite** *time.*
in'definitely *adverb*: *I am staying here* **indefinitely.**

independent /ˌɪndɪ'pendənt/ *adjective*
able to look after yourself; not governed by anyone or anything else: *Although she is young, she is very* **independent.** *America has not always been* **independent.**
ˌinde'pendence *noun* (*no plural*): *America gained its* **independence** *in 1776.*

index /'ɪndeks/ *noun*
(*plural* **indexes**)
a list in a book of what can be found in it, and on what page

indicate /'ɪndɪkeɪt/ *verb* (*present participle* **indicating**, *past*

indicated)
to show: *On this map, the towns are* **indicated** *by a red dot.*

,indi'cation *noun: There is no* **indication** (= nothing to show) *that you have worked hard.*

'indicator *noun:*
On a car,
the **indicator**
flashes if
the driver is
going to turn. indicator

indignant /ɪn'dɪgnənt/ *adjective*
angry because of something that appears wrong: *I was* **indignant** *because I felt that I had been punished unfairly.*
in'dignantly *adverb: "It isn't fair!" she said* **indignantly.**

indirect /ˌɪndɪ'rekt/ *adjective*
not direct; not straight: *We went to the house by an* **indirect** *road.*
,indi'rectly *adverb*

individual[1] /ˌɪndɪ'vɪdʒʊəl/ *noun*
a person: *If any* **individuals** *are seen leaving school early, they will be punished.*

individual[2] *adjective*
single; for one person only: *The children had* **individual** *desks.*
,indi'vidually *adverb: The children were taught* **individually,** *not in a group.*

indoor /'ɪndɔːʳ/ *adjective*
inside a building: *If it rains, we play* **indoor** *games.*

indoors /ɪn'dɔːz/ *adverb*
inside a building: *Let's stay* **indoors** *today.*

°**industry** /'ɪndəstrɪ/ *noun*
(*plural* **industries**)
making things in factories: *Our town has a lot of* **industry.** *What are the important* **industries** *in the town?*
industrial /ɪn'dʌstrɪəl/ *adjective:*

an **industrial** *town* (= with a lot of industry)

infant /'ɪnfənt/ *noun*
a baby or young child

infect /ɪn'fekt/ *verb*
to give an illness to: *One of the boys in the class had a fever and he soon* **infected** *other children.*
in'fection *noun: My brother has a throat* **infection.**
in'fectious *adjective: An* **infectious** *illness is one that you can give to other people.*

infinite /'ɪnfɪnət/ *adjective*
endless; so large that it cannot be imagined: **Infinite** *space surrounds the Earth.*
'infinitely *adverb: It is* **infinitely** (= very much) *easier to drive a car than to repair it.*

inflate /ɪn'fleɪt/ *verb* (*present participle* **inflating,** *past* **inflated**)
to fill with air: *to* **inflate** *a tyre*

influence[1] /'ɪnflʊəns/ *noun*
something that changes what happens: *My teacher's* **influence** *made me study science at college.*
influential /ˌɪnflʊ'enʃl/ *adjective*
having great influence

influence[2] *verb* (*present participle* **influencing,** *past* **influenced**)
to change what happens: *My teacher* **influenced** *my decision to study science.*

influenza /ˌɪnflu:'enzə/ *or* **flu** /flu:/ *noun* (*no plural*)
an illness which causes fever, headache, and other discomfort

inform /ɪn'fɔːm/ *verb*
to tell: *The headmistress* **informed** *us that the school would be closed for one day next week.*

°**information** /ˌɪnfə'meɪʃn/ *noun* (*no plural*) facts; knowledge; things you want to know: *What* **information** *is on a map?*

informal /ɪnˈfɔːml/ *adjective*
happening or done in an easy way, not according to rules: *It's not a formal party, it's an informal one so you can wear what you like.*
inˈformally *adverb*

ingredient /ɪŋˈgriːdɪənt/ *noun*
something you put in when making something: *Flour is an ingredient of this cake.*

inhabitant /ɪnˈhæbɪtənt/ *noun*
someone who lives in a place: *the inhabitants of a village*

inherit /ɪnˈherɪt/ *verb*
to get something from someone when they die: *He inherited the farm from his parents.*
inheritance *noun*: *The farm is his inheritance.*

initial¹ /ɪˈnɪʃl/ *noun*
the first letter of a name, used to stand for the name: *His name is John Smith, so his initials are J.S.*

initial² *adjective*
first: *Her initial plan was to walk to town but then she decided to go by bus.* **initially** *adverb*

inject /ɪnˈdʒekt/
verb
to give someone medicine through the skin, with a needle

injection

injection *noun*: *The doctor gave him an injection.*

injure /ˈɪndʒər/ *verb* (*present participle* **injuring**, *past* **injured**)
to harm; wound: *There were two people injured in the car accident.*
injury *noun* (*plural* **injuries**) a wound; damage: *The people in the accident had serious injuries.*

injustice /ɪnˈdʒʌstɪs/ *noun*
being unfair; something unfair:
The teacher did him an injustice when she called him a cheat.

° **ink** /ɪŋk/ *noun* (*no plural*)
a coloured liquid used for writing, printing, etc.

inland¹ /ˈɪnlənd/ *adjective*
far from the sea: *an inland town*

inland² /ɪnˈlænd/ *adverb*
away from the sea: *We went twenty kilometres inland, up the river.*

in-law /ˈɪn lɔː/
used after a word to mean a person related to you through your wife or husband: *Your ˈmother-in-ˌlaw is your wife's (or husband's) mother.*

inn /ɪn/ *noun*
a place which sells drinks and food, and is sometimes a hotel as well: *The travellers stopped to eat at a small inn.*

inner /ˈɪnər/ *adjective*
further in, or in the middle: *The inner room was reached through the kitchen.*

innocent /ˈɪnəsnt/ *adjective*
not guilty
innocence *noun* (*no plural*): *Her innocence has been proved.*

inquire /ɪnˈkwaɪər/ *verb*
(*present participle* **inquiring**, *past* **inquired**)
to ask: *If you want to know anything, just inquire at this office.*
inquiry *noun*: *She made an inquiry about jobs.*

insane /ɪnˈseɪn/ *adjective*
mad: *He must be insane to drive his car so fast.*

° **insect** /ˈɪnsekt/ *noun*
a small animal without bones that has six legs: *Bees and ants are insects.*

insert /ɪnˈsɜːt/ *verb*
to put in: *Insert this card in your book to mark the page.*

○ **inside¹** /ɪnˈsaɪd/ *noun*
the part that is in the middle of something, contained by something or facing inwards: *The outside of an orange is bitter, but the* **inside** *is sweet. Have you seen the* **inside** *of the house?*

○ **inside²**
preposition, adverb, adjective
in; to or on the inside of something: *She put the money* **inside** *her bag. Don't stand out there in the sun; come* **inside**. *We eat the* **inside** *part of this fruit.*

insist /ɪnˈsɪst/ *verb*
to say with great firmness: *I* **insist** *that you come to school now. Mr Brown* **insists** **on** *seeing you, Headmaster.*

inspect /ɪnˈspekt/ *verb*
to look at carefully, to see if there is anything wrong: *He* **inspected** *the car before he bought it. The government sent someone to* **inspect** *our school.*
inspection *noun: He made an* **inspection** *of the school.*
inspector *noun* 1 a person who inspects: *The School* **Inspector** *visited our school.* 2 a police officer

install /ɪnˈstɔːl/ *verb*
to fit machinery, etc.: *We have* **installed** *a telephone in the office.*
installation /ˌɪnstəˈleɪʃn/ *noun*

instance /ˈɪnstəns/ *noun*
an example: *An* **instance** *of his bad behaviour is that he ran away from school.*

instant /ˈɪnstənt/ *adjective*
happening or working at once: **Instant** *coffee is made as soon as you pour water on it.*
instantly *adverb* at once

○ **instead** /ɪnˈsted/ *adverb*
in place of someone or something:
I didn't have a pen, so I used a pencil **instead**.
instead of *preposition* in place of: *I came* **instead of** *my brother.*

instinct /ˈɪnstɪŋkt/ *noun*
a natural force which makes you do things when you haven't been taught to do them; natural feelings: *Babies drink from their mothers* **by instinct**.
instinctive *adjective: A baby's cry is* **instinctive**.

institute /ˈɪnstɪtjuːt/ *noun*
a group, or the building it uses, of people who want to study or talk about a special thing
institution *noun: A hospital is an* **institution** *for ill people* (=a building specially for them).

instruct /ɪnˈstrʌkt/ *verb*
to teach: *She* **instructed** *me in the use of the telephone.*
instruction *noun: Read the* **instructions** *on the packet.*
instructor *noun: He is a sports* **instructor**.

○ **instrument**
/ˈɪnstrəmənt/
noun
a tool used
for doing
something
special: *A pen* **musical instruments**
is an
instrument *for writing. Do you play any* **musical instrument** (=thing to make music)?

insult¹ /ɪnˈsʌlt/ *verb*
to be rude to: *He* **insulted** *her by calling her a stupid fool.*

insult² /ˈɪnsʌlt/ *noun*
something rude said to someone: *He shouted* **insults** *at the boys.*

insurance /ɪnˈʃʊərəns/ *noun*
(*no plural*)
money paid to a company which

will pay a large amount if you are in an accident, die, etc.

intelligent /ɪn'telɪdʒənt/ *adjective*
being quick at thinking; clever
intelligence *noun* (*no plural*)

○ **intend** /ɪn'tend/ *verb*
to plan to do something: *Today, I* **intend** *to finish reading this book.*
intention *noun: I began reading* **with the intention of** *finishing the book, but I never did.*

○ **interest**[1] /'ɪntrest/ *noun*
wanting to know more about something; getting pleasure from studying something: *She* **takes an interest in** *everything around her. His chief* **interest** (= thing he is interested in) *is football.*

○ **interest**[2] *verb*
to make someone want to know more, or get pleasure from studying: *I am very* **interested in** *stamps. I find them* **interesting.**

interfere /ˌɪntə'fɪər/ *verb*
(*present participle* **interfering,** *past* **interfered**)
to prevent someone doing what he wants to; to get in the way: *I was playing with Jane but Anne* **interfered** *and spoiled the game.*
interference *noun*

interior /ɪn'tɪərɪər/ *noun* (*no plural*)
the inside: *The* **interior** *of the box was black.*

internal /ɪn'tɜːnl/ *adjective*
of or on the inside: *Although the man who had fallen looked all right, he was hurt* **internally.**

international /ˌɪntə'næʃənl/ *adjective*
of, for or by many countries: *an* **international** *agreement*

interrupt /ˌɪntə'rʌpt/ *verb*
to say something when someone else is already speaking: *It is rude to* **interrupt.**

interval /'ɪntəvl/ *noun*
a time or space between things: *In between parts of a play, there is often an* **interval.** *There were trees* **at intervals** *along the road.*

interview[1] /'ɪntəvjuː/ *noun*
a meeting to decide if a person is suitable for a job, or to ask his opinions: *to go for an* **interview**

interview[2] *verb*
to talk to someone to see if he is suitable for a job, or to ask his opinions

○ **into** /'ɪntə; *strong* 'ɪntuː/ *preposition*
1 to or towards the middle of: *Come* **into** *the classroom.*
2 (used to show how people or things change): *She made the material* **into** *a dress. He cut the cake* **into** *six pieces.*

intransitive /ɪn'trænsətɪv/ *noun, adjective*
a verb whose action is not done to something or somebody; a verb that does not take an object (see): *When he had finished, he sat down. "Finish" and "sit" are* **intransitive** *verbs here.* Look at **transitive.**

introduce /ˌɪntrə'djuːs/ *verb*
(*present participle* **introducing,** *past* **introduced**)
1 to give someone's name when they first meet someone else: *He* **introduced** *his friend to me.*
2 to bring in a new thing: *to* **introduce** *a new subject in a school*
introduction /ˌɪntrə'dʌkʃn/ *noun* **1** introducing someone or something **2** a piece of writing at the beginning of a book telling us about it

invade /ɪn'veɪd/ *verb* (*present participle* **invading,** *past* **invaded**)
to attack and go into someone's

land, house, etc.: *The army* **invaded** *the town.* **invasion** *noun*

invalid /ˈɪnvəlɪd/ *noun*
a person made weak by illness: *He helps to look after his grandfather who is an* **invalid.**

invent /ɪnˈvent/ *verb*
to think of and plan something completely new: *Who* **invented** *the telephone?*
> **invention** *noun: the* **invention** *of the telephone*
> **inventor** *noun* a person who invents

inverted commas
/ɪnˌvɜːtɪd ˈkɒməz/ *plural noun*
the signs ' ' or " ", used in writing to show what somebody says: *"Please be quiet", said Sarah.*

investigate /ɪnˈvestɪgeɪt/ *verb*
(*present participle* **investigating,** *past* **investigated**)
to find out about something by looking, asking questions, etc.: *The police are* **investigating** *the robbery.*
> **in,vesti'gation** *noun: The police* **investigation** *will take weeks.*

invisible /ɪnˈvɪzɪbl/ *adjective*
not able to be seen: *It was so cloudy that the top of the mountain was* **invisible.**

invite /ɪnˈvaɪt/ *verb* (*present participle* **inviting,** *past* **invited**)
to ask someone to your house, to go out with you, etc.: *She* **invited** *us to her party.*
> **invitation** /ˌɪnvɪˈteɪʃn/ *noun: We had three* **invitations** (= letters inviting us) *to parties.*

involve /ɪnˈvɒlv/ *verb* (*present participle* **involving,** *past* **involved**)
to make be a part of: *All the children were* **involved** *in the school play. This lesson* **involves** (= needs) *a lot of work.*

∘ **inwards** /ˈɪnwədz/ *adverb*
towards the middle or the inside: *She turns her toes* **inwards** *when she walks.*

∘ **iron**[1] /ˈaɪən/
noun
1 (*no plural*) a hard, grey metal
2 an instrument which is heated and then used to make clothes smooth

iron

iron[2] *verb*
to press clothes with a hot iron to make them smooth

irregular /ɪˈregjələr/ *adjective*
not regular: *Your writing is* **irregular:** *some letters are big and some small.* **irregularly** *adverb*

irrigate /ˈɪrɪgeɪt/ *verb*
(*present participle* **irrigating,** *past* **irrigated**)
to make water flow onto: *The fields are* **irrigated** *so that the crops can grow.*
> ,**irri'gation** *noun: We could not grow rice on this land before* **irrigation,** *because there was not enough rain.*

irritate /ˈɪrɪteɪt/ *verb*
(*present participle* **irritating,** *past* **irritated**)
to annoy: *The noise of the children was* **irritating** *me. Insect bites* **irritate** *your skin* (= make it sore).

is /s, z, əz; *strong* ɪz/ *verb*
the part of the verb **be** that we use with **he, she** and **it**: *She* **is** *Peter's sister.* **He's** *her brother. That* **boy's** (= boy is) *in my class.* **He's not** (*or* **he isn't**) *in your class.*

Islam /ˈɪzlɑːm/ *noun*
the religion of the Muslims
> **Is'lamic** *adjective*

° **island** /ˈaɪlənd/ *noun*
a piece of land surrounded by water (see picture on page 185)

isolate /ˈaɪsəleɪt/ *verb* (*present participle* **isolating**, *past* **isolated**)
to separate; set apart from other things or people: *The farm is* **isolated**; *the nearest house is 5 kilometres away.*

issue[1] /ˈɪʃuː/ *verb* (*present participle* **issuing**, *past* **issued**)
to give, send, or come out: *The teacher* **issued** *paper and pencils to all the children.*

issue[2] *noun*
something that comes out: *An* **issue** *of a newspaper is one day's newspaper.*

° **it** /ɪt/ (*plural* **they** /ðeɪ/)
1 the thing or animal or baby that the sentence is about: *I've lost my book, and I can't find* **it** *anywhere.* **It's** (= it is) *not in my room.* **It'll** (= it will) *be Saturday tomorrow.*
2 (used about the weather, time, and dates, and in other phrases): **It** *is very hot today.* **It's** *nearly four o'clock.* **It** *is Thursday, September 2nd.* **It's** *a long way to the town.*

itch[1] /ɪtʃ/ *verb*
to be sore and annoying, so that you want to rub it: *The insect bite* **itched** *all night.*

itch[2] *noun* (*plural* **itches**)
an itching feeling: *I've got an* **itch** *on my back.*

item /ˈaɪtəm/ *noun*
a thing: *There was an interesting* **item** *in the newspaper today. On the desk there were two books, a pen, and some other* **items**.

° **its** /ɪts/
of it; belonging to it: *She gave the baby* **its** *food. The dog hurt* **its** *foot.*

itself /ɪtˈself/ (*plural* **themselves** /ðəmˈselvz/)
the same thing, animal, or baby as the one that the sentence is about: *The baby is too young to feed* **itself**. *The house stands* **by itself** (= alone) *outside the village.*

ivory /ˈaɪvərɪ/ *noun* (*no plural*)
hard, yellowish-white substance taken from the tusks (= long teeth) of elephants

jab /dʒæb/ *verb* (*present participle* **jabbing**, *past* **jabbed**)
to push, usually with something sharp: *I* **jabbed** *the needle into my finger. He kept* **jabbing** *his finger into my back until I turned round.*

jackal /ˈdʒækəl/ *noun*
a wild animal like a small dog that eats meat

jacket /ˈdʒækɪt/ *noun*
1 a short coat with sleeves (= covering for the arms)
2 the outer covering of some things: *The paper cover of some books is called a* **dust jacket**.

jacket

jagged /'dʒægɪd/ *adjective*
having a rough uneven edge with sharp points: *I cut myself on the* **jagged** *edge of the tin.*

jaguar /'dʒægjʊəʳ/ *noun*
a wild animal with a spotted coat which is one of the big cats

jail *or* **gaol** /dʒeɪl/ *noun*
prison: *The man was sent to* **jail.**

jam[1] /dʒæm/ *verb* (*present participle* **jamming**, *past* **jammed**)
1 to press or be pressed together; pack tightly into something: *I tried to* **jam** *all my clothes into a case, but they wouldn't fit.*
2 to get stuck or stop all movement: *I can't open this window — it's* **jammed.**

jam[2] *noun*
so many cars, people, etc., crowded together that movement is stopped: *There are always* **traffic jams** *in the city in the morning.*

jam[3] *noun* (*no plural*)
sweet food made of fruit boiled with sugar, usually eaten with bread

○ **January** /'dʒænjʊərɪ/ *noun*
the first month of the year

jar /dʒɑːʳ/ *noun*
a container like a bottle with a short neck and a wide opening: *a* **jar** *of jam* (picture at **bottle**)

jaw /dʒɔː/ *noun*
one of the bony parts of the face in which the teeth are set (picture on page 133)

jazz /dʒæz/ *noun* (*no plural*)
a kind of music with a strong beat: *Do you like listening to* **jazz**?

jealous /'dʒeləs/ *adjective*
1 unhappy because of wanting what someone else has: *I was* **jealous** *of Sarah when she got her new bicycle. I was very* **jealous** *of Sarah's new bicycle.*
2 being afraid of losing what you have: *Sarah is Jane's friend but she is* **jealous** *if Jane plays with other girls.* **jealously** *adverb*
jealousy *noun* (*no plural*): *It is silly to let* **jealousy** *spoil our friendship.*

jeans /dʒiːnz/ *plural noun*
trousers made of a strong cotton cloth, usually blue: *I've got a new* **pair of jeans.**

jeep /dʒiːp/ *noun*
a car which has a strong engine and can be used on bad roads

jeep

jeer /dʒɪəʳ/ *verb*
to laugh rudely at someone: *Don't* **jeer at** *the person who came last in the race — it's very unkind.*

jelly /'dʒelɪ/ *noun*
1 (*plural* **jellies**) a sweet soft food, often tasting of fruit
2 (*no plural*) any other thing that is between liquid and solid: *The medicine was a clear* **jelly.**

jellyfish /'dʒelɪˌfɪʃ/ *noun*
(*plural* **jellyfish** *or* **jellyfishes**)
a soft sea creature that looks like a lump of jelly (see) and can sting

jerk[1] /dʒɜːk/ *verb*
to pull or move suddenly: *She* **jerked** *the rope but it wouldn't move.*

jerk[2] *noun*
a short hard pull or movement: *The old bus started with a* **jerk.**

jersey /'dʒɜːzɪ/ *noun*
a piece of clothing, usually made of wool, that covers the top part of the body. **Sweater** and **jumper** are other words for **jersey**.

jet /dʒet/ *noun*
1 a narrow stream of gas, air, or liquid which comes out of a small

hole: *The fireman sent* **jets** *of water into the burning house.*

2 an aircraft that is pushed through the air by an engine which pushes out hot air behind itself (a **jet engine**)

jetty /'dʒetɪ/ *noun* (*plural* **jetties**)
a kind of wall built out into water, used for getting on and off boats, or for protection against the waves

jewel /'dʒuːəl/ *noun*
a stone which is worth a lot of money and is used as an ornament: *She wore beautiful* **jewels** *round her neck.*

> **jewellery** /'dʒuːəlrɪ/ *noun* (*no plural*) jewels, gold, etc. made into rings, earrings, and other ornaments

jigsaw puzzle /'dʒɪgsɔː ˌpʌzl/ *or* **jigsaw** *noun*
a game in which you must fit together small pieces to make one big picture

jingle /'dʒɪŋgl/ *verb* (*present participle* **jingling**, *past* **jingled**)
to make a ringing noise, like little bells: *The coins* **jingled** *in his pocket.*

○ **job** /dʒɒb/ *noun*
1 a piece of work that must be done: *My mother does all the* **jobs** *about the house.*
2 work that you are paid to do: *What is your* **job**? — *I'm a teacher.* **It's a good job** (= It's lucky) *you were here to help me.*

○ **join**[1] /dʒɔɪn/ *verb*
1 to put or bring two or more things together: *Tie a knot to* **join** *those two pieces of rope. This road* **joins** *the two villages.*
2 to come together; meet: *Where do the two roads* **join**? *Will you* **join** *us for coffee* (= have coffee with us)?

3 to become a member of something: *He* **joined** *the army. Everyone* **joined in** (= was a part of) *the game.*

○ **join**[2] *noun*
a place where two things have been joined together: *There's a* **join** *in this piece of material.*

○ **joint**[1] /dʒɔɪnt/ *noun*
1 a place where things, especially bones, are joined: *Our arms and legs bend at the* **joints** — *the elbows and knees.*
2 a piece of meat for cooking

joint[2] *adjective*
shared by two or more people: *Mr Jones and his two sons are the* **joint** *owners of the business.*
> **jointly** *adverb*

○ **joke**[1] /dʒəʊk/ *noun*
something you say or do to make people laugh: *Our teacher told us a* **joke** *today. We all* **played a joke on** *him* (= did something to make other people laugh at him).

○ **joke**[2] *verb* (*present participle* **joking**, *past* **joked**)
to tell jokes: *I didn't mean that seriously* — *I was only* **joking.**

jolly[1] /'dʒɒlɪ/ *adjective* (**jollier**, **jolliest**)
happy; pleasant: *a* **jolly** *person*

jolly[2] *adverb*
very: *a* **jolly** *good book*

jolt[1] /dʒəʊlt/ *noun*
a sudden shake or shock: *The lorry started with a* **jolt.**

jolt[2] *verb*
to give a jolt; move with a jolt

journal /'dʒɜːnl/ *noun*
1 a sort of newspaper, often for special things: *The doctor reads the* **Journal** *of Medical Science.*
2 a diary (see)
> **journalism** *noun* (*no plural*) the job of a journalist; the writing

that a journalist does

journalist *noun* a person who works for a newspaper, and writes about the news

°**journey** /'dʒɜːnɪ/ *noun*
a trip, usually a long one: *How long is the journey to the coast?*

joy /dʒɔɪ/ *noun*
1 (*no plural*) great happiness: *She was full of joy when her child was born.*
2 something that gives great happiness: *Her child was a joy to her.*
joyful *adjective* showing or giving joy **joyfully** *adverb*

judge¹ /dʒʌdʒ/ *noun*
1 a person who can decide questions of law in a court (see): *The judge decided that the man should go to prison for two years.*
2 a person who decides who wins a competition

judge² *verb* (*present participle* **judging**, *past* **judged**)
1 to decide if something or someone is good or bad, right or wrong, etc.; form an opinion about: *Can you judge which shoes are best?*
2 to act as a judge: *Who's judging the races?*
judgement *noun* **1** the decision made by a judge **2** (*no plural*) what you think or decide: *In her judgement, we shouldn't change our plans.*

judo /'dʒuːdəʊ/ *noun* (*no plural*)
a kind of fighting in which you hold and throw the other person

jug /dʒʌg/ *noun*
a container with a handle for holding and pouring liquids: *a jug of water*

juggle /'dʒʌgl/ *verb* (*present participle* **juggling**, *past* **juggled**)
to throw several things into the air and keep them moving by throwing and catching them, as a trick
juggler *noun*

°**juice** /dʒuːs/ *noun*
the liquid that comes out of fruit and vegetables and also meat: *a glass of orange juice*
juicy *adjective* (**juicier, juiciest**) having a lot of juice: *Oranges are juicy.*

°**July** /dʒuːˈlaɪ/ *noun*
the seventh month of the year

jumble /'dʒʌmbl/ *verb*
(*present participle* **jumbling**, *past* **jumbled**)
to mix up together in an untidy way: *How can I find that letter when all your papers are jumbled up like this?*

°**jump**¹ /dʒʌmp/ *verb*
1 to move the body off the ground, up in the air, or over something: *She jumped up into the chair. The dog jumped over the gate.*
2 to move quickly: *She jumped to her feet* (= stood up quickly).
3 to move suddenly because of fear or surprise: *That sudden noise made me jump.*

°**jump**² *noun*
1 moving the body off the ground: *He went over the fence in one jump.*
2 something that someone jumps over, in a race, etc.: *The horses raced over the jumps.*

jumper /'dʒʌmpəʳ/ *noun*
a piece of clothing,

jumper

usually made of wool, that covers the top part of the body **sweater** and **jersey** are other words for **jumper.**

junction /ˈdʒʌŋkʃn/ noun
a place where two or more things join or meet each other: *Turn left at the* **junction** *of the two roads.*

○ **June** /dʒuːn/ noun
the sixth month of the year

jungle /ˈdʒʌŋgl/ noun
a thick forest in hot countries

junior /ˈdʒuːnɪəʳ/ adjective
1 younger: *She teaches a* **junior** *class.*
2 lower in importance or position: *He has a* **junior** *position in the company.*

junk /dʒʌŋk/ noun (no plural)
useless things that are not wanted: *That room is full of* **junk.**

jury /ˈdʒʊərɪ/ noun (plural **juries**)
a group of people who decide if a person is guilty or not in a law court (see)

○ **just**[1] /dʒʌst/ adverb
1 exactly; no more and no less: *It is his birthday; he is* **just** *ten years old.*
2 to the amount needed, but no more: *I can* **just** *reach the top shelf if I stand on my toes.*
3 a very short time ago; by a short time: *You have* **just** *missed the bus.*
4 only: *I rang up* **just** *to say hello.*
5 (used in some phrases, to make the meaning stronger): *Ada is* **just** *as clever as her brothers. I am* **just** *going to cook a meal; will you stay and eat with us? The last pupil arrived* **just as** (= at the moment when) *the lesson began.*

○ **just**[2] adjective
fair and right: *a* **just** *punishment*

justice /ˈdʒʌstɪs/ noun **1** (no plural) being fair and just: *Everyone should be treated with* **justice.** **2** (no plural) the power of the law: *The criminals were finally* **brought to justice.**

justly adverb

Kk

kangaroo
/ˌkæŋgəˈruː/
noun
an animal living in Australia that jumps along on its large back legs

kangaroo

keen /kiːn/ adjective
eager to do something; liking to do something: *He was* **keen** *to see the new film. Are you* **keen on** *swimming? — Yes, I like it very much.* **keenly** adverb

○ **keep**[1] /kiːp/ verb
(past **kept** /kept/)
1 to have or hold something: *I don't want this book any more, so you can* **keep** *it* (= have it as your own). *Will you* **keep** *this book until next week, and give it back to me then?*
2 to store something in a place: *Always* **keep** *your money in a safe place.*
3 to give food, clothes, and things that are needed to someone: *He has to earn quite a lot of money to* **keep** *his wife and six children.*

4 to stay or make someone stay: *Her illness* **kept** *her in hospital for three weeks.* **Keep** *still while I'm cutting your hair. He* **keeps** *telling me* (= he tells me often) *but I always forget. Danger —* **keep out! Keep off** *the grass!*

'**keeper** *noun* a person who keeps or looks after something

keep² *noun (no plural)*
the cost of someone's food, clothes, etc.: *He* **earns his keep** *by working with his uncle.*

kennel /'kenl/ *noun*
a small house for a dog

kerb /kɜːb/ *noun*
a line of raised stones separating the pavement (= place where you walk) from the road (picture at **pavement**)

kerosene /'kerəsiːn/ *or* **paraffin** *noun (no plural)*
a colourless oil that can be burnt and used for cooking and lighting

kettle /'ketl/ *noun*
a metal pot with a lid and a handle and a long curved mouth for pouring; it is used for boiling water: *Will you* **put the kettle on?**

○ **key** /kiː/ *noun*

keys

1 a metal instrument used for locking and unlocking things: *We have a* **key** *for the door of the house and a* **key** *for starting the car.*
2 a small part of a machine or musical instrument, that is pressed: *There are black and white* **keys** *on a piano* (see). *On a typewriter* (see), *each* **key** *has a letter on it.*
3 an answer, or something that helps you to understand: *The answers are in the* **key** *at the back of the book.*

'**keyhole** *noun* the part of a lock that a key fits into

khaki /'kɑːkɪ/ *adjective, noun (no plural)*
a yellow-brown colour; a strong cotton cloth of this colour

○ **kick¹** /kɪk/ *verb*
to hit something with the foot; move the foot suddenly as if to hit something: *Don't* **kick** *the ball into the road. The baby was lying on its back,* **kicking** *its legs in the air.*

○ **kick²** *noun*
1 an act of kicking: *If the door won't open, give it a* **kick.**
2 a feeling of pleasure or excitement: *I* **get a kick out of** *driving fast.*

kid /kɪd/ *noun*
1 a young goat
2 a child or young person

kidnap /'kɪdnæp/ *verb*
(*present participle* **kidnapping,** *past* **kidnapped**)
to take someone away and ask for money in return for bringing them back safely **kidnapper** *noun*

kidney /'kɪdnɪ/ *noun*
one of the two parts inside the body which remove waste liquid from the blood (picture on p. 133)

○ **kill** /kɪl/ *verb*
to make someone or something die: *Ten people were* **killed** *in the train crash.*

'**killer** *noun* a person or thing that kills: *The* **killer** *was put in prison.*

kilogram /'kɪləgræm/ *or* **kilogramme** *noun*
a measure of weight; 1,000 grams

○ **kilo** /'kiːləʊ/ *noun* a short way of writing or saying kilogram: *a* **kilo** *of sugar*

○**kilometre** /'kɪləmiːtə^r, kɪ'lɒmɪtə^r/ *noun*

a measure of length; 1,000 metres: *It is three* **kilometres** *to the town.* **km** is a short way of writing **kilometre**.

kin /kɪn/ *noun (no plural)*

people in your family: *The dead man's* **next of kin** (=his closest relative) *was told about his death.*

○**kind**[1] /kaɪnd/ *noun*

a sort; type; group: *She is the* **kind** *of woman who helps people. What* **kind** *of car has he got?*

○**kind**[2] *adjective*

good; helpful; wanting to do things that make other people happy: *She was* **kind** *to me when I was unhappy. It's very* **kind** *of you to help me.*

ˌ**kind-'hearted** *adjective: She's very* **kind-hearted** — *she always helps other people when she can.* ˈ**kindness** *noun (no plural): Thank you for all your* **kindness**.

kindle /'kɪndl/ *verb (present participle* **kindling** *past* **kindled**)

to begin to burn; make something burn: *This wet wood won't* **kindle**.

○**king** /kɪŋ/ *noun*

a male ruler of a country, especially one who comes from a family of rulers

ˈ**kingdom** *noun* the land ruled by a king

○**kiss**[1] /kɪs/ *verb*

to touch someone with the lips, as a sign of love or liking: *He* **kissed** *his wife when he said goodbye. He* **kissed** *her goodbye.*

○**kiss**[2] *noun (plural* **kisses**)

an act of kissing: *He gave his daughter a* **kiss**.

kit /kɪt/ *noun*

1 (*no plural*) all the things needed for doing something or going

somewhere: *The soldiers packed their* **kit** *for the journey.*

2 a set of small pieces from which to make something: *We made a model plane out of a* **kit**.

○**kitchen** /'kɪtʃɪn/ *noun*

a room used for cooking

kite /kaɪt/ *noun*

a toy with a light frame covered with plastic or cloth which flies in the air on the end of a long string

kitten /'kɪtn/ *noun*

a young cat

knead /niːd/ *verb*

to mix and press dough (=flour and water) to make bread

○**knee** /niː/ *noun*

the joint in the middle of the leg where the leg bends (picture on page 133)

○**kneel** /niːl/ *verb*

(*past* **knelt** /nelt/)

to go down or stay on the knees: *She* **knelt down** *to pray.*

knew /njuː/ see **know**

knickers /'nɪkəz/ *plural noun*

women's and girls' underclothes for the lower part of the body, not covering the legs

○**knife** /naɪf/ *noun (plural* **knives** /naɪvz/)

a blade with a handle, used for cutting

knives

knight /naɪt/ *noun*

a man who is given a title by the Queen of England, and whose name then has "Sir" in front of it

knit /nɪt/ *verb (present participle* **knitting**, *past* **knitted** *or* **knit**)

to join wool or other thread into a sort of cloth using long needles: *My grandmother* **knitted** *me some socks.*

'knitting *noun* (*no plural*)
making things by knitting; a
piece of knitted work

knob /nɒb/ *noun*
a round lump, handle, or button:
Turn the door **knob** *to open the
door. This machine has lots of*
knobs *on it. Which one starts it?*

° **knock¹** /nɒk/ *verb*
1 to hit something, making a sharp
noise: *Please* **knock** *on the door
before you go in.*
2 to hit or push something: *I*
knocked over *the glass and spilt
the water. The old house was*
knocked down (=pulled down to
the ground). *The bigger man hit
the other one so hard that he*
knocked *him* **out** (=made him fall
down, so that he could not know
or feel anything).

° **knock²** *noun*
the sound of a blow: *a knock at
the door*

° **knot¹** /nɒt/
noun
a fastening
made by tying
two ends of

knots

something together: *to tie a* **knot**
in a piece of string

° **knot²** *verb* (*present participle*
knotting, *past* **knotted**)
to tie something in a knot or with
a knot: *Will you* **knot** *the rope
round the post?*

° **know** /nəʊ/ *verb*
(*past tense* **knew** /njuː/, *past
participle* **known** /nəʊn/)
1 to have in the mind; have learnt:
Do you **know** *what happened? I*
know *how to swim.*
2 to have met or seen before: *I
don't* **know** *that boy; who is he?*

° **knowledge** /'nɒlɪdʒ/ *noun*
(*no plural*)
things that we know: *We go to
school to get* **knowledge** *about
many different things. He has a
good* **knowledge** *of this area* (=he
knows a lot about it).

'knowledgeable *adjective*
having a lot of knowledge

knuckle /'nʌkl/ *noun*
one of the joints in the fingers:
Our fingers bend at the **knuckles.**

Koran /kə'rɑːn/ *noun*
the holy book of the Muslims

LI

label¹ /'leɪbl/
noun
a piece of
paper or other
material fixed
to something
which gives
you

labels

information about it: *A* **label** *on a
parcel tells us where to send it.*

label² *verb* (*present participle*
labelling /'leɪblɪŋ/, *past* **labelled**)

to put or fix a label on something:
The parcel was not **labelled** *so it
got lost.*

laboratory /lə'bɒrətrɪ/ *noun*
(*plural* **laboratories**)
a room or building where scientific
work is done

lab /læb/ is a short way of saying
laboratory.

labour¹ /'leɪbər/ *noun* (*no plural*)
1 hard work done with the hands:
His beautiful home was the result

of many years of **labour.**

2 the workers in a country or factory: *We don't have enough* **labour** *to finish the job.*

labour² *verb*

to work hard: *We* **laboured** *all day to finish the job.*

labourer *noun* a person who works with his hands: *a farm* **labourer**

lace¹ /leɪs/ *noun*

1 a piece of string for fastening a shoe: *I need new* **laces** *for my shoes.*

2 (*no plural*) ornamental cloth with holes in it, made from fine thread: *My dress has lots of pretty* **lace** *around the neck and sleeves.*

lace² *verb* (*present participle* **lacing,** *past* **laced**)

to tie with a lace: **Lace** *your shoes* **up.**

○ **lack¹** /læk/ *verb*

to have too little of something: *He* **lacked** *the strength to lift the box.*

○ **lack²** *noun*

too little of something: *We have a great* **lack** *of water; there has been no rain.*

lad /læd/ *noun*

a boy: *He moved here when he was a young* **lad.**

○ **ladder** /ˈlædəʳ/ *noun*

ladder

two long pieces of wood or metal joined together by shorter pieces that form steps for climbing: *I need a* **ladder** *to reach the roof.*

laden /ˈleɪdn/ *adjective*

carrying something, especially a large amount: *The lorry was* **laden** *with boxes of fruit.*

ladle /ˈleɪdl/ *noun*

a big spoon with a long handle: *She used a* **ladle** *for serving soup.*

○ **lady** /ˈleɪdɪ/ *noun* (*plural* **ladies**)

1 a polite woman

2 the wife of a lord (see)

lag /læg/ *verb* (*present participle* **lagging,** *past* **lagged**)

to move more slowly than others: *The children were tired and* **lagged behind** *their parents.*

laid /leɪd/ see **lay**

lain /leɪn/ see **lie**

lake /leɪk/ *noun*

a big pool of water with land all round it (picture on page 185)

lamb /læm/ *noun*

a young sheep

lame /leɪm/ *adjective* (**lamer, lamest**)

not able to walk easily, usually because of a hurt leg or foot: *My horse is* **lame** *— I can't ride him.*

○ **lamp** /læmp/ *noun*

an apparatus for giving light: *There are electric* **lamps** *in the streets.*

ˈlamp-post *noun* a tall post in the street with a light at the top

ˈlampshade *noun* a cover for a lamp

○ **land¹** /lænd/ *noun*

1 (*no plural*) the dry part of the earth, not covered by the sea: *The* **land** *is very dry; there has been no rain. We travelled* **by land** *until we reached the sea.*

2 a country: *After living in foreign* **lands** *for many years, the man went back home.*

ˈlandˌlady *noun* (*plural* **landladies**) a woman who owns a building which she lets others use or live in, in return for money

ˈlandˌlord *noun* a man who owns a building which he lets others use or live in, in return for money

'Land,rover *noun* a big strong car that can travel over rough ground

landscape /'lænd,skeɪp/ *noun* (*no plural*) the way an area of land looks: *The trees and the mountains made the* **landscape** *very beautiful.*

○**land²** *verb*

1 to come to the ground or the land from the air or water: *The plane will* **land** *in five minutes.*

2 to bring a plane or ship to the ground from the air or water: *He* **landed** *the plane at the airport.*

landing *noun: The plane made a safe* **landing.**

lane /leɪn/ *noun*

a narrow road: *We walked down the* **lane** *to the farm.*

○**language** /'læŋgwɪdʒ/ *noun*

the words people use in speaking and writing: *People in different countries speak different* **languages.**

lantern /'læntən/ *noun*

a lamp in a glass case, often having a handle for carrying it

lap¹ /læp/ *noun*

1 the flat surface formed by the upper parts of the legs when you are sitting down: *Her little girl sat on her* **lap.**

2 the distance once round a track in a race: *a six* **lap** *race*

lap² *verb*

(*present participle* **lapping,** *past* **lapped**)

to drink liquid with the tongue, like a dog: *The dog* **lapped** *its water* (**up**).

larder /'lɑːdə'/ *noun*

a cupboard or small room where food is kept

○**large** /lɑːdʒ/ *adjective* (**larger, largest**)

big; able to hold a lot: *They need a* **large** *house because they have nine children.*

'largely *adverb* mostly: *There are few towns in this area; it is* **largely** *land for farming.*

laser /'leɪzə'/ *noun*

an apparatus with a very strong, very narrow beam (see) of light used to cut metal, etc.

lash¹ /læʃ/ *verb*

1 to hit hard, usually with something like a whip: *The cruel man* **lashed** *the donkey but it would not go any faster.*

2 to fasten something tightly with a rope: *We* **lashed** *the boat to a tree.*

lash² *noun* (*plural* **lashes**)

one of the hairs that grow round the eye: *Mary has beautiful* **lashes.**

eyelash is another word for **lash.**

lasso¹ /lə'suː/ *noun*

a long rope with a rope ring at the end, for catching animals

lasso² *verb* (*present participle* **lassoing,** *past* **lassoed**)

to catch with a lasso: *The farmer* **lassoed** *the cow.*

last¹ /lɑːst/

1 coming after all others: *The* **last** *boy who came in was James. Who came in* **last?**

2 happening just before this time; the time before now: *I saw my friend* **last** *week, but I haven't seen him this week. I haven't seen his brother since* **last** *July* (= July of last year). *When did you* **last** *read an exciting book?*

3 (used in some phrases): *I waited a long time, and* **at 'last** (= in the

lantern

end) *the bus came. That is* **the last**
of the flour; there isn't any more.
'**lastly** *adverb* at the end: **Lastly,**
let me thank you for your help.

last² *verb*

1 to go in time: *Our holiday* **lasted**
ten days.

2 to stay in good condition or
unchanged: *Good shoes* **last**
*longer. She was very angry
yesterday, but it didn't* **last,** *she was
happy again today.*

3 to be enough: *Two loaves of
bread will* **last** *us for two days.*

○ **late** /leɪt/ *adjective, adverb*
(**later, latest**)

1 after the usual or agreed time: *I
was* **late** *for school because I got
up* **late.**

2 near the end (of a day, year, etc.):
It is very **late** — *I should be in bed.
He began the work in* **late** *May.*

'**lately** *adverb* not long ago:
Have you been on a bus **lately?**

'**latest** *adjective* newest: *Have
you heard the* **latest** *news? Please
arrive by 9 o'clock* **at the latest**
(=and no later).

lather /'lɑːðəʳ/ *noun* (*no plural*)
the white soapy mass on the top of
water that has soap in it

latitude /'lætɪtjuːd/ *noun*
(*no plural*)
a position on the earth shown on
maps by lines (lines of latitude)
that go from east to west. Look at
longitude. (picture on page 185)

latter /'lætəʳ/ *adjective*

1 the second of two: *Richard and
Paul came in together; the* **latter**
(= Paul) *was wearing his coat.*

2 later in time: *In the* **latter** *years
of his life, my grandfather never
went out of the house.*

○ **laugh¹** /lɑːf/ *verb*
to make a sound that shows you

are pleased, happy, or think
something is funny: *We all* **laughed**
loudly when she made a joke.

laughter /'lɑːftəʳ/ *noun* (no
plural): *loud* **laughter**

○ **laugh²** *noun*
laughter: *We had a good* **laugh** *at
his joke.*

launch¹
/lɔːntʃ/ *noun*
a small boat
driven by an
engine

launch

launch² *verb*
to put a ship into the water or to
send a spaceship into space

laundry /'lɔːndrɪ/ *noun*

1 (*plural* **laundries**) a place where
clothes and sheets are washed

2 (*no plural*) the clothes and sheets
that are washed together at one
time: *Will you carry the* **laundry**
into the kitchen?

lava /'lɑːvə/ *noun* (*no plural*)
very hot liquid rock that comes out
of the top of a volcano (=a
mountain that explodes)

lavatory /'lævətrɪ/ *noun*
(*plural* **lavatories**)

1 a container joined to a waste
pipe, used for passing body waste

2 a room with this in it: *Where is
the ladies'* **lavatory** *please?* **toilet** is
another word for **lavatory.**

○ **law** /lɔː/ *noun*
a rule made by the government
that all people must obey: *There is
a* **law** *to stop people driving too
fast in towns. It is* **against the law**
(=not allowed by the law) *to steal.*

'**lawful** *adjective: It is not* **lawful**
to steal.

lawyer /'lɔːjəʳ/ *noun* a person
who has studied the laws of our
country and helps us to
understand them

lawn /lɔːn/ *noun*

an area of short grass outside a house or in a park

'**lawn mower** *noun* a machine for cutting a lawn

○ **lay**[1] /leɪ/ *verb* (*past* **laid** /leɪd/)

1 to put down; put in a certain place: **Lay** *the book on the table.*
2 to make eggs and send them out of the body: *The hen* **laid** *three eggs.*

lay[2] see **lie**

layer /'leɪəʳ/ *noun*

a covering that is spread on top of another thing or in between two other things: *This cake has a* **layer** *of chocolate in the middle.*

○ **lazy** /'leɪzɪ/ *adjective*
(**lazier, laziest**)

not wanting to work: *a* **lazy** *pupil*
lazily *adverb*

○ **lead**[1] /liːd/ *verb* (*past* **led** /led/)

1 to show someone the way, usually by going in front: *He* **led** *us to his home. The path* **led** *to his home.*
2 to be the chief person in doing a thing; be first or at the front, especially in a race or competition: *After the first half of the race I was* **leading.**

'**leader** *noun: Our teacher is the* **leader** — *she will show us where to go.*

○ **lead**[2] /liːd/ *noun*

1 (*no plural*) guiding; going in front: *We all followed the teacher's* **lead.** *Sarah was* **in the lead** (=in front) *during the race.*
2 a piece of rope, leather, etc., for holding an animal: *Please keep your dog* **on a lead.**

lead[3] /led/ *noun*

1 (*no plural*) a soft grey metal
2 the part inside a pencil, that we write with

○ **leaf** /liːf/ *noun*
(*plural* **leaves** /liːvz/)

one of the green flat parts of a plant or tree which grow out of branches or stems: *Some plants have* **leaves** *that grow straight out of the ground.* (picture at **flower**)

leaflet /'liːflɪt/ *noun*

a piece of paper with an advertisement or a notice printed on it

league /liːg/ *noun*

1 a group of people, countries, etc. who join together to help each other: *the* **League** *of Nations*
2 a group of people or teams that play against each other in a competition: *Our team plays in the football* **league.**

leak[1] /liːk/ *noun*

a hole or crack through which gas or liquid may pass in or out: *There's a* **leak** *in the roof — the rain's coming in.*

'**leaky** *adjective* (**leakier, leakiest**) having a leak: *The roof is* **leaky** *and the rain comes in.*

leak[2] *verb*

to escape through a hole or crack; let gas or liquid escape: *The roof* **leaks;** *it lets the rain come in.*

○ **lean**[1] /liːn/ *verb*
(*past* **leaned** *or* **leant** /lent/)
1 to bend forwards, sideways, backwards, or towards: *Do not* **lean** *out of the window too far because you might fall out.*

lean

2 to put a thing against or on another thing to support it: *She* **leant** *her bicycle against the wall.*

lean[2] *adjective*

not containing fat; thin: **lean** *cattle*

leap[1] /liːp/ *verb* (*past* **leaped** *or* **leapt** /lept/)
to jump: *The dog* **leapt** *over the fence.*

leap[2] *noun*
a jump: *The dog made a* **leap** *over the fence.*

'**leap year** *noun* a year, once every four years, in which February has 29 days instead of 28 days: *1984 and 1988 are* **leap years.**

◦**learn** /lɜːn/ *verb* (*past* **learned** *or* **learnt**)
1 to get knowledge of something or of how to do something: *Have you* **learnt** *to swim? I am* **learning** *English.*
2 to fix in the memory: *She* **learnt** *the whole lesson so that she could repeat it the next day.*

◦**least** /liːst/
1 the smallest amount or number: *None of us had much money, but I had* (*the*) **least** *of all. I had the* **least** *money of us all. They arrived when I* **least** *expected them* (=when I did not expect them at all).
2 (used in some phrases): *He's going away for* **at least** (=not less than) *a week. I'm* **not in the least** (=not at all) *interested in what she says. I don't like rain or storms, and* **least of all** (=especially not) *thunder.*

◦**leather** /'leðəʳ/ *noun* (*no plural*)
the skin of a dead animal specially prepared for use: **leather** *shoes*

◦**leave**[1] /liːv/ *verb* (*present participle* **leaving**, *past* **left** /left/)
1 to go away (from): *The train* **leaves** (*the station*) *in five minutes.*
2 to let a thing stay in a place: *When I went to school I* **left** *my books at home.*
3 to let things stay as they are: *

Leave *the cakes alone — you can eat them later.*

leave[2] *noun*
a short time away from work: *The soldiers had six weeks'* **leave.**

leaves /liːvz/ see **leaf**

lecture[1] /'lektʃəʳ/ *noun*
a talk given to teach a large number of people: *The students have* **lectures** *every day.*

lecture[2] *verb* (*present participle* **lecturing**, *past* **lectured**)
to give a lecture: *I am going to* **lecture** *to my students today.*
lecturer *noun*

led /led/ see **lead**

ledge /ledʒ/ *noun*
a narrow shelf, such as at the bottom of a window, or a narrow flat piece of rock, on which you can stand: *a window* **ledge**

left[1] /left/ see **leave**

◦**left**[2] *noun* (*no plural*), *adjective, adverb*
the opposite side to the right side: *The school is on the* **left** *of the road and his house is on the right. Turn* **left** *at the corner.*

'**left-'handed** *adjective: If you do most things with your left hand, you are* **left-handed.**

◦**leg** /leg/ *noun*
1 one of the parts of the body of a man or animal used for walking: *Men have two* **legs** *and dogs have four* **legs.** (picture on page 133)
2 one of the parts on which chairs, tables, etc. stand: *a chair with a broken* **leg**

legal /'liːgl/ *adjective*
allowed by the law: *Stealing is not* **legal.**

legend /'ledʒənd/ *noun*
a story about people who lived in the past, which may not be true

legible /'ledʒəbl/ *adjective*
easy to read: **legible** *writing*

leisure /'leʒəʳ/ *noun* (*no plural*)
the time when you are not at work
and can do what you want: *What
do you do in your* **leisure** *time?*

lemon /'lemən/ *noun*
a yellow fruit with a sour taste,
from the lemon tree which grows
in hot places

lemonade /ˌlemə'neɪd/ *noun*
(*no plural*)
a drink made from lemons

○ **lend** /lend/ *verb* (*past* **lent** /lent/)
to let someone use or have
something for a time, after which
he must give it back: *Can you* **lend**
me that book for a few days?

○ **length** /leŋθ/ *noun* (*no plural*)
the distance from one end of
something to the other; how long
something is: *Mary's dress is not
the right* **length**; *it is too short.*
(picture on page 185)
'**lengthy** *adjective* (**lengthier,
lengthiest**) long: *a lengthy speech*

lengthen /'leŋθən/ *verb*
to make longer: *to* **lengthen** *a dress*

lens /lenz/
noun (*plural*
lenses)
one of the
shaped pieces
of glass used to bend light in an
instrument for seeing things
clearly, like a pair of glasses, a
camera, or microscope

leopard /'lepəd/ *noun*
(*plural* **leopard** or **leopards**)
a wild animal with a spotted coat
which is one of the big cats and
lives in Africa and Asia

○ **less** /les/
1 smaller; not so much: *I don't
want all that bread — please give
me* **less**. *I would like* **less** *bread,*
please.
2 (used in some phrases): *He does*
less and less *work* (=a smaller
amount of work) *every day — he's
very lazy.*

lessen /'lesn/ *verb*
to make or become less

○ **lesson** /'lesn/ *noun*
something you must learn; a time
when you must learn things in
schools: *We had a history* **lesson** *at
school this morning.*

○ **let** /let/ *verb* (*present participle*
letting, *past* **let**)
1 to allow: *My mother wouldn't* **let**
*me go to the film. Hold the ladder
for me and don't* **let go** (=stop
holding it). *They won't* **let** *people
in without a ticket. She promised
to come and help, but then she* **let**
us **down** (=didn't do what she had
promised).
2 to allow someone to use a house
or some land in return for money:
They **let** *their house to another
family when they went away.*
3 (used when you ask someone to
do something with you): **Let's** *go
down to the river and swim.*

○ **letter** /'letəʳ/ *noun*
1 one of the signs we use to write
words: *A, B, C, and D are the first
four* **letters** *in the alphabet.*
2 a written message sent to
someone by post: *to post a* **letter**
'**letter box** *noun* **1** a box in the
street or post office where letters
are put to be sent
2 a hole or box for letters in the
front of a building

lettuce /'letɪs/ *noun*
a vegetable with large soft green
leaves which are eaten without
cooking

○ **level**[1] /'levl/ *adjective*
1 flat; without higher or lower

places: *We need a* **level** *piece of ground to play football on.*
2 equal: *I was* **level** *with my friend in the examination; we got the same number of marks.*

○ **level²** *noun*
a place or position of a particular height: *The house was built on two* **levels.**

level³ *verb (present participle* **levelling,** *past* **levelled)**
to make something flat: *We* **levelled** *the piece of ground so that we could play football on it.*

lever¹ /ˈliːvəʳ/ *noun*
a long bar for lifting or moving heavy things

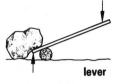

lever

lever² *verb*
to move something with a lever: *I* **levered** *the lid off the box with a stick.*

liable /ˈlaɪəbl/ *adjective*
likely: *You are* **liable** *to* (=likely to) *be caught if you steal.*

liar /ˈlaɪəʳ/ *noun*
someone who tells lies

liberty /ˈlɪbətɪ/ *noun (no plural)*
being free and not forced to do what other people order: *The prisoner was given his* **liberty** *and allowed to leave the prison.*

○ **library** /ˈlaɪbrərɪ/ *noun*
(plural **libraries)**
a collection of books that people can borrow or a room or building where they are kept: *Our town has a very good* **library.**
librarian /laɪˈbreərɪən/ *noun* a person who works in a library

lice /laɪs/ see **louse**

licence /ˈlaɪsəns/ *noun*
a piece of paper showing that the law allows you to do something,

like drive a car: *The policeman asked to see his* **ˈdriving licence.**
license *verb (present participle* **licensing,** *past* **licensed)** to give someone a licence

lick /lɪk/ *verb*
to touch a thing with the tongue: *The cat cleaned itself by* **licking** *its hair.*

○ **lid** /lɪd/ *noun*
a cover for a box, pan, or other container, which can be taken off

lids

○ **lie¹** /laɪ/ *verb (present participle* **lying,** *past tense* **lay** /leɪ/, *past participle* **lain** /leɪn/)
1 to have your body flat on something: *He was* **lying** *in the shade of the tree. She* **lay** *down* (=got into a lying position) *on her bed.*
2 to stay or be: *The plates* **lay** *on the table.*

○ **lie²** *verb (present participle* **lying,** *past* **lied)**
to say things that are not true: *I'm sorry I* **lied** *to you.*

○ **lie³** *noun (plural* **lies)**
things said which are not true: *Why did you tell me a* **lie?**

lieutenant /lefˈtenənt/ *noun*
an officer in the army, navy (see), or police

life /laɪf/ *noun*
1 *(no plural)* the ability that we have to grow and feel: *Animals and plants have* **life,** *which makes them different from stones and water.*
2 *(plural* **lives** /laɪvz/) the time that someone is alive: *He has lived in the same village all his* **life.**
3 *(plural* **lives)** the way someone lives or spends their time: *He leads a happy* **life** *in the country.*

4 (*no plural*) activity; strength; cheerfulness: *The children were jumping about and full of* **life.**

'**life,time** *noun* the time for which someone is alive: *In my father's* **lifetime** *there have been many changes in the village.*

◦ **lift¹** /lɪft/ *verb*
to pick up, often to put in a higher place: "**Lift** *me* **up** *so I can see over the fence,*" *said the little girl.*

lift² *noun*
1 a machine that carries people or things between floors of a tall building
2 a free ride in a vehicle: *He gave me a* **lift** *to the station in his car.*

◦ **light¹** /laɪt/ *noun*
1 (*no plural*) the thing that allows our eyes to see, that there is not enough of when it is dark: *The sun gives us* **light** *during the day.*
2 a thing that gives out light: *We use* **lights** *in the house at night so that we can see.*

'**lighting** *noun* (*no plural*): *The* **lighting** *in this room is not bright enough for me to read.*

◦ **light²** *adjective*
1 not dark in colour; brightly coloured and having a lot of white: *a* **light** *blue sky*
2 easy to lift; not heavy; *The basket is very* **light:** *I can easily pick it up.*

'**lighten** *verb* to make light or more light in weight or colour

◦ **light³** *verb* (*past* **lit** /lɪt/ *or* **lighted**)
to make a thing like a lamp, fire, or cigarette burn or give out light: *Will you* **light** *the fire for me. A* **lighter** *is an instrument for lighting a cigarette or pipe.*

◦ **lightning** /'laɪtnɪŋ/ *noun* (*no plural*)
a bright flash of light in the sky, followed by thunder, that happens during a storm

lightning

◦ **like¹** /laɪk/ *verb* (*present participle* **liking**, *past* **liked**)
to find pleasant; enjoy: *Do you* **like** *your teacher? I* **like** *bananas.*

liking *noun: I* **have a liking for** *bananas.*

◦ **like²** *preposition*
1 in the same way as: *I wish I could sing* **like** *her.*
2 with the same qualities as: *Mary's dress is red,* **like** *mine.*

◦ **likely** *adjective*
1 expected: *The train is* **likely** *to be late.*
2 suitable: *She is the most* **likely** *girl to win the prize.*

'**likeness** *noun* being or looking the same: *There is a* **likeness** *between the three brothers.*

'**likewise** *adverb* in the same way; the same; also: *Paul always finishes his work — you should do* **likewise.**

lily /'lɪlɪ/ *noun* (*plural* **lilies**)
a plant with beautiful flowers and thick roots

◦ **limb** /lɪm/ *noun*
a part of the body such as an arm or leg: *Men and women have four* **limbs;** *two arms and two legs.*

lime /laɪm/ *noun*
a green fruit with a sour taste from a tree of the orange family which grows in hot places

◦ **limit¹** /'lɪmɪt/ *noun*
as far as you can or are allowed to go; the edge of an area of ground; a greatest amount or furthest distance: *The* '**speed limit** *is the fastest speed you are allowed to drive a car at. There is a* **limit** *to*

the amount of money I can afford.
The fence shows the **limit** of the
field.

○ **limit**[2] *verb*

to stop a thing from going past a
point or level: *My mother* **limits**
the amount of food that I eat.

limp[1] /lɪmp/ *adjective*

not firm or stiff: *When flowers are
dying, their stems become* **limp.**

limp[2] *verb*

to walk as if one leg or foot has
been hurt: *He* **limped** *off the
football field.*

limp[3] *noun*

the way we walk when one leg is
hurt: *to walk with a* **limp**

○ **line**[1] /laɪn/ *noun*

1 a long very narrow mark: *Write
on the* **lines** *of the paper.*

2 people or things one after the
other or beside each other; a row:
How many **lines** *of words are there
on this page?*

3 a long piece of string or rope: *We
have a* **washing line** *from which we
hang clothes to dry.*

line[2] *verb (present participle* **lining,**
past **lined)**

1 to stand in a line: *People* **lined**
*the streets to see the famous man
go past.* **Line up** *please, children!*
2 to cover the inside, sides, or edges
of something: *The box was* **lined**
*with soft paper to protect the
things inside.*

linen /'lɪnɪn/ *noun (no plural)*

cloth made from threads from the
stem of a certain plant: *Tablecloths
and sheets are often made of* **linen.**

lining /'laɪnɪŋ/ *noun*

the cloth covering the inside of a
piece of clothing: *The* **lining** *of my
coat is torn.*

link[1] /lɪŋk/ *noun*

one of several rings, usually

made of metal,
fitted together
in a long
line: *A lot of*
links *fitted*

link

together form a chain.

link[2] *verb*

to join together or be joined with:
The two towns are **linked** *by a
railway.*

○ **lion** /'laɪən/ *noun
(plural* **lion** *or* **lions)**

a wild animal which is one of the
big cats and lives in Africa
lioness /laɪə'nes/ *noun (plural
lionesses) a female lion (picture
on page 17)

○ **lip** /lɪp/ *noun*

one of the soft red edges round the
mouth: *We move our* **lips** *when we
speak.* (picture on page 133)
'**lip,stick** *noun* colour that
women put on their lips

○ **liquid** /'lɪkwɪd/ *noun*

a thing like water or milk that can
be poured **liquid** *adjective*

○ **list**[1] /lɪst/ *noun*

a lot of names of things written
down one under another: *I must
make a list of things to buy.*

list[2] *verb*

to write or say as a list: *I* **listed** *the
things I wanted to buy.*

○ **listen** /'lɪsn/ *verb*

to try to hear a thing; take notice
of what someone is saying: **Listen**
*to the noise of the wind in the
trees. You should* **listen** *to the
teacher if you want to learn.*

lit /lɪt/ see **light**[3]

literature /'lɪtrətʃəʳ/ *noun
(no plural)*

good books and writing that
people like to read: *Newspapers
are not* **literature;** *you usually read
them only once.*

○ **litre** /ˈliːtəʳ/ noun
a measure of liquid: *The bottle holds a* **litre** *of beer. A* **litre** *is equal to about 1¾ pints* (see).

litter /ˈlɪtəʳ/ noun
1 (*no plural*) waste paper and other things left lying on the ground: **litter** *on the streets of a town*
2 a lot of animals born together: *a* **litter** *of puppies* (= young dogs)

○ **little**[1] /ˈlɪtl/ adjective
(**littler, littlest**)
small; not big; young: *We live in a* **little** *house. The mother was carrying her* **little** *girl.*

○ **little**[2] (**less** /les/, **least** /liːst/)
1 some, but not much: *There isn't much tea, but we only need a* **little** *for a cup of tea. Put a* **little** *salt on the meat. I feel a* **little** *better.*
2 a very small amount: *You eat very* **little** *— that's why you're so thin. I have too* **little** *time to finish this work. I go there very* **little** (= not often).

○ **live**[1] /lɪv/ verb (*present participle* **living**, *past* **lived**)
1 to have life; not to be dead: *My grandfather is still* **living**, *but my grandmother is dead.*
2 to stay in a place or at a house; have your home somewhere: *I* **live** *in a town.*
3 to keep alive by eating something or by earning some money: *Cows* **live** *on grass. I can* **live** *on very little money.*
living adjective alive

live[2] /laɪv/ adjective
having life; not dead: *a* **live** *animal*
lively adjective (**livelier, liveliest**):
A **lively** *person is full of life and is always doing things.*

liver /ˈlɪvəʳ/ noun
a large part inside the body which cleans the blood (picture on p.133)

lizard /ˈlɪzəd/ noun
an animal with four short legs which has a skin like a snake

lizard

○ **load**[1] /ləʊd/ noun
things that are carried, especially by a train, lorry, or ship: *The lorry was carrying a* **load** *of bananas.*

○ **load**[2] verb
1 to put a load on a lorry, ship, or other thing for carrying loads: *We* **loaded** *the lorry with bananas.*
2 to put pieces of metal (bullets) in a gun so that they can be fired out of it

○ **loaf** /ləʊf/ noun
(*plural* **loaves** /ləʊvz/)
a piece of baked bread before it is cut up: *to bake a* **loaf** *of bread*

loan[1] /ləʊn/ noun
a thing, especially money, lent to another person: *I asked the bank for a* **loan**.

loan[2] verb
to give a loan: *The bank* **loaned** *me some money.*

loathe /ləʊð/ verb (*present participle* **loathing**, *past* **loathed**)
to hate: *I* **loathe** *washing dishes.*

lobster /ˈlɒbstəʳ/ noun
a sea animal with a shell, a tail, and ten legs

local /ˈləʊkl/ adjective
in the area near a place; near where you live: *My children go to the* **local** *school.*

locate /ləʊˈkeɪt/ verb (*present participle* **locating**, *past* **located**)
1 to put something in a place: *The new building will be* **located** *in the centre of town.*
2 to find the place where a thing is: *I cannot* **locate** *the shop.*
lo'cation noun: *Have they*

lock

decided on the **location** of the new building yet?

○ **lock¹** /lɒk/ noun

an instrument for fastening

locks

things like doors, gates, or drawers, that can only be opened or closed with the right key

○ **lock²** verb

to close a lock with a key: *My father accidentally* **locked** *me* **out** *of the house* (= he locked the door so that I could not get back into the house).

locker /'lɒkəʳ/ noun

a small cupboard, often with a lock, for keeping things: *At the station there were* **lockers** *where people could leave suitcases.*

locust /'ləʊkəst/ noun

an insect that is a kind of grasshopper (see) and lives in large groups

lodge /lɒdʒ/ verb (*present participle* **lodging**, *past* **lodged**)

to pay to live in a room in someone else's house: *My friend* **lodges** *in my uncle's house.*

'**lodger** noun: *My friend is a* **lodger** *in my uncle's house.*

'**lodgings** plural noun: *My friend lives in* **lodgings.**

○ **log** /lɒg/ noun

a large piece of wood as it comes from a tree: *We put* **logs** *on the fire.*

○ **lonely** /'ləʊnlɪ/ adjective (**lonelier, loneliest**)

unhappy because you are alone: *People who have no friends can be* **lonely.**

○ **long¹** /lɒŋ/ adjective

1 measuring a great distance or time from one end to the other: *I take a* **long** *time to walk to school because it is a* **long** *way.*

2 measuring distance or time from one end to the other: *This piece of string is 30 centimetres* **long.** *How* **long** *do you take to walk home?*

○ **long²** adverb

1 for a long time: *He said he'd waited so* **long** *that he couldn't stay any* **longer.**

2 at a distant time: *He died* **long** *ago.* **Not long** (= a short time) *after that, he got married.*

3 (used in some phrases): *You can go out* **as long as** (= if) *you promise to be back before 9.*

long³ verb

to want something very much: *I* **longed for** *a bicycle.*

longitude /'lɒndʒɪtjuːd/ noun (*no plural*)

a position on the earth shown on maps by lines (lines of longitude) that go from north to south. Look at **latitude.** (picture on page 185)

○ **look¹** /lʊk/ verb

1 to point the eyes towards a thing to try to see it: *The teacher told us to* **look** *at the blackboard.* **Look out** (= be careful), *there's a car coming. The children were* **looking for** (= trying to find) *a ball. My friend* **looked after** (= cared for) *my dog while I was on holiday. When you do not understand a word, you can* **look it up** (= find it) *in this dictionary. We are all* **looking forward** *to our holiday* (= waiting for it and thinking about it with pleasure).

2 to seem to be: *That dog* **looks** *dangerous. That* **looks like** *an interesting film.*

○ **look²** noun

1 looking; using the eyes: *Have a* **look** *at this book.*

2 the way something appears: *I*

don't like the **look** *of it* (= I think it is bad).

3 the expression on a face: *an angry* **look**

looks *plural noun* the way a person appears: **Good 'looks** (= beauty) *are not as important as kindness.*

loom /luːm/ *noun*
a machine for weaving cloth

loop /luːp/ *noun*
a ring made by a thing like rope or string crossing itself: *She put a* **loop** *of rope around the cow's neck.*

○ **loose** /luːs/ *adjective*
(looser, loosest)
free or able to move easily; not tight: *The dog was tied up but the rope broke and now the dog is* **loose.**

'loosen *verb: My belt is too tight; I must* **loosen** *it.*

lord /lɔːd/ *noun*
a title for a man, used before his name

○ **lorry** /'lɒrɪ/
noun
(plural
lorries)
a large

lorry

vehicle that is moved by a motor, for carrying heavy goods. **truck** is another word for **lorry.**

○ **lose** /luːz/ *verb* (*present participle* **losing,** *past* **lost** /lɒst/)
1 not to keep; not to have something any more: *I cannot find my watch; I must have* **lost** *it. My father has* **lost** *his job.*
2 not to do well; not to win: *Our team* **lost** *the football match.*

○ **loss** /lɒs/ *noun* (*plural* **losses**)
losing or a thing that is lost: *The* **loss** *of my watch meant that I had to buy a new one.*

lost /lɒst/ *adjective* not knowing where you are: *The little boy went for a walk and got* **lost.**

○ **lot** /lɒt/ *noun* or **lots** *plural noun* a large amount or number; much: *There was* **a lot of** *mud on the ground. I picked* **lots** *of flowers.*

lotion /'ləʊʃn/ *noun*
a liquid for putting on the skin or wounds: *Put this* **lotion** *on the insect bites to stop them hurting.*

lotus /'ləʊtəs/ *noun* (*plural* **lotuses**)
a water plant of Asia with white or pink flowers and round leaves on tall stems

○ **loud** /laʊd/ *adjective*
having or making a lot of noise; easily heard: *The teacher's voice is very* **loud;** *we can all hear it.*
'loudly *adverb*
loud'speaker *noun* an electric instrument for making sounds: *There is a* **loudspeaker** *in a radio.*

lounge /laʊndʒ/ *noun*
a room in a house or hotel with comfortable chairs

louse /laʊs/ *noun*
(*plural* **lice** /laɪs/) a small insect without wings that lives on the skin of animals, birds, and people
lousy /'laʊzɪ/ *adjective* (**lousier, lousiest**) **1** having lice **2** bad: *What a* **lousy** *day I've had!*

○ **love**[1] /lʌv/ *verb* (*present participle* **loving,** *past* **loved**)
1 to have a very strong warm feeling for someone: *Mothers and fathers* **love** *their children.*
2 to like very much: *Maria* **loves** *reading.*
'lovable *adjective* so nice as to be loved very much: *a* **lovable** *child*
'loving *adjective* showing that you love someone: *He gave her a* **loving** *kiss.* **'lovingly** *adverb*

love

○**love**[2] *noun* (*no plural*)
strong warm feeling: *The boy* **fell in love with** *the girl* (=he started to love her).

lovely /ˈlʌvlɪ/ *adjective* (**lovelier, loveliest**)
very much liked; very beautiful: *a* **lovely** *cool drink*

○**low** /ləʊ/ *adjective*
1 near the ground; not high: *a* **low** *fence/***low** *prices*
2 not loud; not high in sound: *a* **low** *voice*
lower /ˈləʊəʳ/ *verb* to make a thing nearer the ground or less high or loud: *They* **lowered** *the load to the ground. Please* **lower** *your voice.*
lowland /ˈləʊlənd/ *noun* land that is flat and has no mountains

loyal /ˈlɔɪəl/ *adjective*
able to be trusted by a friend or by your country: *The people stayed* **loyal** *to their country in the war.*
loyalty *noun* (*plural* **loyalties**): *The government was sure of the people's* **loyalty.**

○**luck** /lʌk/ *noun* (*no plural*)
the good and bad things that happen to you by chance: *It was good* **luck** *that I met you here; I did not expect to see you.*
ˈ**lucky** *adjective* (**luckier, luckiest**) having or bringing good luck: *I was* **lucky** *that I met you here. Some people think that black cats are* **lucky** (=bring good luck). ˈ**luckily** *adverb*

luggage /ˈlʌgɪdʒ/ *noun*
(*no plural*)
the bags, suitcases, and other things you take with you when you travel

luggage

lukewarm /ˌluːkˈwɔːm/ *adjective*
not very warm but not cold: *The water was* **lukewarm.**

lullaby /ˈlʌləbaɪ/ *noun*
(*plural* **lullabies**)
a soft song to send someone to sleep

○**lump** /lʌmp/ *noun*
1 a hard piece of something, without a special shape: *a* **lump** *of rock*
2 a swelling on the body: *I have a* **lump** *on my head where I hit it against the door.*
ˈ**lumpy** *adjective* full of lumps, usually when you do not want them

lunatic /ˈluːnətɪk/ *noun*
a mad person: *He must be a* **lunatic** *to drive his car so fast.*

lunch /lʌntʃ/ *noun* (plural **lunches**)
the meal you eat in the middle of the day

lung /lʌŋ/ *noun*
one of the two parts inside the chest with which we breathe (picture on page 133)

lurk /lɜːk/ *verb*
to wait in hiding, especially for some bad purpose: *There's someone* **lurking** *behind that bush.*

lust /lʌst/ *noun* (*no plural*)
a very strong feeling of wanting something, often something bad or wrong: *a* **lust** *for money*

luxury /ˈlʌkʃərɪ/ *noun*
1 (*no plural*) great comfort: *They live* **in luxury** *in a very big house.*
2 (*plural* **luxuries**) something that you do not really need, but that is very pleasant: *Going to school in a car is a* **luxury.**
luxurious /lʌgˈzʊərɪəs/ *adjective* fine and expensive; very comfortable: *a* **luxurious** *hotel*

lying /ˈlaɪ-ɪŋ/ *see* **lie**[1] *and* [2]

Mm

°machine /mə'ʃiːn/ *noun*
an instrument made up of many parts, used to do work: *A* **sewing-machine** *helps us to sew things more quickly.*

ma'chine-,gun *noun*
a gun that fires continuously while the trigger (see) is pressed

°ma'chinery *noun* (*no plural*)
parts of a machine or a number of machines together: *The new factory contained a lot of* **machinery.**

mackintosh /'mækɪntɒʃ/ *noun*
(*plural* **mackintoshes**)
a coat made to keep out the rain
mack or **mac** /mæk/ are short ways of saying and writing **mackintosh.**

°mad /mæd/ *adjective* (**madder, maddest**)
1 having a sick mind: *He behaves very strangely — I think he's* **mad.**
2 very foolish: *You're* **mad** *to drive your car so fast.* **madly** *adverb*

madam /'mædəm/ *noun*
a polite way of speaking or writing to a woman: *I began my letter "Dear* **Madam".**

made /meɪd/ see **make**

magazine /ˌmægə'ziːn/ *noun*
a paper-covered book containing stories, articles, and pictures: **Magazines** *are sold weekly or monthly.*

magic¹ /'mædʒɪk/
noun (*no plural*)
1 strange or wonderful things that happen by a special power; the power to do strange things: *Some people say they can cure illnesses by* **magic.**
2 clever or strange tricks done to amuse people
magical *adjective:* a **magical** *cure*
magically *adverb*
magician /mə'dʒɪʃn/ *noun* a person who can do magic: *There was a* **magician** *at the party.*

magic² *adjective*
about or having magic

magnet /'mægnɪt/ *noun*
a piece of iron which draws other pieces of iron towards it: *The* **magnet** *picked up the pins.*
magnetic /mæg'netɪk/ *adjective*

magnificent /mæg'nɪfɪsnt/ *adjective*
very great; very fine: *What a* **magnificent** *building!*
magnificently *adverb*

magnify /'mægnɪfaɪ/ *verb*
(*present participle* **magnifying,** *past* **magnified**)
to make things look larger than they really are: *We use a* **'magnifying ,glass** *to see small objects more clearly; it is an instrument which* **magnifies** *things.*

maid /meɪd/ *noun*
a woman servant

maiden /'meɪdn/ *noun*
an unmarried woman: *A woman's* **'maiden ,name** *is her name before she is married.*

mail /meɪl/ (*no plural*)
the letters and parcels sent or brought by post: *The* **mail** *arrived late today.*

main /meɪn/ *adjective*
chief; most important: *the* **main** *road into town*
  '**mainly** *adverb: This school is* **mainly** *for boys; there are only a few girls in it.*

maintain /meɪn'teɪn/ *verb*
to support; look after: *He has worked hard to* **maintain** *his family. The car has always been properly* **maintained.**
  maintenance /'meɪntɪnəns/ *noun* (*no plural*): *He took a course to learn about* **car maintenance.**

° **maize** /meɪz/ *or* **corn** *noun* (*no plural*)
a tall grain plant with big white or yellow seeds used as food

cob   **maize**

majestic /mə'dʒestɪk/ *adjective*
very fine; important-looking: *a* **majestic** *figure*
  majestically *adverb*

major[1] /'meɪdʒəʳ/ *adjective*
chief; most important: *a* **major** *city*
  majority /mə'dʒɒrətɪ/ *noun* the largest part or number: *The* **majority** *of children in our class have brown eyes; only two have blue eyes.*

major[2] *noun*
an officer in the army

° **make** /meɪk/ *verb* (*present participle* **making,** *past* **made** /meɪd/)
1 to produce; build: *He* **made** *a model plane out of wood. Who is* **making** *all that noise?*
2 to earn; gain; win: *He* **makes** *a lot of money every week — he's got a good job.*

3 to force someone to do something, or cause something to happen: *I don't like milk, but she* **made** *me drink it. That dress* **makes** *you look very pretty.*
4 (used in some phrases): *He* **made up his mind** (=decided) *to become a doctor. The boy* **made up** *a story; it was not true. She* **made up** *her face* (=put special paint and powder on it) *to look prettier.*
  '**make-up** *noun* (*no plural*) special powder and paint put on the face: *to wear* **make-up**

malaria /mə'leərɪə/ *noun* (*no plural*)
an illness in which the person has very high fevers, caused by being bitten by a kind of mosquito (see)

° **male**[1] /meɪl/ *adjective*
belonging to the sex that does not give birth to young: *A lion is a* **male** *animal; a lioness is a female animal.*

° **male**[2] *noun*
a male person or animal: *Men and boys are* **males.**

malnutrition /ˌmælnju:'trɪʃn/ *noun* (*no plural*)
the unhealthy condition caused by not having enough food

mammal /'mæml/ *noun*
an animal which is fed on its mother's milk when it is young: *A cow is a* **mammal;** *her calves drink her milk.*

° **man** /mæn/ *noun*
1 (*plural* **men** /men/) a fully grown human male
2 (*plural* **men**) a person; a human being: **Men** *have lived here for thousands of years.*
3 (*no plural*) all humans: **Man** *uses animals in many ways.*
  man'kind *noun* (*no plural*) all human beings

man-'made *adjective* made by people, not grown or produced naturally: *a* **man-made** *material*

manage /'mænɪdʒ/ *verb* (*present participle* **managing**, *past* **managed**)
1 to succeed in doing something: *He* **managed** *to avoid an accident.*
2 to handle; have power over someone or something: *The horse was difficult to* **manage.** *He* **managed** *the supermarket when the owner was away.*

management *noun* **1** the people who control a business **2** (*no plural*) managing: *A business can't do well without good* **management.**

manager *noun* a person who looks after a business

mane /meɪn/ *noun*
the long hair on the necks of some animals (picture at **animal** and **horse**)

° **mango** /'mæŋgəʊ/ *noun* (*plural* **mangoes**)
a sweet juicy fruit with one large seed from a tree which grows in hot countries

mangrove /'mæŋgrəʊv/ *noun*
a tree that grows in water near hot sea coasts and has roots hanging from its branches into the water

manner /'mænər/ *noun*
the way in which something is done or happens: *Why are you talking in such a strange* **manner?** **Manners** *are the way you behave. You should have* **good manners** *all the time. You should be* **well-mannered** *not* **ill-mannered.**

manual /'mænjʊəl/ *adjective*
using the hands: **manual** *work*
manually *adverb: The work was done* **manually** (= by people), *not by a machine.*

manufacture[1] /ˌmænjʊ'fæktʃər/ *verb* (*present participle* **manufacturing**, *past* **manufactured**)
to make things in large numbers, usually by machinery: *to* **manufacture** *goods in a factory*

manufacture[2] *noun* (*no plural*)
making things in large numbers: *the* **manufacture** *of cars*

° **many** /'menɪ/ (**more, most**)
a lot; a large number of: **How many** *bananas are in the basket? There are not* **many** *there.*

° **map** /mæp/ *noun*
a flat drawing of a large surface: *In the library there are* **maps** *of towns,*

map

countries, and the world.

marble /'mɑːbl/ *noun*
1 (*no plural*) a hard stone which can be made smooth and shiny and is used in making buildings
2 a small glass or stone ball used in a game: *to play* **marbles**

march[1] /mɑːtʃ/ *verb*
to walk with regular steps: *The soldiers* **marched** *along the street.*

march[2] *noun* (*plural* **marches**)
1 a way of walking with regular steps; the distance of a walk
2 a piece of music to which soldiers march

° **March** *noun*
the third month of the year

margarine /ˌmɑːdʒə'riːn/ *noun* (*no plural*)
a food made from animal or vegetables fats: *We use* **margarine** *in cooking, and eat it on bread.*

margin /'mɑːdʒɪn/ *noun*
the space at each edge of a page without writing or printing

○**mark**[1] /mɑːk/ *noun*

1 a spot or line on the surface of something: *You have a dirty* **mark** *on your face. The black cat has a white* **mark** *on its ear.*

2 a sign; something written to show something: *It is dangerous to swim beyond this* **mark**. *The teacher gave me a good* **mark** *for my story.*

○**mark**[2] *verb*

1 to put a sign on something: *He* **marked** *the floor with chalk. The teacher* **marked** *my examination* (=saw how many questions I had right).

2 to put a spot or line on something: *She* **marked** *her white dress when she sat on the grass.*

○**market** /ˈmɑːkɪt/ *noun*
a place where people can bring goods to sell

marry /ˈmærɪ/ *verb* (*present participle* **marrying**, *past* **married**)

1 to take someone as a husband or wife: *I am going to* **marry** *John.*

2 to join as husband and wife: *They were* **married** *by a priest.*

marriage /ˈmærɪdʒ/ *noun*: *My sister's* **marriage** *took place at eleven o'clock today.*

marsh /mɑːʃ/ *noun*
(*plural* **marshes**)
low, wet ground: *When they tried to cross the* **marsh**, *their shoes sank into the soft ground.*

marvellous /ˈmɑːvələs/ *adjective*
wonderful: *a* **marvellous** *film*

masculine /ˈmæskjʊlɪn/ *adjective*
like or of a man

mask /mɑːsk/
noun
a covering to hide the face:
We all wore

mask

masks *at the party and no one knew who we were.*

○**mass** /mæs/ *noun* (plural **masses**)

1 a large quantity of something with no special shape: *Before the rain, the sky was a* **mass** *of clouds.*

2 a large number of people

massacre[1] /ˈmæsəkə(r)/ *verb* (*present participle* **massacring** /ˈmæsəkrɪŋ/, *past* **massacred**)
to kill a lage number of people: *They cruelly* **massacred** *all the people in the village.*

massacre[2] *noun*
the cruel killing of many people

mast /mɑːst/
noun
a tall length of wood or metal: *The* **mast** *on a ship holds the flag and sails. A radio or television* **mast** *is a metal post which sends out signals.*

masts

master /ˈmɑːstə(r)/ *noun*

1 the chief person; the person who has power over people who live or work with him: *The dog obeyed his* **master.**

2 a word used in front of a boy's name: *The letter was addressed to "***Master** *Peter Jones".*

○**mat** /mæt/ *noun*
a floor covering made of woven straw, wood, etc.

○**match**[1] /mætʃ/ *noun*
(*plural* **matches**)
a small stick with something on the end which burns when it is rubbed or struck: *It is dangerous to play with* **matches**; *you might burn yourself.*

○**match**[2] *noun* (*plural* **matches**)
a game between two people or two teams: *a football* **match**

Roland Ayotte

° **match**[3] *verb*
to be like something else in size, shape, etc.: *These shoes do not* **match**; *one is large and the other is small.*

mate[1] /meɪt/ *noun*
1 a friend: *The people we work with are called* '**workmates** *and our friends at school are called* '**classmates.**
2 one of a male and female pair of animals or birds

mate[2] *verb* (*present participle* **mating**, *past* **mated**)
to join together to have young: *Birds* **mate** *in the spring.*

° **material** /məˈtɪərɪəl/ *noun*
1 anything from which something can be made: *Wood and iron are* **materials**; *we can make many things from them.*
2 (*no plural*) cloth: *blue cotton* **material**

mathematics /ˌmæθəˈmætɪks/
plural noun (*used with a singular verb*)
the study or science of numbers: *In our* **mathematics** *class we study arithmetic, algebra, and geometry.*
maths /mæθs/ is a short way of saying or writing **mathematics**.
ˌmatheˈmatical *adjective*

matron /ˈmeɪtrən/ *noun*
1 a woman who looks after the children in a school where children live: *Go and see* **matron** *if you feel ill.*
2 a chief nurse in a hospital

matter[1] /ˈmætəʳ/ *noun*
1 (*no plural*) the substance of which things are made: *Everything we can see and touch is made up of* **matter.**
2 something important; something about which we must talk or think: *I have an important* **matter** *to talk*

to you about. **As a matter of fact** (=really; in fact) *I'm only thirty-five, so don't say I'm old.*
3 something wrong; something which troubles us: **What is the matter** *with her? She's crying.*

° **matter**[2] *verb*
to be important: *It doesn't* **matter** *if I miss this bus, I can walk.*

mattress /ˈmætrɪs/ *noun*
(*plural* **mattresses**)
a large flat bag full of soft material on which we sleep: **Mattresses** *are filled with feathers, cotton, or straw* (see).

mature /məˈtjʊəʳ/ *adjective*
fully grown: *You are a* **mature** *man now; you are no longer a boy.*

maximum[1] /ˈmæksɪməm/ *noun*
the largest possible amount, number, or size: *I can swim a* **maximum** *of 1 mile.*

maximum[2] *adjective*
biggest; largest: *"What's the* **maximum** *distance you've swum?"*

° **May** /meɪ/ *noun*
the fifth month of the year

° **may** *verb*
1 (used to show that something is possible but is not sure to happen): *He* **may** *come tonight, or he* **may** *wait until tomorrow.*
2 be allowed to: *Please* **may** *we go home now?*
3 (showing a hope that something will happen): **May** *the best team win!*

maybe /ˈmeɪbɪ/ *adverb*
perhaps; possibly: *Are you coming to ·the party? —* **Maybe**, *I don't know yet.*

me /miː/
the person who is speaking, (used in sentences like this): *I need that book, so please give it to* **me.** *Give* **me** *the book.*

○ **meal** /miːl/ *noun*
the food we eat at regular times: *I always enjoy my evening* **meal.**

mean[1] /miːn/ *adjective*
unkind; not wanting to share with or help other people: *Peter's father was very* **mean;** *he never gave Peter any new clothes.*

○ **mean**[2] *verb* (*past* **meant** /ment/)
1 to be the same as; have as a meaning: *The word "house"* **means** *a building where people live.*
2 to plan or want to do something: *I* **meant** *to give you this book today, but I forgot.*
'**meaning** *noun* what something is or stands for; what should be understood from something: *If you don't understand a word, look up its* **meaning** *in this book.*

means /miːnz/ *plural noun*
1 something which helps us to do what we want to do: *He climbed the tree* **by means of** *a ladder.*
2 money: *He wants to go to college, but his family haven't the* **means** *to help him.*

meanwhile /ˈmiːnwaɪl/ *or* **meantime** /ˈmiːntaɪm/ *adverb, noun*
the time before something happens or while something else is happening: *They'll arrive in a few minutes —* **meanwhile,** *we'll have a cup of tea. You get the table ready and* **in the meantime** (=while you are doing it) *I'll cook the fish.*

○ **measure**[1] /ˈmeʒəʳ/ *noun*
the size, weight, or amount of anything: *A metre is a* **measure** *of length.*

○ **measure**[2] *verb* (*present participle* **measuring,** *past* **measured**)
to find out the size, weight, or amount of anything: *Mother* **measured** *me to see what size of dress I should have.*
measurement *noun: We take the* **measurements** *of something to see how long, tall, or wide it is.*

○ **meat** /miːt/ *noun* (*no plural*)
the parts of an animal's body used as food: *We always cook* **meat.**

mechanic /mɪˈkænɪk/ *noun*
a person who has been trained to work with machines
mechanical *adjective* of a machine; done or made by machine **mechanically** *adverb*

medal /ˈmedl/ *noun*
a piece of metal like a coin given to someone who has done something special

medal

○ **medicine** /ˈmedsɪn/ *noun*
1 (*no plural*) the science of treating and understanding illnesses: *A person who wants to become a doctor has to study* **medicine.**
2 things which we drink or eat when we are ill, to help us to get better
medical /ˈmedɪkl/ *adjective: He is a* **medical** *student. The doctor gave him a* **medical** *examination.*

medium /ˈmiːdjəm/ *adjective*
not big or small; of middle size or amount: *She is of* **medium** *height.*

○ **meet** /miːt/ *verb* (*past* **met** /met/)
1 to come together: *I* **met** *my teacher in the street today. Let us* **meet** *at your house tonight.*
2 to get to know someone: *I would like you to* **meet** *my father.*
'**meeting** *noun: Many people came to the* **meeting** *in the hall.*

melody /ˈmelədɪ/ *noun* (*plural* **melodies**)

a number of musical sounds coming one after the other in a song or tune (see): *I like that song; it has a pleasant* **melody.**

melon /'melən/ *noun*
a large round fruit with watery juice inside

° **melt** /melt/ *verb*
to make or become a liquid by heating: *Iron will* **melt** *when it is made very hot.*

° **member** /'membər/ *noun*
a person who belongs to a group: *I am a* **member** *of our school football club.*
membership *noun* (*no plural*)
belonging to a group or the people who belong to it

° **memory** /'memrɪ/ *noun*
(*plural* **memories**)
1 the ability to remember things: *Grandmother* **has a good memory;** *she can remember things which happened many years ago.*
2 a thought about the past; something remembered: *I had happy* **memories** *of my school.*

men /men/ see **man**

menace /'menɪs/ *noun*
a danger: *A man who drives fast is a* **menace** *to other people.*

° **mend** /mend/ *verb*
to repair or fix something broken or with a hole in it: *Can you* **mend** *the hole in my shirt?*

mental /'mentl/ *adjective*
of or done with the mind: *A* **mental** *hospital is for people who have an illness of the mind.*
mentally *adverb: He added the numbers* **mentally;** *he did not need a pencil and paper.*

° **mention** /'menʃn/ *verb*
to speak about in a few words: *On the telephone, he* **mentioned** *that he had been ill.*

menu /'menjuː/ *noun*
a list of food that you can choose to eat, in a hotel, etc.

merchant /'mɜːtʃənt/ *noun*
a person who buys and sells goods, often buying from and selling to people in other countries: *a* **fruit merchant**

mercury /'mɜːkjʊrɪ/ *noun*
(*no plural*)
a silver-coloured metal

mercy /'mɜːsɪ/ *noun* (*no plural*)
kindness shown to other people by a person who does not have to be kind: *The soldier showed* **mercy** *to his prisoner and set him free.*
merciful *adjective* showing mercy **mercifully** *adverb*
merciless *adjective* cruel; without mercy **mercilessly** *adverb*

mere /mɪər/ *adjective*
only; not more than: *A* **mere** *child cannot do the work of a man.*
'merely *adverb: I* **merely** *looked at the chocolate; I did not eat it.*

merit[1] /'merɪt/ *noun* (*no plural*)
greatness; goodness

merit[2] *verb*
to deserve: *His work* **merits** *a prize.*

merry /'merɪ/ *adjective* (**merrier, merriest**)
happy; full of laughter: *a* **merry** *expression on her face*
merrily *adverb*
'merry-go-₁round *noun* a big machine that you can ride on for pleasure while it turns round and round

mess[1] /mes/ *noun* (*plural* **messes**)
many things mixed up together, often dirty: *Your room is* **in a mess.** *Please tidy it.*
'messy *adjective* (**messier, messiest**): *a* **messy** *room*

mess[2] *verb*

1 to make something dirty or untidy; make something not happen in the right way: *I've just cleaned the floor, and you've* **messed** *it* **up** *again by dropping bits of paper everywhere!*

2 to play instead of working; be silly: *Stop* **messing about** — *finish your work.*

º **message** /'mesɪdʒ/ *noun*

news or an order sent from one person to another: *I have sent mother a* **message** *to tell her I shall be home late.*

messenger /'mesɪndʒəʳ/ *noun* a person who takes a message

met /met/ see **meet**

º **metal**[1] /'metl/ *noun*

a substance such as iron, tin, gold, etc.

º **metal**[2] *adjective*

made of metal: *a* **metal** *box*

meter /'miːtəʳ/ *noun*

a machine used for measuring: *The electricity* **meter** *in our house shows how much electricity we have used.*

method /'meθəd/ *noun*

the way in which something is done: *Our teacher is showing us a new* **method** *of writing.*

º **metre** /'miːtəʳ/ *noun*

a measure of length equal to 100 centimetres (see) or 39 inches (see)

metric /'metrɪk/ *adjective: The* **metric system** *of measurement and counting uses* **metres** *for measuring length,* **grams** *for measuring weight, and* **litres** *for measuring liquid.*

miaow /mɪ'aʊ/ *verb*

to make the sound a cat makes

mice /maɪs/ see **mouse**

microcomputer

/'maɪkrəʊkəm,pjuːtəʳ/ *noun*

a small computer (see) that you can use at home or at school

microphone

/'maɪkrəfəʊn/ *noun*

an instrument which carries sounds a long distance or makes sounds louder

microphone

º **microscope** /'maɪkrəskəʊp/ *noun*

an instrument which helps us to see very small things by making them look much bigger: *She looked at the insect* **under a microscope.**

midday /,mɪd'deɪ/ *noun* (*no plural*)

the middle of the day; 12 o'clock **noon** is another word for **midday.**

º **middle**[1] /'mɪdl/ *noun*

the part which is the same distance from the two ends or sides of something: *Please stand* **in the middle** *of the room. I woke* **in the middle** *of the night.*

º **middle**[2] *adjective*

in the centre: *Which book do you want? I'll have the* **middle** *one. A* **middle-aged** *person is between forty and sixty years old.*

midnight /'mɪdnaɪt/ *noun*

(*no plural*)

12 o'clock at night

º **might**[1] /maɪt/ *verb*

1 past tense of **may**: *I asked if I* **might** *borrow the book.*

2 (used to show that something is possible, but not certain or likely): *Jane* **might** *come later, but I don't think she will.*

3 a very polite way of asking for something: **Might** *I borrow your pen?*

might[2] *noun* (*no plural*)

strength; power: *He tried* **with all**

his **might** *to open the door but it stayed shut.*

'**mighty** *adjective* (**mightier, mightiest**): *He gave it a* **mighty** *push and it opened.*

migrate /maɪ'greɪt/ *verb* (*present participle* **migrating,** *past* **migrated**)
1 to move from one place to another: *People* **migrate** *to find work.*
2 to travel at the same time every year from one part of the world to another: *Some birds* **migrate** *to find warmer weather.*
   mi'gration *noun*

mild /maɪld/ *adjective*
gentle; not rough: *The weather is* **mild** *today; it is neither hot nor cold.* '**mildly** *adverb*

° **mile** /maɪl/ *noun*
a measure of length equal to 1,760 yards or 1.6 kilometres

° **military** /'mɪlɪtrɪ/ *adjective*
of soldiers: *a* **military** *government*

° **milk**[1] /mɪlk/ *noun* (*no plural*)
the white liquid that comes from female animals as food for their young: *We drink cows'* **milk.**
   milkman /'mɪlkmən/ *noun*
   (in Britain) a person who takes milk to people's houses

° **milk**[2] *verb*
to get milk from an animal: *to* **milk** *a cow*

mill /mɪl/ *noun*
1 a place where corn is made into flour
2 a place where things are made by machinery: *Cotton is made in a cotton* **mill.**

millet /'mɪlɪt/ *noun* (*no plural*)
a grain plant with small seeds

millimetre /'mɪlɪmiːtər/ *noun*
a measure of length; $1/1000$ of a metre. **mm** is a short way of writing **millimetre.**

million /'mɪljən/ *noun, adjective*
the number 1,000,000
   millionaire /ˌmɪljə'neər/ *noun* a person who is very very rich

mime /maɪm/ *verb*
(*present participle* **miming,** *past* **mimed**)
to use actions instead of speech to show the meaning of something
   mime *noun* (*no plural*)

mimic /'mɪmɪk/ *verb*
(*present participle* **mimicking,** *past* **mimicked**)
to copy someone's speech or actions to make people laugh: *He* **mimicked** *the teacher's voice.*
   mimic *noun*

mince[1] /mɪns/ *verb*
(*present participle* **mincing,** *past* **minced**)
to cut meat up into very small pieces: *We* **mince** *meat in a machine called a* **mincer.**

mince[2] *noun* (*no plural*)
meat which has been minced: *We had* **mince** *for dinner.*

° **mind**[1] /maɪnd/ *noun*
thoughts; a person's way of thinking or feeling: *Her* **mind** *is full of dreams about becoming famous. He* **made up his mind** (=decided) *to work hard at school. I was going to buy some chocolate but I* **changed my mind** *and bought some apples instead.*

° **mind**[2] *verb*
1 to look after: *Will you* **mind** *the children while I go out?*
2 to dislike: *Do you* **mind** *if I smoke?*
3 to take notice of: **Mind** *the step! Don't fall over it.*

° **mine**[1] /maɪn/
something that belongs to the person speaking: *That bicycle is* **mine** *— I bought it yesterday.*

° **mine**² *noun*
a deep hole in the ground from which people dig out coal, iron, gold, etc.

mine³ *verb* (*present participle* **mining**, *past* **mined**)
to dig out something from a mine: *They* **were mining** *for silver.*
miner *noun*

° **mineral** /'mɪnrəl/ *noun*
a substance like iron, coal, or oil which is dug out of the ground
'mineral ,water *noun* (*no plural*)
a drink with a sweet taste and a little gas in it

miniature /'mɪnətʃəʳ/ *adjective*
very small: *a* **miniature** *railway*

minimum¹ /'mɪnɪməm/ *noun*
the smallest possible amount, number, or size: *You must get a* **minimum** *of 40 questions right to pass the examination.*

minimum² *adjective*
smallest: *The* **minimum** *pass mark in the examination is 40 out of 100.*

minister /'mɪnɪstəʳ/ *noun*
1 an important person in the government
2 a Christian priest
ministry *noun* (*plural* **ministries**)
a part of the government: *the* **Ministry** *of Education*

minor /'maɪnəʳ/ *adjective*
smaller; not very important: *A* **minor** *illness is not a serious one.*
minority /mɪ'nɒrətɪ/ *noun* (*no plural*) the smaller part or number: *Only a* **minority** *of the children were noisy, the majority were quiet.*

minus /'maɪnəs/ *preposition*
less: *10* **minus** *2 is 8* (10−2=8).

° **minute**¹ /'mɪnɪt/ *noun*
a measure of time, of which there are 60 in an hour: *He'll be here* **in a minute** (=soon).

minute² /maɪ'njuːt/ *adjective*
very small: **minute** *writing*

miracle /'mɪrəkl/ *noun*
a wonderful happening which cannot be explained so is thought to be caused by God
miraculous /mɪ'rækjʊləs/ *adjective:* *a* **miraculous** *cure for an illness* **miraculously** *adverb*

° **mirror** /'mɪrəʳ/ *noun*
a flat piece of glass with a shiny back in which we can see ourselves: *She looked at herself in the* **mirror.**

mirror

misbehave /ˌmɪsbɪ'heɪv/ *verb* (*present participle* **misbehaving**, *past* **misbehaved**)
to behave badly; do something bad: *The teacher was angry because the children were* **misbehaving.**

mischief /'mɪstʃɪf/ *noun* (*no plural*)
foolish actions which may cause harm or damage: *Those boys have been* **up to mischief** *again; they've put water all over the floor.*
mischievous /'mɪstʃɪvəs/ *adjective:* **mischievous** *children*

misery /'mɪzərɪ/ *noun* (*no plural*)
great unhappiness: *the* **misery** *of the people who had lost their homes in the fire*
miserable /'mɪzrəbl/ *adjective:* *I'm feeling* **miserable**; *I'm tired, cold, and very hungry.*

misfortune /mɪs'fɔːtʃən/ *noun*
bad luck; something bad which happens to you: *to suffer a* **misfortune**

° **miss** /mɪs/ *verb*
1 not to hit or catch something: *He threw the ball to me, but I* **missed**

it and it landed on the ground. I was late because I **missed** *the bus.*
2 not to be where it should be: *A book is* **missing** *from my desk. When she read the list of names aloud, she* **missed** *my name* **out** (=she did not say it).
3 to feel sad when someone is not there: *We shall all* **miss** *you when you go away.*

Miss /mɪs/ *noun (plural* **Misses)**
the title of a girl or unmarried woman: *We call our teacher* **Miss** *Johnson.*

missile /'mɪsaɪl/ *noun*
something which is thrown or fired to harm or damage: *Spears and arrows are* **missiles.** *Men make rockets* (see) *to use as* **missiles.**

missionary /'mɪʃənrɪ/ *noun (plural* **missionaries)**
a person whose work is to teach others about his religion
    mission *noun* the place where missionaries work

mist /mɪst/ *noun*
a thin cloud near the ground: *We couldn't see through the* **mist.**
    misty *adjective* (**mistier, mistiest**): **misty** *weather*

○ **mistake¹** /mɪ'steɪk/ *noun*
a wrong thought or act: *You have* **made a mistake** *here; this 3 should be 5. I took your pen* **by mistake.**

○ **mistake²** *verb*
(*present participle* **mistaking,** *past tense* **mistook** /mɪ'stʊk/, *past participle* **mistaken**)
to think or act wrongly: *I am sorry, I* **mistook** *you for* (=thought that you were) *someone I know.*

mistress /'mɪstrɪs/ *noun*
(*plural* **mistresses)**
a woman teacher

○ **mix** /mɪks/ *verb*
to put different things together to make something new; join together: *We* **mix** *flour and water to make bread.*
    mixture /'mɪkstʃər/ *noun: A* **mixture** *is what we make by putting different things together.*

moan /məʊn/ *verb*
to make a low sound of pain: *The child lay* **moaning** *gently.*
    moan *noun*

mock /mɒk/ *verb*
to laugh unkindly at someone: *You shouldn't* **mock** *the way he walks.*

○ **model¹** /'mɒdl/ *noun*
1 a small copy of something: *a* **model** *of an aeroplane*
2 a small object which is going to be copied in a much larger size: *The builder had a* **model** *of the new house.*

model² *verb*
(*present participle* **modelling,** *past* **modelled)**
to make the shape of something; make a small copy of something: *to* **model** *animals in clay*

model³ *adjective*
made in a small size: *a* **model** *car*

○ **moderate** /'mɒdrət/ *adjective*
neither high nor low, fast nor slow, large nor small: *a* **moderate** *speed*
    moderately *adverb*

○ **modern** /'mɒdn/ *adjective*
of the present time; not old: **modern** *clothes/***modern** *music*

modest /'mɒdɪst/ *adjective*
not making oneself noticed or telling other people about what you do well: *She is very* **modest** *about the prizes she has won.*
    modesty *noun (no plural)*

moist /mɔɪst/ *adjective*
a little wet; not dry: *His eyes were* **moist** *with tears.*
    moisture /'mɔɪstʃər/ *noun (no plural)* small drops of water;

wetness: *The sun dries the* **moisture** *on the ground.*

mole[1] /məʊl/
noun
a small
animal which
makes and
lives in holes underground

mole

'**mole-ˌhill** *noun* a small heap of earth thrown up by a mole when it is digging

mole[2] *noun*
a small round dark spot on the skin

molecule /'mɒlɪkjuːl/ *noun*
the smallest part which a substance can be broken up into without changing its form: *A* **molecule** *is made up of atoms* (see).

moment /'məʊmənt/ *noun*
a very short time: *He will be here* **in a moment. At the moment** (=now) *I am working.*

monarch /'mɒnək/ *noun*
a king or queen
monarchy *noun* (*plural* **monarchies**) a country that has a monarch: *Britain is a* **monarchy.**

monastery /'mɒnəstrɪ/ *noun*
(*plural* **monasteries**)
a place where monks (see) live

○ **Monday** /'mʌndeɪ, −dɪ/ *noun*
the second day of the week

○ **money** /'mʌnɪ/ *noun* (*no plural*)
coins and paper banknotes: *He* **makes a lot of money** *selling clothes.*

monk /mʌŋk/ *noun*
one of a group of men who live together and have given their lives to a religion

○ **monkey** /'mʌŋkɪ/ *noun*
the animal that is most like a human in shape but which usually has a long tail and lives in trees (picture on page 17)

monotony /mə'nɒtənɪ/ *noun*
(*no plural*)
lack of change; being the same all the time: *The* **monotony** *of his voice sent me to sleep.*
monotonous *adjective: a* **monotonous** *voice which sent me to sleep*

monsoon /mɒn'suːn/ *noun*
a wind to the south of Asia; the rain which comes with the wind in the wet season

monster /'mɒnstər/ *noun*
an animal or person with a strange or unusual shape, often very big
monstrous /'mɒnstrəs/ *adjective* big and ugly

○ **month** /mʌnθ/ *noun*
one of the twelve periods of time which make a year
'**monthly** *adjective, adverb: A* **monthly** *paper is printed every month. We read it* **monthly.**

monument /'mɒnjʊmənt/ *noun*
something which is built to help us to remember a person or an event

moo /muː/ *verb*
to make the noise that a cow makes

mood /muːd/ *noun*
the way we feel at any one time: *The beautiful sunny morning put me in a happy* **mood.**

○ **moon** /muːn/
noun
the large
body in the
sky which
shines at night: *When we can see all of the moon, we call it a* **full moon.** *When we can only see a small thin part of the moon we call it a* **new moon.** (picture on p.259)

moon

'**moonˌlight** *noun* (*no plural*)

moor /mɔːr/ *verb*
to tie up a boat

moral /'mɒrəl/ *noun*
a lesson about what is right and wrong which we learn from a story or happening: *The* **moral** *of the story was that we should be kind to other people.*

° **more** /mɔːʳ/
1 a larger amount or number: *The other children only have a little bread, but I have* **more***. I have* **more** *bread than them. I like football* **more** *than swimming. I run* **more** *quickly than Simon.*
2 (used in some phrases): *Next year my brother is going to get a job, so he won't come to school* **any more** (=again). *It is* **more and more** *difficult to find work.*

° **morning** /'mɔːnɪŋ/ *noun*
the time from when the sun rises to midday

Morse code /ˌmɔːs 'kəʊd/ *noun* (*no plural*)
a way of sending messages using flashing lights or sounds

Moslem /'mʊzlɪm/ *noun, adjective*
Muslim

° **mosque** /mɒsk/ *noun*
a Muslim religious building where people pray

° **mosquito** /mɒ'skiːtəʊ/ *noun* (*plural* **mosquitoes**)
a fly that drinks blood and can carry malaria (see) from one person to another

moss /mɒs/ *noun* (*no plural*)
a bright green plant that grows flat on wet ground and stones

° **most** /məʊst/
1 the largest amount or number: *You all ate a lot of rice, but David ate* **most***. He ate* **the most** *of all. I gave him* (**the**) **most** *rice because he was very hungry.*
2 very: *You have been* **most** *kind.*
3 (used in some phrases): *It will*

take you an hour **at** (**the**) **most** (=not more than an hour) *to get to the village.*

'**mostly** *adverb* almost all: *The earth here is* **mostly** *clay.*

moth /mɒθ/ *noun*
an insect with four wings, like a butterfly (see) but usually flying at night

° **mother** /'mʌðəʳ/ *noun*
a female parent: *the* **mother** *of three sons*
'**mother-in-ˌlaw** *noun* (*plural* **mothers-in-law**) the mother of your wife or husband

motion /'məʊʃn/ *noun* (*no plural*)
movement: *You must not get out of the car when it is* **in motion***.*
motionless *adjective: The cat sat* **motionless** (=not moving).

motive /'məʊtɪv/ *noun*
the reason for doing something: *His* **motive** *for working so hard is that he needs money.*

° **motor** /'məʊtəʳ/ *noun*
an engine that makes things move or work
'**motorˌboat** *noun* a small boat with an engine
'**motorˌcar** *noun* a vehicle on wheels, driven by an engine, that you can travel in **car** is the usual word for a **motorcar***.*
'**motorˌcycle**
noun
a big bicycle worked by an engine
motorbike is another word for a **motorcycle***.*

motorcycle

'**motorist** *noun* a person who drives a motorcar
'**motorˌway** *noun* a wide road built for vehicles to travel long distances fast

mould[1] /məʊld/ *verb*
to make something into the shape we want it to be: *We* **mould** *clay with our fingers.*

mould[2] *noun*
a hollow container which shapes whatever we pour into it

mould[3] *noun* (*no plural*)
a greenish-white substance which grows on food and clothes if they are left in warm wet air

'**mouldy** *adjective* (**mouldier, mouldiest**): **mouldy** *bread*

mound /maʊnd/ *noun*
a heap of earth; a small hill: *Your dog has dug up a* **mound** *of earth.*

mount[1] /maʊnt/ *verb*
to climb up something; to get on a horse or bicycle

mount[2] *noun*
a mountain, usually used in names: **Mount** *Everest*

○ **mountain** /'maʊntɪn/ *noun*
a very high hill: *Mount Everest is the highest* **mountain** *in the world.*

mourn /mɔːn/ *verb*
to be very sad especially for someone who is dead: *She* **mourned for** *her dead child.*

'**mourning** *noun* (*no plural*): *She was* **in mourning** *for her child.*

mouse
/maʊs/ *noun*
(*plural* **mice**
/maɪs/)
a small

mouse

animal with a long tail which may live in houses and eat stored food

moustache /məˈstɑːʃ/ *noun*
the hair that grows above a man's mouth (picture at **beard**)

○ **mouth** /maʊθ/ *noun*
the opening in our faces through which we speak and take in food (picture on page 133)

'**mouthful** *noun* the amount of food or drink that fills your mouth

○ **move** /muːv/ *verb* (*present participle* **moving**, *past* **moved**)
1 to go from one place to another: *The teacher asked Peter to* **move** *to the front of the room. That family* **moved house** *last week.*
2 to take something from one place and put it in another: *Who has* **moved** *my book? I left it here.*

'**movement** *noun*: *She watched the dancer and tried to copy her* **movements** (= how she moved).

mow /məʊ/ *verb* (*present participle* **mowing**, *past tense* **mowed**, *past participle* **mown**)
to cut grass: *to* **mow** *the grass*

○ **Mr** /'mɪstər/ *noun*
a word put before a man's name: *This is* **Mr** *Brown.*

○ **Mrs** /'mɪsɪz/ *noun*
a word put before a married woman's name: *This is* **Mrs** *Brown.*

○ **much** /mʌtʃ/ (**more, most**)
1 a lot; a large amount of: *The baby can't eat* **much** *food. "Did you pay* **much** *for that old bicycle?" "No,* **not much**.*" "How* **much** *did you pay?" His garden is* **much** *larger than mine.*
2 often: *I don't see her* **much** *because she lives so far away.*
3 (used in some phrases): *Thank you* **very much**. *How* **much** *longer can you wait? He talks* **too much**.

○ **mud** /mʌd/ *noun* (*no plural*)
wet earth

'**muddy** *adjective* (**muddier, muddiest**): *When it rains the ground becomes very* **muddy**.

muddle[1] /'mʌdl/ *noun*
a mixed-up state: *She was in a* **muddle**; *she couldn't even remember what day it was.*

muddle[2] *verb*

(*present participle* **muddling** /ˈmʌdlɪŋ/, *past* **muddled**)

to put into disorder; mix up: *If your mind is* **muddled** *you can't think clearly.*

mug /mʌg/ *noun*

a big cup with straight sides

mug

mule /mjuːl/ *noun*

an animal whose parents were a horse and a donkey (see)

multiply /ˈmʌltɪplaɪ/ *verb* (*present participle* **multiplying**, *past* **multiplied**)

to increase by a number of times: *2* **multiplied** *by 3 is 6* $(2 \times 3 = 6)$.

multiplication /ˌmʌltɪplɪˈkeɪʃn/ *noun* (*no plural*)

mumble /ˈmʌmbl/ *verb* (*present participle* **mumbling**, *past* **mumbled**)

to speak in a way that is difficult to hear or understand: *He* **mumbled** *something to me but I could not hear what he said.*

mummy /ˈmʌmɪ/ *noun*

(*plural* **mummies**)

a word for mother used by children

mumps /mʌmps/ *noun* (*no plural*)

an illness which causes fever and swellings in the neck and throat

murder[1] /ˈmɜːdəʳ/ *verb*

to kill a person when you have decided to do it

murderer *noun* a person who murders someone

murder[2] *noun*

an act of murdering: **Murder** *is a serious crime.*

murmur /ˈmɜːməʳ/ *verb*

to make a soft sound; speak quietly: *The child* **murmured** *in her sleep.* **murmur** *noun*

○ **muscle** /ˈmʌsl/ *noun*

one of the pieces of stretchy

muscles

material in the body which can tighten to move parts of the body: *We use our* **muscles** *to bend our arms and legs.*

museum /mjuːˈzɪəm/ *noun*

a building in which interesting objects are kept and shown to visitors

mushroom /ˈmʌʃruːm/ *noun*

a plant which is not green and is a fungus (see) that we can eat

○ **music** /ˈmjuːzɪk/ *noun* (*no plural*)

1 the pleasant sounds made by voices or by instruments: *to listen to* **music**

2 a written or printed set of musical notes: *a* **sheet of music**

musical *adjective* of music; skilled in music: *She is very* **musical**. *She plays and sings well.*

musician /mjuːˈzɪʃn/ *noun* a person who plays an instrument or writes music

○ **Muslim** /ˈmʊzlɪm/ *noun, adjective*

a follower of the religion that believes in the teachings of Mohammed as written in the Koran (see)

○ **must** /məst; *strong* mʌst/ *verb*

1 (used with another verb to show what is necessary or what has to be done): *I* **must** *shut the door, or the rain will come in. You* **mustn't** (= must not) *be late for school.*

2 (showing what is sure or likely): *It is very late; it* **must** *be nearly 12 o'clock. I can't open the door — somebody* **must have** *locked it.*

mustard /ˈmʌstəd/ *noun*

(*no plural*)

a yellow powder made from the

seeds of a plant, used mixed with water to give a hot taste to food

mutter /'mʌtəʳ/ *verb*
to speak in a low voice: *He was* **muttering** *on the telephone so I asked him to speak more clearly.*

mutton /'mʌtn/ *noun* (*no plural*)
meat from a sheep eaten as food

° **my** /maɪ/
belonging to the person speaking: *I hurt* **my** *knee when I fell off* **my** *bicycle.*

myself /maɪ'self/
1 the same person as the one who is speaking: *I looked at* **myself** *in the mirror. I played* **by myself** (=alone). *I did the sums* **by myself** (=without help).
2 (used to give **I** a stronger meaning): *I made this shirt* **myself.**

mystery /'mɪstərɪ/ *noun*
(*plural* **mysteries**)
a strange thing which we cannot explain: *Who had taken the money? It was a* **mystery.**
mysterious /mɪ'stɪərɪəs/ *adjective*

Nn

° **nail**[1] /neɪl/ *noun*
1 a small piece of metal,

nail
nails

pointed at one end and flat at the other: *He fastened the lid to the box with* **nails.**
2 the hard parts at the end of the fingers and toes: *Sarah cut her* **'fingernails** *but forgot to cut her* **'toenails.** (picture on page 133)

° **nail**[2] *verb*
to fasten or fix with a nail: *Will you* **nail** *the sign* **on**/**to** *the door?*

naked /'neɪkɪd/ *adjective*
1 without clothes: *The* **naked** *baby sat in the bath.*
2 not covered: *a* **naked** *flame*

° **name**[1] /neɪm/ *noun*
the word used in speaking to or about a person or thing: *My* **name** *is Jane Smith. What is the* **name** *of this town?*

° **name**[2] *verb* (*present participle* **naming**, *past* **named**)
to give a name to someone or something: *They* **named** *the baby Ann.*
'namely *adverb* that is: *Ask the smallest girl in the class,* **namely** *Sarah.*

nanny /'nænɪ/ *noun*
(*plural* **nannies**)
a woman whose job is to look after children

nap /næp/ *noun*
a short sleep: *to have a* **nap**

napkin /'næpkɪn/ *noun*
a square of cloth or paper used at meals to keep one's clothes, hands, and mouth clean

nappy /'næpɪ/ *noun*
(*plural* **nappies**)
a piece of cloth or paper worn between a baby's legs and round its bottom: *The baby has a wet* **nappy** *— will you change it?*

○ **narrow** /ˈnærəʊ/ *adjective*
not wide; small from side to side:
a **narrow** *path*

nasty /ˈnɑːstɪ/ *adjective* (**nastier, nastiest**)
not pleasant: **nasty** *medicine*

nation /ˈneɪʃn/ *noun*
all the people belonging to a country and living under its government: *The whole* **nation** *supported the government.*

national /ˈnæʃənl/ *adjective* of or belonging to a country: *a* **national** *holiday*

nationality /ˌnæʃəˈnælətɪ/ *noun* (*plural* **nationalities**) belonging to a country: *Richard is American, John is British — they have different* **nationalities.**

native[1] /ˈneɪtɪv/ *noun*
a person born in a certain place: *Mary is a* **native** *of Australia.*

native[2] *adjective*
belonging to or being the place where one was born

○ **nature** /ˈneɪtʃəʳ/ *noun*
1 (*no plural*) the world and everything in it which man has not made: *In* **nature** *study, we learn about plants, insects, and animals.*
2 the character of a person or thing: *Peter has a happy* **nature**; *he is a* **good-natured** *boy.*

natural /ˈnætʃrəl/ *adjective*
1 made by nature: *Rubber in its* **natural** *state is a liquid.* **2** usual: *It is* **natural** *for a cat to catch mice.*

naturally *adverb* **1** by nature: *Her hair is* **naturally** *wavy.* **2** as you would expect: **Naturally,** *I want to win the race.*

naughty /ˈnɔːtɪ/ *adjective* (**naughtier, naughtiest**)
not well-behaved: *the* **naughtiest** *boy in the class* **naughtily** *adverb*

navigate /ˈnævɪgeɪt/ *verb* (*present participle* **navigating**, *past* **navigated**)
1 to decide the way a ship or plane should go: *He* **navigated** *the plane through the low cloud.*
2 to go through or across by sea or air: *He was the first man to* **navigate** *the Atlantic alone.*
ˌnaviˈgation *noun* (*no plural*).

navy /ˈneɪvɪ/ *noun* (plural **navies**)
the warships of a country; the officers and men of these ships: *My son is in the* **navy.**

naval /ˈneɪvl/ *adjective*

○ **near** /nɪəʳ/ *adjective, adverb, preposition*
not far; close; at a short distance: *Our school is very* **near.** *My aunt lives quite* **near.** *He sat in a chair* **near** *the window.*

nearby /nɪəˈbaɪ/ *adjective, adverb*
close; not far away: *We swim in a* **nearby** *river. Is the school* **nearby?**

nearly /ˈnɪəlɪ/ *adverb*
almost: *We have* **nearly** *finished.*

○ **neat** /niːt/ *adjective*
clean and well arranged: *She always kept her room* **neat.**
ˈneatly *adverb*

○ **necessary** /ˈnesəsrɪ, ˈnesəserɪ/ *adjective*
which we must do or must have: *Good food is* **necessary** *to good health.*

necessity /nəˈsesətɪ/ *noun* (*plural* **necessities**) something we need

○ **neck** /nek/ *noun*
the part of the body between the head and shoulders (picture on page 133)

necklace

necklace /'neklɪs/ *noun: The girl is wearing a bead* **necklace.**

° **need**[1] /niːd/ *noun*

1 (*no plural*) not having something that is necessary: *The hungry children were* **in need of** *food.*

2 something that is necessary: *The mother looks after all her children's* **needs** — *she gives them food and clothes and other things.*

° **need**[2] *verb*

1 to not have something that is necessary: *I* **need** *a hammer and some nails to mend this chair.*

2 to have to: *You* **needn't** *go home yet* — *it's only two o'clock.*

° **needle** /'niːdl/ *noun*

a thin piece of pointed metal with a hole at one end for thread: *She used a* **needle** *to sew the button onto the shirt.*

negative /'negətɪv/ *noun*

the piece of film from which we make a photograph

neglect[1] /nɪ'glekt/ *verb*

not to look after someone or something: *The animals were thin and ill because the farmer had* **neglected** *them.*

neglect[2] *noun* (*no plural*)

the action of neglecting: *The animals were ill because of the farmer's* **neglect.**

negro /'niːgrəʊ/ *noun*
(*plural* **negroes**)

a person from one of the black-skinned African races: *There are many* **negroes** *in America.*

negress /'niːgrɪs/ *noun* (*plural* **negresses**) a negro woman

° **neighbour** /'neɪbər/ *noun*

someone who lives very near you: *My next-door* **neighbour** *lives in the house next to mine.*

neighbourhood *noun* the area around a place: *You will find several shops in the* **neighbourhood.**

° **neither** /'naɪðər, 'niːðər/

not one and not the other of two: **Neither** *boy could swim, but they both wanted to learn.* **Neither** *Peter* **nor** *James can swim. Sarah can't reach the top shelf, and* **neither** *can I* (= I can't reach it either).

nephew /'nefjuː/ *noun*

the son of one's brother or sister

nerve /nɜːv/ *noun*

a very small part in the body like a thread which carries feelings and messages to and from the brain

'nervous *adjective* afraid: *The old woman felt* **nervous** *as she tried to cross the busy road.*

'nervously *adverb*

nest /nest/ *noun*

the home built by a bird or by some animals and insects: *The bird laid three eggs in her* **nest.**

° **net** /net/ *noun*

material with open spaces between knotted thread, string, or wire: *The footballer* net

kicked the ball into the back of the **net.** *A* **'fishing net** *is spread out under water to catch fish.*

° **'network** *noun* a large group of lines, wires, etc. which cross or meet each other: *a railway* **network**

° **never** /'nevər/ *adverb*

not at any time; not ever: *I'll* **never** *forget her kindness. My brother* **never** *lets me ride my bicycle.* **Never mind** (= don't worry), *you can ride mine.*

nevertheless /ˌnevəðəˈles/ *adverb*
but; yet: *He was very tired; nevertheless he didn't stop working.*

° **new** /njuː/ *adjective*
1 not used or worn; not old: *a new dress*
2 not seen or known before: *She is learning a new language. He was new to the town; he had never been there before.*
  '**newly** *adverb* recently; freshly: *The house was newly built.*

° **news** /njuːz/ *plural noun* (*used with a singular verb*)
things which have just happened: *We listen to the news on the radio.*
  ° **newspaper** /ˈnjuːspeɪpər/ *noun*
a paper printed daily or weekly with news, notices, etc. in it
  paper is another word for **newspaper.**

° **next** /nekst/ *adjective, adverb*
1 nearest; without anything between: *Jane sits at the next desk. My next door neighbour lives in the house next to mine.*
2 coming after without anything between: *It was Saturday, so the next day was Sunday. What did you do next?*

nibble /ˈnɪbl/ *verb* (*present participle* **nibbling,** *past* **nibbled**)
to take little bites of food: *Aren't you hungry? You're only nibbling your food.*

° **nice** /naɪs/ *adjective* (**nicer, nicest**)
pleasant; good: *This shop sells nice fruit.*
  '**nicely** *adverb*: *The child was nicely dressed.*

nickname /ˈnɪkneɪm/ *noun*
a name given to someone which is not his real name: *John's nickname is "Tiny" because he is very small.*

niece /niːs/ *noun*
the daughter of one's brother or sister

° **night** /naɪt/ *noun*
the time when it is dark and the sun cannot be seen: *It rained during the night.*

nine /naɪn/ *noun, adjective*
the number 9: **Nine** *and one is ten* $(9+1=10)$.
  ninth /naɪnθ/ *noun, adjective*
number 9 in order; 9th: *It's my ninth birthday today.*

nineteen /naɪnˈtiːn/ *noun, adjective*
the number 19
  nineteenth *noun, adjective*
number 19 in order; 19th

ninety /ˈnaɪntɪ/ *noun, adjective*
the number 90
  ninetieth *noun, adjective*
number 90 in order; 90th

° **no** /nəʊ/
1 a word we use to answer a question, to show that something is not true, or that we do not agree with something: *Shall we go for a walk? —* **No,** *I'm busy.*
2 not a; not any: *There are* **no** *children in the classroom.*

noble /ˈnəʊbl/ *adjective* (**nobler, noblest**)
1 of one of the old important families
2 showing courage to help others; good in character: *It was a* **noble** *act when he saved his friend from drowning.* **nobly** *adverb*

° **nobody** /ˈnəʊbədɪ/ *or* **no one** /ˈnəʊ wʌn/
not anybody; no person: *I knocked on the door but* **nobody** *opened it.*

nod[1] /nɒd/ *verb* (*present participle* **nodding,** *past* **nodded**)
to bend the head forward quickly: *She* **nodded** *to show that she agreed with me.*

nod[2] *noun*

an act of nodding: *He greeted me with a* **nod.**

○ **noise** /nɔɪz/ *noun*

a loud sound, often unpleasant: *Planes make a lot of* **noise.** *My car's making strange* **noises.**

'**noisily** *adverb*

'**noisy** *adjective* (**noisier, noisiest**): *"What a* **noisy** *class you are!" said the teacher.*

nomad /'nəʊmæd/ *noun*

a person who travels about with his tribe and who has no fixed home

no'madic *adjective*

○ **none** /nʌn/

not one; not any: **None** *of the pupils knew the answer. I've eaten all the bread and there is* **none** *left.*

nonsense /'nɒnsəns/ *noun*

(*no plural*)

something which has no sense or meaning: *She told me that the moon was made of cheese. What* **nonsense!**

noon /nuːn/ *noun* (*no plural*)

the middle of the day; 12 o'clock: *At* **noon,** *the sun is high in the sky.*

○ **no one** /'nəʊ wʌn/

nobody

○ **nor** /nɔːʳ/

a word used between two choices after **neither** or **not**: **Neither** *Anna* **nor** *Maria likes cooking. This job will* **not** *be finished today,* **nor** *tomorrow.*

normal /'nɔːml/ *adjective*

usual; not special: *It is* **normal** *to find your lessons difficult sometimes; everybody does.*

normally *adverb*: **Normally** *I get up at seven o'clock, but today I got up at nine o'clock.*

○ **north** /nɔːθ/

noun, adjective, adverb

the direction that is on the left when you look towards the rising sun: *We travelled* **north** *for two days. There is a strong* **north** *wind* (=coming from the north).

northern /'nɔːðən/ *adjective* in or of the north

northwards *adverb* towards the north: *to travel* **northwards**

○ **nose** /nəʊz/ *noun*

the part of the face through which we breathe and with which we smell: *She had to* **blow her nose** *to clear it when she had a cold.* (picture on page 133)

nostril /'nɒstrɪl/ *noun*

one of the two holes in the nose (picture on page 133)

○ **not** /nɒt/ *adverb*

a word that gives the opposite meaning to another word or a sentence: *He is* **not** *at school, because he* **isn't** (=is not) *well.*

○ **note**[1] /nəʊt/

noun

1 a single sound in music

notes

2 a short written message: *Mary sent her mother a* **note.**

3 a few words written down to help us remember something: *Please* **make a note** *of my new address.*

4 a piece of paper money: *She collected the money from the bank in new* **notes. banknote** is sometimes used instead of **note.**

'**notebook** *noun: We used a* **notebook** *to write down things which we must remember.*

○ **note**[2] *verb* (*present participle* **noting,** *past* **noted**)

to look at or listen to carefully so that one can remember: *The pupil* **noted** *what the teacher said.*

○ **nothing** /'nʌθɪŋ/

not any thing: *There is* **nothing** *in*

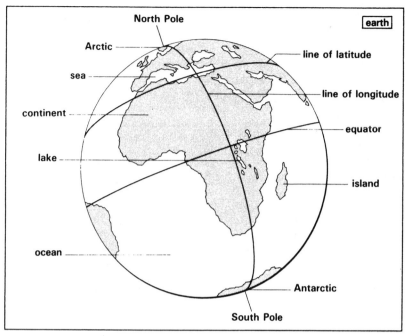

earth

North Pole
Arctic
sea
continent
lake
ocean
line of latitude
line of longitude
equator
island
Antarctic
South Pole

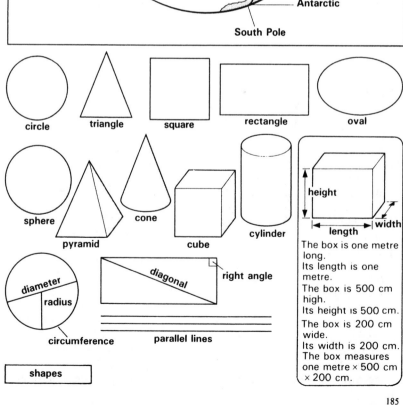

circle
triangle
square
rectangle
oval

sphere
pyramid
cone
cube
cylinder

height
length
width

diameter
radius
circumference

diagonal
right angle

parallel lines

The box is one metre long.
Its length is one metre.
The box is 500 cm high.
Its height is 500 cm.
The box is 200 cm wide.
Its width is 200 cm.
The box measures one metre × 500 cm × 200 cm.

shapes

this box — it's empty. I got this bicycle **for** *nothing* (= free).

○ **notice**[1] /'nəʊtɪs/ *noun*

a warning; news in writing that something is going to happen or has happened: *The* **notice** *on the door said that the library was closed. There were lots of notices on the* **notice-board** (= a piece of wood on a wall on which you put a notice).

○ **notice**[2] *verb* (*present participle* **noticing**, *past* **noticed**)

to see: *The prisoner* **noticed** *that the door was open and ran away.*

noticeable *adjective: The hole in your trousers is not* **noticeable**; *no one will see it.*

nought /nɔːt/ *noun*

the number 0: *When we write a thousand* (*1,000*), *we write three* **noughts** *after the one.* **zero** *is another way of saying* **nought.**

○ **noun** /naʊn/ *noun*

a word that is the name of a person, place, animal, or thing: *In the sentence "The boy threw a stone at the dog" "boy" "stone" and "dog" are* **nouns.**

novel /'nɒvl/ *noun*

a long written story usually printed as a book

novelist *noun* a person who writes novels

○ **November** /nəʊ'vembər/ *noun*

the 11th month of the year

○ **now** /naʊ/ *adverb*

1 at the present time: *We used to live in a village, but* **now** *we live in a city. I must go* **now** — *I can't wait any longer.*

2 (used to call attention): *Now, children, what are you doing?*

'nowadays *adverb* in these times: **Nowadays** *people can fly all over the world in planes.*

○ **nowhere** /'nəʊ,weər/ *adverb*

not anywhere; in, at or to no place: *We looked for the key everywhere but it was* **nowhere** *to be found* (= we couldn't find it anywhere).

nuclear /'njuːklɪər/ *adjective*

using the very great power made by splitting an atom (see) or joining atoms: *A* **nuclear** '**bomb** *is the most powerful weapon we have.*

nucleus /'njuːklɪəs/ *noun* (*plural* **nuclei**)

the central part of something, round which other parts gather: *A* **nucleus** *is the central part of an atom* (see).

nudge[1] /nʌdʒ/ *verb* (*present participle* **nudging**, *past* **nudged**)

to push someone lightly with the elbow: *He* **nudged** *him to wake him up.*

nudge[2] *noun*

an act of nudging: *He gave him a* **nudge.**

○ **nuisance** /'njuːsns/ *noun* (*no plural*)

someone or something which troubles us: *What a* **nuisance**! *I've missed my train.*

○ **number**[1] /'nʌmbər/ *noun*

1 words or figures like one, two, and three or 1, 2, and 3

2 more than one person or thing, in a group: *Birds gather in large* **numbers** *beside the river.*

numerous /'njuːmərəs/ *adjective: Your work has* **numerous** (= very many) *mistakes in it.*

number[2] *verb*

to give a figure to something: *The pages of the book were* **numbered** *1 to 268.*

numeral /'njuːmərəl/ *noun*

a sign used to represent a number: *3 is a* **numeral.**

nun /nʌn/ *noun*
one of a group of women who live together and have given their lives to God

°**nurse**[1] /nɜːs/ *noun*
1 a person who is trained to look after people who are ill: *She works as a **nurse** in a hospital.*
2 a woman who is trained to look after young children

°**nurse**[2] *verb (present participle* **nursing**, *past* **nursed**)

to care for sick people: *She **nursed** her mother when she was ill.*

°**nut** /nʌt/ *noun*
1 a fruit of a plant or tree, with a hard shell
2 a shaped piece of metal which we put on the end of a bolt (see)

nylon /ˈnaɪlɒn/ *noun (no plural)*
a strong thread, made by machines: ***Nylon** is used to make stockings (see) and clothes.*

Oo

oak /əʊk/ *noun*
a tree with hard wood

oar /ɔːʳ/ *noun*
a long bar of wood with a flat blade at the end, used to make a boat move

oar

oasis /əʊˈeɪsɪs/ *noun*
(*plural* **oases** /-siːz/)
a place in the desert where there is water and where trees can grow

oath /əʊθ/ *noun*
a very serious promise: *In court we **take an oath** to tell the truth.*

oats /əʊts/ *noun*
a grain plant

°**obey** /əʊˈbeɪ/ *verb*
to do what you are told to do: *You should **obey** your teacher.*
obedience /əˈbiːdɪəns/ *noun*
(*no plural*) *The dog has learned* **obedience**. *It obeys its owner.*
obedient /əˈbiːdɪənt/ *adjective*

°**object**[1] /ˈɒbdʒɪkt/ *noun*
1 a thing: *What is that big red **object** over there?*
2 an aim or purpose

object[2] *noun*
the person or thing that the action

of a verb is done to; the noun that usually follows the verb: *In the sentence "Jane bought the bread", bread is the **object**.*
Look at **subject**.

object[3] /əbˈdʒekt/ *verb*
to say that you do not like or agree with something: *She **objected to** our plan.*
objection *noun: She had strong* **objections** *to the plan.*

oblige /əˈblaɪdʒ/ *verb (present participle* **obliging**, *past* **obliged**)
to make someone do something: *It was raining so hard that I was* **obliged** *to stay at home.*
obligation /ˌɒblɪˈɡeɪʃn/ *noun* a duty; something we must do

oblong /ˈɒblɒŋ/ *noun, adjective*
a flat shape with four straight sides and four equal angles, that is longer than it is wide

observe /əbˈzɜːv/ *verb (present participle* **observing**, *past* **observed**)
1 to watch something carefully; see and notice something: *The policeman asked if we had* **observed** *anything unusual.*
2 to say

187

observation /ˌɒbzə'veɪʃn/ *noun*
(*no plural*) **1** watching carefully:
The police kept the man **under
observation. 2** something said

obstacle /'ɒbstəkl/ *noun*
something that gets in the way; a
difficulty: *The lorry had to go
slowly because of fallen trees and
other* **obstacles** *on the road.*

obstinate /'ɒbstɪnət/ *adjective*
having a strong will; not willing to
change easily

obstruct /əb'strʌkt/ *verb*
to get in the way of something or
stop it completely: *The road was*
obstructed *by a fallen tree.*
    ob'struction *noun: There was
    an* **obstruction** *on the road.*

obtain /əb'teɪn/ *verb*
to get: *I haven't been able to*
obtain *that book.*

obvious /'ɒbvɪəs/ *adjective*
clear and easy to see or
understand: *It is* **obvious** *that she
is very clever.*
    obviously *adverb:* **Obviously** *the
    thief got in through the door —
    the lock is broken.*

occasion /ə'keɪʒn/ *noun*
a time when something happens,
often something special: *My son's
first birthday is an important*
occasion.
    occasional *adjective* happening
    from time to time
    occasionally /ə'keɪʒnəlɪ/
    *adverb: We go for walks in the
    fields* **occasionally.**

occupy /'ɒkjʊpaɪ/ *verb* (*present
participle* **occupying,** *past*
occupied)
1 to live or be in a place: *Three
families* **occupy** *that big house.*
2 to use time to do something:
While he was waiting, he **occupied**
himself by reading a book. This

work keeps us fully **occupied**
(=busy).
    occupation /ˌɒkjʊ'peɪʃn/ *noun*
    1 a job; a way of using time:
    What is his **occupation?** *He is a
    teacher.* **2** *(no plural)* being in a
    certain place or space

occur /ə'kɜːᵣ/ *verb* (*present
participle* **occurring,** *past*
occurred)
1 to happen, especially of
something unexpected: *The
accident* **occurred** *at five o'clock.*
2 to come into the mind: *That idea
has never* **occurred to** *me before.*

ocean /'əʊʃn/ *noun*
a very large sea: *the* **Atlantic Ocean**
(picture on page 185)

○ **o'clock** /ə'klɒk/ *adverb*
a word used when saying what
hour of the day it is: *What time is
it? It's four* **o'clock** *exactly.*

○ **October** /ɒk'təʊbəᵣ/ *noun*
the tenth month of the year

octopus /'ɒktəpəs/
noun (*plural*
octopuses)
a soft sea
creature,
sometimes very

octopus

large, which has eight long limbs

○ **odd** /ɒd/ *adjective*
1 strange or unusual: *It's* **odd** *that
he hasn't telephoned me.*
2 (of a number) that cannot be
divided by two: *7 and 9 are* **odd**
*numbers, but 6 and 8 are even
numbers.*
3 one of a pair, or not fitting
together as a pair: *I've found an*
odd *shoe — where is the other
one? You've got* **odd** *socks on —
one's blue and the other is green!
In that cupboard there's a box full
of* **odds and ends** (=different
things which are not important).

odour /'əʊdə^r/ *noun*
a smell: *a strange* **odour**

° **of** /əv; *strong* ɒv/ *preposition*
1 belonging to: *a friend* **of** *mine*
2 containing: *a cup* **of** *tea/a kilo* **of** *butter*
3 from among: *I gave my friend some* **of** *my pencils.*
4 made from: *a dress* **of** *cotton*
5 about: *I often think* **of** *you.*
6 (used in some phrases): *He died* **of** *his wounds. England is north* **of** *France.*

of course /əv 'kɔːs/ see **course**

° **off** /ɒf/ *adverb, preposition*
1 away from; from a place: *Take* **off** *that wet shirt, and clean the mud* **off** *your shoes. The dog ran* **off** *down the road.*
2 not on or not working: *Is the light in the kitchen on or* **off**? *I turned it* **off**. *Sunday is my only day* **off** (=when I don't work).
3 at a distance: *My house is not far* **off**.
4 not good or fresh: *If you leave meat in the sun it will go* **off**.

offend /ə'fend/ *verb*
to make someone feel unhappy or angry: *I* **offended** *him by not answering his letter.*
offence *noun* 1 something that is wrong; a crime: *It is an* **offence** *to ride a bicycle at night without lights.* 2 (*no plural*) making someone angry or unhappy; rudeness: *He* **took offence** *because I didn't answer his letter.*

° **offer**¹ /'ɒfə^r/ *verb*
to say or show that we are ready to give or do something: *James* **offered** *me an orange, but I didn't take it. Sarah* **offered** *to carry the box for her mother.*

° **offer**² *noun*
1 when we say we are ready to give or do something: *Thank you for your* **offer** *of help.*
2 the thing we offer: *He would not sell us the car because our* **offer** (=the money we offered) *was too low.*

° **office** /'ɒfɪs/ *noun*
a place where business and paper work is done: *She works in an* **office**.

° **officer** /'ɒfɪsə^r/ *noun*
1 a person who can give orders to other people, in the army, etc.
2 a person who has an important job in the government, a business, etc.: *A policeman is also called a* **police officer**.

official¹ /ə'fɪʃl/ *adjective*
of or from the government or someone important: *an* **official** *letter*

official² *noun*
a person who works in the government: *an* **official** *in the department of health*

° **often** /'ɒfn/ *adverb*
many times: *I* **often** *see her because she lives near me.* **How often** *have you been abroad? Not* **often**, *only twice.*

° **oil**¹ /ɔɪl/ *noun*
(*no plural*)
thick liquid
that comes
from plants or
animals, from
under the

oil rig

ground or under the sea, used for cooking, burning, or for making machines work smoothly: *An* '**oil well** *is a hole made in the ground to get* **oil** *out. The tall machinery above it is called an* '**oil rig**.

° **oil**² *verb*
to put oil on something: *You should* **oil** *that machine often.*

ointment /'ɔɪntmənt/ *noun*
(*no plural*)
smooth oily medicine that can be rubbed on the skin

° **old** /əʊld/ *adjective*
1 not young; having lived a long time: *My grandmother is very* **old**.
2 the word we use to show our age: *How* **old** *are you? I am eleven years* **old**.
3 not new: **old** *clothes/an* **old** *building*
4 having lasted for a long time: *We are very* **old** *friends — we've known each other since we were children.*
   old-'fashioned *adjective* not modern; not common any more: **old-fashioned** *clothes*

olive /'ɔlɪv/ *noun*
a small fruit which is green or black, from the olive tree
   ˌolive 'oil *noun* (*no plural*) oil made from olives and used for food

omelet /'ɒmlɪt/ *noun*
eggs beaten together and cooked in hot fat in a flat pan

omit /ə'mɪt/ *verb* (*present participle* **omitting**, *past* **omitted**)
to leave out; not include: *You have* **omitted** *my name from the list.*

° **on** /ɒn/ *preposition, adverb*
1 (used to show where something is): *I put the glass* **on** *the shelf. There is a list of our lessons* **on** *the wall. The town stands* **on** *the hill.*
2 (used with days or dates, to show when): *The party is* **on** *March 12th. We gave Julie a present* **on** *her birthday.*
3 about: *a lesson* **on** *history*
4 in use; working: *Is the light in the kitchen off or* **on**? *I'll turn it* **on**.
5 continuously; without stopping; further: *I stopped for a rest and James went* **on** *alone.*

6 covering the body: *When I heard the door bell I was in the bath with nothing* **on**, *so I put my clothes* **on** *quickly.*
7 (used in some other ways): *What's* **on** *television tonight?* (=what film or pictures are being shown) **On** *her arrival* (=when she arrived) *she telephoned her mother. Did you come by car or* **on** *foot?* (=walking)

° **once** /wʌns/ *adverb*
1 one time: *I have been to America* **once**, *but my friend has been* **more than once**.
2 some time ago: *My grandmother was* **once** *a teacher in this school.*
3 when: *It was easy* **once** *I learnt how to do it.*
4 (used in some phrases): *Go* **at 'once** (=without waiting), *or you will be late. You can't do three different things* **at once** (=at the same time). *If you can't do it the first time, try* **once more** (=again).

° **one** /wʌn/
1 the number 1: *Only* **one** *person came to the meeting.* **One** *and two make three* $(1+2=3)$.
2 a single thing or person: *Have you any books on farming? — I'd like to borrow* **one** (=a book on farming). *That girl has only got* **one** *shoe on, I wonder where the other* **one** *is.*
3 a: *John telephoned me* **one** *day last week.*
4 the same: *They all ran in* **one** *direction.*
5 any person: **One** *should try to help other people. Mary and I like* **one a'nother** (=Mary likes me and I like her).

oneself /wʌn'self/
the same person as **one** in the sentence: *Sometimes it's nice to sit* **by oneself** (=alone) *and read.*

onion /'ʌnjən/
noun
a round
white
vegetable

onions

with a strong smell, which is made up of one skin inside another

° **only** /'əʊnlɪ/ *adjective, adverb*
1 that is the one person or thing of the same kind or in the same group: *She is the* **only** *girl in her family; all the other children are boys. James is an* **only child** (= his parents have no other children).
2 and nothing more; and no one else: *I don't want to buy anything; I'm* **only** *looking. The sign on the door said "Ladies* **only**".
3 but: *I'll lend you my book,* **only** *you must take care of it.*
4 (used to make something stronger): **If only** *she would come!* (= I want her to come very much) *They've* **only just** *arrived* (= they arrived a very short time ago).

onto /'ɒntə; *strong* 'ɒntʊ/
preposition
to a place: *He climbed* **onto** *a rock.*

onwards /'ɒnwʊdz/ *adverb*
forward in time or space: *They hurried* **onwards**. *From Monday* **onwards** *I shall be in another class.*

ooze /uːz/ *verb* (*present participle* **oozing**, *past* **oozed**)
to move or flow slowly: *The blood* **oozed** *out of the meat.*

° **open**[1] /'əʊpən/ *adjective*
1 not shut or covered: *She's not asleep; her eyes are* **open**. *There is an* **open** *market in the village.*
2 ready for business: *The bank isn't* **open**.
3 not surrounded by other things: *We drove through* **open** *country, where there were no towns or villages. The party was held* **in the open air** (= outside).

° **open**[2] *verb*
1 to make something open or become open: **Open** *your books at page three. The door* **opened** *and my sister walked in.*
2 to start: *The shop doesn't* **open** *until 10 o'clock.*

opener *noun* an instrument for opening things: *a tin-opener*
opening /'əʊpnɪŋ/ *noun* a space or a way through something: *He put a gate across the* **opening** *in the fence.*

opera /'ɒprə/ *noun*
a kind of play which has songs and music instead of spoken words

operate /'ɒpəreɪt/ *verb* (*present participle* **operating**, *past* **operated**)
1 to work or make something work: *Do you know how to* **operate** *this machine?*
2 to cut the body of someone who is ill, to make the unhealthy part better: *The doctors* **operated on** *her stomach.*

operation *noun* **1** (*no plural*) the way a thing works; making something work: *The* **operation** *of a sewing-machine is easy.* **2** cutting a part of the body of someone who is ill: *an* **operation** *on her stomach*
operator /'ɒpəreɪtər/ *noun* **1** a person who makes a machine work: *a telephone* **operator**

° **opinion** /ə'pɪnjən/ *noun*
what someone thinks about something: *He asked his father's* **opinion** *about his plans.* **In my opinion** (= I think), *you're wrong.*

opponent /ə'pəʊnənt/ *noun*
someone who is on the opposite side, in playing or fighting: *We beat our* **opponents** *at football.*

opportunity /ˌɒpə'tjuːnətɪ/ *noun*
(*plural* **opportunities**)
a chance or time to do something:

I have been offered a job. It's a great **opportunity.**

oppose /ə'pəuz/ *verb*
(*present participle* **opposing,** *past* **opposed**)
to be against something; not agree with something: *My mother is* **opposed to** *the new plan.*
  opposition /ˌɒpə'zɪʃn/ *noun:* **opposition** *to his plan*

opposite[1] /'ɒpəzɪt/ *noun*
a person or thing that is as different as possible from another: *High is the* **opposite** *of low.*

° **opposite**[2] *adjective*
1 as different as possible: *The buses went in* **opposite** *directions — one went south and the other went north.*
2 facing: *The library is on the* **opposite** *side of the road from the school.*

° **opposite**[3] *preposition*
facing: *The library is* **opposite** *the school.*

optician /ɒp'tɪʃn/ *noun*
a person who makes and sells glasses for the eyes

option /'ɒpʃn/ *noun*
a choice; the power to choose: *Since the train didn't come, and there was no bus, I had no* **option** *but to wait* (=there was nothing I could do except wait).
  optional *adjective* that you can choose: *Is English an* **optional** *lesson, or does everyone have to learn it?*

° **or** /əʳ; *strong* ɔːʳ/
(used when giving a choice): *Will you have tea* **or** *coffee? I don't know where I left my book —* **either** *at school* **or** *on the bus.*

oral /'ɔːrəl/ *adjective*
spoken, not written: *We're having an* **oral** *test in class this week.*

° **orange**[1] /'ɒrɪndʒ/ *noun*
a round sweet juicy fruit from the orange tree

° **orange**[2] *noun, adjective*
(of) the colour of the skin of an orange when it is ripe; a mixture of yellow and red

orbit[1] /'ɔːbɪt/ *noun*
the path of one thing moving around another in space (picture on page 259)

orbit[2] *verb*
to move in an orbit round something: *The spaceship* **orbited** *the moon.*

orchard /'ɔːtʃəd/ *noun*
a field where fruit trees grow

orchestra
/'ɔːkɪstrə/
noun
a large group
of people who
play musical
instruments
together

orchestra

° **order**[1] /'ɔːdəʳ/ *noun*
1 (*no plural*) being carefully arranged; neatness: *You must try to keep these important papers* **in order.** *The teacher kept the children* **in order** (=made them stay calm and quiet). *The telephone is* **out of order** (=not working).
2 (*no plural*) a special way things are arranged or placed: *The words in this book are in alphabetical* **order** — *so "apple" comes before "banana", and "many" comes before "mend".*
3 something that tells someone what they must do: *Soldiers have to obey* **orders.**
4 (used in some phrases): *He stood on a chair* **in order to** (=so that he could) *reach the top shelf.*

° **order**² *verb*
to say that something must be done, made, brought, etc.: *The officer* **ordered** *the soldiers to attack. I* **ordered** *a new suit from the shop.*

° **ordinary** /'ɔːdnrɪ/ *adjective*
usual or common; not special: *It was a very* **ordinary** *day today — I got up, went to school, came home, ate a meal, and went to bed.* **ordinarily** /'ɔːdɪnrəlɪ, ɔːdɪ'nerəlɪ/ *adverb*

ore /ɔːʳ/ *noun*
a kind of rock or earth in which metal is found: *iron* **ore**

organ /'ɔːɡən/ *noun*
1 a part of an animal or a plant that has a special purpose: *The eyes are the* **organs** *of sight.*
2 a musical instrument which has long pipes. Air goes through the pipes to make the sounds.

° **organize** /'ɔːɡənaɪz/ *verb* (*present participle* **organizing**, *past* **organized**)
to arrange in a careful way; put in order; plan: *Jane* **organized** *the party. She asked people to come and bought the food and drinks.*
organization *noun* **1** (*no plural*) arranging or planning: *Good* **organization** *makes your work easier.* **2** a group of people with a special purpose, like a club or a business: *This country is a member of the United Nations* **Organization.**

origin /'ɒrədʒɪn/ *noun*
the place or people that someone or something comes from: *Many Americans are African* **by origin.**
original /ə'rɪdʒɪnl/ *adjective* **1** first; earliest: *Who was the* **original** *owner of this house?* **2** new and different: *an* **original** *idea for a game* **3** not copied:

This is the **original** *painting, and these others are copies.*
originally /ə'rɪdʒɪnəlɪ/ *adverb* in the beginning: *I live here now, but I wonder who lived here* **originally?**

° **ornament** /'ɔːnəmənt/ *noun*
something which we have because it is beautiful, not because it is useful: *That pot is an* **ornament;** *we don't use it.*
ornamental /ˌɔːnə'mentl/ *adjective: an* **ornamental** *pot*

orphan /'ɔːfn/ *noun*
someone whose mother and father are dead
orphanage *noun* a home for orphan children

ostrich /'ɒstrɪtʃ/ *noun* (*plural* **ostriches**)
a very large bird with long legs which is black and white and cannot fly

ostrich

° **other** /'ʌðəʳ/
1 not the same; a different one; *I sleep in this room, and my brother sleeps in the* **other** *room. Alice didn't like that dress, so she asked to see some* **others.**
2 someone or something not mentioned specially: *The blue pen is mine and all the* **others** (=the other pens) *are yours.*

otherwise /'ʌðəwaɪz/ *adverb*
1 if not: *You should go now,* **otherwise** *you'll miss the bus.*
2 except for that: *I've got one more page to write;* **otherwise** *I've finished.*
3 differently: *We were going to play football, but it was so hot that we decided to do* **otherwise** (=to do something different).

° **ought** /ɔːt/ *verb*
(used to show what someone should or must do, or what is right): *He* **ought to** *take care of his children.*

ounce /aʊns/ *noun*
a measure of weight equal to 28.35 grams (see): *There are 16* **ounces** *in one pound.* **oz** is a short way of writing **ounce.**

° **our** /aʊəʳ/ *adjective*
belonging to us: *We put* **our** *books in* **our** *bags.*

° **ours** /aʊəz/
something that belongs to us: *They left their books at school but we took* **ours** *home.*

ourselves /aʊə'selvz/
the same people as *we* or *us* in the sentence: *We hid* **ourselves** *in the cupboard. We did that* **by ourselves** (= no one helped us). *Our mother never lets us go on the train* **by ourselves** (= without another person).

° **out** /aʊt/ *adverb*
1 not in or inside; away from: *Shut the gate or the dog will get* **out.** *She opened the bag and took* **out** *the money.*
2 not at home or in an office: *My father is* **out** *this morning, but he will be in this afternoon.*
3 not shining or burning: *The lights were* **out** *and the house was dark. The fire went* **out.**
4 (used in sentences like this): *When he called* **out** (= loudly) *I heard him. I feel tired* **out** (= completely tired). *This list is for last year; it's* **out of date** (= old) *now.*

out'door *adjective* not in a building: *an* **outdoor** *pool*
out'doors *adverb:* *A farmer works* **outdoors.**

° **'outer** *adjective* on the outside or edge of something; far away from the middle: *The* **outer** *walls of the house were made of brick.*
'outing *noun* a trip or short journey

outfit /'aʊtfɪt/ *noun*
a set of clothes, especially for a special purpose: *The football team were wearing yellow* **outfits.**

outline /'aʊtlaɪn/ *noun*
a line showing the shape of something: *He drew the* **outline** *of a house on the paper.*

° **outside**[1] /'aʊtsaɪd/ *noun*
the outer part or surface of something: *The* **outside** *of an orange is bitter, but the inside is sweet.*

° **outside**[2] /aʊt'saɪd/
preposition, adverb, adjective
1 to or on the outside of something: **Outside** *the house there was a notice saying "For Sale". The box was red* **outside** *and green inside. The* **outside** *parts of some fruit are not good to eat.*
2 not in a building: *Come* **outside** *and see my bicycle.* **Outside** *the house is a large yard.*

outskirts /'aʊtskɜːts/ *plural noun*
the parts of a town which are not in the centre: *We live on the* **outskirts** *of the city.*

outstanding /aʊt'stændɪŋ/ *adjective*
very good: *an* **outstanding** *pupil*

outwards /'aʊtwʊdz/ *adverb*
towards the outside; away from the middle

oval /'əʊvl/ *noun, adjective*
a round flat shape like an egg (picture on page 185)

oven /'ʌvn/ *noun*
a box which can be made hot to cook food in

○ **over** /ˈəʊvəʳ/ *preposition, adverb*
1 above: *The lamp is hanging* **over** *the table.*
2 covering: *My father went to sleep with a newspaper* **over** *his face.*
3 across; from one side to the other: *He jumped* **over** *the wall. I can see our neighbour* **over** *the fence.*
4 down to a lying position: *He knocked the bottle* **over** *and the oil ran out.*
5 finished: *When we arrived the film was* **over.**
6 more; more than: *Children* **over** *12 don't come to this school.*
7 in every part: **All over** *the world, people like music.*
8 from the start to the finish; again: *Think it* **over** *before you decide. We played the songs* **over and over (again)** (= many times).
9 not used: *If there is any food left* **over** *after dinner, keep it for tomorrow.*

overall /ˈəʊvərɔːl/
noun
a garment
that is put
over
other clothes
to keep them
clean

overall   overalls

overalls /ˈəʊvərɔːlz/ *plural noun*
loose trousers with a top part, worn over other clothes to keep them clean

overboard /ˈəʊvəbɔːd/ *adverb*
over the side of a boat into the water: *He fell* **overboard.**

overcoat /ˈəʊvəkəʊt/ *noun*
a warm coat worn outside when it is cold

overflow /ˌəʊvəˈfləʊ/ *verb*
to flow over the edge of something: *If you put too much water in the pot, it will* **overflow.**

overhead /ˌəʊvəˈhed/ *adverb*
above our heads; in the sky: *The plane flew* **overhead.**

overlook /ˌəʊvəˈlʊk/ *verb*
1 to have or give a sight of something from above: *The house on the hill* **overlooks** *the village.*
2 not to see or notice: *You have* **overlooked** *several of the mistakes in this work.*

overnight /ˌəʊvəˈnaɪt/
adjective, adverb
for the whole night: *We stayed* **overnight** *with my sister.*

overseas /ˌəʊvəˈsiːz/
adverb, adjective
to, in, or of places across the sea from your own country: *My brother lives* **overseas. Overseas** *trade is important to our country.*

overtake /ˌəʊvəˈteɪk/ *verb*
(*present participle* **overtaking,** *past tense* **overtook** /ˌəʊvəˈtʊk/, *past participle* **overtaken**)
to pass another person or vehicle going in the same direction: *The car* **overtook** *the lorry.*

○ **owe** /əʊ/ *verb* (*present participle* **owing,** *past* **owed**)
1 to have to give or pay: *The food cost £3, but I only paid £2 so I still* **owe** *£1.*
2 to feel grateful to someone for something: *He* **owes** *his teachers a lot, because he got a very good job when he left school.*
'owing to *preposition* because of: *They could not cross the river* **owing to** *the flood.*

owl /aʊl/
noun
a large bird
that flies at
night and
kills small
animals for food

owl

° **own**[1] /əʊn/

belonging to oneself: *I like writing with my* **own** *pen. That bicycle isn't his* **own**; *his brother lent it to him. She lives* **on her own** (= with nobody else).

° **own**[2] *verb*

1 to have something that belongs to you: *Who* **owns** *this house?*

2 (used in sentences like this):

When the teacher asked us who had taken the book, John **owned up** (= said he had done it).

'owner *noun* a person who owns something

° **ox** /ɒks/ *noun*

(*plural* **oxen** /'ɒksn/)

a bull (= male cow) which is stopped from having young ones and is used for work on farms

---

Pp

---

pace[1] /peɪs/ *noun*

a step: *He ran forward ten* **paces**.

pace[2] *verb* (*present participle* **pacing**, *past* **paced**)

to walk with slow regular steps: *The lion was* **pacing** *up and down.*

pack[1] /pæk/ *verb*

to put things together in a container: *She* **packed** (*her clothes*), *as she was going away. I can't* **pack** (= fit) *any more books into the box.*

pack[2] *noun*

1 a container of things packed together: *His clothes were in a* **pack** *on his back. He bought a* **pack** *of cards.*

2 a group of animals that hunt together

package /'pækɪdʒ/ *noun*

a parcel: *a* **package** *of books*

packet /'pækɪt/ *noun*

a small container or parcel: *a* **packet** *of cigarettes*

pad /pæd/ *noun*

1 a mass of soft material used to protect a part of the body or a wound

2 a number of sheets of paper stuck together at one edge: *a* **pad** *of writing paper*

paddle[1] /'pædl/ *noun*

a piece of wood with a broad end used for moving a boat through water (picture at **canoe**)

paddle[2] *verb* (*present participle* **paddling**, *past* **paddled**)

1 to move a boat through water using a paddle

2 to walk in water without shoes: *We* **paddled** *in the sea.*

paddy /'pædɪ/ *or* **'paddy field** *noun*

a field for growing rice

padlock

/'pædlɒk/

noun

a lock that

can be used

on doors, boxes, etc.

padlock

° **page** /peɪdʒ/ *noun*

one of the sheets of paper in a book: *The book has 120* **pages**.

paid /peɪd/ see **pay**

pail /peɪl/ *noun*

a bucket

° **pain** /peɪn/ *noun*
a feeling of hurting: *He had a* **pain** *in his head.*
'**painful** *adjective: His head was very* **painful** (= hurt a lot).
pains *plural noun: She* **took pains** (= took trouble, tried hard) *to dress nicely.*

° **paint**¹ /peɪnt/ *noun*
a sticky coloured substance that is used to cover walls, or to colour pictures: *She brought a box of* **paints** *to school. There's* **paint** *on your clothes.*

° **paint**² *verb*
to cover or colour with paint: *He* **painted** *the wall yellow. She* **painted** *a (picture of a) boat.*
'**painter** *noun* a person who paints, either pictures or things like houses, as a job
'**painting** *noun* a painted picture: a **painting** *of a boat*

° **pair** /peəʳ/ *noun*
1 two things of the same kind thought of together: *a* **pair of socks**
2 something with two parts joined together: *a* **pair of scissors**

palace /'pæləs/ *noun*
a large building where an important person, like a king, lives

° **pale** /peɪl/ *adjective* (**paler, palest**)
light or white in colour: *The sky was* **pale** *blue. The baby had* **pale** *skin.*

° **palm**¹ /pɑːm/ *noun*
a tree with a long trunk without branches and a group of large leaves at the top: *Coconuts grow on* **palm trees.**

palm

palm² *noun*
the wide part inside the hand: *He put the insect on the* **palm** *of his hand.*

° **pan** /pæn/ *noun*
a round metal pot for cooking things over heat: *She fried the eggs in a* **frying pan.** *He heated some milk in a* **saucepan.**

panda /'pændə/ *noun*
a large black and white animal like a bear (see) which lives in China

pane /peɪn/ *noun*
a piece of glass used in windows: *Who broke this* **pane** *of glass?*

panel /'pænl/ *noun*
a flat piece of wood used in a door or on a wall

panic¹ /'pænɪk/ *noun*
a sudden fear which can spread quickly: *He felt* **panic** *as the wind blew the flames towards his home.*

panic² *verb* (*present participle* **panicking,** *past* **panicked**)
to feel panic: *He* **panicked** *and ran as fast as he could to safety.*

pant /pænt/ *verb*
to breathe quickly: *He was* **panting** *when he reached the top of the hill.*

pantomime /'pæntəmaɪm/ *noun*
a funny play, usually telling an old story, with songs and dances in it

pantry /'pæntrɪ/ *noun*
(*plural* **pantries**)
a small room in which food is kept

pants /pænts/
plural noun
1 a piece of clothing worn under other clothes from the middle of the body to the top of the legs
2 trousers

pants

°**paper** /ˈpeɪpəʳ/ *noun*

1 (*no plural*) sheets of thin material used for writing, wrapping, etc.: *These pages are made of* **paper.**

2 a newspaper

3 paper with writing or printing on it: *I left my* **papers** *on my desk.*

'**paper clip** *noun: A* **paper clip** *is used to hold papers together.*

parachute /ˈpærəʃuːt/ *noun*

a large round piece of cloth that fills with air, and lets someone

parachute

fall slowly to earth from an aeroplane

parade[1] /pəˈreɪd/ *noun*

a number of people walking or marching together to be seen

parade[2] *verb* (*present participle* **parading,** *past* **paraded**)

to walk in a parade: *The soldiers* **paraded** *through the town.*

paradise /ˈpærədaɪs/ *noun*

a place of complete happiness; heaven (see)

paraffin /ˈpærəfɪn/ *or*

kerosene /ˈkerəsiːn/ *noun* (*no plural*)

a colourless oil that can be burnt and used for cooking and lighting

paragraph /ˈpærəgrɑːf/ *noun*

a piece of writing that begins on a new line: *Read from your book, starting at the second* **paragraph.**

parallel /ˈpærəlel/ *adjective*

always the same distance away from each other: **parallel** *lines* (see picture on page 185)

paralyze /ˈpærəlaɪz/ *verb* (*present participle* **paralyzing,** *past* **paralyzed**)

to prevent someone from being able to move some or all of his body: *The climber was* **paralyzed** *in a fall, and couldn't walk.*

paralysis /pəˈræləsɪs/ *noun* (*no plural*) being unable to move

°**parcel** /ˈpɑːsl/ *noun*

something wrapped in paper and tied, for posting or carrying: *She sent a* **parcel** (*of books*) *to her brother.*

pardon[1] /ˈpɑːdn/ *noun* (*no plural*)

forgiveness: *If someone says something that you do not hear, you can say* **"I beg your pardon?"** *or* **"Pardon?"** *so they will say it again.*

pardon[2] *verb*

to forgive: **Pardon me** — *I didn't hear what you said.*

°**parent** /ˈpeərənt/ *noun*

a father or mother

parish /ˈpærɪʃ/ *noun* (*plural* **parishes**)

an area looked after by one Christian priest or served by one church

°**park**[1] /pɑːk/ *noun*

a large piece of ground in a town used by the public for pleasure: *We were playing in the* **park.**

°**park**[2] *verb*

to leave a car, bus, etc.: *She* **parked** (*the car*) *near the bank.*

parliament /ˈpɑːləmənt/ *noun*

a group of people chosen by the people of a country to make laws

parrot /ˈpærət/ *noun*

a brightly coloured bird with a short curved beak (see)

parrot

°**part**[1] /pɑːt/ *noun*

1 some of a thing or things: *I ate*

part *of the apple, and gave the rest to Jane. A day is divided into 24* **parts,** *called hours.*

2 a share in an activity: *We all* **took part in** *the race.*

3 a character in a play or film: *James acted the* **part** *of the soldier in the play.*

'**partly** *adverb: The accident was* **partly** *my fault* (=it was also other people's fault).

part[2] *verb*

to separate; leave one another: *The friends* **parted:** *Jane went home and Mary went to the library.*

participle /ˈpɑːtɪsɪpl/ *noun*

one of two forms of a verb: *The* **past participle** *of "sing" is "sung" and the* **present participle** *is "singing".*

particular /pəˈtɪkjʊləʳ/ *adjective*

1 special; separate from others: *Have you a* **particular** *reason for choosing this book?*

2 liking things to be just right: *I'm not* **particular** *about my clothes; I don't mind what I wear.*

particularly *adverb: It is* **particularly** *hot today.*

partner /ˈpɑːtnəʳ/ *noun*

a person who is close to another in work, play, etc.: *a dance* **partner** */a business* **partner**

°**party** /ˈpɑːtɪ/ *noun (plural* **parties)**

1 a meeting of friends to enjoy themselves, eat, drink, etc.: *a birthday* **party**

2 a group of people who have the same interests, aims, etc.: *Our teacher is taking a* **party** *of children to the library.*

3 a group of people with the same opinions in politics (see): *Are you a member of a political* **party**?

°**pass**[1] /pɑːs/ *verb*

to move up to, across, and past: *We*

passed *a sign saying "Welcome to the city". How much time has* **passed** *since you came to this school? Please* **pass** (=give) *me your books. The government has* **passed** (=agreed to make) *a new law. Seven children* **passed** *the examination* (=got good enough marks in it). *I* **passed the time** (=did something to amuse myself while waiting) *by counting the cars that drove past the school.*

pass[2] *noun (plural* **passes)**

1 getting good enough marks in an examination: *In this class there were seven* **passes.**

2 a high mountain road

3 a paper allowing you to go somewhere or have something: *I showed my* **pass** *to the man at the factory gate, and was allowed in.*

passage /ˈpæsɪdʒ/ *noun*

1 a narrow path or part of a building: *Sarah's mother was waiting in the* **passage** *outside the doctor's room.*

2 part of a written work: *He read a* **passage** *on rice farming from the geography book.*

°**passenger** /ˈpæsɪndʒəʳ/ *noun*

a person who rides in a car, bus, train, etc., but does not drive it: *There were ten* **passengers** *in the bus. This is a* **passenger** *train, not a goods train.*

passer-by /ˌpɑːsə ˈbaɪ/ *noun (plural* **passers-by)**

someone who goes past, especially in the street: *A* **passer-by** *told me the time.*

passion /ˈpæʃn/ *noun*

a very strong feeling, especially of love or anger: *She spoke with* **passion** *about human rights.*

passionate *adjective* with very strong feelings: *She made a* **passionate** *speech.*

passive /'pæsɪv/ *adjective*
having the action done by someone to something or someone else: *In the sentence "The ball was kicked by John", "was kicked" is a* **passive** *verb.*
The opposite of **passive** is **active**.

passport /'pɑːspɔːt/ *noun*
a little book with your photograph and facts about you in it, which you must have if you are going abroad

° **past**[1] /pɑːst/ *noun* (*no plural*)
all the time which has already gone: **In the past,** *I have always lived in a village; in the future, I shall live in the town.*

° **past**[2] *adjective*
of time, events, etc. in the past: *I've been ill for the* **past** *two weeks.*

° **past**[3] *preposition, adverb*
up to and beyond; by: *Did he drive* **past** *the school? Yes, he drove* **past**, *but he didn't stop. It is* **past** *3 o'clock.*

° **past**[4] *noun, adjective*
talking about an action that has already happened: *The sentence "We saw them yesterday" has the verb in the* **past**. Look at **tense**.

paste /peɪst/ *noun* (*no plural*)
a soft mixture such as that made from flour and water

pastime /'pɑːstaɪm/ *noun*
something that you do for fun: *Swimming is my favourite* **pastime**.

pat[1] /pæt/ *verb* (*present participle* **patting**, *past* **patted**)
to touch lightly with the open hand: *She* **patted** *the baby's cheek.*

pat[2] *noun*
a light touch; patting: *a* **pat** *on the cheek*

patch[1] /pætʃ/ *noun*
a piece of material used for covering a hole in something

patch[2] *verb*
to put a patch on: *You can* **patch** *a bicycle tyre with a piece of rubber.*

patch

° **path** /pɑːθ/ *noun*
a track for walking on: *There was a narrow* **path** *through the forest.*

patient[1] /'peɪʃnt/ *adjective*
able to bear something or wait for something calmly: *I know your leg hurts, just be* **patient** *until the doctor arrives.*
   patience *noun* (*no plural*): *Have* **patience**; *the bus will come soon.*
   patiently *adverb*: *He sat* **patiently** *waiting for the bus.*

patient[2] *noun*
a person who is ill: *The doctor visited his* **patients** *in hospital.*

patrol[1] /pə'trəʊl/ *noun*
1 a small group of policemen or soldiers
2 (*no plural*) keeping watch: *The policeman was* **on patrol**.

patrol[2] *verb* (*present participle* **patrolling**, *past* **patrolled**)
to go round watching for thieves, fires, etc.: *Every hour a policeman* **patrolled** *our street.*

patter /'pætər/ *verb*
to make a light knocking noise: *The rain* **pattered** *on the roof.*

° **pattern** /'pætn/ *noun*
1 an ornamental arrangement of shapes and colours: *a* **pattern** *of flowers on dress material*
2 something you copy if you want to make something: *You can make a dress from this paper* **pattern**.

pause[1] /pɔːz/ *noun*
a short time when you stop what you are doing: *There was a* **pause** *in the talk when Mary came in.*

pause² *verb* (*present participle* **pausing**, *past* **paused**)
to stop for a short time: *When he had run up the hill, he* **paused** *for a minute to rest.*

pavement /ˈpeɪvmənt/ *noun*
a path at the side of a road for people to walk on

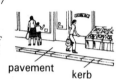

pavement   kerb

paw /pɔː/ *noun*
the foot of an animal such as a dog or cat

pawpaw /ˈpɔːpɔː/ *noun*
a large fruit grown in hot places that has a sweet yellow inside

° **pay**¹ /peɪ/ *verb* (*present participle* **paying**, *past* **paid**)
to give money to someone in exchange for goods or something done for you: *He* **paid** *£3 for the book. Can you lend me some money — I can* **pay** *you* **back** (=return it) *tomorrow!*
  '**payment** *noun*: *He gave the man £3 in* **payment** *for the book.*

° **pay**² *noun* (*no plural*)
the money received for work

pea /piː/ *noun*
a round seed that is used for food

° **peace** /piːs/ *noun* (*no plural*)
1 a time when there is no war or fighting: *War started again after six years of* **peace**.
2 quietness; calm: *the* **peace** *of the country*
  '**peaceful** *adjective* quiet: *It's* **peaceful** *at home when the children are at school.*

peach /piːtʃ/ *noun* (*plural* **peaches**)
a juicy fruit with one large seed and a soft skin

peacock /ˈpiːkɒk/ *noun*
a bird with a large brightly coloured tail

peak /piːk/ *noun*
1 a pointed hill or mountain
2 the front part of a cap (=sort of hat) which sticks forward over the eyes

peal /piːl/ *noun*
a ringing noise, or loud noise: *the* **peal** *of bells/a* **peal** *of thunder*
  peal *verb*

peanut /ˈpiːnʌt/ *noun*
another name for groundnut (see), especially when it is ready for eating

pear /peəʳ/ *noun*
a juicy yellow or green fruit

pearl /pɜːl/ *noun*
a small round white thing, found in the shells of some fish, which is used as an ornament: *Her ring had* **pearls** *on it.*

pebble /ˈpebl/ *noun*
a small stone

peck /pek/ *verb*
to cut or lift with the beak (=bird's mouth): *The hens* **pecked** *at the corn.*

peculiar /pɪˈkjuːljəʳ/ *adjective*
odd; strange; unusual: *a* **peculiar** *smell*

pedal¹ /ˈpedl/ *noun*
the part of a machine which you move with the foot: *a bicycle* **pedal** (picture at **bicycle**)

pedal² *verb* (*present participle* **pedalling**, *past* **pedalled**)
to move pedals with the feet: *We* **pedalled** *slowly up the hill.*

pedestrian /pəˈdestrɪən/ *noun*
a person walking: *This path is only for* **pedestrians**.

peel¹ /piːl/ *noun* (*no plural*)
the outside part of a fruit or

201

vegetable: *Apples have red or green* **peel.**

peel[2] *verb*
to take the peel off: *Please* **peel** *this banana.*

peep[1] /piːp/ *verb*
to look quickly, and sometimes secretly: *I* **peeped**. *through the window to see if she was there.*

peep[2] *noun*
a quick look: *I had a* **peep** *at your new dress.*

peg /peg/ *noun*
1 a wooden or metal hook for hanging clothes, etc.
2 an instrument used to fasten clothes to a string while they are drying: *She hung up the shirt with two* **(clothes) pegs.**

○ **pen**[1] /pen/ *noun*
an instrument for writing which uses a coloured liquid **(ink)** to make marks on paper

pen[2] *noun*
a place for keeping cattle or sheep shut in

penalty /'penltɪ/ *noun*
(plural **penalties)**
a punishment: *What is the* **penalty** *for dangerous driving?*

pence /pens/ see **penny**

○ **pencil** /'pensl/ *noun*
a writing instrument made of wood with a hard grey substance in it which marks the paper

penetrate /'penɪtreɪt/ *verb (present participle* **penetrating,** *past* **penetrated)**
to go into or through: *The knife* **penetrated** *her finger and made it bleed.*

penknife
/'pen,naɪf/
noun (plural
penknives /-naɪvz/)

penknife

a small knife with a folding blade that can be carried in your pocket

penny /'penɪ/ *noun (plural* **pence** *or* **pennies)**
a British coin; there are 100 pence in a pound

pension /'penʃn/ *noun*
money given to someone regularly when they leave work when they are old

○ **people** /'piːpl/ *noun*
the plural noun for **person:** *I saw many* **people** *at the dance.*

○ **pepper** /'pepər/ *noun*
1 *(no plural)* a powder made from the seeds of some plants and used to give food a hot taste
2 the fruit of pepper plants, which can be eaten raw or used in cooking

peppermint /'pepəmɪnt/ *noun*
1 *(no plural)* oil from a plant which is used to give a taste to sweets
2 a sweet that tastes of this

per /pər; *strong* pɜːr/ *preposition*
for each; during each: *How much do you earn* **per** *week? The fruit costs 30 pence* **per** *kilo.*
per cent /pə'sent/ *noun* out of a hundred: *"Sixty* **per cent (60%)** *of the pupils are boys" means that of every hundred pupils, sixty are boys.*

perch /pɜːtʃ/ *verb*
to sit on something narrow: *Birds* **perched** *on the branch.*

○ **perfect**[1] /'pɜːfɪkt/ *adjective*
so good that it cannot be made better: *His reading is* **perfect.**
perfectly *adverb* **1** completely: **perfectly** *happy* **2** in a perfect way: *He reads* **perfectly.**

perfect[2] /pə'fekt/ *verb*
to make very good or perfect: *They worked hard to* **perfect** *their dance.*
per'fection *noun (no plural)*

perform /pə'fɔːm/ *verb*
to act: *The children* **performed** *a play. The singer* **performed** (=sang) *beautifully. I am going to* **perform** (=do) *a difficult job.*
performance *noun:* *Her* **performance** *in the play was very good. The* **performances** (=times when the play is acted, music is played, etc.) *are on the 5th and 6th of this month.*

perfume /'pɜːfjuːm/ *noun* (*no plural*)
a sweet smell; liquid that has a sweet smell: *She was wearing a strong* **perfume.**

○ **perhaps** /pə'hæps/ *adverb*
possibly; it may be: **Perhaps** *our team will win.*

○ **period** /'pɪərɪəd/ *noun*
a length of time: *the happiest* **period** *in my life*

perish /'perɪʃ/ *verb*
to die: *The plants all* **perished** *because there was no rain.*

permanent /'pɜːmənənt/ *adjective*
not changing or moving; fixed: *I have a* **permanent** *job here.*
permanently *adverb*

○ **permit**[1] /pə'mɪt/ *verb* (*present participle* **permitting,** *past* **permitted**)
to allow: *Do you* **permit** *your children to smoke?*
○ **per'mission** *noun* (*no plural*): *You must* **ask permission** *if you want to leave early.*

permit[2] /'pɜːmɪt/ *noun*
a piece of paper saying you are allowed to do something

○ **person** /'pɜːsn/ *noun* (*plural* **people** /'piːpl/ *or* **persons**)
a human being; man, woman, or child: *We need a* **person** *to help us.*
personal *adjective* belonging to or for one person; of one's own:

a **personal** *letter/a* **personal** *friend*
personally *adverb:* **Personally** (=my own opinion is that), *I think he is dishonest, but many people trust him.*

○ **persuade** /pə'sweɪd/ *verb* (*present participle* **persuading,** *past* **persuaded**)
to talk with someone until they agree with what you say: *He* **persuaded** *her to go to school, even though she did not want to.*
persuasion /pə'sweɪʒn/ *noun* (*no plural*): *After a lot of* **persuasion,** *she agreed to go.*

pest /pest/ *noun*
a person or animal that is harmful or annoying: *Insects which eat crops are* **pests.**

pet /pet/ *noun*
1 an animal you look after and keep in your house: *She has two cats as* **pets.**
2 a favourite child: *She's the teacher's* **pet.**

petal /'petl/ *noun*
one of the parts of a flower that are usually brightly coloured (picture at **flower**)

petition /pə'tɪʃn/ *noun*
a letter to a powerful person asking for something: *The villagers all signed a* **petition** *asking for a hospital to be built.*

○ **petrol** /'petrəl/ *noun* (*no plural*)
a liquid used in cars to make the engine work

philosophy /fɪ'lɒsəfɪ/ *noun* (*no plural*)
the study of life and what it means, how we should live, etc.

phone[1] /fəun/ *noun*
a short way of saying **telephone**
phone[2] *verb* (*present participle* **phoning,** *past* **phoned**)
to telephone: *I* **phoned** *my parents.*

°**photograph**¹ /ˈfəʊtəɡrɑːf/ *noun*
a picture made by a camera
photo /ˈfəʊtəʊ/ is a short word
for **photograph.**

°**photograph**² *verb*
to take a photograph of: *We*
photographed *the school team.*
photographer /fəˈtɒɡrəfəʳ/
noun a person who takes
photographs
phoˈtography *noun* (*no plural*)
the art or business of producing
photographs

phrase /freɪz/ *noun*
a group of words that does not
make a full sentence: *"Later that*
day" and "on the way home" are
phrases. Look at **clause.**

physical /ˈfɪzɪkl/ *adjective*
of or about the natural world or
the body: **Physical** *geography is the*
study of mountains, rivers, seas,
and rocks. **Physical** *fitness is*
having a strong healthy body.

physician /fɪˈzɪʃn/ *noun*
a doctor

physics /ˈfɪzɪks/ *plural noun* (*used*
with a singular verb)
the study of natural forces
physicist *noun* a person who
studies physics

piano
/pɪˈænəʊ/
noun
a musical
instrument
·with strings
piano

piano

inside a large wooden frame
pianist /ˈpiːənɪst/ *noun*
a person who plays a piano

°**pick**¹ /pɪk/ *verb*
1 to choose: *I* **picked** *a book to read.*
2 to take up or off with the fingers:
We **picked** *apples (from the tree).*
Pick up *your coat, it should not be*
on the floor!

pick² *noun* (*no plural*)
choice: **Take your pick** (=choose
which you want) *of these books.*

pickaxe /ˈpɪkæks/ *or* **pick** *noun*
a sharp metal tool with a long
handle, for making holes in rock
or hard ground

picnic /ˈpɪknɪk/ *noun*
a meal eaten outside, when you are
away from home: *We had a* **picnic**
by the sea.

°**picture**¹ /ˈpɪktʃəʳ/ *noun*
something represented on paper,
either as a drawing or painting, or
as a photograph: *She drew a*
picture *of me.*

picture² *verb* (*present participle*
picturing, *past* **pictured**)
to imagine: *She* **pictured** *herself at*
school in a foreign country.

°**piece** /piːs/ *noun*
a part of something, or single
thing: *He took a* **piece** *of the cake.*
This page is a **piece** *of paper. The*
plate which I dropped lay **in pieces**
on the floor.

pierce /pɪəs/
verb (*present participle* **piercing,**
past **pierced**)
to make a hole in: *The needle*
pierced *the material.*

°**pig** /pɪɡ/ *noun*
an animal that is kept for its meat

pigeon /ˈpɪdʒən/ *noun*
a bird that is grey or green with
short legs and makes a soft noise

piglet /ˈpɪɡlət/ *noun*
a young pig (see)

°**pile**¹ /paɪl/ *noun*
a number of things put on top of
each other: *a* **pile** *of books*

°**pile**² *verb* (*present participle* **piling,**
past **piled**)
to put in a pile: *She* **piled** *the*
books on the table.

pilgrim /'pɪlgrɪm/ *noun*
a person who goes to pray at a holy place far away from his home
pilgrimage *noun* a journey to a holy place

pill /pɪl/ *noun*
a small ball of medicine which you swallow

pillar /'pɪləʳ/ *noun*
a strong, usually round, stone or metal post: *The roof of the church was supported by stone* **pillars.**

pillow /'pɪləʊ/ *noun*
a soft thing to put your head on when you are in bed
'**pillowcase** *noun* a cloth bag to keep a pillow clean

pilot /'paɪlət/ *noun*
1 a person who drives an aeroplane
2 a person who guides ships into harbour or along rivers

pin[1] /pɪn/
noun
a pointed bit of metal
used for

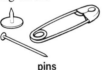

pins

fastening paper, cloth, etc.: *A* '**safety pin** *has a metal covering over the pointed end. A* '**drawing pin** *is a thin nail with a flat head that is used for fastening papers to a board or wall.*

pin[2] *verb* (*present participle* **pinning,** *past* **pinned**)
to fasten with a pin

pinch[1] /pɪntʃ/ *verb*
1 to take something between the fingers and press it: *She* **pinched** *my arm hard, and it still hurts.*
2 to steal: *He* **pinched** *an apple.*

pinch[2] *noun*
a small amount: *A* **pinch of salt** *is the amount you can pick up between your finger and thumb.*

pine /paɪn/ *noun*
a tree that has leaves like needles

pineapple
/'paɪnæpl/ *noun*
the large juicy fruit of the pineapple plant

pineapple

° **pink** /pɪŋk/ *noun, adjective*
(of) the colour made by mixing red and white

pint /paɪnt/ *noun*
a measure of liquid, equal to 0.57 litres: *There are eight* **pints** *in a gallon.*

pioneer /ˌpaɪə'nɪəʳ/ *noun*
someone who goes somewhere or does something before other people: *His grandfather was one of the* **pioneers** *of flying.*

pip /pɪp/ *noun*
the seed of some fruits

° **pipe** /paɪp/ *noun*
a tube: *The water flows along a* **pipe** *to our houses. The man was smoking a* **pipe** (=a short tube with tobacco (see) in it).

pirate /'paɪərət/ *noun*
a robber of ships

pistol /'pɪstl/ *noun*
a small gun

pit /pɪtɪ/ *noun*
1 a deep hole in the ground
2 a mine

pitch[1] /pɪtʃ/ *noun* (*plural* **pitches**)
1 a part of a field on which games are played
2 how high or low a sound is: *a* **high-pitched** *voice*

pitch[2] *verb*
to put up: *The girls* **pitched** *a tent.*

° **pity**[1] /'pɪtɪ/ *noun*
the sadness that you feel when someone else is hurt, in trouble, etc.: *I felt great* **pity** *for the woman whose baby died.* **It's a pity** (=it makes us sorry) *that you have to go so soon.*

pity[2] *verb* (*present participle* **pitying**, *past* **pitied**)

to feel sadness for someone else: *We all **pitied** the woman whose baby died.*

place[1] /pleɪs/ *noun*

1 where something is: *The right **place** for the bowl is on the shelf.*
2 space for something: *There are no **places** left to sit on the train.*
3 a town, village, etc.: *What is this **place** called?*
4 a building: *A school is a **place** to learn things.*

place[2] *verb* (*present participle* **placing**, *past* **placed**)

to put: *She **placed** a book on the table.*

plain[1] /pleɪn/ *adjective*

easy to see, hear, or understand; simple: *He made it **plain** that he did not like me. She wore a **plain** brown dress.*

plainly *adverb*: *It was **plainly** (=clearly) too hot to be working in the sun.*

plain[2] *noun*

a flat piece of country

plait[1] /plæt/ *verb*

to twist together three or more pieces of rope, hair, etc.

plait[2] *noun*

a length of something that is plaited: *She wore her hair in **plaits**.*

plait

plan[1] /plæn/ *noun*

1 something you have decided to do, and how to do it: *We listened as he told us his **plan** for starting a football club.*
2 a drawing of a new building

plan[2] *verb* (*present participle* **planning**, *past* **planned**)

to think about what you are going

to do and how to do it: *The government **plans** to build a bridge.*

plane /pleɪn/ *noun*

a short word for **aeroplane**

planet /'plænɪt/ *noun*

one of the large masses like the Earth that go round a sun

plank /plæŋk/ *noun*

a long, flat, thin piece of wood

plant[1] /plɑːnt/ *noun*

something living that is not an animal: *Trees and vegetables are **plants**.*

plant[2] *verb*

to put in the ground to grow: *Have you **planted** any vegetables yet?*

plan'tation *noun* a large piece of land on which tea, sugar, cotton, or rubber is grown

plaster[1] /'plɑːstəʳ/ *noun*

1 (*no plural*) a soft white material which is spread on walls and becomes hard and smooth when it is dry
2 a piece of cloth with medicine on it which you can stick over a cut

plaster[2] *verb*

to cover with plaster or other soft material

plastic /'plæstɪk/ *adjective, noun*

a strong man-made substance used for strong containers, toys, etc.: *If you drop a **plastic** bowl, it will not break.*

plate /pleɪt/ *noun*

a flat dish: *a **plate** of food*

platform /'plætfɔːm/ *noun*

1 a part of a station where you get on and off trains: *The train at **Platform** 2 goes to the city.*
2 a raised part: *The headmaster stood on a **platform** at one end of the hall.*

play[1] /pleɪ/ *verb*

1 to amuse yourself; take part in

a game: *The children were* **playing**
with a ball. He **plays** *football.*
2 to make sounds on a musical
instrument: *She* **plays** *the drum.*
'**player** *noun: a football* **player**
'**playground** *noun: All the
schoolchildren ran about in the
playground.*

°**play**² *noun*
1 (*no plural*) amusement: *The
children were* **at play** *in the yard.*
2 a story acted in a theatre, as a
film, on the radio, etc.: *She is in a*
play *about a famous singer.*

°**pleasant** /'plezt/ *adjective*
nice; enjoyable: *We spent a*
pleasant *day in the country.*
pleasantly *adverb*

°**please**¹ /pliːz/ *verb* (*present
participle* **pleasing**, *past* **pleased**)
to give happiness or pleasure to: *I
am* **pleased** *that you have a new
job. He is* **pleased with** *his new job.*
°**pleasure** /'pleʒəʳ/ *noun: It gives
me* **pleasure** *to see you looking
happy. I will help you* **with
pleasure** (=willingly).

°**please**²
a word added to a question or an
order, to make it polite: **Please**
bring your book to me.

°**plenty** /'plentɪ/
a lot; enough: *We have* **plenty of**
*time to catch the train. She
thought there wasn't enough
bread, but there was* **plenty.**
plentiful *adjective: Fruit is*
plentiful *in summer.*

pliers /'plaɪəz/
plural noun
a tool like
scissors used for

pliers

cutting wire or for holding things:
Have you got **a pair of pliers?**

plot¹ /plɒt/ *noun*
a small piece of ground, especially
for growing vegetables

plot² *noun*
1 a secret plan, usually to do
something wrong
2 the story of a book, film, etc.:
The film had an exciting **plot.**

plot³ *verb* (*present participle*
plotting, *past* **plotted**)
to plan (something wrong): *We
were* **plotting** *to rob a bank.*

plough¹ /plaʊ/ *noun*
an instrument for cutting up and
turning over the earth

plough² *verb*
to cut up the earth with a plough:
A farmer must **plough** *the land
before planting crops.*

pluck /plʌk/ *verb*
to pull off: *When you kill a
chicken to eat, you have to* **pluck**
it (=pull the feathers off).

plug¹ /plʌg/   socket
noun
1 a round
piece of
rubber, plastic,
etc. which
stops water

plugs

running   out   of   a   basin
2 a metal and plastic thing joined
to an electric wire, which you put
into holes called electric sockets
(see) in the wall

plug² *verb* (*present participle*
plugging, *past* **plugged**)
1 to put a plug in something: *How
can I* **plug** *the hole in this bucket?*
2 to put an electric plug in a special
part (**socket**) in a wall: *to* **plug in**
a lamp

plum /plʌm/ *noun*
a sweet juicy red fruit with one
large seed

plumbing /'plʌmɪŋ/ *noun*
(*no plural*)
all the water pipes, containers, etc.
put in a building so that there can

be running water: *A* **plumber** /'plʌmə^r/ *is a person who fits and mends the* **plumbing.**

plump /plʌmp/ *adjective*
nicely fat: *the baby's* **plump** *arms*

plural /'pluərəl/ *adjective, noun*
more than one: *"Dogs" is the* **plural** *of "dog".* The opposite of **plural** is **singular.**

plus /plʌs/ *preposition*
added to; and: *Four* **plus** *two is six* $(4+2=6)$.

p.m. /piː'em/
in the afternoon or evening: *It is 4.30* **p.m.**

° **pocket** /'pɒkɪt/ *noun*
a piece of material sewn onto clothes to make a little bag to keep things in
'**pocket money** *noun* money given to a child every week to spend as he or she wants

pod /pɒd/ *noun*
in some plants, a long part in

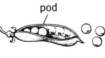
pod

which the seeds grow: *Peas and beans grow in* **pods.**

poem /'pəʊɪm/ *noun*
writing with regular lines and sounds that expresses something in powerful or beautiful language: *He wrote a* **poem** *about war.*
poet *noun: A* **poet** *writes poems.*
poetry *noun (no plural)* poems

° **point**[1] /pɔɪnt/ *verb*
to show, especially with a finger stretched out: *The signpost* **pointed** *to the school. He* **pointed** *his pen at the student and said "Go on reading".*
'**pointed** *adjective* sharp at one end: *a* **pointed** *stick*

° **point**[2] *noun*
1 a sharp end: *the* **point** *of a nail*

2 importance; purpose: *I don't see the* **point** *of waiting for her, she is probably not coming.*
3 mark: *Our team won ten* **points.**
4 time: *At the* **point** *when I left, the teacher was reading a story.*

poison[1] /'pɔɪzn/ *noun (no plural)*
a substance which kills or harms you if it gets into your body
poisonous *adjective*

poison[2] *verb*
to kill with poison: *The farmer* **poisoned** *the rats.*

poke /pəʊk/ *verb (present participle* **poking,** *past* **poked)**
to push a pointed thing into someone or something: *He* **poked** *the fire with a stick.*

° **pole**[1] /pəʊl/ *noun*
a long narrow piece of wood: *A* **pole** *for a flag is called a* **flagpole.**

pole[2] *noun*
one end of the Earth: *The* **North Pole** *is the part of the Earth that is furthest north; the* **South Pole** *is the furthest south.* (picture at **earth**)

° **police** /pə'liːs/ *noun (no plural)*
the people who make sure that everyone obeys the law: *Policemen and policewomen work at a police station.*

policy /'pɒləsɪ/ *noun (plural* **policies)**
a general plan: *It is the* **policy** *of the government to improve education.*

polish[1] /'pɒlɪʃ/ *verb*
to rub something so that it shines: *He* **polished** *the car.*

polish[2] *noun (no plural)*
an oily substance which helps to make things shine

° **polite** /pə'laɪt/ *adjective* (**politer, politest)**
having a kind and respectful way

of behaving; not rude: *You should be* **polite** *to everyone.*

politics /'pɒlətɪks/ *plural noun*
the study of government; how countries should be governed: *an argument about* **politics**

    political /pə'lɪtɪkl/ *adjective* of or about government: *A* **political party** *is a group of people who agree about politics.*

    politician /,pɒlə'tɪʃn/ *noun* a person who takes part, or wants to take part in the government of a country

polytechnic /,pɒlɪ'teknɪk/ *noun*
a college where you can study technical (see) subjects

pond /pɒnd/ *noun*
a pool of water: *a* **pond** *with fish in it*

°**pool** /puːl/ *noun*
an area of a liquid: *There were* **pools** *of water in the holes in the road. a* '**swimming pool**

°**poor** /pʊəʳ/ *adjective*
1 not having much money: *a* **poor** *family*
2 needing kindness or help: *The* **poor** *animal hadn't been fed.*
3 not good: *Your writing is* **poor.**

pop[1] /pɒp/ *noun*
a sudden noise like the sound of the top being pulled out of a bottle

pop[2] *noun* (*no plural*)
music or songs that many younger people like and dance to: *A* **pop group** *plays* **pop music.**

pope /pəʊp/ *noun*
the head of the Roman Catholic (see) church

°**popular** /'pɒpjʊləʳ/ *adjective*
liked by many people: *She is* **popular** *at school. This dance is* **popular** *with young people.*

    popularity /,pɒpjʊ'lærətɪ/ *noun* (*no plural*)

population /,pɒpjʊ'leɪʃn/ *noun*
the number of people living in a place: *What is the* **population** *of this city?*

pork /pɔːk/ *noun* (*no plural*)
meat from pigs

porridge /'pɒrɪdʒ/ *noun* (*no plural*)
food made by boiling grain in water until it is very soft

°**port** /pɔːt/ *noun*
a harbour, or a town with a harbour

porter /'pɔːtəʳ/ *noun*
a person who carries bags and other things for people

portion /'pɔːʃn/ *noun*
a part or share of something: *She only eats a small* **portion** *of food.*

portrait /'pɔːtreɪt/ *noun*
a picture of a person: *He painted a* **portrait** *of his daughter.*

°**position** /pə'zɪʃn/ *noun*
1 a place where a person or thing is: *The telephone is in a bad* **position** — *I cannot reach it.*
2 a job: *He has an important* **position** *in the company.*
3 the state or condition of a person: *I am not* **in a position** *to lend you money* (= I am unable to).

positive /'pɒzətɪv/ *adjective*
sure: *I am* **positive** *that I gave you his address.*

    positively *adverb: I* **positively** *hate* (=hate very much) *fish.*

possess /pə'zes/ *verb*
to have or own: *She* **possesses** *some interesting pictures.*

    pos'session *noun: He had few* **possessions** (=things he owned).

°**possible** /'pɒsəbl/ *adjective*
able to happen: *Is it* **possible** *to get to the city by train, or must I take a bus?*

°**possi'bility** *noun* (*plural* **possibilities**): *Is it a* **possibility** *that you will work abroad?*

'possibly *adverb: I can't* **possibly** *eat all that food* (= I cannot do it at all). *You may* **possibly** (= It may happen that) *get a new job.*

°**post**[1] /pəʊst/ *noun*
a thick bar of wood, metal, or stone fixed in the ground: *The fence was held up by wooden* **posts.**

°**post**[2] *verb*
to send a letter or parcel

°**post**[3] *noun* (*no plural*)
the way of sending letters, etc.; mail (see): *You can send letters* **by post.**

'postage *noun* (*no plural*) the amount of money paid for something posted: (*Postage*) **stamps** *show how much* **postage** *has been paid.*

'postcard *noun* a small card which you can write a message on and send by post

postcard

'postman *noun* a man who collects and gives out letters and parcels

'post office *noun* a place where you can buy stamps, post parcels, etc.

post[4] *noun*
a job: *I am hoping to get a better* **post** *next year.*

poster /'pəʊstə[r]/ *noun*
a large printed paper advertising something

postpone /pəs'pəʊn/ *verb*
(*present participle* **postponing,** *past* **postponed**)
to change the time of some event to a later time: *We* **postponed** *the*

match from March 5th to March 19th.

°**pot** /pɒt/ *noun*
a container, especially a round one, made of baked clay: *She made a* **pot** *of coffee. The flowers were growing in* (**flower**) **pots.**

'pottery *noun* (*no plural*) dishes, pots, etc. made of baked clay; the art of making these things

potato /pə'teɪtəʊ/ *noun*
(*plural* **potatoes**)
a vegetable found under the ground and cooked before eating

poultry /'pəʊltrɪ/ *noun* (*no plural*)
hens and other birds kept for eggs or meat

pounce /paʊns/ *verb* (*present participle* **pouncing,** *past* **pounced**)
to jump on suddenly: *The cat* **pounced** *on the bird.*

°**pound**[1] /paʊnd/ *noun*
the money used in Britain and some other places: *I bought a car for five hundred* **pounds** (*£500*).

pound[2] *noun*
a measure of weight equal to ·454 kilograms (see): *a* **pound** *of rice* **lb** *is a short way of writing* **pound.**

pound[3] *verb*
to crush by hitting hard and often: *She* **pounded** *the corn.*

°**pour** /pɔː[r]/ *verb*
to flow or cause to flow: *She* **poured** *the tea* (*from the teapot into the cups*). *It was* **pouring** (*with rain*).

poverty /'pɒvətɪ/ *noun* (*no plural*)
the state of being poor: *She has lived* **in poverty** *all her life.*

°**powder** /'paʊdə[r]/ *noun* (*no plural*)
fine grains like dust: *They washed the clothes with soap* **powder.**

°**power** /'paʊə[r]/ (*no plural*)
strength or force: *The* **power** *of*

falling water is used to make electricity. The teacher has **power** *over his pupils* (= he can tell them what to do, punish them, etc.).
powerful *adjective: The headmaster is a* **powerful** *man.*

practical /'præktɪkl/ *adjective*
about or good at doing rather than thinking: *He is very* **practical** — *he can make or mend almost anything.*
practically *adverb* almost: *I've* **practically** *finished* — *I'll come in a minute.*

°**practice** /'præktɪs/ *noun*
(*no plural*) doing something to improve how you do it: *You need more* **practice** *before you can play for our team.*

°**practise** /'præktɪs/ *verb* (*present participle* **practising**, *past* **practised**)
to go on doing something so as to become better at it: *You won't become a good singer if you don't* **practise.**

°**praise**[1] /preɪz/ *verb* (*present participle* **praising**, *past* **praised**)
to speak well of; say that you admire: *She* **praised** *her daughter's hard work.*

°**praise**[2] *noun* (*no plural*)
praising; admiration: *He gave a speech in* **praise** *of the school.*

pram /præm/ *noun*
a wheeled vehicle for a baby which is pushed by hand

°**pray** /preɪ/ *verb*
to talk to God or a god; ask for something: *She* **prayed** *silently.*
prayer /preəʳ/ *noun* praying; words said in praying

preach /priːtʃ/ *verb*
to give a religious talk; talk to people about how they should live, etc. '**preacher** *noun*

precaution /prɪ'kɔːʃn/ *noun*
something that is done to prevent something else happening: *He took the* **precaution** *of locking his door when he went out.*

precious /'preʃəs/ *adjective*
worth a lot of money; very much loved: *a* **precious** *stone*

predict /prɪ'dɪkt/ *verb*
to say what is going to happen: *The teacher* **predicted** *that we would all pass the examination.*
prediction *noun*

prefect /'priːfekt/ *noun*
a boy or girl who helps to keep the pupils in order in a school

prefer /prɪ'fɜːʳ/ *verb*
(*present participle* **preferring**, *past* **preferred**)
to like better: *Which of these two dresses do you* **prefer?**
preference /'prefrəns/ *noun*

prefix /'priːfɪks/ *noun*
(*plural* **prefixes**)
letters that can be added to the beginning of another word to change the meaning: *If we add the* **prefix** *"un" to the word "happy", we make the word "unhappy".* Look at **suffix.**

pregnant /'pregnənt/ *adjective*
about to have a child: *A woman is* **pregnant** *for nine months before a child is born.*

prejudice /'predʒədɪs/ *noun*
an opinion formed before you know all the facts about something: *Why have you a* **prejudice** *against women drivers? They can drive just as well as men.*

°**prepare** /prɪ'peəʳ/ *verb*
(*present participle* **preparing**, *past* **prepared**)
to make ready: *I* **prepared** *the ground for the seeds.*
preparation /ˌprepə'reɪʃn/ *noun*

preposition /ˌprepəˈzɪʃn/ *noun*
a word like *to, for, on, by,* etc.; a word which is put in front of a noun to show where, when, how, etc.: *She sat* **by** *the fire. They went* **to** *town.*

prescription /prɪˈskrɪpʃn/ *noun*
a paper written by a doctor, ordering medicine for someone: *The doctor wrote me a* **prescription** *for medicine for my cough.*

° **present**[1] /ˈprezənt/ *adjective*
1 here; in this place: *There are twenty children* **present.**
2 now: *What is your* **present** *job?*

° **present**[2] *noun*
this time: **At present,** *he is on holiday.*
presently *adverb* in a short time

° **present**[3] *noun, adjective*
talking about an action that is happening now: *The sentence "We see them every day" has the verb in the* **present.** Look at **tense.**

° **present**[4] *noun*
something given to someone: *He gave his mother a* **present.**

present[5] /prɪˈzent/ *verb*
to give: *He* **presented** *me with some flowers.*

preserve /prɪˈzɜːv/ *verb* (*present participle* **preserving,** *past* **preserved**)
to keep from being damaged, or from going bad: *You can* **preserve** *meat or fish in salt.*
preservation /ˌprezəˈveɪʃn/ *noun*

president /ˈprezɪdənt/ *noun*
1 the head of government in many countries that do not have a king
2 the head of a big company, a club, etc.

° **press**[1] /pres/ *verb*
1 to push steadily on: *He* **pressed** *the doorbell.*
2 to make flat: *I've* **pressed** *your trousers with the iron.*
pressure /ˈpreʃər/ *noun* (*no plural*): *Do not put much* **pressure** *on the handle, it may break.*

press[2] *noun*
1 (*plural* **presses**) a machine for printing
2 (*no plural*) newspapers: *He works for the* **press.**

° **pretend** /prɪˈtend/ *verb*
to do something to make people believe something untrue: *He* **pretended** *that he was ill so that he could stay at home.*

° **pretty**[1] /ˈprɪtɪ/ *adjective* (**prettier, prettiest**)
beautiful: *a* **pretty** *girl*

pretty[2] *adverb*
fairly; quite: *It was a* **pretty** *serious accident.*

° **prevent** /prɪˈvent/ *verb*
to stop something happening: *Try to* **prevent** *fires in dry weather.*
prevention *noun* (*no plural*): **Prevention** *of illness is better than curing it.*

previous /ˈpriːvɪəs/ *adjective*
happening before; coming before in time: *In my* **previous** *job, I used to travel to the city every day.*
previously *adverb*

prey /preɪ/ *noun* (*no plural*)
something that is hunted and caught: *The big bird carried its* **prey** *in its claws* (= hooked toes).

° **price** /praɪs/ *noun*
the money that you must pay for something: *The* **price** *of that house is high.*

° **prick** /prɪk/ *verb*
to make a small wound with something sharp: *The needle* **pricked** *her hand.*

° **prickle** /'prɪkl/
noun
a sharp part
of a plant or
animal
prickly
adjective
(**pricklier,**
prickliest) having sharp pieces on
it

prickles

° **pride** /praɪd/ *noun* (*no plural*)
the feeling of having a high
opinion of yourself or things that
are yours; being proud: *She
showed us her new home with
great* **pride.**

° **priest** /priːst/ *noun*
a religious person whose job is to
lead ceremonies, say prayers, and
look after the religious part of
people's lives

primary /'praɪmərɪ/ *adjective*
first: *A* **primary** *school is the first
school you go to.*

prime minister /ˌpraɪm 'mɪnɪstər/
noun
the head of government in many
countries

primitive /'prɪmətɪv/ *adjective*
early in history; simple: **Primitive**
people used **primitive** *tools.*

prince /prɪns/ *noun*
1 the son of a king or queen
2 the ruler of a country

princess /prɪn'ses/ *noun*
1 the daughter of a king or queen
2 the wife of a prince

principal[1] /'prɪnsɪpl/ *adjective*
the most important; chief: *What is
your* **principal** *reason for staying
here?* **principally** *adverb*

principal[2] *noun*
the head of a school, college, etc.

principle /'prɪnsɪpl/ *noun*
a rule for living in a way you think
is right: *It is a* **principle** *of mine to*

help people when I can.

° **print**[1] /prɪnt/ *verb*
to press words and pictures on
paper or cloth by machine: *You are
reading a* **printed** *book.*
printer *noun*

print[2] *noun*
something printed: *The book was
in large* **print** (=had big letters).

° **prison** /'prɪzn/ *noun*
a place where criminals are kept as
a punishment: *He was in* **prison**
for ten years.
prisoner *noun* someone who is
kept in prison

private /'praɪvɪt/ *adjective*
belonging to one person or group;
not public: *This is* **private** *land,
you can't walk across it. Can I
speak to you* **in private** (=with no
one else there)? **privately** *adverb*

privilege /'prɪvɪlɪdʒ/ *noun*
a favour allowed to one or only a
few people: *I had the* **privilege** *of
meeting the queen.*

° **prize** /praɪz/ *noun*
something that you win: *I won a
prize for running.*

probable /'prɒbəbl/ *adjective*
likely: *It is* **probable** *that I shall be
working here next year.*
probably *adverb: It will* **probably**
rain.

problem /'prɒbləm/ *noun*
a difficult question; a cause of
worry: *The* **problem** *was how to
move the heavy machinery.*

proceed /prə'siːd/ *verb*
to go; go on: *After stopping to rest,
they* **proceeded** *up the hill.*

process /'prəʊses/ *noun*
(*plural* **processes**)
a number of actions one after
another: *Building a car is a long
process.

213

procession
/prəˈseʃn/
noun
a number of
people

procession
following one another: *They watched the* **procession** *go past.*

○ **produce**[1] /prəˈdjuːs/ *verb* (*present participle* **producing**, *past* **produced**)
to make or bring out: *That factory* **produces** *cars. He* **produced** *some sweets from his pocket.*

○ **product** /ˈprɒdʌkt/ *noun: The company sells plastic* **products.**

○ **production** /prəˈdʌkʃn/ *noun* (*no plural*) making: *the* **production** *of cars*

produce[2] /ˈprɒdjuːs/ *noun* (*no plural*)
something produced by growing or farming: *The farmer's* **produce** *was vegetables and fruit.*

profession /prəˈfeʃn/ *noun*
an employment which needs special learning: *Teaching is a* **profession.**

professional *adjective: He got* **professional** *advice* (= from someone who has learnt the profession) *from his doctor.*

professor /prəˈfesəʳ/ *noun*
a teacher of the highest class in a university (see)

profit /ˈprɒfɪt/ *noun*
money gained when you sell something for more than you paid for it: *The fruit seller made a penny* **profit** *on each orange.*

profitable *adjective: Selling oranges is* **profitable.**

programme /ˈprəʊɡræm/ *noun*
1 a list of things which are planned to happen: *A* **programme** *for a play contains a list of the actors' names and other information*

about the play.
2 something sent out by radio or television: *We watched a* **programme** *about farming.*

progress[1] /ˈprəʊɡres/ *noun* (*no plural*)
going forward; becoming better: *You have made* **progress** *with your English.*

progress[2] /prəˈɡres/ *verb*
to go forward; get better: *Our company cannot* **progress** *until we employ more people.*

project /ˈprɒdʒekt/ *noun*
a plan for a special thing: *a* **project** *to build a new road*

prominent /ˈprɒmɪnənt/ *adjective*
1 noticeable, especially because it is tall or large: *a* **prominent** *nose*
2 important: *a* **prominent** *doctor*

○ **promise**[1] /ˈprɒmɪs/ *verb* (*present participle* **promising**, *past* **promised**)
to say you will do something: *She* **promised** *her brother that she would write to him. She* **promised** *to write to him.*

○ **promise**[2] *noun*
something you have said you will do: *She* **made a promise** *to her brother. He* **broke his promise** *and did not come to see me.*

promote /prəˈməʊt/ *verb* (*present participle* **promoting**, *past* **promoted**)
to give someone a better job: *Our teacher has been* **promoted** *to headmaster.*

promotion *noun: Our teacher has got a* **promotion.**

prompt /prɒmpt/ *adjective*
quick; without delay: *a* **prompt** *answer*

pronoun /ˈprəʊnaʊn/ *noun*
a word like *he, she, it, they,* etc., which is used instead of using a

noun again: *Instead of saying "Peter went to school" we can use a* **pronoun** *and say "He went to school".*

pronounce /prə'naʊns/ *verb* (*present participle* **pronouncing,** *past* **pronounced**)
to speak the sounds of a word: *How do you* **pronounce** *this word?*
pronunciation /prə,nʌnsɪ'eɪʃn/ *noun* (*no ·plural*) the way of saying words: *What is the* **pronunciation** *of this word?*

° **proof** /pruːf/ *noun* (*no plural*)
facts which prove something: *Have you any* **proof** *that he took the money?*

propeller
/prə'pelər/ *noun*
a wheel of curved blades which turn quickly to make a ship or aeroplane move

propeller

proper /'prɒpər/ *adjective*
correct; right for the time and place: *You aren't wearing* **proper** *clothes for this hot weather.*
properly *adverb*: *You haven't done the job* **properly** *— you'll have to do it again.*

° **property** /'prɒpətɪ/ *noun* (*plural* **properties**)
something, usually land or buildings, belonging to someone: *This book is not your* **property.**

prophet /'prɒfɪt/ *noun*
1 someone who says what is going to happen in the future
2 a man who believes that God has told him to teach or lead a special religion: *Mohammed is the* **prophet** *of the Muslims.*
prophecy /'prɒfəsɪ/ *noun* (*plural* **prophecies**) what

someone says will happen; the words of a prophet

proportion /prə'pɔːʃn/ *noun*
the amount of something compared to something else: *The* **proportion** *of girls to boys in the school is about equal.*

propose /prə'pəʊz/ *verb* (*present participle* **proposing,** *past* **proposed**)
1 to give as an idea: *He* **proposed** *that we should go for a walk.*
2 to ask someone to marry you: *He* **proposed** *to her, and she accepted.*
proposal *noun*

prosper /'prɒspər/ *verb*
to do well; become rich: *His company is* **prospering.**
prosperity /prɒ'sperətɪ/ *noun* (*no plural*)
prosperous /'prɒspərəs/ *adjective*: *a* **prosperous** *family*

° **protect** /prə'tekt/ *verb*
to prevent someone or something from being harmed, damaged, etc.: *The fence is to* **protect** *the farmer's cattle.*
° **pro'tection** *noun* (*no plural*): *Her coat gave her* **protection** *from the rain.*

protest[1] /prə'test/ *verb*
to say strongly that you do not agree with something: *The children* **protested** *when they were punished unfairly.*

protest[2] /'prəʊtest/ *noun*
a complaint: *The people made a* **protest** *about the rise in prices.*

Protestant /'prɒtɪstənt/ *noun, adjective*
(a person) belonging to a Christian church that is not Roman Catholic (see)

° **proud** /praʊd/ *adjective*
having a high opinion of yourself or of something that is yours: *He*

is **proud** *of his daughter's ability to speak four languages. She is too* **proud** *to walk to school with the other children.* 'proudly *adverb*

° **prove** /pruːv/ *verb* (*present participle* **proving**, *past* **proved**)
to show that something is true: *I can* **prove** *that you were in town — James saw you there.*

proverb /ˈprɒvɜːb/ *noun*
a short well-known saying

provide /prəˈvaɪd/ *verb* (*present participle* **providing**, *past* **provided**)
to give: *We* **provided** *food for the hungry children.*
  provided (that) if and only if: *You may go out,* **provided (that)** *you come home before dark.*
  ° **provision** /prəˈvɪʒn/ *noun*: *The* **provision** *of food for all the children was difficult. When I went fishing, I took a day's* **provisions** (= food and drink).

province /ˈprɒvɪns/ *noun*
an area of a country, often having its own government for education, hospitals, etc.
  provincial /prəˈvɪnʃl/ *adjective*

° **public**[1] /ˈpʌblɪk/ *adjective*
open to everyone; for the use of the people in general: *This is a* **public** *park, we can all go into it. I do not want to speak about it* **in public** (= with other people there).

° **public**[2] *noun* (*no plural*)
people: *The* **public** *can use this park.*

publish /ˈpʌblɪʃ/ *verb*
to print and sell: *This company* **publishes** *children's books.*
  publication /ˌpʌblɪˈkeɪʃn/ *noun*: *The* **publication** *of his book will be next month.*
  'publisher *noun* a person or company that publishes

puff[1] /pʌf/ *verb*
to breathe quickly: *I was* **puffing** *after swimming so far.*

puff[2] *noun*
a short burst of air, smoke, etc.: *A* **puff** *of wind blew the papers off the table.*

° **pull**[1] /pʊl/ *verb*
to move something towards yourself or by going in front of it: *He* **pulled** *his hand out of the hot water. A horse* **pulled** *the cart along the road. The house is going to be* **pulled down**, *as it is not safe.*

° **pull**[2] *noun*
an act of pulling: *He gave a* **pull** *on the rope.*

pullover
/ˈpʊləʊvəʳ/ *noun*
a woollen garment that covers the top part of the body, and is pulled over the head

pullover

pulse /pʌls/ *noun*
the beating of your heart: *The doctor* **felt her pulse** *on her wrist.*

° **pump**[1] /pʌmp/ *noun*
a machine for making liquid or gas move: *A bicycle* **pump** *puts air into the tyres.*

° **pump**[2] *verb*
to move something with a pump: **Pump up** (= put air into) *your tyres before you go.*

pumpkin /ˈpʌmpkɪn/ *noun*
a large round yellow fruit that is used as a vegetable

punch[1] /pʌntʃ/ *verb*
1 to hit: *He* **punched** *him on the nose.*
2 to make a hole in: *He* **punched** *two holes in the tin of oil, and then poured it out.*

punch[2] *noun* (*plural* **punches**)
a blow: *a* **punch** *on the nose*

punctual /'pʌŋktʃʊəl/ *adjective*
coming at the right time; not late: *She is always* **punctual,** *but her friend is always late.*
punctually *adverb*

punctuate /'pʌŋktʃʊeɪt/ *verb* (*present participle* **punctuating,** *past* **punctuated**)
to put punctuation (see) into writing

punctuation /ˌpʌŋktʃʊ'eɪʃn/ *noun* (*no plural*)
signs like , ; . and ? used to end or break up writing

puncture[1] /'pʌŋktʃər/ *noun*
a hole, especially in a tyre

puncture[2] *verb* (*present participle* **puncturing,** *past* **punctured**)
to make a hole in: *The nail* **punctured** *the tyre.*

○ **punish** /'pʌnɪʃ/ *verb*
to make someone do something he does not like because he has done something wrong: *The teacher* **punished** *the noisy children by making them stay after school.*
punishment *noun:* *They deserved their* **punishment.**

○ **pupil** /'pjuːpl/ *noun*
a person being taught, especially at a school

puppet /'pʌpɪt/ *noun*
a small figure of a person or animal which is moved by someone and appears to move and speak

puppy /'pʌpɪ/ *noun*
(*plural* **puppies**)
a young dog

○ **pure** /pjʊər/ *adjective*
(**purer, purest**)
without anything mixed with it; clean: *The water in mountain rivers is usually* **pure.**

purple /'pɜːpl/ *noun, adjective*
(of) the colour made by mixing red and blue together

○ **purpose** /'pɜːpəs/ *noun*
a reason for doing something; aim: *He went to town with the* **purpose** *of buying a new television. The girl broke a cup* **on purpose** (= she had planned to do it).

purr /pɜːr/ *verb*
(of cats) to make a soft low noise showing pleasure

purse /pɜːs/ *noun*
a small bag for carrying money

pursue /pə'sjuː/ *verb* (*present participle* **pursuing,** *past* **pursued**)
to go after someone hoping to catch him

○ **push**[1] /pʊʃ/ *verb*
to press or lean against, so as to move: *They* **pushed** *the door open.*

○ **push**[2] *noun*
an act of pushing: *She gave a hard* **push,** *and the door opened.*

○ **put** /pʊt/ *verb* (*present participle* **putting,** *past* **put**)
to move to a place; to place: *He* **put** *the cups on the table. The thief was* **put** *in prison.* **Put** *the lights* **on** (= turn them on); *it's too dark to read. He* **put out** *the light* (= turned it off) *and went to sleep.*

puzzle[1] /'pʌzl/ *noun*
1 a difficult question to answer: *It's a* **puzzle** *where all my money goes each week.*
2 a game which is difficult to understand or do: *A jigsaw* **puzzle** *is a picture which has been cut up into bits, and you must make the picture again.*

puzzle[2] *verb* (*present participle* **puzzling,** *past* **puzzled**)
to be difficult to understand: *The new machine* **puzzled** *me until Sarah explained how it worked.*

pyjamas /pə'dʒɑːməz/ *noun*
a loose shirt and trousers that you wear in bed: *a pair of* **pyjamas**

pyramid /'pɪrəmɪd/ *noun*
a solid shape which is square at the base and pointed at the top (picture on page 185)

Qq

quack /kwæk/ *verb*
to make a noise like a duck (see)

qualify /'kwɒlɪfaɪ/ *verb* (*present participle* **qualifying**, *past* **qualified**)
to finish training to do some special work: *He is a* **qualified** *doctor.*

   qualification /ˌkwɒlɪfɪ'keɪʃn/ *noun*: *What* **qualifications** (=special training or knowledge) *have you got to have for this job?*

° **quality** /'kwɒlɪtɪ/ *noun* (*plural* **qualities**)
how good something is: *We only sell cloth of the finest* **quality**. *Her best* **qualities** (=good things in her character) *are courage and cheerfulness.*

quantity /'kwɒntətɪ/ *noun* (*plural* **quantities**)
an amount: *He ate a small* **quantity** *of rice.*

° **quarrel**[1] /'kwɒrəl/ *noun*
an angry argument: *We had a* **quarrel** *about money.*

° **quarrel**[2] *verb* (*present participle* **quarrelling**, *past* **quarrelled**)
to have an argument: *Those children are always* **quarrelling** *over little things.*

quarry /'kwɒrɪ/ *noun* (*plural* **quarries**)
a hole in the ground where people dig up stone or sand

quart /kwɔːt/ *noun*
a measure of liquid equal to 1.13 litres: *There are two* **pints** *in a* **quart** *and four* **quarts** *in a gallon.*

° **quarter** /'kwɔːtəʳ/ *noun*
1 one of four equal parts of something; ¼: *There were four of us, so we divided the orange into* **quarters** *and each ate a piece. He was waiting for a* **quarter** *of an hour* (=15 minutes). *It's* (**a**) **quarter to** *six* (=15 minutes before 6 o'clock). *I must leave at* (**a**) **quarter past** *six* (=15 minutes after 6 o'clock).
2 a part of a town

quarters /'kwɔːtəz/ *plural noun*
a place where people live, especially if they live where they work: *The soldiers'* **quarters** *are in that long building over there.*

quay /kiː/ *noun*
a place where boats tie up and unload: *The* **quay** *looked like a long stone road going into the sea.*

queen /kwiːn/ *noun*
1 the female ruler of a country, especially one who comes from a family of rulers
2 the wife of a king

queer /kwɪəʳ/ *adjective*
odd; strange: *He has some* **queer** *opinions on education.*

   'queerly *adverb*

Roland Cepotte

quench /kwentʃ/ *verb*
to stop thirst or fire: *The cold beer* **quenched** *his thirst.*

query[1] /'kwɪərɪ/ *noun*
(*plural* **queries**)
a question: *I have several* **queries** *about the work you gave me.*

query[2] *verb* (*present participle* **querying,** *past* **queried** /'kwɪərɪd/)
to ask about something, usually to make sure that it is right: *If you think the price is too high, you should* **query** *it.*

° **question**[1] /'kwestʃən/ *noun*
1 something you ask someone: *You haven't answered my* **question.**
2 something to be talked about; a difficulty: *We talked about the* **question** *of private education. I want to buy the house, but it's a* **question** *of money — I haven't got enough.*

° **question**[2] *verb*
to ask about something: *I* **questioned** *the teacher about the work she had given us. I do not* **question** (=doubt) *his honesty.*

question mark /'kwestʃən ˌmɑːk/ *noun*
the sign ?, used in writing at the end of a sentence which asks a question: *Where are you going?*

queue[1] /kjuː/
noun
a line of people waiting for

queue

something: *a queue for a bus*

queue[2] *verb* (*present participle* **queuing,** *past* **queued**)
to stand in a line to wait for something: *We* **queued** *for the bus.*

° **quick** /kwɪk/ *adjective*
fast; not slow; happening in a short time: *We had a* **quick** *meal and then ran to catch the train. This is the* **quickest** *way to get to school.*
'**quickly** *adverb*

° **quiet**[1] /'kwaɪət/ *adjective*
1 having or making very little noise: *The streets were* **quiet** *at night. He has a* **quiet** *voice, I cannot hear what he says.*
2 not active: *I had a* **quiet** *day reading at home.* **quietly** *adverb*

quiet[2] *noun* (*no plural*)
silence; a time when there is no noise: *Your brother needs* **peace and quiet** *because he's working.*

quilt /kwɪlt/ *noun*
a soft, thick covering for a bed

° **quite** /kwaɪt/ *adverb*
1 completely; perfectly: *I* **quite** *agree with you. That fruit is not* **quite** *ripe.*
2 rather; not very much: *I was* **quite** *busy last week.*

quiver /'kwɪvəʳ/ *verb*
to shake a little: *The bridge* **quivered** *as the lorry crossed it.*

quiz /kwɪz/ *noun* (*plural* **quizzes**)
a game in which people try to answer questions correctly

quote /kwəʊt/ *verb* (*present participle* **quoting,** *past* **quoted**)
to say or write something that has been said or written before by someone else: *He* **quoted** *the saying "Every dog has his day", meaning that he would get a chance in life sometime.*
quo'tation *noun: Which book do these* **quotations** (=things quoted) *come from?*

Rr

rabbit /ˈræbɪt/ *noun*

a small animal with long ears and long back legs which lives in holes under the ground

○**race**[1] /reɪs/ *noun*

a group of human beings, animals or plants different from other groups in shape, colour, size, etc.: *White people are of a different race to black people.*

racial /ˈreɪʃl/ *adjective*

○**race**[2] *noun*

a competition to see who can run, swim, walk, etc., fastest: *Jane can run fast — she usually wins races.*

race[3] *verb* (*present participle racing, past raced*)

to try to run or go faster than: *Paul raced (against) John in the one mile race.*

rack /ræk/ *noun*

a frame on which things can be kept:

rack

The bottles were stored in a rack.

racket /ˈrækɪt/ *noun*

an instrument used in games like tennis (see) to hit the ball

radar /ˈreɪdɑːʳ/ *noun* (*no plural*)

a way of finding out the position of something by using radio waves: *The aeroplane could land at night because the pilot (=driver) was using radar.*

radiator /ˈreɪdɪeɪtəʳ/ *noun*

1 an instrument for cooling the engine of a car

2 an instrument for sending out heat in a house

○**radio** /ˈreɪdɪəʊ/ *noun*

1 (*no plural*) sending out or receiving sounds by electrical waves: *Ships send messages to each other by radio.*

2 (*plural radios*) a machine which receives the waves and plays them to you: *He was listening to music on the radio.*

radius /ˈreɪdɪəs/ *noun*

(see picture on page 185)

raft /rɑːft/ *noun*

large pieces of wood joined together to make a rough flat boat

rag /ræg/ *noun*

1 an old torn garment

2 a piece of cloth: *She washed the floor with a rag.*

rage /reɪdʒ/ *noun*

fierce anger; bad temper: *My father was in a rage last night.*

raid[1] /reɪd/ *noun*

a sudden attack

raid[2] *verb*

to attack: *They raided the village.*

rail /reɪl/ *noun*

a fixed metal bar: *Trains run on two rails. You can hang clothes from a rail.*

railing *noun* a rail in a fence: *There were railings round the park.*

○**railway** /ˈreɪlweɪ/ *noun*

1 a track made of rails for trains to go on: *We went to the ˈrailway ˌstation to catch a train.*

2 the tracks, stations, etc. used in carrying people and goods by train: *a book about railways*

rain^1 /reɪn/ *verb*
(of water) to fall from the sky: *It* **rained** *last night.*

rain^2 *noun*
(*no plural*)
water falling
from the sky:
There was **rain**
in the night.

rainbow

rainbow
/'reɪnbəʊ/
noun an arch of colours in the sky, especially after rain

'**raincoat** *noun* a coat that keeps out the rain

'**rainy** *adjective: Last week was very* **rainy**; *rain fell every day.*

° **raise** /reɪz/ *verb* (*present participle* **raising,** *past* **raised**)
to lift up; make higher: *He* **raised** *his arms above his head. Her wages were* **raised** *last week.*

raisin /'reɪzn/ *noun*
a small dried grape (see)

rake^1 /reɪk/
noun
a tool for
pulling
leaves, etc.

rake

together on the ground, and for making ground level

rake^2 *verb* (*present participle* **raking,** *past* **raked**)
to pull a rake over; gather with a rake

ran /ræn/ see **run**

ranch /rɑːntʃ/ *noun*
a large cattle farm

rang /ræŋ/ see **ring**

° **range** /reɪndʒ/ *noun*
1 a line of mountains or hills
2 a number of different things: *We sell a wide* **range** *of goods.*
3 the distance something can reach or travel: *What is the* **range** *of your gun* (=how far can you fire it)?

rank /ræŋk/ *noun*
a group or class thought of as higher or lower than other groups: *A general is an army officer with a high* **rank.**

ransom /'rænsəm/ *noun*
money paid so that a prisoner is made free: *The rich man was asked to pay a high* **ransom** *for his daughter who was taken away by criminals.*

rapid /'ræpɪd/ *adjective*
quick; fast
rapidly *adverb: He talked so* **rapidly** *that I could not understand him.*

rare /reə^r/ *adjective* (**rarer, rarest**)
not happening often; not often seen: *That bird is very* **rare** *in this country.*
'**rarely** *adverb: She is old and* **rarely** *goes out.*

rascal /'rɑːskl/ *noun*
a bad person; a badly-behaved child

rash^1 /ræʃ/ *adjective*
acting quickly without thinking enough what might happen: *It was* **rash** *to say you would buy it when you haven't any money.*
'**rashly** *adverb*

rash^2 *noun*
red spots on the skin: *With some illnesses, you get a* **rash.**

° **rat** /ræt/ *noun*
a small animal like a mouse (see) but larger, which often eats food or grain that is stored

° **rate** /reɪt/ *noun*
1 the money paid for a fixed amount of work; the amount produced, bought, used, etc. in a period of time: *He was paid at the* **rate** *of £3 an hour.*
2 the speed of something: *She learns at a quick* **rate.**

°**rather** /ˈrɑːðəʳ/
a little: *This shirt is* **rather** *tight; I need a bigger one.*

ration[1] /ˈræʃn/ *verb*
to limit the goods that someone can have: *The government had to* **ration** *petrol during the war.*

ration[2] *noun*
a fixed amount of something that is given or allowed: *Have you used your* **ration** *of petrol for this week?*

rattle[1] /ˈrætl/ *verb* (*present participle* **rattling**, *past* **rattled**)
to shake, making a noise: *She* **rattled** *some coins in the box.*

rattle[2] *noun*
a toy which a baby shakes to make a noise

ravine /rəˈviːn/ *noun*
a deep narrow area between hills or mountains

°**raw** /rɔ/ *adjective*
1 not cooked: **raw** *meat*
2 in the natural state; not changed: *Clay and water are the* **raw** *materials used for making pots.*

ray /reɪ/ *noun*
a line of light: *the* **rays** *of the sun*

razor /ˈreɪzəʳ/ *noun*
an instrument with a sharp blade, used especially for removing hair from men's faces

razors

°**reach**[1] /riːtʃ/ *verb*
1 to get to a place; arrive at: *This train* **reaches** *the village at twelve o'clock. I have* **reached** *the age when I can leave school.*
2 to stretch out your hand: *I* **reached up** *and took an apple from the tree.*

°**reach**[2] *noun* (*no plural*)
the distance that we can reach: *The book was* **within reach** (=I could reach it). *The ball was* **out of reach** (=I couldn't reach it).

react /rɪˈækt/ *verb*
to act because of something that has happened: *How did your mother* **react to** *the news? She* **reacted** *by getting very angry.*
reˈaction *noun*

°**read** /riːd/ *verb* (*present participle* **reading**, *past* **read** /red/)
to look at words and understand them: *She* **read** *the newspaper. He* **read** *the story to his son. I like* **reading.**
ˈreader *noun* **1** a person who reads **2** a book for teaching reading

°**ready** /ˈredɪ/ *adjective*
1 in the right way or order for use; prepared: *I am not* **ready** *to go out yet; I have not got my keys or my money. He got his tools* **ready** *to start the job.*
2 willing: *I'm always* **ready** *to help.*
readily *adverb*: *I can* **readily** (=easily and willingly) *believe that she is lazy at home — she is very lazy at school.*

°**real** /riːl/ *adjective*
being in fact; not imagined: *That is a* **real** *dog, not a toy.*
ˈreally *adverb*: *I am* **really** (=truly) *worried about my work. He is* **really** (=very) *nice!* **Really,** *Jane, you are behaving badly.*

realize /ˈrɪəlaɪz/ *verb* (*present participle* **realizing**, *past* **realized**)
to know or understand something as true, especially suddenly: *When I heard the noise on the roof, I* **realized** *that it was raining.*
ˌrealiˈzation *noun*

reap /riːp/ *verb*
to cut a crop and gather it: *They* **reaped** *the corn.*

rear[1] /rɪəʳ/ *adjective*

at the back: *the* **rear** *wheels of a car*

rear[2] *noun*

the back part: *We sat at the* **rear** *of the bus.*

rear[3] *verb*

to keep (animals, children, etc.) while they grow up: *to* **rear** *sheep/to* **rear** *a family*

○ **reason**[1] /'riːzn/ *noun*

1 why something is done or happens: *The* **reason** *she was ill was that she had eaten bad meat.* **2** (*no plural*) the power of thinking and deciding: *Use your* **reason** — *you can't expect to pass the examination if you don't work!*

reasonable *adjective* **1** having good sense: *Don't be afraid to talk to the teacher, she's very* **reasonable.** **2** fair: *a* **reasonable** *price* **reasonably** *adverb*

○ **reason**[2] *verb*

to argue in a thoughtful way: *He* **reasoned with** *the boy who had run away, and made him see that it was a silly thing to do.*

reassure /ˌriːə'ʃʊəʳ/ *verb* (*present participle* **reassuring**, *past* **reassured**)

to help feel safe and comfortable: *When the child was afraid in the storm, his parents* **reassured** *him.*

rebel[1] /rɪ'bel/ *verb* (*present participle* **rebelling**, *past* **rebelled**)

to fight against a leader or government: *The students* **rebelled** *against their government.*

re'bellion *noun: When a lot of people rebel, there is a* **rebellion.**

rebel[2] /'rebl/ *noun*

a person who rebels

○ **receive** /rɪ'siːv/ *verb* (*present participle* **receiving**, *past* **received**)

to get something given to you: *Did*

you **receive** *any letters today?*

receipt /rɪ'siːt/ *noun: When you have paid for something, a* **receipt** (=a piece of paper showing that you have paid) *is given to you.*

receiver *noun:*

The part of a telephone you speak into and

receiver

listen at is called a **receiver.**

reception /rɪ'sepʃn/ *noun: A party for a special event is called a* **reception.** *The place where you go to see if there is a room for you in a hotel is called the* **reception desk,** *or just* "**Reception**".

recent /'riːsnt/ *adjective*

happening a short time ago: *a* **recent** *visit to the city*

recently *adverb: I have been abroad* **recently.**

recipe /'resəpɪ/ *noun*

a piece of writing telling you how to cook something: *In the* **recipe,** *it says that I must use two eggs.*

reckless /'reklɪs/ *adjective*

careless and dangerous: *His* **reckless** *driving caused a serious accident.* **recklessly** *adverb*

reckon /'rekən/ *verb*

1 to guess: *I* **reckon** *he must have finished eating by now.*

2 to add or count: *She* **reckoned** (**up**) *the money we owed her.*

recognize /'rekəgnaɪz/ *verb* (*present participle* **recognizing**, *past* **recognized**)

1 to know someone or something again: *I* **recognized** *Peter although I hadn't seen him for 10 years. I don't* **recognize** *this word — what does it mean?*

2 to know as true: *Everyone* **recognizes** *that Richard is the best*

recommend

player in the team.

recognition /ˌrekəgˈnɪʃn/ *noun*

recommend /ˈrekəˈmend/ *verb*
1 to tell someone that a person or thing is good, useful, etc.: *If you are going to the city, I* **recommend** *the new hotel — it is very nice.*
2 to advise: *I* **recommended** *him to stay at school for another year, and then to try to go to college.*
recommenˈdation *noun: I went to the new hotel on your* **recommendation.**

record[1] /rɪˈkɔːd/ *verb*
1 to write the story of, or make pictures of: *The newspapers* **recorded** *the interesting news story.*
2 to store sounds electrically so that they can be listened to: *The songs were* **recorded** *by the radio company.*
recording *noun: We made a* **(tape) recording** *of the songs.*

record[2] /ˈrekɔːd/ *noun*
1 a round thin flat piece of plastic that stores sounds, and which we play on a machine (a **record player**) to hear the sounds

record player

2 information that is written down and kept: *The doctor keeps a* **record** *of all the serious illnesses in the village.*
3 something done better, quicker, etc. than anyone else has done it: *He holds the world* **record** *for the high jump. Can anyone* **break his record** *(= do better)?*

recover /rɪˈkʌvə(r)/ *verb*
to get better, or get back to a usual state: *She has had a bad illness, but she is* **recovering** *now. I* **recovered** *(= got back) the money I had lost.*

recovery *noun: She made a quick* **recovery** *after her illness.*

recreation /ˌrekrɪˈeɪʃn/ *noun*
rest or play after you have been working: *Football is the boys' usual* **recreation** *after school.*

recruit[1] /rɪˈkruːt/ *noun*
a new member of a group, especially of the armed forces

recruit[2] *verb*
to find or get someone as a recruit: *to* **recruit** *new police officers*

rectangle /ˈrektæŋgl/ *noun*
a flat shape with four straight sides and four equal angles, that is larger than it is wide (picture on page 185)
rectangular /rekˈtæŋgjʊlə(r)/ *adjective: a* **rectangular** *table*

○ **red** /red/ *noun, adjective* **(redder, reddest)**
(of) the colour of blood: *The sticks in the fire became* **red** *as they burnt. She was dressed* **in red.**

reduce /rɪˈdjuːs/ *verb (present participle* **reducing,** *past* **reduced)**
to get or make smaller or less: *They've* **reduced** *the prices in the shop, so it's a good time to buy.*
reduction /rɪˈdʌkʃn/ *noun*

reed /riːd/ *noun*
a tall plant like grass, which grows in or near water

reel /riːl/ *noun*
a round thing on which thread, film, etc. can be wound: *a* **reel** *of cotton*

reels

refer /rɪˈfɜː(r)/ *verb (present participle* **referring,** *past* **referred)**
1 to go to a person, book, etc., to get a piece of knowledge: *I* **referred to** *the dictionary to find out the meaning of the word.*

2 to speak about: *The teacher* **referred to** *Jane's good work when she spoke to her parents.*

reference /'refrəns/ *noun: A dictionary is a* **reference book** (=a book that you can refer to if you want to know things). *When I was looking for a job, I asked my head teacher to give me a* **reference** (=to write about me to people who might employ me).

referee /ˌrefə'riː/ *noun*
a person who watches a game and decides if it is fair

eflect /rɪ'flekt/ *verb*
1 to throw back light, heat, a picture, etc.: *A mirror* **reflects** *a picture of you when you look in it.*
2 to think: *He* **reflected** *before answering my question.*
re'flection *noun* **1** throwing back light, heat, etc.
2 what we see in a mirror: *He saw his* **reflection** *in the mirror.*
3 (*no plural*) thinking: *After a minute's* **reflection,** *he answered.*

refresh /rɪ'freʃ/ *verb*
to make someone feel better, less tired, etc.: *A cool drink* **refreshed** *me after my long walk. I had a* **refreshing** *drink.*
refreshments *plural noun* food and drink: *We bought* **refreshments** *at the football match.*

refrigerator /rɪ'frɪdʒəreɪtə^r/ *noun*
a machine for keeping food cold and fresh: *We have a* **refrigerator** *in our kitchen.*
fridge /frɪdʒ/ is a short way of saying **refrigerator.**

refuge /'refjuːdʒ/ *noun*
somewhere safe: *He* **took refuge** *from the storm in a hut.*
refugee /ˌrefjuː'dʒiː/ *noun* a person who has to leave his own country because he is in danger

refuse /rɪ'fjuːz/ *verb*
(*present participle* **refusing,** *past* **refused**)
not to allow; not to agree or accept: *She* **refused** *to let me help.*
refusal *noun: her* **refusal** *of my help*

regard[1] /rɪ'gɑːd/ *verb*
to think of or see: *We* **regard** *him as our cleverest student.*
regarding *preposition* about: *I wrote a letter* **regarding** *my daughter's school examinations.*

regard[2] *noun* (*no plural*)
care: *He always says what he thinks, without* **regard** *for other people's feelings.*
regardless *adverb: He says what he thinks,* **regardless** *of other people's feelings.*
regards *plural noun* best wishes: *Give my* **regards** *to your parents.*

regiment /'redʒɪmənt/ *noun*
a large group of soldiers; part of an army

region /'riːdʒən/ *noun*
an area: *This is a farming* **region.**

register[1] /'redʒɪstə^r/ *noun*
a list: *The teacher kept a* **register** *of the names of the children.*

register[2] *verb*
1 to have your name put on a list: *He* **registered** *the birth of his child.*
2 to show: *The machine* **registered** *how fast we were going.*
ˌregi'stration *noun*

regret[1] /rɪ'gret/ *verb*
(*present participle* **regretting,** *past* **regretted**)
to be sorry about something: *I* **regret** *spending so much money on a car. I* **regret** *to say I cannot come.*

regret[2] *noun*
a feeling of being sorry: *He told me* **with regret** *that he could not come to the party.*

° **regular** /'regjʊlə^r/ *adjective*

1 happening or being at fixed times: *He is a* **regular** *visitor — he comes every Sunday.*

2 ordinary; usual: *Is he your* **regular** *doctor?*

regularity /ˌregjʊ'lærətɪ/ *noun* (*no plural*): *The clock ticked with great* **regularity.**

'**regularly** *adverb*: *Take the medicine* **regularly** *three times a day.*

regulation /ˌregjʊ'leɪʃn/ *noun*

a rule: *It is a* **regulation** *of the football club that dogs are not allowed inside.*

rehearse /rɪ'hɜːs/ *verb* (*present participle* **rehearsing,** *past* **rehearsed**)

to do or say again and again, to make it as good as possible: *He* **rehearsed** *his speech last night.*

rehearsal *noun*: *All the children in the play must come to the* **rehearsal.**

reign[1] /reɪn/ *verb*

to be king or queen

reign[2] *noun*

the time when a king or queen reigns: *He has had a long* **reign.**

rein /reɪn/ *noun*

a long narrow piece of leather used to handle a horse: *The rider pulled on the* **reins,** *and the horse stopped.*

reins

reject /rɪ'dʒekt/ *verb*

to decide not to have; throw away: *We* **rejected** *his idea for a music club, and decided to have an art club instead.*

rejoice /rɪ'dʒɔɪs/ *verb* (*present participle* **rejoicing,** *past* **rejoiced**)

to be very happy

relate /rɪ'leɪt/ *verb* (*present participle* **relating,** *past* **related**)

1 to have a connection with: *This film* **relates** *to what we were learning about metals last week.*

2 to tell: *I* **related** *my adventure to my family.*

related *adjective* connected; of the same family: *I am* **related to** *him — he's my uncle.*

re'lation *noun* a member of the same family: *Some of my* **relations,** *my mother's aunt and uncle, live in America.*

relationship *noun* **1** being related: *"Do you know her* **relationship** *to that girl?" "She's her sister."* **2** feelings between people: *The teacher has a very good* **relationship** *with her students.*

° **relative** /'relətɪv/ *noun* a relation

relax /rɪ'læks/ *verb*

to become less worried, angry, tight, etc. *Don't worry about it, just try to* **relax.**

ˌ**relax'ation** *noun* (*no plural*)

release[1] /rɪ'liːs/ *verb* (*present participle* **releasing,** *past* **released**)

to let go: *I* **released** (*my hold on*) *the horse and it ran away. Four prisoners were* **released.**

release[2] *noun*

letting go: *After their* **release,** *the prisoners came home.*

relieve /rɪ'liːv/ *verb* (*present participle* **relieving,** *past* **relieved**)

to make pain or trouble less: *The medicine* **relieved** *his headache. I was* **relieved** *when he arrived home safely.*

relief *noun* (*no plural*): *I felt great* **relief** *when I heard I had passed the examination.*

° **religion** /rɪ'lɪdʒən/ *noun*

1 (*no plural*) belief in one or more

gods: *Almost every country has some form of* **religion.**

2 a special set of beliefs in one or more gods: *Hinduism and Buddhism are Eastern* **religions.**

religious *adjective*

reluctant /rɪˈlʌktənt/ *adjective*
not willing: *The child was* **reluctant** *to leave her mother.*

rely /rɪˈlaɪ/ *verb (present participle* **relying,** *past* **relied)**
to trust in: *You can* **rely on** *me to help you.*

reliable *adjective: He is a* **reliable** *person; if he says he will do something, he will do it.*

remain /rɪˈmeɪn/ *verb*
to stay: *I went to the city, but my brother* **remained** *at home. We* **remained** *friends for many years.*

remainder *noun* the rest; what is left: *I will go ahead with three of you, and the* **remainder** *(of the group) can wait here.*

remains *plural noun* parts which are left: *We found the* **remains** *of a meal on the table.*

remark[1] /rɪˈmɑːk/ *noun*
something said: *He made a rude* **remark** *about the woman who passed us.*

remark[2] *verb*
to say; notice: *"That is where Jane lives,"* *she* **remarked.**

remarkable *adjective* unusual, usually in a good way: *Your work has been* **remarkable** *this week.*

remarkably *adverb*

remedy /ˈremədɪ/ *noun*
(*plural* **remedies**)
a way of making something better: *a* **remedy** *for an illness*

° **remember** /rɪˈmembər/ *verb*
to keep in the mind; not to forget: *Did you* **remember** *to feed the animals?*

° **remind** /rɪˈmaɪnd/ *verb*
to make someone remember; **Remind** *me to write to my uncle. That man* **reminds** *me of* (=is like) *my teacher.*

remote /rɪˈməʊt/ *adjective*
far away; far from where people live: *They have a* **remote** *farm in the hills.*

remotely *adverb: He is not* **remotely** (=not in any way) *like me.*

remove /rɪˈmuːv/ *verb (present participle* **removing,** *past* **removed)**
to take and move to somewhere else: *Will you* **remove** *your books from my desk?*

removal *noun: That company does* **removals** (=carries things for other people who are moving to live in another house).

renew /rɪˈnjuː/ *verb*
1 to get or give a new thing or a thing of the same sort: *He* **renewed** *his car licence* (=paper saying that he was allowed to keep a car).

2 to start again: *The soldiers* **renewed** *their attack on the town.*

rent[1] /rent/ *noun*
money paid regularly for the use of a house, office, etc.: *He pays 100 dollars a week* **rent.**

rent[2] *verb*
to have the use of or let someone use a house, etc. in return for rent: *My father* **rents** *an office in the city.*

° **repair**[1] /rɪˈpeər/ *verb*
to make something that is broken or old good again; mend: *Have you* **repaired** *the bicycle yet?*

° **repair**[2] *noun*
mending: *I haven't paid for the* **repairs** *to my bicycle.*

repay /rɪˈpeɪ/ *verb (present participle* **repaying,** *past* **repaid)**

to give money back to someone: *I will* **repay** *you tomorrow.*

repeat /rɪ'piːt/ *verb*
to say or do again: *Could you* **repeat** *the question?*
   repetition /ˌrepɪ'tɪʃn/ *noun: I want no* **repetition** *of your bad behaviour.*

replace /rɪ'pleɪs/ *verb* (*present participle* **replacing**, *past* **replaced**)
1 to put something back in its place: *When you have finished using the axe, please* **replace** *it.*
2 to put a new or different thing in place of something: *The man who sold me the radio said he would* **replace** *it if it didn't work.*
   replacement *noun: This radio does not work; I must get a* **replacement**.

reply[1] /rɪ'plaɪ/ *verb* (*present participle* **replying**, *past* **replied**)
to give an answer: *I asked him how he was, and he* **replied** *that he was well. "I'm well," he* **replied**.

reply[2] *noun* (*plural* **replies**)
an answer: *His* **reply** *was, "I'm very well, thank you."*

report[1] /rɪ'pɔːt/ *verb*
to give the story of; tell about the facts of: *The newspaper* **reported** *that there had been a fire in the village. We* **reported** *the robbery to the police.*

report[2] *noun*
facts told or written: *The newspaper* **report** *was on the front page.*

   reporter *noun* a person who writes reports in newspapers or tells news stories on television or radio

° **represent** /ˌreprɪ'zent/ *verb*
1 to act for: *Mr Johnson* **represented** *his company at the meeting.*

2 to be a sign of: *The sign "&"* **represents** *the word "and".*
   representative /-tətɪv/ *noun: a* **representative** *of a company*

reproach /rɪ'prəʊtʃ/ *verb*
to blame someone in a sad way, not an angry way: *Do not* **reproach** *yourself, it was not your fault.*

reproduce /ˌriːprə'djuːs/ *verb* (*present participle* **reproducing**, *past* **reproduced**)
1 to produce young: *Cats often* **reproduce** *twice a year.*
2 to make a copy of: *I* **reproduced** *the drawing I had seen.*
   reproduction /ˌriːprə'dʌkʃn/ *noun* **1** (*no plural*) producing young ones: *human* **reproduction** **2** a copy: *a* **reproduction** *of a famous picture*

reptile /'reptaɪl/ *noun*
a cold-blooded animal such as a snake

lizard
snake
crocodile
reptiles

republic /rɪ'pʌblɪk/ *noun*
a country whose head is a president, not a king

reputation /ˌrepjʊ'teɪʃn/ *noun*
the opinion that people have about someone or something: *This hotel has the best* **reputation** *in the city.*

request[1] /rɪ'kwest/ *verb*
to ask: *May I* **request** *you to be quiet in the hospital?*

° **request**[2] *noun*
something that you ask: *She* **made a request** *for some water.*

require /rɪ'kwaɪər/ *verb* (*present participle* **requiring**, *past* **required**)
to need: *I* **require** *two children to help me.*
   requirement *noun: If you have any* **requirements** (= *if you need anything*), *ask me.*

rescue[1] /'reskjuː/ *verb* (*present participle* **rescuing,** *past* **rescued**)
to save: *We* **rescued** *the boy who fell into the river.*

rescue[2] *noun*
saving: *We came to his* **rescue** *and pulled him out of the river.*

research[1] /rɪ'sɜːtʃ, 'riːsɜːtʃ/ *noun* (*no plural*)
careful study, especially to find out something new: *scientific* **research**/*medical* **research**

research[2] /rɪ'sɜːtʃ/ *verb*
to study something to find out new things: *to* **research** *into the causes of an illness*

resemble /rɪ'zembl/ *verb* (*present participle* **resembling,** *past* **resembled**)
to be like: *She* **resembles** *her mother in the way she moves her hands when she talks.*
   resemblance *noun: There is no* **resemblance** *between the two brothers.*

resent /rɪ'zent/ *verb*
to feel angry with someone: *I* **resent** *what you said about me — it's not true.*
   resentment *noun* (*no plural*)

reserve[1] /rɪ'zɜːv/ *verb* (*present participle* **reserving,** *past* **reserved**)
to keep something for someone: *I have* **reserved** *a room for you at the hotel.*
   reservation /ˌrezə'veɪʃn/ *noun: If you want to go to the concert, you'll have to make a* **reservation,** *or there will be no tickets.*

reserve[2] *noun*
1 an amount of something that has been stored: *We have large* **reserves** *of oil.*
2 a place where wild animals live and are protected: *Africa has many* **game reserves.**

reservoir /'rezəvwɑːr/ *noun*
a place where a lot of water is stored: *This* **reservoir** *gives water to the whole city.*

residence /'rezɪdəns/ *noun*
1 a house: *a* **residence** *in the country*
2 (*no plural*) having your home in a place: *to* **take up residence** *in a town*
   residential /ˌrezɪ'denʃl/ *adjective: a* **residential** *area of a town* (=where people live)

resign /rɪ'zaɪn/ *verb*
1 to leave your job: *to* **resign** *from a job*
2 to accept something unpleasant calmly: *I* **resigned myself to** *a long wait.*
   resignation /ˌrezɪg'neɪʃn/ *noun*
1 a letter saying you are leaving your job: *I sent in my* **resignation** *last week.* **2** (*no plural*) accepting

resist /rɪ'zɪst/ *verb*
1 to refuse to do or accept something: *I can't* **resist** *eating chocolates.*
2 to be strong against: *Will this new wall* **resist** *the force of the sea?*
   resistance *noun*

resolve /rɪ'zɒlv/ *verb* (*present participle* **resolving,** *past* **resolved**)
to decide: *I* **resolved** *to work hard until the examination.*
   resolution /ˌrezə'luːʃn/ *noun: I made a* **resolution** *to work hard.*

resources /rɪ'zɔːsɪz/ *plural noun*
money, goods, etc. that help you to do things: *A country's* **natural resources** *are things which grow or are found there that can be used by the people or sold abroad.*

○**respect**[1] /rɪ'spekt/ *noun*
1 (*no plural*) a good opinion of someone: *He has great* **respect** *for his parents.*

2 way: *In some* **respects,** *he is like his father.*

> **respectable** *adjective:* *a* **respectable** *young man* (of good character)

° **respect**[2] *verb*
to feel respect for: *All the children* **respected** *their teacher.*

respond /rɪˈspɒnd/ *verb*
to answer: *How did she* **respond to** *your question? She* **responded** *by laughing.*

> **response** *noun:* *I've had no* **response** *to my letter.*

responsible /rɪˈspɒnsəbl/ *adjective*
taking care of someone or something, and taking the blame if anything goes wrong: *I am* **responsible** *for my sister until she gets a job. Simon is a* **responsible** *boy; we can leave him to look after the smaller children.*

> **responsibility** /rɪˌspɒnsəˈbɪlətɪ/ *noun* (*plural* **responsibilities**): *My children are my* **responsibility.**

° **rest**[1] /rest/ *noun*
1 a time of quiet away from work or play: *I had an hour's* **rest** *after work.*
2 (*no plural*) that or those left behind: *Have you seen* **the rest** *of the children?*

° **rest**[2] *verb*
1 to have a quiet time away from work or play: *I* **rested** *for an hour before I went out.*
2 to put or be placed: *I* **rested** *my elbows on the table.*

restaurant /ˈrestrɒnt/ *noun*
a place where you can buy and eat food

restore /rɪˈstɔːʳ/ *verb* (*present participle* **restoring,** *past* **restored**)
1 to repair, so that it looks new: *to* **restore** *an old building*
2 to give back

restrain /rɪˈstreɪn/ *verb*
to stop or hold back: *I can't* **restrain** *my anger when I hear of people being cruel to animals.*

restrict /rɪˈstrɪkt/ *verb*
to keep within a limit: *Swimming is* **restricted** *to this part of the river only — the rest is dangerous.*

° **result**[1] /rɪˈzʌlt/ *noun*
what happens because something else has happened: *What was the* **result** *of your examination — did you pass or fail?*

° **result**[2] *verb*
to happen as a result; have as a result: *The accident* **resulted in** *three people being killed.*

resume /rɪˈzjuːm/ *verb* (*present participle* **resuming,** *past* **resumed**)
to start again: *We shall* **resume** *our work in a quarter of an hour.*

retain /rɪˈteɪn/ *verb*
to keep; keep in: *I have* **retained** *my job for a year.*

retire /rɪˈtaɪəʳ/ *verb* (*present participle* **retiring,** *past* **retired**)
to stop work because of old age or illness: *He* **retired** *from the business when he was 65.*

> **retirement** *noun:* *She plans to spend her* **retirement** *travelling.*

retreat[1] /rɪˈtriːt/ *verb*
to go back or away from something or someone: *The soldiers had to* **retreat** *when they were beaten in battle.*

retreat[2] *noun*
retreating

° **return**[1] /rɪˈtɜːn/ *verb*
1 to come or go back: *I was* **returning** *from school when I saw him.*
2 to give back: *Could you* **return** *the book I lent you?*

° **return**[2] *noun*
coming or going back: *On my*

return *from work, I saw the door was open. I would like a* **return ticket** (=to go to a place and come back from it).

reveal /rɪ'viːl/ *verb*
to say or show something that was covered up or secret before: *I lifted the cloth to* **reveal** *a bicycle.*

revenge /rɪ'vendʒ/ *noun*
(*no plural*)
doing something bad to someone who has done something bad to you: *I broke Mary's pen by accident, and* **in revenge** *she tore up my school work.*

reverend /'revrənd/ *noun*
a title for a Christian priest: *We say the* **Reverend** *Richard Jones, but we write* **Rev.** *Richard Jones.*

reverse¹ /rɪ'vɜːs/ *verb* (*present participle* **reversing**, *past* **reversed**)
1 to turn over or around: *If you* **reverse** *this sentence, you read it from the end to the beginning.*
2 to make something go backwards: *The driver* **reversed** *the lorry into the narrow road.*

reverse² *noun*
the opposite: *You think I gave him the fruit, but the* **reverse** *is true: he gave it to me.*

review¹ /rɪ'vjuː/ *noun*
a piece of writing telling you about a book, film, etc.

review² *verb*
to look at books, films, etc. and say what you think about them

revise /rɪ'vaɪz/ *verb* (*present participle* **revising**, *past* **revised**)
1 to look through again and change things where needed: *He was* **revising** *what he had written.*
2 to learn and practise things, especially for an examination: *I've been* **revising** *all week.*

   revision /rɪ'vɪʒn/ *noun*

revive /rɪ'vaɪv/ *verb*
(*present participle* **reviving**, *past* **revived**)
to come or bring back to strength or life: *He managed to* **revive** *the woman he saved from the river.*

revolt¹ /rɪ'vəʊlt/ *verb*
1 to fight in a mass against leaders or government: *The soldiers* **revolted** *against their officers.*
2 to make someone feel ill, by being very unpleasant: *I was* **revolted** *by the bad smell.*
   revolting *adjective*: *What a* **revolting** *smell!*

revolt² *noun*
when a lot of people fight against their leaders or government: *The army officers led a* **revolt** *against the king.*

revolve /rɪ'vɒlv/ *verb* (*present participle* **revolving**, *past* **revolved**)
to go round and round: *The wheels* **revolved** *quickly. The Earth* **revolves** *round the sun.*
   revolution /ˌrevə'luːʃn/ *noun* **1** a great change, especially in the government of a country: *The army officers led a* **revolution** *against the king.* **2** going round like a wheel

reward¹ /rɪ'wɔːd/ *noun*
something given in return for good work, kindness, bravery, etc.: *He has had a hard life, and if he is rich now, it is a fair* **reward.**

reward² *verb*
to give a reward to: *The police said they would* **reward** *anyone who found the stolen car.*

rhinoceros /raɪ'nɒsərəs/ *noun*
(*plural* **rhinoceroses**)
a large wild animal with a hard skin and two horns on its nose, which lives in Africa and Asia (picture on page 17)

rhino /'raɪnəʊ/ is a short way of saying and writing **rhinoceros**.

rhyme[1] /raɪm/ *noun*
1 words with the same sounds, like "pot", "lot", and "got"
2 a short thing you say or sing which has rhymes in it

rhyme[2] *verb* (*present participle* **rhyming**, *past* **rhymed**)
(of words) to end with the same sound: *Weigh* **rhymes** *with play*.

rhythm /'rɪðəm/ *noun*
a regular sound like a drum in music: *I can't dance to music without a good* **rhythm**.

rib /rɪb/ *noun*
one of the narrow bones which go round your chest (picture on p.133)

ribbon /'rɪbən/ *noun*
a long narrow piece of material used for tying things: **ribbons** *in her hair*

° **rice** /raɪs/ *noun* (*no plural*)
a grain plant grown in hot countries with seeds which are used as food

° **rich** /rɪtʃ/ *adjective*
1 having a lot of money
2 cooked with a lot of oil, sugar, etc. *I don't like* **rich** *food*.
'**riches** *plural noun* money and goods; things that cost a lot of money: *She gave away all her* **riches**.

° **rid** /rɪd/ *preposition*
free of: *We* **got** **rid of** *the insects by killing them*.

riddle /'rɪdl/ *noun*
a question which is a trick, which makes people laugh: *Here is a* **riddle** *for you: "Why is 'smiles' the longest word in the world? Because it is made of two s's with a 'mile' between them."*

° **ride**[1] /raɪd/ *verb* (*present participle* **riding**, *past tense* **rode** /rəʊd/, *past participle* **ridden** /'rɪdn/)
to go along on or in something: *She was* **riding** *a bicycle. They* **rode** *in the back seat of the bus.*
'**rider** *noun: The bicycle* **rider** *was hurt in the accident.*

° **ride**[2] *noun*
an act of riding: *He went for a* **ride** *in his car.*

ridge /rɪdʒ/ *noun*
a long narrow raised part of something, such as the top of a hill: *The waves had pushed the sand into little* **ridges**.

ridiculous /rɪ'dɪkjʊləs/ *adjective*
not reasonable; silly: *Don't be* **ridiculous** — *you can't play outside in the storm.*

rifle /'raɪfl/ *noun*
a long gun fired from the shoulder

rifle

° **right**[1] /raɪt/ *adjective*
1 correct; good: *He showed us the* **right** *way to build a boat. It is* **right** *that everyone should go to school. This is the* **right** *time to ask her.*
2 the opposite of left
,**right**-'**handed** *adjective: If you do most things with your right hand, you are* **right-handed**.

° **right**[2] *noun*
1 (*no plural*) what is fair and good: *You must learn the difference between* **right** *and wrong*.
2 what is or should be allowed by law: *We must work for equal* **rights** *for everyone*.
3 the side opposite to the left side: *The school is on the left of the road, and his house is on the* **right**.

° **right**[3] *adverb*
1 correctly: *I did all my sums* **right**.
2 towards the right side: *Turn* **right** *at the corner*.

3 completely; all the way: *I read* **right** *to the end of the book.*

4 directly; straight: *That's our house,* **right** *in front of you.*

rim /rɪm/ *noun*

the edge of something: *a pattern round the* **rim** *of a plate*

rind /raɪnd/ *noun*

the hard outer part of fruit, cheese, etc.; skin

° **ring**¹ /rɪŋ/ *noun*

1 a round shape: *The children sat in a* **ring** *round the teacher.*

2 something round: *She wore a gold ring on her finger. He hung the keys on a* **ring.**

° **ring**² *verb* (*present participle* **ringing,** *past tense* **rang** /ræŋ/, *past participle* **rung** /rʌŋ/)

1 to make a sound like a bell: *He heard the telephone* **ringing.** *He* **rang** *the bell but no one came to the door.*

2 to speak to on the telephone: *I* **rang (up)** *Peter to see if he could come to dinner. I* **gave him a ring.**

rinse /rɪns/ *verb* (*present participle* **rinsing,** *past* **rinsed**)

to wash the soap out of: *I* **rinsed** *the clothes I had washed.*

riot¹ /'raɪət/ *noun*

fighting against something by an angry crowd of people: *There was a* **riot** *when the workers were told they had lost their jobs.*

riot² *verb*

to fight in an angry crowd: *They* **rioted** *in the streets.*

rip /rɪp/ *verb* (*present participle* **ripping,** *past* **ripped**)

to tear: *When Paul was climbing over the fence, he* **ripped** *his trousers on a nail.*

° **ripe** /raɪp/ *adjective*

full-grown and ready to eat: *This fruit isn't* **ripe** *yet — we can't eat it.*

ripple¹ /'rɪpl/ *noun*

a little wave: *There were* **ripples** *on the pool as the wind grew stronger.*

ripple² *verb* (*present participle* **rippling,** *past* **rippled**)

to move in little waves: *The water* **rippled** *as the bird swam along.*

° **rise**¹ /raɪz/ *verb* (*present participle* **rising,** *past tense* **rose** /rəʊz/, *past participle* **risen** /'rɪzn/)

to come or get up: *The sun* **rose** *at seven o'clock. The land* **rises** *steeply from the river.*

rise² *noun*

an increase: *a* **rise** *in prices*

° **risk**¹ /rɪsk/ *noun*

the chance of being in danger: *He took a* **risk** *when he crossed the old bridge* (=there was a chance it might fall down).

° **risk**² *verb*

to take a chance of something bad happening; put in danger: *He* **risked** *his life when he saved the child from the fire.*

rival /'raɪvl/ *noun*

a person who tries to do better than another: *She and I are* **rivals** *for the swimming prize.*

rivalry *noun: There is great* **rivalry** *between the two sisters.*

° **river** /'rɪvəʳ/ *noun*

a continuous flow of water along a course to the sea: *The longest* **river** *in Africa is the Nile.*

° **road** /rəʊd/ *noun*

a hard, wide tract that people and traffic can use: *Do you like to travel* **by road** *or by rail* (=by bus, car, etc., or by train)?

roam /rəʊm/ *verb*

to wander: *The visitors* **roamed** *around the town.*

roar¹ /rɔːʳ/ *verb*

to make a deep, angry noise, like a lion

roar[2] *noun*

a sound of roaring: *The lion gave a loud* **roar.**

roast /rəʊst/ *verb*

to cook in an oven (see) without water, or over a fire: *The meat is* **roasting.**

° **rob** /rɒb/ *verb* (*present participle* **robbing,** *past* **robbed**)

to take money, goods, etc. from a person or place, when it is not yours; steal from: *While he was away, his house was* **robbed.**

'robber *noun* a person who robs
'robbery *noun* (*plural* **robberies**): *a bank* **robbery**

robe /rəʊb/ *noun*

a long loose piece of clothing that covers much of the body

robot /'rəʊbɒt/ *noun*

a machine that does some of the work a person can do

° **rock**[1] /rɒk/ *noun*

1 (*no plural*) stone: *Mountains are made of* **rock.**

2 a large piece of stone
'rocky *adjective* (**rockier, rockiest**) *a rocky shore*

rock[2] *verb*

to move from side to side: *When I stepped onto the side of the boat, it* **rocked.**

rocket /'rɒkɪt/ *noun*

1 a thing driven into the air by burning gas, used to lift a weapon or a spaceship from the ground (picture on page 259)

2 a firework (=toy which bursts with a loud noise and pretty lights) which goes up into the air

rod /rɒd/ *noun*

a thin bar: *You catch fish with a* **fishing rod.**

fishing rod

rode /rəʊd/ see **ride**

rogue /rəʊg/ *noun*

a bad or dishonest person

role /rəʊl/ *noun*

a character in a play or film: *He played the* **role** *of the old king in our school play.*

° **roll**[1] /rəʊl/ *verb*

1 to move along by turning over and over: *The ball* **rolled** *under the table.*

2 to make a rounded shape by turning something over and over: **Roll** *the picture* **up** *so that it does not get damaged.*

3 to make flat by passing something over and over: *She* **rolled out** *the flour and water mixture to make bread.*

4 to make a long loud noise: *We heard the drums* **roll.**

° **roll**[2] *noun*

1 something rolled up into a long round shape: *a* **roll** *of cloth*

2 a small round piece of bread

3 a list of names, such as children in a class

4 a long steady sound of drums

Roman Catholic /ˌrəʊmən 'kæθəlɪk/ *or* **Catholic** *noun, adjective*

(a Christian) belonging to the church whose head is the Pope

° **romance** /rəʊ'mæns/ *noun*

1 being in love: *a* **romance** *between a king and a poor girl*

2 a story about love
romantic *adjective*

° **roof** /ruːf/ *noun*

the top covering of a building, car, etc.: *There is a cat on our* **roof.**

° **room** /ruːm/ *noun*

1 one of the parts of a house separated by walls and doors: *We sleep in the* **'bedroom,** *and wash in the* **'bathroom.**

2 (*no plural*) space; enough space: *There isn't* **room** *for anyone else in the car. This desk takes up a lot of* **room.**

° **root** /ruːt/ *noun*
the part of a plant which grows downwards, and is usually below the ground (picture at **flower**)

° **rope** /rəʊp/ *noun*
very thick string

rose[1] /rəʊz/ see **rise**

rose[2] *noun*
a beautiful and sweet-smelling flower

rot /rɒt/ *verb* (*present participle* **rotting,** *past* **rotted**)
to go bad and soft because it is old or wet: *The ripe fruit began to* **rot** *when no one came to pick it.*
   '**rotten** *adjective: The fish is* **rotten;** *you must not eat it.*

rotate /rəʊ'teɪt/ *verb* (*present participle* **rotating,** *past* **rotated**)
to go round like a wheel: *The Earth* **rotates** *round the sun.*
   ro'tation *noun: The* **rotation** *of the Earth round the sun takes one year.*

° **rough** /rʌf/ *adjective*
1 not smooth; uneven: *a* **rough** *surface*
2 not calm or gentle; wild: *The sea was* **rough** *in the storm.*
3 not finished: *a* **rough** *drawing*
   '**roughly** *adverb* **1** about: *I had* **roughly** *four kilometres to go.* **2** wildly: *He played* **roughly** *with the baby.*

° **round**[1] /raʊnd/ *adjective*
like a ring or cirle: *A ball is* **round.**

° **round**[2] *or* **around** /ə'raʊnd/ *adverb, preposition*
1 with a movement like a circle: *The Earth turns* **round** *once every day.*
2 going around; on all sides: *She*

wore a belt **round** *her dress. The children stood* **round** *the teacher.*
3 to the other way: *You're going the wrong way; you should turn* **round** *and go back.*
4 to different places: *They walked* **round** (*the town*) *for an hour.*

roundabout
/'raʊndəbaʊt/
noun
1 a round
machine on
which children
can ride,
sitting on
wooden animals
roundabouts
2 a place where traffic goes in a circle and where roads cross each other

route /ruːt/ *noun*
a way to a place: *We came by a longer* **route** *than usual.*

routine /ruː'tiːn/ *noun*
a set way of doing things: *I arrive at nine o'clock, teach until twelve thirty and then have a meal: that is my morning* **routine.**

° **row**[1] /rəʊ/ *noun*
a line: *a* **row** *of pots on a shelf*

row[2] /raʊ/ *noun*
a quarrel; a loud noise: *The two men were having a* **row.**

row[3] /rəʊ/ *verb*
to move oars (see) through water to make a boat move

royal /'rɔɪəl/ *adjective*
of, belonging to, or like a king or queen: *the* **royal** *family*
   royalty *noun* (*no plural*) a member of a king or queen's family

° **rub** /rʌb/ *verb* (*present participle* **rubbing,** *past* **rubbed**)
to move something back and forward over something else: *She* **rubbed** *her shoes with a cloth to*

make them shine. He rubbed out the writing (=used a piece of rubber to rub the writing off the paper).

○ **rubber** /'rʌbəʳ/ *noun*
1 (*no plural*) a soft material from a tree that can be stretched and that goes back into shape when it is let go: *Tyres are made of* **rubber.**
2 a piece of this material used for getting rid of pencil marks

,**rubber 'band** *noun* a piece of rubber in a ring shape that is used to fasten things together

rubbish /'rʌbɪʃ/ *noun* (*no plural*)
1 things which you do not want and will throw away: *The cupboard was full of old papers, broken toys, and other* **rubbish.**
2 anything silly: *I thought that story was* **rubbish.**

○ **rude** /ruːd/ *adjective*
(**ruder, rudest**)
not polite or kind; saying unpleasant things: *He was punished because he was* **rude** *to his teacher.*

rug /rʌg/ *noun*
a thick floor mat; a large thick cloth to wrap round you to keep you warm

rugged /'rʌgɪd/ *adjective*
rough and wild; full of rocks: **rugged** *country*

ruin¹ /'ruːɪn/ *verb*
to destroy: *She poured water all over my painting, and* **ruined** *it.*

ruin² *noun*
a building that has been destroyed: *We saw the* **ruins** *of the church.*

○ **rule**¹ /ruːl/ *verb* (*present participle* **ruling,** *past* **ruled**)
1 to be the king or most powerful person of: *Who* **rules** *this country?*
2 to make a straight line: *He* **ruled** *a line under his name.*

'ruler *noun*
1 someone who governs a country

ruler

2 a piece of wood, plastic, or metal with a straight edge to help you to draw lines

○ **rule**² *noun*
1 a law; thing that you must or must not do: *The school* **rules** *must be obeyed.*
2 (*no plural*) government

rum /rʌm/ *noun* (*no plural*)
a strong alcoholic drink made from sugar

rumble /'rʌmbl/ *verb* (*present participle* **rumbling,** *past* **rumbled**)
to make a long low noise, like thunder in the distance

rumour /'ruːmɔʳ/ *noun*
something that people tell each other but that may not be true: *I heard a* **rumour** *that the headmaster is leaving.*

○ **run**¹ /rʌn/ *verb* (*present participle* **running,** *past tense* **ran** /ræn/, *past participle* **run**)
1 to move on your feet very quickly: *He* **ran** *across the road.*
2 to work or make work: *This machine is not* **running** *correctly. She is* **running** *a school in the city.*
3 to make a journey: *Trains* **run** *every hour.*
4 (used in sentences like these): *The river has* **run dry** (=become dry). *The wall* **runs** (=goes) *round the village. We have* **run out of** (=we have no more of) *sugar. A dog was* **run over** (=a car or bus went over the dog) *outside our school. He stole the fruit and then* **ran away** (=escaped quickly).

○ **run**² *noun*
1 a time of running: *to go for a run*

2 a journey: *There are no stops on the* **run** *to the coast.*

3 a point in the game of cricket

rung[1] /rʌŋ/ see **ring**

rung[2] *noun*
one of the bars in a ladder (picture at **ladder**)

rural /'ruərəl/ *adjective*
in, of, or belonging to the country; not of the town: *Crops are grown in* **rural** *areas.*

rush[1] /rʌʃ/ *verb*
to hurry; go fast: *She* **rushed** *into the room to tell us the news.*

rush[2] *noun* (*no plural*)
hurry: *I can't stop; I'm* **in a rush.**

rust[1] /rʌst/ *noun* (*no plural*)
red-brown substance that forms on iron when it has been wet: *an old car with a lot of* **rust**

'rusty *adjective* (**rustier, rustiest**)
covered with rust: *a* **rusty** *car*

rust[2] *verb*
to become covered with rust: *If you leave your metal tools outside in the rain, they will* **rust.**

rustle[1] /'rʌsl/ *verb* (*present participle* **rustling**, *past* **rustled**)
to make a light sound like paper being moved: *The leaves* **rustled** *in the wind.*

rustle[2] *noun* (*no plural*)
a light sound of rustling: *the* **rustle** *of paper*

rut /rʌt/ *noun*
a deep narrow track made by a wheel in soft ground

Ss

sack /sæk/ *noun*
a large bag made of strong material: *a* **sack** *of rice*

sacred /'seɪkrɪd/ *adjective*
religious; holy: *a* **sacred** *building*/**sacred** *writings*

sacrifice[1] /'sækrɪfaɪs/ *noun*
1 something killed and offered to a god
2 something important to you that you give up for some good purpose: *Her parents made many* **sacrifices** *so that she could study abroad.*

sacrifice[2] *verb* (*present participle* **sacrificing**, *past* **sacrificed**)
1 to offer to a god: *They* **sacrificed** *a goat.*
2 to give up: *She* **sacrificed** *her job so that she could help her parents.*

○ **sad** /sæd/ *adjective* (**sadder, saddest**)
not happy; feeling sorrow: *I am very* **sad** *to hear that your father has died.* **sadly** *adverb*

saddle /'sædl/ *noun*
a seat for the rider of a horse or bicycle (picture at **bicycle**)

safari /sə'fɑːri/ *noun*
a journey to hunt or look at wild animals, especially in Africa

○ **safe**[1] /seɪf/ *adjective*
not in danger; not dangerous: *It is good to be* **safe** *at home on a night like this. The bridge is* **safe** *to walk on.* **'safely** *adverb*

'safety *noun* (*no plural*) a safe place: *They ran to* **safety,** *away from the fire. A* **safety pin** *has a cover over its point.*

safe[2] *noun*

a strong box or cupboard that can be locked, for keeping things safely

sag /sæg/ *verb* (*present participle* **sagging,** *past* **sagged**)

to hang down heavily: *The bed sags in the middle, and is uncomfortable.*

said /sed/ see **say**

sail[1] /seɪl/ *noun*

a large cloth used to catch the wind and move a boat

sail

sail[2] *verb*

1 to travel on water: *His ship sails today.*

2 to direct a boat with sails: *She sailed the boat without any help.*

'**sailor** *noun* a person who works on a ship

saint /seɪnt/ *noun*

a person who has lived a very good and religious life

St /sənt/ is a short way of writing **saint:** St *Peter's Church*

sake /seɪk/ *noun*

used with **for,** to show purpose or reason: *Your sister is trying to read; please be quiet for her sake. I stopped smoking for the sake of my health. Oh,* **for goodness' sake,** *hurry up!*

salad /'sæləd/ *noun*

a dish of cold, usually raw vegetables

salary /'sælərɪ/ *noun* (*plural* **salaries**)

a fixed amount of money paid to someone every month for the work done

○ **sale** /seɪl/ *noun*

1 selling: *He got four pounds from the* **sale** *of his drawing. That house is* **for sale** (=waiting to be sold).

2 a time when prices are low: *The shoe shop is having a* **sale** *this week.*

salesman /'seɪlzmən/ *noun* (*plural* **salesmen**) *or* **saleswoman** /'seɪlz,wʊmən/ *(plural* **saleswomen**) a person whose job is to sell goods

salmon /'sæmən/ *noun* (*plural* **salmon**)

a large river and sea fish

○ **salt** /sɔːlt/ *noun* (*no plural*)

a white chemical found in sea-water, rocks, etc., which we add to our food to make it taste better

'**salty** *adjective* (**saltier, saltiest**) having a lot of salt

salute[1] /sə'luːt/ *noun*

a mark of respect to someone, done by holding your hand stiffly against the side of your head

salute[2] *verb* (*present participle* **saluting,** *past* **saluted**)

to hold up your hand as a salute: *The soldier* **saluted** *his officer.*

○ **same** /seɪm/ *adjective*

1 not different; alike in one or more ways: *Your pen is* **the same** *as mine.*

2 being one person or thing; not another: *We go to* **the same** *school.*

sample[1] /'sɑːmpl/ *noun*

a single piece taken as an example of what something is like: *a* **sample** *of his work*

sample[2] *verb* (*present participle* **sampling,** *past* **sampled**)

to try: *I have* **sampled** *all the cakes and I like Jane's best.*

○ **sand** /sænd/ *noun* (*no plural*)

fine powder, usually white or yellow, made of rock, often found next to the sea and in deserts

sands *plural noun* places covered with sand

'**sandy** *adjective* (**sandier, sandiest**): *a* **sandy** *shore*

sandal
/'sændl/
noun
an open shoe
that can be
put on
easily

a pair of sandals

sandwich /'sændwɪtʃ/ *noun*
(*plural* **sandwiches**)
two pieces of bread put together
with something else in between
them: *I made a chicken* **sandwich.**

sane /seɪn/ *adjective*
(**saner, sanest**)
not mad; reasonable: *I don't think
a* **sane** *person would drive as
dangerously as he did.*

sang /sæŋ/ see **sing**

sank /sæŋk/ see **sink**

sap /sæp/ *noun* (*no plural*)
the liquid inside a plant which
feeds it

sardine /sɑːˈdiːn/ *noun*
a small fish that is usually put into
tins and used for food

sat /sæt/ see **sit**

satellite /'sætəlaɪt/ *noun*
something which moves round the
Earth or another planet (=mass
like the Earth which goes round
the sun): *They receive television
pictures by* **satellite** (=pictures sent
out in one part of the world, which
hit a man-made satellite and come
back to Earth in a different place).
(picture on page 259)

satisfy /'sætɪsfaɪ/ *verb* (*present
participle* **satisfying,** *past* **satisfied**)
1 to be enough or good enough
for: *This work does not* **satisfy** *me.*
2 to make sure: *I* **satisfied** *my
employer that I had finished.*
    satisfaction /ˌsætɪsˈfækʃn/
noun (*no plural*) being satisfied;
pleasure: *He looked at his work
with a smile of* **satisfaction.**

° **satisˈfactory** *adjective* enough
or good enough

° **Saturday** /'sætədeɪ, -dɪ/ *noun*
the seventh day of the week

sauce /sɔːs/ *noun*
a liquid that we put on or eat with
food to improve its taste

saucepan /'sɔːspən/ *noun*
a pan with a handle for cooking
things over heat

saucer /'sɔːsər/ *noun*
a small plate that a cup stands on
(picture at **cup**)

sausage
/'sɒsɪdʒ/
noun
finely
chopped
meat cooked inside a thin skin

sausages

savage /'sævɪdʒ/ *adjective*
wild and fierce: *a* **savage** *animal*

° **save** /seɪv/ *verb* (*present participle*
saving, *past* **saved**)
1 to help someone or something to
be safe: *I* **saved** *the animals from
the flood.*
2 to keep something until it is
wanted: *If you* **save** (*money*) *now,
you will be able to buy a car soon.*
3 to use less: *We should* **save** *oil,
or else there won't be any left in
the world.*
    savings *plural noun* money that
you keep without spending: *He
used his* **savings** *to buy the
bicycle.*

saviour /'seɪvjər/ *noun*
someone who saves others from
danger or evil

saw[1] /sɔː/ see **see**

saw[2] *noun*
a tool
with a
blade with
metal teeth, used for cutting
through wood or metal

saw

teeth

saw³ *verb* (*present participle* **sawing**, *past tense* **sawed**, *past participle* **sawn**)
to use a saw to cut something: *He* **sawed** *the wood into three pieces.*

° **say** /seɪ/ *verb* (*present participle* **saying**, *past* **said** /sed/)
to speak something: *He* **said** (*that*) *he wanted to go to town. "I'm going to town", he* **said.**

  'saying *noun* a wise statement that is often said: *"Every dog has his day" is a* **saying,** *meaning that everyone gets his chance of doing well.*

scab /skæb/ *noun*
a hard covering which grows over a wound

scaffolding /'skæfəldɪŋ/ *noun* (*no plural*)
a framework of bars fixed to a building for the builders to stand on while they work

scald /skɔːld/ *verb*
to burn with steam or boiling water

scale /skeɪl/ *noun*
1 marks on a measuring instrument: *A machine for weighing people has a* **scale** *from one pound to 300 pounds on it.*
2 the way distances or sizes are shown on a map, a model, etc.: *The* **scale** *of this map is one centimetre to the kilometre* (=on this map, every centimetre represents one kilometre of country).
3 a set of musical notes going up or down in order
4 a round shiny part of the skin: *Fish have* **scales.** (picture at **fish**)

scales /skeɪlz/ *plural noun* a machine for weighing things or people

scales

scalp /skælp/ *noun*
the skin and hair of the head

scamper /'skæmpər/ *verb*
to run lightly and quickly: *The dog* **scampered** *along the road.*

scandal /'skændl/ *noun*
something which causes a lot of people to talk and show that they do not approve: *There was a great* **scandal** *when we found out that the doctor had been sent to prison for stealing.*

scar¹ /skɑːr/ *noun*
a mark left on the skin where a wound has been

scar² *verb* (*present participle* **scarring**, *past* **scarred**)
to make a scar: *His face was badly* **scarred** *after the car accident.*

scarce /skeəs/ *adjective*
not often seen or found; uncommon: *That bird has become* **scarce** *in this country.*

  'scarcely *adverb:* *There is* **scarcely** (=almost not) *enough food.*

scare¹ /skeər/ *verb* (*present participle* **scaring**, *past* **scared**)
to make someone afraid: *I was* **scared of** *the big dog.*

  'scarecrow *noun* a wooden figure dressed in old clothes and put in a field of crops to frighten birds away

scare² *noun*
something that makes you afraid

scarf /skɑːf/ *noun* (*plural* **scarves**)
a piece of cloth worn round the neck or head

scarlet /'skɑːlət/ *noun, adjective*
bright red: **scarlet** *drops of blood*

° **scatter** /'skætər/ *verb*
to go or make things or people go in different directions: *The farmer* **scattered** *the corn in the yard for the hens.*

°**scene** /siːn/ *noun*

1 what we see in a special place: *The teacher saw a busy* **scene** *as she entered the classroom.*

2 the place where something happens: *a crowd at the* **scene** *of the accident*

3 a short part of a play: *This play is divided into three acts, and each act has three* **scenes.**

'**scenery** *noun* (*no plural*) **1** what we see of the country: *The* **scenery** *in the mountains is very beautiful.* **2** the painted pictures at the back of a stage

scent /sent/ *noun*

1 a nice smell: *the* **scent** *of flowers*

2 (*no plural*) liquid having a nice smell: *What a lovely smell! Are you wearing* **scent?**

schedule /'ʃedjuːl, 'ske-/ *noun*

a list of times when buses or trains should come or when things are to be done: *The next thing on our* **schedule** *is to telephone our friends.*

scheme[1] /skiːm/ *noun*

a plan: *He thought of a* **scheme** *to get some money.*

scheme[2] *verb* (*present participle* **scheming,** *past* **schemed**)

to make plans, especially dishonest ones

scholar /'skɒlə^r/ *noun*

1 a person who has studied and knows a lot about a special thing

2 a clever student who has been given money so that he or she can continue to study

scholarship *noun* money given to a clever student so that he or she can continue to study

°**school** /skuːl/ *noun*

a place where children go to learn: *Children who go to* **school** *are* **schoolchildren.**

°**science** /'saɪəns/ *noun*

the study of nature and the way things in the world are made, behave, etc.: *The chief* **sciences** *are chemistry, physics* (see), *and biology* (see).

°ˌscien'**tific** *adjective* of or about science: **scientific** *studies*

'**scientist** *noun* a person who studies or practises science

°**scissors** /'sɪzəz/ *plural noun*

an instrument for cutting with two blades joined together: *Have you got a* **(pair of) scissors?**

a pair of scissors

°**scold** /skəʊld/ *verb*

to tell someone angrily that they have done wrong: *My mother* **scolded** *me when I dropped the plates.*

scoop /skuːp/ *verb*

to take out with the hands or a spoon: *She* **scooped** *flour out of the bag.*

scorch /skɔːtʃ/ *verb*

to burn lightly, usually so that there is a brown mark: *I* **scorched** *my dress with the iron.*

score[1] /skɔː^r/ *noun*

the marks or points you get in a game or test: *The* **score** *in the football game was 4-1* (four to one team, one to the other).

score[2] *verb* (*present participle* **scoring,** *past* **scored**)

1 to win: *to* **score** *a point*

2 to keep a note of the score: *Will you* **score** *for us when we play?*

scorn[1] /skɔːn/ *verb*

to think that someone or something is worthless; not to respect

scorn[2] *noun* (*no plural*)
lack of respect: *He showed his* **scorn** *for my question by saying he would not answer it.*

scorpion /ˈskɔːpɪən/ *noun*
a small creature which stings with its tail

scorpion

scowl[1] /skaʊl/ *verb*
to look angry, especially by pulling the eyebrows (= hairy lines above the eyes) down

scowl[2] *noun*
an angry look on the face: *a* **scowl** *on his face*

scramble /ˈskræmbl/ *verb* (*present participle* **scrambling**, *past* **scrambled**)
to climb on hands and knees: *The children* **scrambled** *up the hill.*

scrap /skræp/ *noun*
a small piece: *a* **scrap** *of paper*

scrape /skreɪp/ *verb* (*present participle* **scraping**, *past* **scraped**)
to rub with a sharp instrument such as a knife: **Scrape** *the mud off your shoes with this knife.*

scratch[1] /skrætʃ/ *verb*
to make marks with something pointed: *The stick* **scratched** *the side of the car. He* **scratched** *the insect bite on his leg (with his nails).*

scratch[2] *noun* (*plural* **scratches**)
a mark or small wound made by scratching: *a* **scratch** *on her hand*

scream /skriːm/ *verb*
to give a loud high cry: *She* **screamed** *with fear.* **scream** *noun*

screech /skriːtʃ/ *verb*
to give a loud high noise: *The car tyres* **screeched** *on the road as it turned too fast.* **screech** *noun*

screen /skriːn/ *noun*
1 a flat, square surface on which pictures can be shown: *a television* **screen**
2 a covered frame used to stop someone being seen, protect from the cold, etc.

° **screw**[1] /skruː/ *noun*
a thing like a nail which can be pushed into something by being turned round and round

screwdriver

screw

'screwdriver *noun: You turn the screws round and round with a* **screwdriver.**

° **screw**[2] *verb*
to turn round and round; fix or fasten with screws, or by turning round and round: *She* **screwed** *the top onto the bottle. He* **screwed** *the mirror onto the wall.*

scribble /ˈskrɪbl/ *verb* (*present participle* **scribbling**, *past* **scribbled**)
to write quickly or carelessly

scripture /ˈskrɪptʃəʳ/ *noun*
1 an old religious writing
2 learning about religion

scrub /skrʌb/ *verb* (*present participle* **scrubbing**, *past* **scrubbed**)
to rub with a hard brush

sculptor /ˈskʌlptəʳ/ *noun*
a person who cuts shapes from wood, stone, or metal
sculpture /ˈskʌlptʃəʳ/ *noun* a figure made from wood, stone, etc.; the art of making these figures

° **sea** /siː/ *noun*
a large mass of salt water that surrounds the land (see picture on page 185)

'sea-shell *noun* the shell of a

small sea animal

'seaside *noun: We are going to the* seaside *for our holiday.*

seal[1] /siːl/ *noun*

an animal with a thick coat and flat limbs for swimming which lives on cold sea coasts

seal[2] *verb*

to close firmly so that it cannot open by mistake: *We* seal *the back of envelopes* (=paper covers for letters).

seam /siːm/ *noun*

a line of sewing where two pieces of cloth are joined together

° search[1] /sɜːtʃ/ *verb*

to look for: *I* searched *everywhere for the book.*

° search[2] *noun (plural* searches)

an act of searching: *After a long* search, *they found the lost child.*

° season /'siːzn/ *noun*

one of the four parts of the year; a special time of year: *Summer is the hottest* season.

° seat /siːt/ *noun*

a place to sit, or a thing to sit on: *I could not find a* seat *on the bus. Please* take a seat (=sit down).

° second[1] /'sekənd/ *noun*

a very short length of time; there are 60 seconds in a minute

° second[2]

the one after the first; 2nd: *This is the* second *time I have met him. I came* second *in the race.*

secondary school /'sekəndrɪ/ *noun*

a school you go to after primary (see) school, when you are 11 or 12

° secret /'siːkrɪt/ *noun, adjective*

something that has not been told to other people: *Don't tell anyone about our plan,* keep it a secret — *it's a* secret *plan.*

° secretary /'sekrətrɪ/ *noun* (*plural* secretaries)

1 a person who does office work, writes letters, arranges journeys, etc. for an employer

2 in some countries, a government officer

section /'sekʃn/ *noun*

a part: *One* section *of the class was reading and the other* section *was writing.*

secure /sɪ'kjʊəʳ/ *adjective*

1 safe: *I don't feel* secure *when I am alone in the house.*

2 strong and fixed firmly: *This lock is* secure.

se'curity *noun (no plural): The government looks after the* security *of the country.*

° see /siː/ *verb (present participle* seeing, *past tense* saw /sɔː/, *past participle* seen /siːn/)

1 to use the eyes to know something: *I can* see *two ships in the harbour.*

2 to understand: *I don't* see *what you mean.*

3 (used in sentences like these): Please see *who is at the door* (=go and look). *She* sees (=meets) *him after work. I'll* see *if I can help you* (=I will think about it and act if possible). See to (=Do what is needed about) *the dinner, will you?*

° seed /siːd/ *noun*

a small grain from which a plant grows

seek /siːk/ *verb* (*present participle* seeking, *past* sought /sɔːt/)

to look for: *We* sought *an answer to the question, but couldn't find one.*

° seem /siːm/ *verb*

to appear as or to: *The man* seemed *to be ill.*

seep /siːp/ *verb*
(of a liquid) to flow slowly from or through: *Rain* **seeped** *through the roof.*

seesaw /'siːsɔː/ *noun*
a long piece of wood balanced in the middle, so that when a person sits at each end, they can swing up and down

seesaw

seize /siːz/ *verb* (*present participle* **seizing,** *past* **seized**)
to take hold of quickly and firmly or roughly

seldom /'seldəm/ *adverb*
only a few times; not often: *The children are* **seldom** *ill.*

select /sɪ'lekt/ *verb*
to choose: *I was* **selected** *for the team.*
se'lection *noun* (*no plural*) some examples: *Here is a* **selection** *of our books.*

° **self** /self/ *noun* (*plural* **selves**)
your own person: *Have you got* **yourself** *a job? I cut* **myself** *on a knife. He can look after* **himself.**
'**selfish** *adjective* always thinking of yourself and not other people: *Don't be* **selfish.**
'**selfishly** *adverb*
'**selfishness** *noun* (*no plural*)

° **sell** /sel/ *verb* (*present participle* **selling,** *past* **sold** /səʊld/)
to give in exchange for money: *She* **sold** *her old bicycle to me.*
'**seller** *noun*

semicircle /'semɪsɜːkl/ *noun*
half a circle: *Halfway between new moon and full moon, the moon is a* **semicircle.**

semicolon /ˌsemɪ'kəʊlən/ *noun*
the sign ; used in writing to separate parts of a sentence: *It was a long walk; I'm very tired.*

senate /'senət/ *noun*
one of the groups which make up the government in some countries
senator *noun* a member of a senate

° **send** /send/ *verb* (*present participle* **sending,** *past* **sent**)
to cause a person or thing to go somewhere: *She* **sent** *me a present.* **Send** *him to me when he gets in.* *She* **sent for** *the doctor* (=asked the doctor to come).

senior /'siːnjəʳ/ *adjective*
1 older: *She teaches a* **senior** *class.*
2 higher in position or importance: *She used to be a junior manager, but now she has a* **senior** *position in the company.*

° **sense**[1] /sens/ *noun*
1 hearing, seeing, tasting, feeling, and smelling are the five senses: *He has a good* **sense** *of smell.*
2 (*no plural*) good understanding and reasonable ideas: *What she is saying doesn't* **make sense.**
sen'sation *noun* **1** feeling: *a* **sensation** *of pain* **2** excited interest: *Her strange clothes caused a* **sensation** *in the village.*
'**sensible** *adjective* reasonable: *If you are* **sensible** *you will study for another year.*
'**sensitive** *adjective: She is* **sensitive to** *what people think of her* (=she worries about what people think).

sense[2] *verb* (*present participle* **sensing,** *past* **sensed**)
to know through the senses; feel: *The dog* **sensed** *that I was afraid.*

° **sentence** /'sentəns/ *noun*
a group of words which makes a statement and contains a verb: *This is a* **sentence.**

° **separate**[1] /'seprət/ *adjective*
different: *They have gone to* **separate** *places.*

° **separate**[2] /'sepəreɪt/ *verb* (*present participle* **separating,** *past* **separated**)
1 to go in different directions: *The two children* **separated** *at the end of the road.*
2 to make, become, or keep in different places: *A fence* **separated** *the cows from the pigs.*
ˌsepaˈration *noun* time away from each other

° **September** /sep'tembə^r/ *noun*
the ninth month of the year

sergeant /'sɑːdʒənt/ *noun*
an officer in the army or police force

serial /'sɪərɪəl/ *noun*
a story which is told or written in parts

series /'sɪərɪz/ *noun* (*plural* **series**)
a number of things coming one after the other: *He saw a* **series** *of white arrows painted on the road.*

° **serious** /'sɪərɪəs/ *adjective*
1 not cheerful or full of fun: *He is a* **serious** *boy. Be* **serious** *for a minute and listen to me.*
2 important: *How to stop people dying of hunger is a* **serious** *question.* **seriously** *adverb*

sermon /'sɜːmən/ *noun*
a talk given by a priest in a church

serve /sɜːv/ *verb* (*present participle* **serving,** *past* **served**)
1 to do work for other people; be useful to; sell things to: *The girl in the shop* **served** *me.*
2 to give food to: *Please* **serve yourselves** (=take what food you want)! *The chicken was* **served** *with rice.*
'**servant** *noun* a person who works for someone in his house

service /'sɜːvɪs/ *noun*
1 something that you do for others: *We need the* **services** *of a doctor.*
2 selling in a shop: *The* **service** *in this shop is always slow; the girls are very lazy.*
3 something that people can use to help them: *The train* **service** *to the capital is very good.*
4 a church ceremony: *Morning* **service** *will be at 11 o'clock.*

session /'seʃn/ *noun*
a meeting of people for some purpose: *a dancing* **session**

° **set**[1] /set/ *noun*
1 a group of things thought of together: *I have bought a* **set** *of shelves for the kitchen.*

television set / set

2 an electrical instrument, especially a radio or television

° **set**[2] *verb* (*present participle* **setting,** *past* **set**)
1 to put: *I* **set** *the flowers on the table.*
2 to make something happen: *I* **set fire to** (=made burn) *the paper.*
3 give work to: *The teacher* **set** *us a test.*
4 to go down in the sky: *The sun was* **setting.**
5 to go: *He* **set off/set out** *on his journey.*
6 to put ready: *I* **set** *the table for dinner.*

settle /'setl/ *verb* (*present participle* **settling,** *past* **settled**)
1 to go and live in a place: *My son has* **settled** *happily in America.*
2 to make comfortable or calm: *He* **settled** (*himself*) *down with a book*

seven

3 to rest on something: *The insect* **settled** *on a leaf.*
4 to decide something: *We have* **settled** *who will pay for the meal.*
settlement *noun: We reached a* **settlement** *about which of us should pay for the meal. The* **settlement** *of Africa by white people started 500 years ago.*
settler *noun: The first white* **settlers** *in Africa were farmers.*

seven /'sevn/ *noun, adjective*
the number 7
seventh *noun, adjective* number 7 in order; 7th

seventeen /ˌsevn'tiːn/ *noun, adjective*
the number 17
seventeenth *noun, adjective* number 17 in order; 17th

seventy /'sevntɪ/ *noun, adjective*
the number 70
seventieth *noun, adjective* number 70 in order; 70th

° **several** /'sevrəl/ *adjective*
more than two, but not many: *She has* **several** *friends in the town.*

° **severe** /sə'vɪəʳ/ *adjective* (**severer, severest**)
hard; hard to bear: *a* **severe** *punishment/a* **severe** *pain*
severely *adverb*

° **sew** /səʊ/ *verb* (*present participle* **sewing**, *past tense* **sewed**, *past participle* **sewn**)
to mend or make by using a needle and thread: *I like* **sewing**. *He* **sewed** *a button onto his shirt.*
sewing *noun* something being sewn
'sewing machine *noun: A* **sewing machine** *helps us to sew things quickly.*

sewing machine

° **sex** /seks/ *noun*
1 being male or female: *Which* **sex** *is your cat?*
2 what is done between a male and a female to make babies

shabby /'ʃæbɪ/ *adjective*
rather old, cheap, or dirty: **shabby** *clothes*

° **shade**[1] /ʃeɪd/ *noun*
1 (*no plural*) shelter from the sun or other light: *They sat in the* **shade** (*of a tree*).
2 a sort of colour: *I want a darker* **shade** *of blue; this* **shade** *is too light.*
shady *adjective* (**shadier, shadiest**): *It's cool and* **shady** *under the tree.*

° **shade**[2] *verb* (*present participle* **shading**, *past* **shaded**)
to shelter from light: *I* **shaded** *my eyes with my hand.*

° **shadow** /'ʃædəʊ/ *noun*
a dark shape made by something when it blocks the light: *The* **shadows** *of the trees grew longer as the afternoon went on.*

shaft /ʃɑːft/ *noun*
1 a long thin pole: *the* **shaft** *of an arrow*
2 a long hole leading to a mine

° **shake** /ʃeɪk/ *verb*
(*present participle* **shaking**, *past tense* **shook** /ʃʊk/ *past participle* **shaken**)
to move quickly from side to side, up and down, etc.: *The house* **shook** *as the heavy lorry went past. She* **shook** *the box to see if there was any money in it. I asked her if she wanted me, but she* **shook** *her head* (=meaning "no").

° **shall** /ʃəl; *strong* ʃæl/ *verb*
1 (a word used instead of **will** with **I** and **we** to say that something is going to happen): *I* **shall** *work*

tomorrow. We **shan't** (= shall not) go out, **we'll** (= we shall) *stay indoors.*

2 (used with **I** and **we** in questions when asking or offering to do something): **Shall** *we all go to the film tonight?*

Look at **will** and **should**.

shallow /'ʃæləʊ/ *adjective*
not deep: *The sea is* **shallow** *here.*

○ **shame** /ʃeɪm/ *noun*
the feeling you have when you have done something wrong or silly: *When his teacher told his parents about his behaviour, he felt great* **shame. What a shame** (= I'm sorry) *that you can't come to dinner tomorrow!*

shampoo[1] /ʃæm'puː/ *noun*
a special soap for washing the hair

shampoo[2] *verb*
to wash with shampoo

shan't /ʃɑːnt/ see **shall**

○ **shape**[1] /ʃeɪp/ *noun*
the form of something: *What is the* **shape** *of a coin? It is round.*

shape[2] *verb* (*present participle* **shaping,** *past* **shaped**)
to make into a certain shape: *He* **shaped** *a pot out of the clay.*

○ **share**[1] /ʃeə^r/ *verb* (*present participle* **sharing,** *past* **shared**)
to divide something so that two or more people can have some: *We* **shared** *the sweets.*

○ **share**[2] *noun*
a part that has been divided: *We gave each of the five children an equal* **share.**

shark /ʃɑːk/ *noun*
a large fierce fish

shark

○ **sharp** /ʃɑːp/ *adjective*
1 pointed or having a cutting edge:

a **sharp** *knife/a needle with a* **sharp** *point*
2 sudden or quick: *There is a* **sharp** *bend in the road. He said something* **sharp** *to the little girl* (=sudden and angry) *and she started to cry.*
3 able to see things far away or very small: **sharp** *eyes*
'**sharply** *adverb*

sharpen /'ʃɑːpən/ *verb*
to make sharp: *to* **sharpen** *a knife*

shatter /'ʃætə^r/ *verb*
to break into many pieces: *The glass* **shattered** *when I dropped it.*

shave[1] /ʃeɪv/ *verb* (*present participle* **shaving,** *past* **shaved**)
to take hair from the face or body by cutting it very close: *My father* **shaves** *every day.*

shave[2] *noun*
an act of shaving: *He had a* **shave** *before he went out. When an accident nearly happens, we say it is* **a close shave** *or* **a narrow shave.**

shawl /ʃɔːl/ *noun*
a long piece of cloth worn round the shoulders and head

○ **she** /ʃɪ; *strong* ʃiː/ (*plural* **they**)
the female person or animal that the sentence is about: **She** *is my sister —* **she's** (=she is) *nine and* **she's** (=she has) *got brown eyes. That's a good cow —* **she** *gives a lot of milk.*

shear /ʃɪə^r/ *verb*
to cut wool from a sheep or goat
shears *plural noun* large scissors for shearing, for cutting plants, etc.

shed[1] /ʃed/ *noun*
a small wooden hut

shed[2] *verb* (*present participle* **shedding,** *past* **shed**)
to let fall: *Some trees* **shed** *their leaves in cold weather.*

sheep

°sheep /ʃiːp/ *noun*
(*plural* **sheep**)
an animal that is kept for meat and for the wool from its thick coat

sheep

sheer /ʃɪəʳ/ *adjective*
straight down; very steep: *There was a sheer drop from where we stood to the sea below us.*

sheet /ʃiːt/ *noun*
a large flat piece of something: *Everyone had two sheets of paper to draw on. There are sheets (= pieces of thin cloth) on our beds.*

°shelf /ʃelf/ *noun* (*plural* **shelves**)
a board fixed to a wall or in a cupboard for putting things on: *He took the cup off the shelf.*

°shell /ʃel/ *noun*
the hard outside covering of some fish, fruit, or of eggs: **Shellfish** *are good to eat.*

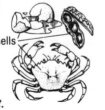
shells

°shelter¹ /ˈʃeltəʳ/ *noun*
somewhere you can be protected from the weather, war, etc.: *He stood in the shelter at the bus stop. We took shelter under the trees when it rained.*

°shelter² *verb*
to protect: *We sheltered under the tree.*

shepherd /ˈʃepəd/ *noun*
someone who looks after sheep

shield¹ /ʃiːld/ *noun*
a piece of wood or metal that soldiers used to hold in front of them to protect their bodies in battle

shield² *verb*
to protect by holding something over or in front of: *He shielded his eyes from the sun.*

shift¹ /ʃɪft/ *verb*
to move: *Shall I shift the chairs?*

shift² *noun*
1 a set of people who work together at one time: *Peter is on the day shift and I am on the night shift.*
2 the length of time that one group works

°shine /ʃaɪn/ *verb* (*present participle* **shining**, *past* **shone** /ʃɒn/)
to give out light, or to throw back light: *The sun shines. The water shone in the sunlight.*
'shiny *adjective* (**shinier, shiniest**): shiny shoes

°ship /ʃɪp/ *noun*
a large boat that goes on the sea
shipping *noun* (*no plural*) ships

°shirt /ʃɜːt/ *noun*
a piece of clothing that covers the upper part of the body and the arms

shirt   sleeve

shiver /ˈʃɪvəʳ/ *verb*
to shake with cold or fear: *He shivered as he heard the strange noise in the night.* **shiver** *noun*

°shock¹ /ʃɒk/ *noun*
1 the feeling caused by an unpleasant surprise; something causing this feeling: *It was a great shock for him when his wife died.*
2 a pain caused by electricity going through you: *An electric shock can kill you.*

°shock² *verb*
to give a shock: *I was shocked when I heard about your accident.*

○ **shoe** /ʃuː/ *noun*
a covering for the foot with a hard bottom part to walk on: **a pair of shoes**

'**shoelace** *noun* a string used to fasten a shoe

shone /ʃɒn/ see **shine**

shook /ʃʊk/ see **shake**

shoot[1] /ʃuːt/ *verb*
(*present participle* **shooting**, *past* **shot** /ʃɒt/)
1 to fire at and hit: *He* **shot** *the bird with his gun.*
2 to move quickly: *He* **shot** *out of school when the bell rang.*

shoot[2] *noun*
part of a plant that leaves will grow from

○ **shop**[1] /ʃɒp/ *noun*
a place where you can go and buy things

'**shop**,**keeper** *noun* a person who runs a shop

shop[2] *verb* (*present participle* **shopping**, *past* **shopped**)
to buy things: *We often* **shop** *in Kings' Road.*

'**shopping** *noun* (*no plural*) **1** buying things: *I have to* **go shopping** *this afternoon.* **2** the things that are bought: *a bag of* **shopping**

○ **shore** /ʃɔːʳ/ *noun*
the flat land at the edge of the sea or a large area of water: *We walked along the* **seashore.**

○ **short** /ʃɔːt/ *adjective*
not very tall; not long: *It's a* **short** *distance to school. Mary is much* **shorter** *than her mother. Are you* **short** *of* (= do you need) *money?*

'**shortage** *noun* not enough: *a* **shortage** *of water*

shorten /'ʃɔːtn/ *verb*
to make shorter: *to* **shorten** *a dress*

shorts /ʃɔːts/
plural noun
trousers which stop above the knee: (**a pair of**) **shorts**

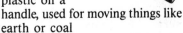
shorts

shot[1] /ʃɒt/ see **shoot**

shot[2] *noun*
1 the sound of a bullet (= hard thing) fired from a gun: *There was a* **shot**, *and the bird fell dead.*
2 a try: *He's* **having a shot** *at cooking the dinner.*

○ **should** /ʃəd; *strong* ʃʊd/ *verb*
1 ought to; have a duty to; would be wise to: *You* **should** *go home now, or your mother will be angry. You* **shouldn't** *stay here anyway.*
2 (the word for **shall** in the past): *I told my mother I* **should** *be late home.*
3 (used in sentences with **if**): *If you* **should** *find my pen, please send it to me.*

○ **shoulder** /'ʃəʊldəʳ/ *noun*
the top part of the body where the arms join it (picture on page 133)

○ **shout**[1] /ʃaʊt/ *verb*
to speak in a loud voice: *He is rather far away, but if you* **shout**, *he may hear you.*

shout[2] *noun*
an act or sound of shouting: *to give a* **shout**

shovel[1] /'ʃʌvl/ *noun*
a wide piece of metal or plastic on a handle, used for moving things like earth or coal

shovel

shovel[2] *verb* (*present participle* **shovelling**, *past* **shovelled**)
to move with a shovel

○ **show**[1] /ʃəʊ/ *verb* (*present participle* **showing**, *past tense* **showed**, *past*

participle **shown**)

1 to let someone see something: *He* **showed** *me his new radio. Can you* **show** *me the way to Gabriel's house? Her dress was torn, but it didn't* **show** (=people couldn't see it). *The girl* **showed off** (=let people see) *her new dress. That child* **shows off** (=wants people to notice him, so behaves in a loud or silly way).

2 to explain; make clear: *The teacher* **showed** *us how to draw.*

○ **show**² *noun*

1 a lot of things gathered together for people to see: *Many people went to see the flower* **show.**

2 something that people like to go and watch, especially a play, singing, etc.

shred /ʃred/ *noun*
a small piece torn off: *The cat tore the paper* **to shreds.**

shrewd /ʃruːd/ *adjective*
clever, especially about business

shriek /ʃriːk/ *verb*
to make a high loud cry: *She* **shrieked** *in fear.* **shriek** *noun*

shrill /ʃrɪl/ *adjective*
having a loud, high sound that seems to go through your head: *a* **shrill** *voice*

shrine /ʃraɪn/ *noun*
a holy place

shrink /ʃrɪŋk/ *verb*
(*present participle* **shrinking,** *past tense* **shrank** /ʃræŋk/, *past participle* **shrunk** /ʃrʌŋk/)
to get smaller: *The dress* **shrank** *when I washed it.*

shrub /ʃrʌb/ *noun*
a small low tree

shrug /ʃrʌg/ *verb* (*present participle* **shrugging,** *past* **shrugged**)
to lift and drop the shoulders to show that you do not know or do not care: *She* **shrugged** (**her shoulders**) *and said "I don't know."*

shudder /ˈʃʌdəʳ/ *verb*
to shake with fear, dislike, etc.: *He* **shuddered** *when he saw the dead animal.* **shudder** *noun*

○ **shut** /ʃʌt/ *verb* (*present participle* **shutting,** *past* **shut**)
to move something so that it is not open; close: *Please will you* **shut** *the door? He decided to* **shut down** (=close for ever) *the shop.* **Shut up!** (=a rather rude way of saying Be quiet!)

shutter *noun* a cover for a window to keep out the light

shy /ʃaɪ/ *adjective* (**shier, shiest**)
rather afraid to be with other people: *The child was* **shy** *and hid behind his mother.* **'shyly** *adverb*

sick /sɪk/ *adjective*
1 bringing or wanting to bring food up from the stomach: *She feels* **sick** *in buses.*
2 ill: *My father is a very* **sick** *man.* **'sickness** *noun* illness; disease

○ **side** /saɪd/ *noun*
1 one of the parts of something that is not the top, bottom, back, or front: *He went round to the* **side** *of the house. I have a pain in my left* **side** (=the left part of my body). *The chair had arms at the* **sides.** *He stood at the* **side** (=edge) *of the street. You have only written on one* **side** *of the paper, why don't you write on* **both sides?**
2 a team: *Which* **side** *do you want to win?*

○ **'sideways** *adverb* **1** to one side: *He stepped* **sideways** *off the path to let me pass.* **2** turned so that the side is at the front or on top: *We turned the table* **sideways** *to get it into the room.*

sigh[1] /saɪ/ *verb*
to breathe once deeply, as when you are tired, sad, etc.

sigh[2] *noun*
an act or sound of sighing: *"I wish I had finished this work," she said with a* **sigh.**

○ **sight** /saɪt/ *noun*
1 (*no plural*) the power to see: *She lost her* **sight** *in an accident.*
2 a thing seen: *The fire was a frightening* **sight.** *The visitors to the town went* **sightseeing** (=looking at all the interesting things to see).
3 (*no plural*) seeing: *I caught* **sight of** (=saw) *an empty seat at the back of the bus. When he came* **into sight** (=was seen), *I waved.*

○ **sign**[1] /saɪn/ *noun*
a movement, mark, or words which have a message for the person who sees it or them: *He made a* **sign** *for me to follow him. The* **sign** *by the road said "No Parking"* (=you cannot leave your car here).
'signpost *noun*

signpost

○ **sign**[2] *verb*
to write your name
signature /'sɪgnətʃər/ *noun* a name written in the usual way

○ **signal**[1] /'sɪgnəl/ *noun*
a movement or thing which tells you what to do: *The railway* **signal** *showed that the train could pass.*

○ **signal**[2] *verb* (*present participle* **signalling**, *past* **signalled**)
to give a signal: *The teacher* **signalled** *to the boy to begin.*

significant /sɪg'nɪfɪkənt/ *adjective*
having a special meaning: *It is* **significant** *that the animals are*

excited: *I think a storm is coming.*
significance *noun* (*no plural*)
meaning: *What is the* **significance** *of this speech?*

○ **silence** /'saɪləns/ *noun* (*no plural*)
complete quiet: *They worked* **in silence.**
○ **silent** *adjective* without any noise; completely quiet
silently *adverb: The children worked* **silently.**

silk /sɪlk/ *noun* (*no plural*)
a fine cloth made from the threads that come from a silkworm (see)

silkworm /'sɪlkwɜːm/ *noun*
a caterpillar (see) that makes the soft threads from which the material called silk can be made

○ **silly** /'sɪlɪ/ *adjective* (**sillier, silliest**)
not reasonable or clever: *Don't be* **silly,** *that insect can't hurt you.*

silver /'sɪlvər/ *noun* (*no plural*)
1 a soft shiny grey-white metal used for ornaments, old coins, etc.
2 the colour of this metal

similar /'sɪmɪlər/ *adjective*
like: *My new dress is* **similar to** *the one you have. Our dresses are* **similar.**
similarity /ˌsɪmɪ'lærətɪ/ *noun* (*plural* **similarities**) likeness: *a* **similarity** *between the sisters*

○ **simple** /'sɪmpl/ *adjective* (**simpler, simplest**)
1 easy to understand: *a* **simple** *question*
2 not ornamented; plain: **simple** *clothes/* **simple** *food*
3 not very clever: *a* **simple** *child*
simply *adverb*

simplify /'sɪmplɪfaɪ/ *verb* (*present participle* **simplifying**, *past* **simplified**)
to make simple: *The English in this story has been* **simplified** *to make it easier to understand.*

sin /sɪn/ *noun*

something people think is a very bad act; something your religion teaches you is wrong: *It's a* **sin** *to tell lies.*

° **since** /sɪns/

between a time in the past and now; after: *He came to school last week, but I haven't seen him* **since.** *She has been ill* **since** *Christmas. It is six years* **since** *we first met. We have been friends* **ever since** (*then*).

° **sincere** /sɪn'sɪəʳ/ *adjective*

true and real; not pretending: *He was* **sincere** *in his wish to help us.*
sincerely *adverb: You can end a letter to someone you know with* **"Yours sincerely"** *and then write your name.*

° **sing** /sɪŋ/ *verb* (*present participle* **singing,** *past tense* **sang** /sæŋ/, *past participle* **sung** /sʌŋ/)

to make music with the voice: *She* **sang** *as she worked. She* **sang** *a song.*

singer *noun* someone who sings

° **single** /'sɪŋgl/ *adjective*

one only: *There is a* **single** *name on the blackboard — whose is it? A* **single** *person is one without a husband or wife. I would like a* **single ticket** (=for one journey only, not a return ticket). *A* **single** *bed is made for one person.*

singular /'sɪŋgjələʳ/ *adjective, noun*

only one: *"Dog" is the* **singular** *of "dogs".* The opposite of **singular** is **plural.**

sink[1] /sɪŋk/ *noun*
a large basin for washing clothes or dishes in

tap
sink

° **sink**[2] *verb* (*present participle* **sinking,** *past tense* **sank** /sæŋk/,

past participle **sunk** /sʌŋk/)

1 to go down: *The sun* **sank** *behind the mountain.*

2 to go down, or make go down in the water: *The ship is* **sinking.**

sip[1] /sɪp/ *verb* (*present participle* **sipping,** *past* **sipped**)

to drink in very small amounts: *She* **sipped** *the hot tea.*

sip[2] *noun*

an act of sipping; a very small amount: *I had a* **sip** *of his drink.*

sir /sɜːʳ/ *noun*

1 a polite way of speaking or writing to a man: *I began my letter "Dear* **Sir".**

2 the title of a knight (see)

siren /'saɪərən/ *noun*

something which makes a loud long warning sound

° **sister** /'sɪstəʳ/ *noun*

1 a girl who has the same parents as you: *She is my* **sister.** *We are* **sisters.**

2 a nurse who looks after a part of a hospital

3 a nun (see)
'sister-in-law *noun* (*plural* **sisters-in-law**) the sister of your wife or husband, or the wife of your brother

° **sit** /sɪt/ *verb* (*present participle* **sitting,** *past* **sat** /sæt/)

to rest on the bottom of the back: *He* **sat** *in a chair. Please* **sit down.**
'sitting-room *noun* a room in a house where we usually sit

site /saɪt/ *noun*

a place where a building is, was, or will be: *The* **site** *of the new hotel is by the sea.*

situate /'sɪtʃʊeɪt/ *verb* (*present participle* **situating,** *past* **situated**)

to put; place: *The house is* **situated** *on a hill.*

,situ'ation *noun* **1** position **2**

state of events: *This **situation** is very difficult. I want to take the job but I don't like the employer.*

six /sɪks/ *noun, adjective*
the number 6: *I want **six** oranges.*
sixth *noun, adjective* number 6 in order; 6th

sixteen /sɪk'stiːn/ *noun, adjective*
the number 16
sixteenth *noun, adjective* number 16 in order; 16th

sixty /'sɪkstɪ/ *noun, adjective*
the number 60
sixtieth *noun, adjective* number 60 in order; 60th

° **size** /saɪz/ *noun*
how big something or someone is: *What **size** is your house? The two books were the same **size**. These shoes are **size** 5.*

skate¹ /skeɪt/ *verb* (*present participle* **skating**, *past* **skated**)
to move smoothly over ice or on wheels over the ground: *She **skated** over the ice towards us. He loves **roller skating**.*

skate² *noun*
a special shoe with wheels or a blade fixed under it: **roller skates**/**ice skates**

skeleton
/'skelɪtən/
noun
the bones of a whole animal or person

sketch¹ /sketʃ/ *noun*
(*plural* **sketches**)
a quick drawing

sketch² *verb*
to draw: *He **sketched** the cat.*

skid /skɪd/ *verb* (*present participle* **skidding**, *past* **skidded**)
to slip sideways on a wet surface: *The car **skidded** on a pool of oil and ran into the fence.*

skill /skɪl/ *noun*
the ability to do something well; something you do well: *He has great **skill** in drawing.*
° **'skilful** *adjective* having or showing skill: *a **skilful** piece of work* **'skilfully** *adverb*

° **skin** /skɪn/ *noun*
the outside of a person, animal, vegetable, or fruit: *You can make shoes from the **skins** of animals.*

skinny /'skɪnɪ/ *adjective* (**skinnier**, **skinniest**) very thin: *a **skinny** child*

skip /skɪp/ *verb* (*present participle* **skipping**, *past* **skipped**)
to jump with short light steps, especially over a rope (**skipping rope**) which is made to swing over the head and under the feet

° **skirt** /skɜːt/ *noun*
a piece of
woman's clothing
that hangs
from the waist

skull /skʌl/ *noun*
the bones of the head (picture at **skeleton**)

° **sky** /skaɪ/ *noun* (*plural* **skies**)
the space above the Earth which we can see if we look up: *The **sky** was blue and clear.*

skyscraper /'skaɪskreɪpəʳ/ *noun*
a very tall building

slab /slæb/ *noun*
a large flat block: *a **slab** of stone*

slack /slæk/ *adjective*
1 loose: *The string around the parcel was **slack**.*
2 careless; not caring: **slack** *work*

slam /slæm/ *verb*
(*present participle* **slamming**, *past* **slammed**)
to shut or put down with a loud noise: *He **slammed** the door angrily. She **slammed** the books down on the table.*

slang /slæŋ/ *noun* (*no plural*)
language you use in ordinary talk, but which is not always suitable or correct: *"Shut up" is* **slang**; *it sounds more polite to say "Please be quiet".*

slant /slɑːnt/ *verb*
to lean or slope

slap[1] /slæp/ *verb* (*present participle* **slapping**, *past* **slapped**)
to hit with the flat inside of the hand

slap[2] *noun*
a hit: *I gave the dog a* **slap.**

slaughter[1] /ˈslɔːtəʳ/ *noun* (*no plural*)
killing, especially of animals or large numbers of people: *the* **slaughter** *of cattle for food*

slaughter[2] *verb*
to kill animals or people in large numbers

slave /sleɪv/ *noun*
a person who is owned by another person and has to work for him and has no freedom: *A long time ago, many black people were taken to America as* **slaves.**
　'**slavery** *noun* (*no plural*) **1** being a slave: *to live in* **slavery 2** having slaves: **Slavery** *was abolished* (= not allowed by law) *a long time ago.*

○ **sleep**[1] /sliːp/ *noun* (*no plural*)
the state of not being awake; a time when we are in this state: *He had a long* **sleep.** *He* **went to sleep** *at two o'clock.*

○ **sleep**[2] *verb* (*past* **slept** /slept/)
to be in sleep; not be awake: *He* **slept** *for two hours.*
　'**sleepy** *adjective* (**sleepier**, **sleepiest**) wanting to sleep: *I felt* **sleepy** *all day.*

sleeve /sliːv/ *noun*
part of a piece of clothing which covers the arm: *His shirt had short* **sleeves.** (picture at **shirt**)

slender /ˈslendəʳ/ *adjective*
thin, in a pleasant way: *a* **slender** *figure*

slice[1] /slaɪs/ *noun*
a flat piece cut from something: *a* **slice** *of meat/of bread*

slice[2] *verb* (*present participle* **slicing**, *past* **sliced**)
to cut into thin flat pieces: *I* **sliced** *the bread.*

○ **slide**[1] /slaɪd/ *verb* (*present participle* **sliding**, *past* **slid** /slɪd/)
to move smoothly over a surface: *She fell over and* **slid** *across the shiny floor.*

slide[2] *noun*
1 a thing which you can sit on and slide down a slope

slide

2 a pin for keeping back the hair

○ **slight** /slaɪt/ *adjective*
small; of no importance: *I have a* **slight** *headache.*
　'**slightly** *adverb:* *Paul is* **slightly** *taller than John.*

slim[1] /slɪm/ *adjective* (**slimmer**, **slimmest**)
thin: *He is not* **slim** *enough to wear these tight trousers.*

slim[2] *verb* (*present participle* **slimming**, *past* **slimmed**)
to get thinner: *He will have to* **slim** *if he wants to wear the trousers.*

sling[1] /slɪŋ/ *noun*
a piece of cloth passed round something to support it: *He had to keep his broken arm in a* **sling.**

sling

sling[2] *verb* (*present participle* **slinging**, *past* **slung** /slʌŋ/)
to throw

○ **slip**[1] /slɪp/ *verb* (*present participle* **slipping**, *past* **slipped**)
1 to move smoothly on something by mistake: *She* **slipped** *on the shiny floor and fell.*
2 to move quickly, smoothly, or quietly: *He* **slipped** *the money into his pocket. She* **slipped out** *of the room and no one noticed.*

slip[2] *noun*
1 a mistake: *to make a* **slip**
2 a small piece (of paper)

slipper /'slɪpəʳ/ *noun*
a soft shoe, worn in the house: (**a pair of**) **slippers**

○ **slippery** /'slɪpərɪ/ *adjective*
smooth; likely to slide: *a* **slippery** *floor*

slit[1] /slɪt/ *noun*
a long narrow opening: *He put the letter through a* **slit** *in the door.*

slit[2] *verb* (*present participle* **slitting**, *past* **slit**)
to cut in a thin line: *I* **slit open** *the letter with a knife.*

○ **slope**[1] /sləʊp/ *noun*
a surface which is higher on one side than the other: *He ran up the* **slope** *to the top of the hill.*

○ **slope**[2] *verb* (*present participle* **sloping**, *past* **sloped**)
to lie or move in a slope: *The hill* **slopes** *steeply down to the town.*

slot /slɒt/ *noun*
a narrow opening: *If you put a coin in the* **slot** *of this machine, stamps come out of another* **slot**.

○ **slow** /sləʊ/ *adjective*
taking a long time; not fast: *The bus is very* **slow**. *The clock is (a minute)* **slow** (=it shows a time which is earlier than the real time).
'**slowly** *adverb*

slug /slʌg/ *noun*
a soft creature without

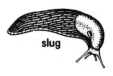
slug

bones or legs that lives on land and eats plants

sly /slaɪ/ *adjective* (**slier, sliest**)
clever in deceiving: *The fruit seller was* **sly** — *he put his best fruit in front but gave people bad ones from behind.* '**slyly** *adverb*

smack[1] /smæk/ *verb*
to hit with the open hand: *He* **smacked** *the naughty child.*

smack[2] *noun*
an act of smacking; a hit: *Don't do that or you'll get a* **smack**.

○ **small** /smɔːl/ *adjective*
little; not large: *Insects are much* **smaller** *than people. He has a* **small** *farm.*

smart /smɑːt/ *adjective*
1 dressed in new-looking, good, clean clothes: *My sister always looks* **smart**. *She always wears* **smart** *clothes.*
2 clever: *He's a* **smart** *businessman.*

smash /smæʃ/ *noun*
to break into pieces: *She* **smashed** *a cup.*

smear[1] /smɪəʳ/ *noun*
to leave a sticky, dirty, or oily mark on: *The child's face was* **smeared** *with chocolate.*

smear[2] *noun*
a mark left by smearing

○ **smell**[1] /smel/ *verb*
(*present participle* **smelling**, *past* **smelt** /smelt/)
1 to discover by taking in air through the nose: *He* **smelt** *the flowers.*
2 to give off something that we discover in this way: *The flowers* **smell** (*very sweet*).

○ **smell²** *noun*
something that we discover through the nose: *There is a* **smell** *of fried chicken in this room.*

○ **smile¹** /smaɪl/ *verb* (*present participle* **smiling**, *past* **smiled**)
to turn up the corners of your mouth to show pleasure, approval, etc.: *She* **smiled** *when she saw me.*

○ **smile²** *noun*
a smiling expression: *a* **smile** *on his face*

○ **smoke¹** /sməʊk/ *noun* (*no plural*)
cloud of gas and bits of ash that comes out of a fire

○ **smoke²** *verb* (*present participle* **smoking**, *past* **smoked**)
1 to give out smoke: *Why is the fire* **smoking** *so much?*
2 to use cigarettes, a pipe, etc.: *Do you* **smoke?**

○ **smooth** /smuːð/ *adjective*
having a flat even surface; not rough: **smooth** *skin*
'smoothly *adverb*

smother /'smʌðəʳ/ *verb*
to stop air from reaching a person or thing: *Don't put that cloth over the baby's face, you'll* **smother** *him!*

smoulder /'sməʊldəʳ/ *verb*
to burn slowly without a flame: *The mat was* **smouldering** *where the burning log had fallen.*

smuggle /'smʌgl/ *verb*
(*present participle* **smuggling**, *past* **smuggled**)
to bring things into a country secretly without paying the money that should be paid: *He was caught* **smuggling** *cameras into the country.* **smuggler** *noun*

snail /sneɪl/ *noun*
a soft creature

shell

snail

256

without bones or legs, but with a round shell on its back, which eats plants

○ **snake** /sneɪk/ *noun*
an animal that has a hard skin and a long body without legs and may have a dangerous bite (picture at **reptile**)

snap¹ /snæp/ *verb* (*present participle* **snapping**, *past* **snapped**)
1 to break with a sharp noise: *The branch* **snapped** *under his foot.*
2 to try to bite: *Your dog* **snapped** *at me.*

snap² *noun*
1 a sharp sound of something breaking
2 a photograph: *holiday* **snaps**

snarl /snɑːl/ *verb*
to make an angry noise, or talk in an angry way: *The two dogs* **snarled** *at each other, and then started fighting.*

snatch /snætʃ/ *verb*
to take quickly and, usually, roughly: *She* **snatched** *the book from my hands.*

sneer /snɪəʳ/ *verb*
to show you have a low opinion of a person or thing by laughing at him or it, or making him or it seem bad or stupid: *James* **sneered at** *my old bicycle. He has a new one.*

sneeze /sniːz/ *verb* (*present participle* **sneezing**, *past* **sneezed**)
to push air out of the lungs (see) suddenly, making a noise through your mouth and nose: *When you have a cold, you* **sneeze** *a lot.*
sneeze *noun*

sniff /snɪf/ *verb*
to take air in through the nose in short breaths; to see what the air smells of: *When she had stopped crying, she* **sniffed** *and dried her eyes.* **sniff** *noun*

R oland Ayotte

snore /snɔːᵣ/ *verb* (*present participle* **snoring**, *past* **snored**)
to make a noise in your nose or throat when you are asleep: *Grandfather was* **snoring**.
snore *noun*

snort /snɔːt/ *verb*
to make an angry noise in the nose
snort *noun*

snow[1] /snəʊ/ *noun* (*no plural*)
very cold rain, which falls in soft white flakes (=pieces)

snow[2] *verb*
(of snow) to come down from the sky: *It's* **snowing**!

° **so** /səʊ/
1 in such a way; to such a point: *I was* **so** *tired that I fell asleep on the bus. I have read 20 pages* **so far** (=up to this time).
2 also: *Ann was there, and* **so** *was Mary*.
3 very; very much: *You have been* **so** *kind to me*.
4 therefore: *I promised to send him a letter.* **so** *I'll write it now*.
5 in order that: *We got up early* **so (that)** *we could go for a swim*.
6 the same; that same thing: *How do you know? Peter told me* **so**.
7 (used to show agreement): *"Look, it's raining!" "***So** *it is!"*

soak /səʊk/ *verb*
1 to leave in a liquid: *She* **soaked** *the dirty clothes in water*.
2 to make very wet: *The rain* **soaked** *us. Our clothes were* **soaking (wet)**.

° **soap** /səʊp/ *noun*
an oily substance that cleans things when it is put with water: *She washed her hands with* **soap**.

soar /sɔːᵣ/ *verb*
1 to fly high in the air
2 to become very high: *Prices are* **soaring** *again*.

sob /sɒb/ *verb* (*present participle* **sobbing**, *past* **sobbed**)
to make the noise of crying: *The child* **sobbed** *loudly*. **sob** *noun*

sober /ˈsəʊbəᵣ/ *adjective*
not drunk (=not having drunk too much alcoholic drink)

soccer /ˈsɒkəᵣ/ *noun* (*no plural*)
football: *a* **soccer** *team*

society /səˈsaɪətɪ/ *noun* (*plural* **societies**)
1 a group of people who live together with shared ideas about how to live: **Society** *makes laws to protect people*.
2 a club; group of people with special interests: *a music* **society**
social /ˈsəʊʃl/ *adjective*: *Man is a* **social** *animal* (=he lives in a group of people). **Social studies** *is the study of how man lives in societies*.

sock /sɒk/ *noun*
a soft covering for the foot and ankle

a pair of socks

socket /ˈsɒkɪt/ *noun*
a hole or set of holes for something to fit into: *an electric* **socket** *in a wall* (picture at **plug**)

sofa /ˈsəʊfə/ *noun*
a long chair for two or more people to sit on

° **soft** /sɒft/ *adjective*
1 not hard; moving inwards when it is pressed: *This orange is* **soft**.
2 feeling smooth and pleasant: **soft** *skin*
3 not loud or noisy: *a* **soft** *voice*
soft 'drink *noun* a drink with no alcohol in it
soften /ˈsɒfn/ *verb* to become or make soft: *The rain* **softened** *the earth*.

softly adverb: He speaks **softly**, so it is difficult to hear what he says.

soil[1] /sɔɪl/ noun (no plural)
earth: This **soil** is very sandy.

soil[2] verb
to make dirty

solar /'səʊlər/ adjective
of or using the sun: **solar** heat

sold /səʊld/ see **sell**

° **soldier** /'səʊldʒər/ noun
a person in the army

sole /səʊl/ noun
the under part of your foot or shoe (picture on page 133)

solemn /'sɒləm/ adjective
serious: a **solemn** face/a **solemn** ceremony **solemnly** adverb

° **solid**[1] /'sɒlɪd/ adjective
1 hard; not liquid or gas: Gold is **solid**, but when you heat it, it becomes liquid.
2 made of one material all the way through; not hollow: This table is **solid** wood.

° **solid**[2] noun
not a liquid or gas: Iron is a **solid**.

solitary /'sɒlɪtrɪ/ adjective
being the only one; alone: There was a **solitary** sheep in the field.

solo /'səʊləʊ/ noun, adjective
something done by one person alone: She sang a **solo**.

solution /sə'luːʃn/ noun
the answer: What is the **solution** to your trouble?

solve /sɒlv/ verb (present participle **solving**, past **solved**)
to find the answer to: to **solve** a crime

° **some** /səm; strong sʌm/
1 an amount of; a number of; not all: She had a big piece of chocolate and she gave me **some**. Would you like **some** bananas? We asked all the class to the party but only **some** of them came.
2 (used when speaking about people or things without saying exactly which ones): **Some** girls are dancing, others are talking.

somebody /'sʌmbədɪ/
or **someone**
1 any person: If you don't know the answer, ask **somebody**.
2 some unknown person, or a person the speaker does not name: There is **somebody** knocking at the door. I know **somebody** who lives near you.

° **somehow** /'sʌmhaʊ/ adverb
in some way: The bridge is broken, but we must cross the river **somehow**.

° **someone** /'sʌmwʌn/
see **somebody**

somersault
/'sʌməsɔːlt/
noun
jumping and
turning upside
down at the
same time: to
do a **somersault**

somersault

something /'sʌmθɪŋ/
a thing, either known or unknown: I want to tell you **something**. She bought **something** to eat.

sometime /'sʌmtaɪm/ adverb
at some time in the past or the future: I hope I'll see you again **sometime**.

° **sometimes** /'sʌmtaɪmz/ adverb
at times; now and then: **Sometimes** I help my mother in the house.

° **somewhere** /'sʌmweər/ adverb
in, to, or at some place: At last he found **somewhere** to park the car.

° **son** /sʌn/ noun
a male child: I have a **son** and a daughter.

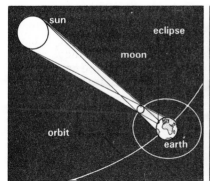

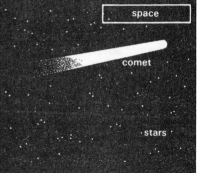

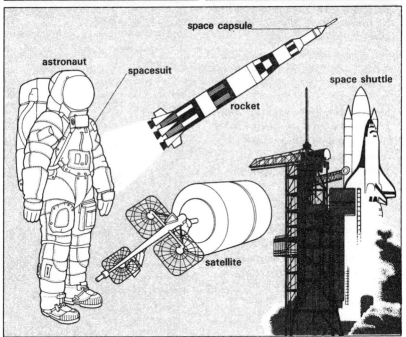

The *Earth* is a *planet.* It moves around the *sun* in an *orbit,* once a year. The sun is a *star.* There are millions of stars in the sky, but all the others are much farther away from us than the sun is, so they look much smaller. We can see them only at night, when the sun is not in the sky.

The *moon* moves around the Earth. If the moon moves between the Earth and the sun it blocks out the sun's light. This is called an *eclipse* of the sun, and it does not happen very often.

A *comet* is a mass with a long tail which moves around the sun, and can sometimes be seen in the sky at night.

○ **song** /sɒŋ/ *noun*
a piece of music with words that are sung

○ **soon** /suːn/ *adverb*
1 in a short time: *Dinner will be ready* **soon.**
2 early: *I made the coffee* **too soon** *and now it is cold. Give me the book* **as soon as** *you can.*

soot /sʊt/ *noun* (*no plural*)
black powder left by smoke

soothe /suːð/ *verb* (*present participle* **soothing,** *past* **soothed**)
to make calm: *She* **soothed** *the child who was afraid.*

○ **sore**[1] /sɔːʳ/ *adjective*
hurting; painful: *My leg is* **sore,** *it hurts.*

○ **sore**[2] *noun*
a painful place on the body, especially where the skin is broken: *He had a* **sore** *on his foot.*

○ **sorrow** /ˈsɒrəʊ/ *noun*
sadness: *He told me with* **sorrow** *that his mother was very ill.*

○ **sorry** /ˈsɒrɪ/ *adjective*
a polite way of saying that you are a little sad, or that you cannot do what is wanted: *Did I stand on your foot?* **Sorry!** *I was* **sorry** *to hear about your illness. I'm* **sorry,** *I can't come to your party.*

○ **sort**[1] /sɔːt/ *noun*
kind; type: *A hammer is a* **sort** *of tool.*

sort[2] *verb*
to put in order; to put things that are alike together: *I* **sorted (out)** *the books into big ones and small ones.*

sought /sɔːt/ see **seek**

soul /səʊl/ *noun*
the part of you that is not body, and that some people think does not die with your body

○ **sound**[1] /saʊnd/ *noun*
something you hear: *the* **sound** *of birds singing*

○ **sound**[2] *verb*
1 to seem, when you hear it: *Your idea* **sounds** *a good one.*
2 to make a sound: *When the bell* **sounds,** *you must come in.*

sound[3] *adjective*
1 healthy or strong: *I've repaired the roof and it's quite* **sound** *now.*
2 (of sleep) deep: *He's in a* **sound** *sleep.*

○ **soup** /suːp/ *noun*
liquid food made from meat, fish, or vegetables: *I had a bowl of chicken* **soup.**

○ **sour** /saʊəʳ/ *adjective*
tasting sharp, like an orange that is not ripe: *The fruit was too* **sour** *to eat. If you leave milk in the sun, it goes* **sour** *quickly.*

source /sɔːs/ *noun*
where something comes from: *The river is the* **source** *of all our water. Bad food is a* **source** *of illness.*

○ **south** /saʊθ/
noun, adjective, adverb
the direction that is on the right when you look at the rising sun: *We travelled* **south** *for two days. There is a strong* **south** *wind* (=coming from the south).
southern /ˈsʌðən/ *adjective* in or of the south
southwards *adverb* towards the south: *to travel* **southwards**

souvenir /ˌsuːvəˈnɪəʳ/ *noun*
a thing that is kept to remember a place or an event

sovereign /ˈsɒvrɪn/ *noun*
a king or queen

sow /səʊ/ *verb* (*past tense* **sowed,** *past participle* **sown**)
to put seeds in the ground so that they will grow into plants

° **space** /speɪs/ *noun*
1 (*no plural*) the empty area that surrounds the sun, the Earth, etc.: *People have travelled through space to the moon.*
2 an empty place: *There is no space for another chair in this room.*
'**spaceman** *noun* (*plural* space**men**): *The first man on the moon was an American spaceman.*
'**spaceship** *noun*: *People who travel in space go in spaceships.*
'**space ,shuttle** *noun* a type of rocket (see) which can return to earth like an aeroplane (picture on page 259)

° **spade** /speɪd/
noun
an instrument used for digging (picture at **dig**)

spanner
/'spænər/
noun
an instrument
for turning nuts and bolts (see), or things that are tight

spanners

spare¹ /speər/ *adjective*
kept in addition to what you have, in case it is needed: *If you have a spare bed, may I stay tonight? Have you any spare time to help me.*

spare² *verb* (*present participle* **sparing,** *past* **spared**)
to be able to give or lend something: *Can you spare me some money? I need to buy food.*

spark /spɑːk/ *noun*
a small piece of burning material: **Sparks** *flew up from the fire.*

sparkle /'spɑːkl/ *verb* (*present participle* **sparkling,** *past* **sparkled**)
to give out bright points of light: *Drops of water sparkled in the sun.*

sparrow /'spærəʊ/ *noun*
a small brownish grey bird

spat /spæt/ see **spit**

° **speak** /spiːk/ *verb*
(*present participle* **speaking,** *past tense* **spoke** /spəʊk/, *past participle* **spoken** /'spəʊkən/)
to say words aloud: *Can your child speak yet? Have you spoken to her about the money? She can speak three languages.*
'**speaker** *noun*

° **spear** /spɪər/
noun
a long thin
weapon with
a pointed end

spear

° **special** /'speʃl/ *adjective*
not usual; important for a reason: *He has a special car because he cannot walk. This is a special day in the history of our country.*
specialist *noun* a person who specializes in something
specially *adverb* **1** for one purpose: *I came here specially to ask you a question.* **2** unusually: *He is not specially clever, but he works hard.*

specialize /'speʃəlaɪz/ *verb* (*present participle* **specializing,** *past* **specialized**)
to study one special thing: *That doctor specializes in children's illnesses.*

species /'spiːʃiz/ *noun*
(*plural* **species**)
sort; type: *a species of animal*

specific /spə'sɪfɪk/ *adjective*
exact; fixed; clear in meaning: *I want a specific answer.*

specimen /'spesɪmən/ *noun*
an example; typical thing: *The doctor took a specimen of blood from his arm.*

speck /spek/ *noun*
a small piece of something: *a speck of paint/of dust*

spectacles /'spektəklz/
plural noun
glasses for the eyes, set in a frame
which rests on the nose and ears:
She wears **spectacles** (picture at
glasses)

spectator /spek'teɪtə^r/ *noun*
someone who watches a sport or
show

° **speech** /spiːtʃ/ *noun*
1 (*no plural*) the ability to speak:
Speech *is learnt in the first years
of life.*
2 (*plural* **speeches**) a long set of
words spoken for people to listen
to: *to make a* **speech**

° **speed** /spiːd/ *noun*
how fast something moves: *The*
speed *of the car was frightening.
He works at a slow* **speed.**
   '**speedily** *adverb*

° **spell** /spel/ *verb* (*past* **spelt** *or*
spelled)
to say the letters that make up a
word: *You* **spell** *dog, D-O-G.*
   '**spelling** *noun: His* **spelling** *is
better than his brother's.*

° **spend** /spend/ *verb* (*present
participle* **spending,** *past* **spent**)
1 to give out money: *How much
money do you* **spend** *each week?*
2 to pass or use time: *I* **spent** *an
hour reading.*

sphere /sfɪə^r/ *noun*
a solid round shape, like a ball
(picture on page 185)
   spherical /'sferɪkl/ *adjective*

spice /spaɪs/ *noun*
a seed, root, or other part of a
plant used to give a strong or hot
taste to food: *Pepper is a* **spice.**
   '**spicy** *adjective* (**spicier, spiciest**)

spider /'spaɪdə^r/ *noun*
a creature with eight legs, which
uses threads from its body to catch
insects in a web (picture at **web**)

spike /spaɪk/
noun
a sharp piece
of metal:
There are

spike

spikes *on the bottom of shoes used
for running.*

spill /spɪl/ *verb* (*present participle*
spilling, *past* **spilt**)
to let fall; to pour out by mistake:
I **spilt** *the coffee — it* **spilt** *all over
my book.*

° **spin** /spɪn/ *verb* (*present participle*
spinning, *past* **spun** /spʌn/)
1 to go round and round fast: *The
wheels of the car were* **spinning**
(*round*).
2 to make thread by twisting
cotton, wool, etc. round
3 to make thread: *Spiders* (see)
spin *threads.*

spine /spaɪn/ *noun*
the long row of bones in your back
(picture on page 133)

spinster /'spɪnstə^r/ *noun*
a woman who is not married

spiral /'spaɪərəl/ *noun, adjective*
a shape that goes round and round
as it goes up: *A spring* (see) *is a*
spiral.

° **spirit** /'spɪrɪt/ *noun*
1 the part of you that is not body,
and that some people think does
not die with your body
2 state of mind: *The children were*
in high spirits (= feeling happy).
3 strong alcoholic drink: *"Rum" is
a* **spirit** *made from sugar.*

spit /spɪt/ *verb* (*present participle*
spitting, *past* **spat** /spæt/)
to throw water with the mouth; to
throw something out of the
mouth: *He* **spat** *into the river. The
child* **spat out** *its food.*

° **spite** /spaɪt/ *noun* (*no plural*)
dislike; wanting to hurt or annoy

another person: *He took my best toy just out of* **spite!**

in spite of even though something else happens: *I went out* **in spite of** *the rain.*

splash[1] /splæʃ/ *noun*
the sound made by something falling into a liquid: *She jumped into the river with a* **splash.**

splash[2] *verb*
to make liquid fall in drops: *The children* **splashed** (*about*) *in the pool. Don't* **splash** *me: I don't want to get wet.*

splendid /'splendɪd/ *adjective*
very great or fine

splinter /'splɪntə`r`/ *noun*
a thin sharp piece of wood or metal: *I have got a* **splinter** *in my finger.*

° **split**[1] /splɪt/ *verb* (*present participle* **splitting,** *past* **split**)
1 to break, especially from one end to the other: *We* **split** *the wood into long thin pieces. My trousers* **split** *when I sat down.*
2 to share: *We* **split** *the work between us.*

split[2] *noun*
a break: *a* **split** *in my trousers*

° **spoil** /spɔɪl/ *verb* (*present participle* **spoiling,** *past* **spoilt**)
to damage something so that it becomes useless: *The rain has* **spoilt** *my painting.*
spoilt *adjective* given everything, so that you become selfish: *a* **spoilt** *child*

spoke[1] /spəʊk/ see **speak**

spoke[2] *noun*
one of the bars joining the outer ring of a wheel to the centre (picture at **bicycle**)

spoken /'spəʊkən/ see **speak:** *Her* **spoken** *English is very good.*

sponge
/spʌndʒ/
noun
a soft sea
creature like
a piece of rubber with many holes; this or a substance like it, used for cleaning

sponge

spool /spuːl/ *noun*
a round thing for winding thread, wire, etc. round

° **spoon** /spuːn/ *noun*
an instrument with a rounded part used for eating liquids, mixing in cooking, etc.
'**spoonful** *noun* (*plural* **spoonsful** *or* **spoonfuls**) the amount a spoon holds: *You must take three* **spoonfuls** *of medicine.*

° **sport** /spɔːt/ *noun*
games and exercises done for pleasure: *Football and running are* **sports.**

° **spot** /spɒt/ *noun*
1 a small mark: *She had* **spots** *on her face when she was ill. A* **spot** *of blood fell on the floor.*
2 a place: *This is a nice* **spot** *for a house.*

spout /spaʊt/ *noun*
part of a container through which liquid is poured

sprain /spreɪn/ *verb*
to damage a joint of your body by turning it suddenly: *He* **sprained** *his ankle when he fell.*

spray[1] /spreɪ/ *verb*
to make wet with small drops: *He* **sprayed** *water over the flowers. He* **sprayed** *the flowers with water.*

spray[2] *noun*
liquid in small drops: *a* **spray** *of water*

° **spread** /spred/ *verb* (*present participle* **spreading,** *past* **spread**)
1 to cover thinly: *She* **spread** *the*

bread with butter (see).
2 to open out: *The bird* **spread** *its wings.*
3 to move over an area: *The illness* **spread** *through the village.*

spring[1] /sprɪŋ/
noun
1 a river coming up from the ground

spring

2 a twisted round piece of metal wire which goes back into shape if you pull it

spring[2] /sprɪŋ/ *verb*
(*present participle* **springing,** *past tense* **sprang** /spræŋ/, *past participle* **sprung** /sprʌŋ/)
to jump: *She* **sprang** *out of her chair to greet her father.*

spring[3] *noun, adjective*
the season after winter, in cool countries, when plants start to grow again: **spring** *flowers*

sprinkle /'sprɪŋkl/ *verb*
(*present participle* **sprinkling,** *past* **sprinkled**)
to scatter: *She* **sprinkled** *sugar on the cakes.*

sprout /spraʊt/ *verb*
to start to grow: *These seeds have* **sprouted** — *you can see little green leaves above the earth.*

spun /spʌn/ see **spin**

spy[1] /spaɪ/ *noun* (*plural* **spies**)
a person whose job is to find out secret information, usually about another country

spy[2] *verb* (*present participle* **spying,** *past* **spied**)
to look at and find out things, especially secretly: *Have you been* **spying on** *me?*

squabble /'skwɒbl/ *verb*
(*present participle* **squabbling,** *past* **squabbled**)
to quarrel about small things: *The children were* **squabbling** *about who had won the game.*
squabble *noun*

° **square**[1] /skweə^r/ *noun*
1 a shape with four equal sides (picture on page 185)
2 an open place in a town: *There was a* **square** *with trees and grass in it in the centre of the city.*

° **square**[2] *adjective*
having four equal sides: *The window was* **square.**

squash[1] /skwɒʃ/ *noun*
a fruit drink: *a glass of orange* **squash**

squash[2] *verb*
to press; hurt or damage by pressing: *We all* **squashed** *into the car. The fruit at the bottom of the box had been* **squashed.**

squeak /skwiːk/ *verb*
to make a high, thin sound: *Rats* **squeak. squeak** *noun*

squeal /skwiːl/ *verb*
to make a loud high cry: *Pigs* **squeal. squeal** *noun*

squeeze /skwiːz/ *verb*
(*present participle* **squeezing,** *past* **squeezed**)
to press sideways: *He* **squeezed** *an orange to get the juice out. The children* **squeezed** *together to make room for me to sit down.*

squirrel /'skwɪrəl/ *noun*
a small animal that has a brown or grey hairy coat and a thick tail and usually lives in trees

stab /stæb/ *verb* (*present participle* **stabbing,** *past* **stabbed**)
to wound with a pointed weapon: *He* **stabbed** *the woman with a knife and she died.*

stable[1] /'steɪbl/ *noun*
a building in which horses are kept

stable[2] *adjective*
firm; steady; not easily moved or
changed: *Is that ladder* **stable?**

stack[1] /stæk/
noun
a large pile: *a*
stack *of books*

stack[2] *verb*
to put in a
stack: *to* **stack**
(up) *books*

stack

stadium /'steɪdɪəm/ *noun*
an open place where games and
races are held; it has seats round it

staff /stɑːf/ *noun* (*no plural*)
a group of people working under
a leader: *the* **staff** *of a school* (=all
the teachers)

° **stage** /steɪdʒ/ *noun*
1 a time or step in a long event:
*When a book has been written, the
next* **stage** *is printing.*
2 a raised floor: *The play was
acted on a* **stage.**

stagger /'stægəʳ/ *verb*
to walk in an unsteady way: *The
wounded man* **staggered** *along.*

stain[1] /steɪn/ *verb*
to make a mark that cannot be
taken away: *The coffee* **stained** *his
shirt brown.*

stain[2] *noun*
a mark: *a coffee* **stain**

° **stairs** /steəz/ *plural noun*
a set of steps leading up and down
inside a building: *The headmaster's room is* **upstairs,** *but to
get to the library you must go*
downstairs.

stake /steɪk/ *noun*
a pointed post in the ground

stale /steɪl/ *adjective*
(staler, stalest)
not fresh; tasting old and dry: **stale**
bread

stalk /stɔːk/ *noun*
the main upright part of a plant
that is not a tree; the long part that
supports leaves or flowers (picture
at **grain**)

stall /stɔːl/ *noun*
a small open shop, especially one
in a market: *a fruit* **stall**

stammer /'stæməʳ/ *verb*
to speak with difficulty, repeating
the same sounds: *"Th-th-thank
you", he* **stammered.**

° **stamp**[1]
/stæmp/
noun **1** a
small piece
of special

stamps

paper that you stick on letters and
parcels to show how much you
have paid to send them: *He collects*
(postage) stamps.
2 an instrument used to make
marks with ink on paper

° **stamp**[2] *verb*
1 to put a stamp on
2 to bring your foot down hard: *He*
stamped *on the insect.*

° **stand**[1] /stænd/ *verb*
(*present participle* **standing,** *past
stood* /stʊd/)
1 to be on your feet: *We* **stood**
outside the shop. **Stand up** (=get
to your feet), *please.*
2 to be: *The house* **stands** *at the
top of the hill.*
3 to mean: *The letters P.J. on his
bag* **stand for** *Peter Johnson.*

stand[2] *noun*
a place for people to watch sports

° **standard** /'stændəd/
noun, adjective
(of) a fixed weight, length, cost, or
quality by which things are
compared: *Your work is of a low*
standard. *It is not* **up to standard**
(=as good as we expect).

stank /stæŋk/ see **stink**

° **star** /stɑːʳ/ *noun*
1 a small point of light that can be seen in the sky at night (picture on page 259)
2 a five-pointed shape (★)

stare /steəʳ/ *verb* (*present participle* **staring**, *past* **stared**)
to look steadily for a long time: *He* **stared** *at the word trying to remember what it meant.*

° **start**¹ /stɑːt/ *verb*
to begin: *If you are ready, you may* **start** *your work. The children* **started** *singing.*

° **start**² *noun*
an act of starting: *We made an early* **start** *in the morning.*

startle /'stɑːtl/ *verb* (*present participle* **startling**, *past* **startled**)
to surprise; give a shock to: *You* **startled** *me when you shouted.*

starve /stɑːv/ *verb* (*present participle* **starving**, *past* **starved**)
to die of hunger: *People* **starve** *because there is not enough for everyone to eat.*
star'vation *noun* (*no plural*)
'starving *adjective* **1** dying of hunger: **starving** *children* **2** very hungry: *I'm* **starving** — *is dinner ready yet?*

° **state**¹ /steɪt/ *verb* (*present participle* **stating**, *past* **stated**)
to say: *He* **stated** *that he had never seen the criminal before.*
'statement *noun* something that is said: *The man made a* **statement** *to the police.*

° **state**² *noun*
1 the condition of something; how good, bad, etc., it is: *This book is in a very bad* **state***. She is in a worried* **state** *of mind.*
2 (a part of) a country, which governs itself: *Mississippi is one of the 50* **states** *in the United* **States** *of America.*
3 a country and its government: *In Britain, the railways are owned by the* **state.**

'statesman *noun* (*plural* **statesmen**) a government leader

° **station** /'steɪʃn/ *noun*
1 a place where buses or trains stop: *a* **railway station***/a* **bus station**
2 a building for some special work: *Policemen work at a* **po'lice station.**

stationary /'steɪʃənrɪ/ *adjective*
not moving; still: *Wait until the bus is* **stationary** *before you get off.*

stationery /'steɪʃənrɪ/ *noun* (*no plural*)
paper, pens, pencils, notebooks, etc.: *The shop that sells* **stationery** *is called a* **stationer's.**

statue /'stætʃuː/ *noun*
a figure of a person or animal made of stone, metal, or wood: *There is* *a* **statue** *of a famous soldier in the park.*

statue

ᵓ **stay** /steɪ/ *verb*
to continue to be: **Stay** *in your classroom until it is time to go home. He* **stayed** *with his father while he was ill.*

° **steady** /'stedɪ/ *adjective, adverb* (**steadier, steadiest**)
1 firm; not moving: *Hold the chair* **steady** *while I stand on it.*
2 regular: *a* **steady** *job/a* **steady** *speed*
steadily *adverb*: *We drove* **steadily** *at 30 miles an hour.*

steak /steɪk/ *noun*
a thick flat piece of meat or fish

° **steal** /stiːl/ *verb* (*present participle* **stealing**, *past tense* **stole** /stəʊl/, *past participle* **stolen**)
1 to take something that does not belong to you, without asking for it: *Who* **stole** *my money?*
2 to move quietly: *She* **stole** *out of the room.*

° **steam¹** /stiːm/ *noun* (*no plural*)
the gas that water becomes when it boils: *There was* **steam** *coming from the cooking-pot.*
'**steam-engine** *noun* an engine that works by the pressure of steam inside it
'**steamer** or '**steam-ship** *noun* a ship driven by a steam-engine

° **steam²** *verb*
1 to give off steam: *The hot water was* **steaming.**
2 to cook by putting in steam

° **steel** /stiːl/ *noun* (*no plural*)
a hard metal made of specially treated iron, used for knives, machines, etc.

° **steep** /stiːp/ *adjective*
having a sharp slope: *a* **steep** *hill*
steeply *adverb*

steer /stɪəʳ/ *verb*
to direct or guide a vehicle: *He* **steered** *the ship carefully between the rocks.*

° **stem** /stem/ *noun*
the central part of a plant from which the leaves or flowers grow (picture at **flower**)

° **step¹** /step/ *verb* (*present participle* **stepping**, *past* **stepped**)
to move the foot in walking or running: *He* **stepped** *over the dog.*

° **step²** *noun*
1 a movement with the foot; the sound of this: *He took a* **step** *towards the door. There was the sound of a* **step** *outside the door.*
2 a flat edge in a set of stairs: *There are two* **steps** *up onto the bus.*
3 an event in a set of events: *The first* **step** *in changing a car tyre is to loosen the wheel. He showed us how to repair the tyre* **step by step.**

stepfather /'stepfɑːðəʳ/ *noun*
a man who marries your mother but is not your father

stepmother /'stepmʌðəʳ/ *noun*
a woman who marries your father but is not your mother: *The children of a* **stepfather** *or* **stepmother** *are your* **stepbrothers** *or* **stepsisters.**

stern /stɜːn/ *adjective*
firm and serious: *a* **stern** *teacher*

stew¹ /stjuː/ *noun*
meat or fish and vegetables, cooked together in liquid

stew² *verb*
to cook slowly in liquid: *You can* **stew** *fruit in water and sugar.*

steward /'stjuːəd/ *noun*
a man who looks after passengers on a boat or plane
,**stewar'dess** *noun* a female steward

° **stick¹** /stɪk/ *noun*
a long thin piece of wood: *We made the fire out of dry* **sticks.** *The old man walked leaning on a* **stick.**

° **stick²** *verb* (*present participle* **sticking**, *past* **stuck** /stʌk/)
1 to fix with a special substance (**glue**): *I* **stuck** *a stamp on the letter.*
2 to put something pointed into: *I* **stuck** *a needle into the cloth.*
3 to stay fixed: *The wheels of the car* **stuck** *in the mud and we could not go on.*
'**sticky** *adjective* (**stickier**, **stickiest**) able to hold things together: *a* **sticky** *sweet*

° **stiff** /stɪf/ *adjective*

1 not able to move or bend easily: *The cards were made of* **stiff** *paper.*

2 difficult: *a* **stiff** *examination*

'**stiffly** *adverb: to walk* **stiffly**

° **still**¹ /stɪl/ *adverb*

1 up to this or that time: *My father* **still** *remembers his first day at school.*

2 even: *The car was very fast, but the plane was faster* **still**.

3 even so: *It was raining, but she* **still** *went out.*

° **still**² *adjective*

not moving; quiet: *The sea was calm and* **still**. *Keep* **still** *while I comb your hair.*

° **sting**¹ /stɪŋ/ *verb*

(*present participle* **stinging**, *past* **stung** /stʌŋ/)

to hurt by pricking the skin: *The bee* **stung** *her leg.*

° **sting**² *noun*

1 the part of an insect which stings

2 the pain or wound of a sting: *The red spot on his arm is a* **sting**.

stink¹ /stɪŋk/ *verb* (*present participle* **stinking**, *past tense* **stank** /stæŋk/, *past participle* **stunk** /stʌŋk/)

to smell very unpleasant

stink² *noun*

a very unpleasant smell

stir /stɜːʳ/ *verb* (*present participle* **stirring**, *past* **stirred**)

1 to mix about with a spoon: *He put sugar in his tea and* **stirred** *it.*

2 to move a little: *The leaves* **stirred** *in the wind.*

° **stitch**¹ /stɪtʃ/ *noun* (*plural* **stitches**)

1 the movement of a needle and

stitches

thread through cloth and out again: *The dress was sewn with small* **stitches**. **2** a turn of wool round a needle in knitting (see)

° **stitch**² *verb*

to sew: *to* **stitch** *a button onto a shirt*

stock¹ /stɒk/ *noun*

a store of goods in a shop: *We have a large* **stock** *of tinned fruit.*

stock² *verb*

to have for sale in a shop: *They do not* **stock** *flowers, only fruit.*

stocking /'stɒkɪŋ/ *noun*

one of a pair of coverings for the legs and feet: *She wore nylon* (=very thin material) **stockings**.

stole /stəʊl/ see **steal**

stolen /'stəʊlən/ see **steal**

° **stomach** /'stʌmək/ *noun*

the part of the body into which the food goes when it is swallowed (picture on page 133)

° **stone** /stəʊn/ *noun*

1 a small piece of rock

2 rock: *This is a* **stone** *building.*

3 the hard inside bit in some fruits

4 a piece of coloured rock of great value that is used as an ornament: *A diamond* (see) *is a* **precious stone**.

stood /stʊd/ see **stand**

stool /stuːl/ *noun*

a chair without a back or sides

stoop /stuːp/ *verb*

to bend the body over forwards: *He* **stooped** *to look under the table.*

° **stop**¹ /stɒp/ *verb* (*present participle* **stopping**, *past* **stopped**)

1 to end; make an end to: *We* **stopped** *eating.*

2 to prevent something happening, moving, etc.: *They* **stopped** *me going out of the door. The driver*

stopped *the car and got out.*
3 to finish moving: *The bus* **stopped.**

stopper *noun*
something which closes an opening, especially of a bottle

° **stop**² *noun*
1 a place where a bus or train stops: *We waited at the* **bus stop.**
2 a dot that you put at the end of a sentence: *This sentence ends with a* **full stop.**

° **store**¹ /stɔːʳ/ *verb* (*present participle* **storing,** *past* **stored**)
to put away or keep for use later: *I* **stored** *all the apples from our trees.*

° **store**² *noun*
1 things kept for future use: *a* **store** *of apples*
2 a large shop
3 a place for keeping things: *a* **store** *for furniture*

storey /ˈstɔːrɪ/ *noun*
one level in a building: *This is a four-* **storey** *building.*

storeys

° **storm** /stɔːm/ *noun*
a time of high winds and sometimes thunder and rain
ˈ**stormy** *adjective* (**stormier, stormiest**): **stormy** *weather*

° **story** /ˈstɔːrɪ/ *noun* (*plural* **stories**)
1 a book about something imaginary that happened: *Please read us a* **story!**
2 a telling of events: *What is the* **story** *of your accident?*

stove /stəʊv/ *noun*
a metal or brick container which is heated and used for cooking or heating: *My mother has a gas* **stove** *for cooking.*

° **straight**¹ /streɪt/ *adjective*
1 not bending or curved: *This road is* **straight.**
2 level: *The picture is not* **straight,** *you must move the left side up.*
3 in order

° **straight**² *adverb*
1 in a straight line: *The car went* **straight** *down the road.*
2 without waiting; directly; without going anywhere else or doing anything else: *He went* **straight** *to his friend to ask for help. I must see you* **straight away** (=now).

straighten /ˈstreɪtn/ *verb* to make or become straight: *She* **straightened** *the picture on the wall.*

strain /streɪn/ *verb*
1 to pull against: *They* **strained** *on the rope to pull the boat in.*
2 to damage a part of the body by pulling or using it wrongly: *I* **strained** *my back when I lifted the box.*
3 to take the lumps out of something by putting it through an instrument with small holes in it: *There are tea leaves in my cup — you haven't* **strained** *the tea.*

strait /streɪt/ *noun*
a narrow piece of water between two pieces of land

° **strange** /streɪndʒ/ *adjective* (**stranger, strangest**)
1 odd; unusual: *a* **strange** *sound*
2 not what you are used to: *a* **strange** *city*
ˈ**strangely** *adverb:* *He acted* **strangely** *when he was ill.*
ˈ**stranger** *noun* a person you do not know

strangle /ˈstræŋgl/ *verb* (*present participle* **strangling,** *past* **strangled**)
to kill by pressing round the throat

269

strap¹ /stræp/ *noun*
a narrow piece of leather, plastic, cloth, etc. used for fastening something

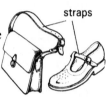

straps

strap² *verb* (*present participle* **strapping**, *past* **strapped**)
to fasten with a strap: *He* **strapped** *the bag onto his bicycle.*

straw /strɔː/ *noun*
1 (*no plural*) dry stems of wheat, rice, etc: *a bag made of* **straw**
2 a dry stem
3 a thin tube for drinking through: *He drank the milk through a* **straw.**

stray¹ /streɪ/ *adjective*
(of animals) not owned by anyone: *a* **stray** *dog*

stray² *verb*
to wander away from home or from the right way: *She* **strayed** *from the road and got lost.*

streak /striːk/ *noun*
a long mark: *a* **streak** *of paint on the wall*

° **stream** /striːm/ *noun*
1 a small river
2 a flow: *a* **stream** *of cars*

° **street** /striːt/ *noun*
a road in a town: *Across the* **street** *from the school is the library. He lives in Park* **Street.**

° **strength** /streŋθ/ *noun* (*no plural*)
being strong: *I haven't the* **strength** *to lift this table.*

strengthen /'streŋθn/ *verb*
to make stronger: *The fence was* **strengthened** *with wire.*

stress¹ /stres/ *noun*
1 (*no plural*) a state of difficulty: *The* **stress** *of working for examinations made him ill.*
2 (*plural* **stresses**) saying a word or a part of a word with special force: *In the word "chemistry" the* **stress** *is on the first part of the word.*

stress² *verb*
to say with special force: *We* **stress** *the first part of the word "chemistry". I must* **stress** *that we haven't much time.*

° **stretch** /stretʃ/ *verb*
1 to make or become larger or longer by pulling; pull tightly: *She* **stretched** *the material. Rubber* **stretches.**
2 to make as long as possible: *He* **stretched** *his legs in front of him.*
3 to try and reach: *I* **stretched out** *my hand towards the book.*

stretcher /'stretʃər/ *noun*
a framework on which an ill person can be carried

stretcher

strict /strɪkt/ *adjective*
severe, especially about behaviour: *Our teacher is* **strict**; *we have to do what she says.*
'**strictly** *adverb* 1 severely. 2 exactly: *What he says is not* **strictly** *true.*

stride¹ /straɪd/ *verb*
(*present participle* **striding**, *past tense* **strode** /strəʊd/, *past participle* **stridden** /'strɪdn/)
to walk with large steps: *He* **strode** *angrily into the classroom.*

stride² *noun*
a large step: *With two* **strides** *he crossed the room.*

strike¹ /straɪk/ *verb*
(*present participle* **striking**, *past* **struck** /strʌk/)
1 to hit: *He* **struck** *me with a stick.*
2 to refuse to work: *The workers were* **striking** *because they wanted more money.*

3 to seem to: **It struck me** *that the room looked different.*

strike² *noun*
refusing to work: *There is a* **strike** *at the factory. The workers are* **on strike.**

° **string** /strɪŋ/ *noun*
1 (*no plural*) thin rope used for fastening things: *The parcel was tied with* **string.**
2 a fine piece of wire used in some musical instruments: *A violin* (see) *has* **strings.**

strip¹ /strɪp/ *noun*
a long narrow piece of something: *a* **strip** *of paper*

strip² *verb*
1 to pull off an outer covering: *He* **stripped** *the paper off the wall.*
2 to take off clothes: *John* **stripped off** *his shirt.*

stripe /straɪp/ *noun*
a long thin line: *A tiger has* **stripes.**
striped *adjective:*
a **striped** *dress*

striped

° **stroke**¹ /strəʊk/ *noun*
a blow: *With one* **stroke** *of his axe, he had cut the tree down.*

stroke² *verb* (*present participle* **stroking,** *past* **stroked**)
to move the hand over gently: *He* **stroked** *the baby's head.*

stroll /strəʊl/ *verb*
to walk slowly: *We* **strolled** *through the park.* **stroll** *noun*

° **strong** /strɒŋ/ *adjective*
1 having power or force: *He is a* **strong** *man. She is a* **strong** *swimmer. a* **strong** *smell of cats*
2 firm: *a* **strong** *fence*
3 having a powerful result: **Strong** *drink can make you feel ill.*

struck /strʌk/ see **strike**

structure /'strʌktʃər/ *noun*
1 a building or framework: *The builders had put up a tall* **structure** *between the shops.*
2 the way something is made: *We learnt about the* **structure** *of the brain today.*

struggle¹ /'strʌgl/ *verb* (*present participle* **struggling,** *past* **struggled**)
to fight: *I* **struggled** *to get free.*

struggle² *noun*
a fight: *We had a* **struggle** *to stop the criminal.*

stubborn /'stʌbən/ *adjective*
not changing your mind or doing what others want: *She won't do what I ask — she's very* **stubborn.**
stubbornly *adverb*

stuck /stʌk/ see **stick**

° **student** /'stju:dənt/ *noun*
a person who is learning, especially at a college or university (see): *He is a* **student** *of history.*

studio /'stju:dɪəʊ/ *noun*
1 a workroom: *a painter's* **studio**
2 a room in which films or radio or television shows are made

° **study**¹ /'stʌdɪ/ *verb* (*present participle* **studying,** *past* **studied**)
to learn about: *I am* **studying** *art.*

° **study**² *noun* (*plural* **studies**)
1 learning: *He will finish his* **studies** *next year.*
2 a room for working in

stuff¹ /stʌf/ *noun* (*no plural*)
any substance or material: *There's some white* **stuff** *on this plate.*

stuff² *verb*
to fill: *The bed was* **stuffed** *with cotton so it was very soft. He* **stuffed** *himself full of food.*
'**stuffy** *adjective* (**stuffier, stuffiest**) with no clean air: *This*

room seems **stuffy** — *open a window.*

stumble /'stʌmbl/ *verb* (*present participle* **stumbling,** *past* **stumbled**)
to walk unsteadily, so that you seem to be falling: *He* **stumbled** *along the road. I* **stumbled** *over a stone and fell.*

stump /stʌmp/ *noun*
what is left when something is cut down: *He sat on a tree* **stump.**

tree stump

stung /stʌŋ/ see **sting**

stunk /stʌŋk/ see **stink**

○ **stupid** /'stjuːpɪd/ *adjective*
not clever; not intelligent: *a* **stupid** *question/a* **stupid** *person*
○ **stu'pidity** *noun* (*no plural*)
'stupidly *adverb*

sturdy /'stɜːdɪ/ *adjective* (**sturdier, sturdiest**)
strong and firm: *The child had* **sturdy** *legs.*

sty /staɪ/ *noun* (*plural* **sties**)
a place for pigs to live in

○ **style** /staɪl/ *noun*
1 a way of doing something: *a hair* **style**
2 the way of dressing that everyone likes at a special time: *That dress is in the latest* **style.**
3 a sort or type: *a new* **style** *of car*

subject[1] /'sʌbdʒekt/ *noun*
1 something studied: *English is one of our school* **subjects.**
2 something talked about: *I was the* **subject** *of their talk.*
3 a person who belongs to a country: *She is a British* **subject.**

subject[2] *noun*
the person or thing that does the action of a verb; the noun that usually goes in front of the verb:

In the sentence "Jane bought the bread", Jane is the **subject.** Look at **object.**

submarine /ˌsʌbməˈriːn/ *noun*
a ship that can go along under the water

submarine

submit /səbˈmɪt/ *verb* (*present participle* **submitting,** *past* **submitted**)
1 to agree to obey
2 to give: *I* **submitted** *my papers to the examiner.*

○ **substance** /'sʌbstəns/ *noun*
a sort of material: *Salt is a* **substance** *we use in cooking.*

subtract /səbˈtrækt/ *verb*
to take away one number from another: *If you* **subtract** *3 from 5, you get 2.* **subˈtraction** *noun*

suburb /'sʌbɜːb/ *noun*
an outer part of a town: *He lives in the* **suburb** *of Greenfield and works in the city.*

succeed /səkˈsiːd/ *verb*
to do well; get what you wanted: *He* **succeeded** *in the examination. His business has* **succeeded,** *and is making a lot of money.*

success /səkˈses/ *noun*
1 (*no plural*) succeeding: *his* **success** *in the examination*
2 (*plural* **successes**) a thing which succeeds: *Her party was a* **success;** *everyone enjoyed it.*
successful *adjective*
successfully *adverb*

such /sʌtʃ/
1 of this or that kind: *Don't play with knives or matches;* **such** *things are not toys.*
2 so unusual in some way: *I have never seen* **such** *a wide river.*
3 (used in some phrases): *They*

wanted some juicy fruit **such as** (=like) *oranges, but there was* **no such** *fruit* (=no fruit of that kind) *in the market.*

suck /sʌk/ *verb*
to draw liquid into the mouth: *The baby was* **sucking** *milk from its mother.*

° **sudden** /'sʌdn/ *adjective*
happening or done unexpectedly: *Her illness was very* **sudden** — *she was well yesterday. a* **sudden illness**
suddenly *adverb:* **Suddenly,** *I heard a loud bang.*

suffer /'sʌfə^r/ *verb*
to be in pain or trouble: *She was* **suffering** *from a headache.*
suffering *noun*

sufficient /sə'fɪʃnt/ *adjective*
enough: *Have you had* **sufficient** *sleep?*

suffix /'sʌfɪks/ *noun*
(*plural* **suffixes**)
letters that are added to the end of another word, to change the meaning: *If we add the* **suffix** *"ful" to the word "hope", we make the word "hopeful".* Look at **prefix.**

° **sugar** /'ʃʊgə^r/ *noun (no plural)*
a substance made from some plants, used to make food sweet

suggest /sə'dʒest/ *verb*
to say to someone that something is a good idea: *I* **suggested** *that it would be quicker to travel by train.*
sug'gestion *noun: He made the* **suggestion** *that we go by train.*

° **suit**¹ /suːt/ *verb*
to be right for; look nice when worn: *It* **suits** *me if you come to work at eight o'clock. That dress* **suits** *you.*
suitable *adjective: This toy is not* **suitable for** *young children.*

° **suit**² *noun*
a set of clothes made from the same material: *His* **suit** *was made up of a jacket* (see) *and trousers.*

suitcase
/'suːtkeɪs/
noun
a large bag
that you put
things in when you travel

suitcase

sulk /sʌlk/ *verb*
to feel angry for a long time, usually silently: *When we told her she couldn't come with us, she went and* **sulked** *in her room.*

sultan /'sʌltən/ *noun*
a Muslim leader

° **sum** /sʌm/ *noun*
an exercise in using numbers: *This* **sum** *is "take 4 away from 9"; the answer to the* **sum** *is 5.*

° **summer** /'sʌmə^r/ *noun, adjective*
the season, in cool countries, when it is warmest: *a* **summer** *holiday*

summit /'sʌmɪt/ *noun*
the top: *a mountain* **summit**

summon /'sʌmən/ *verb*
to call for someone to come to you: *The teacher* **summoned** *all the children to the room.*

° **sun** /sʌn/ *noun*
the large ball of fire in the sky which gives light and heat: *The* **sun** *rose at six o'clock. Sit in the* **sun** *and get warm.* (picture on p.259)
'sunlight *noun (no plural): The* **sunlight** *was very bright.*
'sunny *adjective* (**sunnier, sunniest**): *The day was bright and* **sunny.**
'sunrise *noun: At* **sunrise,** *the sun looks as if it is coming up.*
'sunset *noun: At* **sunset,** *the sun looks as if it is going down.*
'sunshine *noun (no plural): The children played in the* **sunshine.**

sunbathe /'sʌnbeɪð/ *verb*
(*present participle* **sunbathing,**
past **sunbathed**)
to lie in the sun

° **Sunday** /'sʌndeɪ, -dɪ/ *noun*
the first day of the week; the day
on which Christians go to church

sung /sʌŋ/ see **sing**

sunk /sʌŋk/ see **sink**

super /'suːpəʳ/ *adjective*
very nice or exciting: *We had a*
super *day at the seaside.*

superb /suː'pɜːb/ *adjective*
very fine: *Her dancing is* **superb.**

superior /suː'pɪərɪəʳ/ *adjective*
better or higher

superlative /suː'pɜːlətɪv/
noun, adjective
a word or a form of a word that
shows that something is the best,
worst, biggest, smallest, etc. of its
kind: *This pen is quite good, that
one is better, but Peter's pen is* **the
best** *of all. "Best" is a* **superlative.**
Look at **comparative.**

supermarket /'suːpəmɑːkɪt/ *noun*
a big shop where you choose what
you want and pay as you go out

supersonic /ˌsuːpə'sɒnɪk/
adjective
faster than sound: *a* **supersonic**
plane

superstition /ˌsuːpə'stɪʃn/ *noun*
something that people believe that
cannot be proved, and is probably
not true: *Some people think that
the number four is unlucky, but
that is just a* **superstition.**

supervise /'suːpəvaɪz/ *verb*
(*present participle* **supervising,**
past **supervised**)
to watch over people while they
work, to see that they are doing the
right thing: *The teacher* **supervised**
our drawing class.

supervision /ˌsuːpə'vɪʒn/ *noun*
(*no plural*): *We worked under the
teacher's* **supervision.**

supper /'sʌpəʳ/ *noun*
an evening meal

supply[1] /sə'plaɪ/ *noun*
(*plural* **supplies**)
a store which can be used; an
amount: *We keep a large* **supply** *of
food in the house. Our* **supplies**
(=the things we need) *for this
month are in the cupboard.*

supply[2] *verb* (*present participle*
supplying, *past* **supplied**)
to give or sell what is needed: *That
company* **supplies** *paper to the
printers.*

° **support**[1] /sə'pɔːt/ *verb*
1 to hold up: *These posts* **support**
the roof.
2 to help, especially with money:
She **supports** *her husband on the
money she earns from teaching.*
3 to be on the side of: *Which
football team do you* **support?**

° **support**[2] *noun*
something that holds up: *There are
two large wooden* **supports** *that
hold up the roof.*

suppose /sə'pəʊz/ *verb* (*present
participle* **supposing,** *past*
supposed)
1 to think: *What do you* **suppose**
you will do after school?
2 to be expected to; ought to: *What
are you* **supposed to** *be doing when
you have finished your work? You*
aren't supposed to *drink alcohol*
(=you are not allowed to).
    supposing if: **Supposing** (*that*)
    *you catch the next bus, you'll be
    home before 10 o'clock.*

supreme /suː'priːm/ *adjective*
highest; best: *The most important
law court* (see) *is called the*
Supreme Court.

°**sure** /ʃʊəʳ/ *adjective*
without doubt: *I am* **sure** *that I put the money in the box. Please* **make sure** *that the house is locked before you leave.*

'**surely** *adverb:* **Surely** *you locked the door? I would be surprised if you hadn't.*

surf /sɜːf/ *noun*
(*no plural*)
white bubbles
(= water filled
with air) on
waves when
they come
onto land

surf

°**surface** /'sɜːfɪs/ *noun*
the outside, flat part or top of something: *The table had a shiny* **surface,** *but underneath it was dull and rough.*

surgeon /'sɜːdʒən/ *noun*
a doctor who cuts into people's bodies to help cure them

surgery /sɜːdʒərɪ/ *noun*
(*plural* **surgeries**)
1 (*no plural*) when a doctor cuts a part of a person's body to cure him
2 a place you can go to see a doctor or dentist (see)

surname /'sɜːneɪm/ *noun*
a name that is used by a family, usually written last: *He is called Peter Brown. Brown is his* **surname.**

°**surprise**[1] /sə'praɪz/ *noun*
an unexpected event; a feeling caused by this event: *Don't tell him about the present — it's a* **surprise.** *I looked at him* **in surprise** *— I didn't expect to see him again.*

°**surprise**[2] *verb* (*present participle* **surprising,** *past* **surprised**)
to cause the feeling of surprise: *His anger* **surprised** *me — I had thought he was a calm person.*

surrender /sə'rendəʳ/ *verb*
to stop fighting and give yourself to the people you are fighting

°**surround** /sə'raʊnd/ *verb*
to be or go all round something: *The fence* **surrounds** *the school.*
surroundings *plural noun* the area around something: *The house is in beautiful* **surroundings.**

survive /sə'vaɪv/ *verb* (*present participle* **surviving,** *past* **survived**)
to go on living: *The man was very ill, but he* **survived.**
survival *noun* (*no plural*): *The man's* **survival** *was surprising, as the doctors thought he would die. We need food and water for* **survival.**

suspect[1] /sə'spekt/ *verb*
to think that something is true, though you do not know: *He seems poor, but I* **suspect** *that he has quite a lot of money.*
suspicious /sə'spɪʃəs/ *adjective*
feeling that something is wrong: *I am* **suspicious** *of that woman — I think she may have stolen something from our shop.*

suspect[2] /'sʌspekt/ *noun*
someone who is thought to have done wrong: *The police have taken the* **suspect** *to the police station.*

suspend /sə'spend/ *verb*
1 to hang: *The lamp was* **suspended** *from the ceiling.*
2 to delay: *We* **suspended** *the building work during the rain.*
suspense *noun* (*no plural*) delay which frightens or excites people: *Please tell us what happened, we're all waiting* **in suspense.**

°**swallow**[1] /'swɒləʊ/ *verb*
to take food or drink down the throat and into the stomach: *She* **swallowed** *some milk.*

swallow[2] *noun*
a small bird with a tail divided into two parts

swam /swæm/ see **swim**

swamp /swɒmp/ *noun*
land which is always soft and wet

swan /swɒn/ *noun*
a large white water bird with a long curved neck

swarm[1] /swɔːm/ *noun*
a large group, especially of insects: *a swarm of bees*

swarm

swarm[2] *verb*
to move in a large group

sway /sweɪ/ *verb*
to move from side to side: *The trees swayed in the wind.*

swear /sweəʳ/ *verb*
(*present participle* **swearing**, *past tense* **swore** /swɔːʳ/, *past participle* **sworn** /swɔːn/)
1 to use very bad words: *He was so angry that he swore at his mother.*
2 to promise: *I swear I won't tell anyone your secret.*

sweat[1] /swet/ *noun* (*no plural*)
water which comes out of your skin: **Sweat** *poured down his face as he ran.*

sweat[2] *verb*
to give off water through the skin: *She was sweating as she reached the top of the hill.*

sweater /ˈswetəʳ/ *noun*
a thick woollen garment for the top of the body

° **sweep** /swiːp/ *verb*
(*present participle* **sweeping**, *past* **swept** /swept/)
1 to clean with a brush: *I swept the floor.*

2 to move quickly: *The sea swept away* (=moved over and carried away) *the huts.*

° **sweet**[1] /swiːt/ *adjective*
1 like sugar or ripe fruit to taste: *I don't like sweet coffee, I like it better without sugar in it.*
2 pleasant or loving: *What a sweet smile she has!*

° **sweet**[2] *noun*
a small sugary thing to eat

° **swell** /swel/ *verb* (*present participle* **swelling**, *past tense* **swelled**, *past participle* **swollen** /ˈswəʊlən/)
to become larger: *A bee has stung my hand and it is swelling up. After the rain, the river swelled.*
'**swelling** *noun*: *The bee sting has left a swelling on my hand.*

swerve /swɜːv/ *verb* (*present participle* **swerving**, *past* **swerved**)
to move suddenly to one side when you are moving along: *The car swerved to avoid the dog.*

swift /swɪft/ *adjective*
fast: *a swift runner*

° **swim**[1] /swɪm/ *verb*
(*present participle* **swimming**, *past tense* **swam** /swæm/, *past participle* **swum** /swʌm/)
to move through the water by using your legs and arms: *He swam across the river.*
'**swimmer** *noun*
'**swimming** *noun* (*no plural*): *He had some swimming lessons, and now he is good at swimming.*
'**swimming pool** *noun* a pool built for people to swim in

swim[2] *noun*
an act or time of swimming: *to go for a swim*

° **swing**[1] /swɪŋ/ *verb* (*present participle* **swinging**, *past* **swung** /swʌŋ/)
to move freely from a fixed point:

The boy **swung** *on the rope tied to a tree. The door was* **swinging** *in the wind.*

swing[2] *noun*
a seat hanging on ropes or chains

swing

switch[1] /swɪtʃ/ *noun*
(*plural* **switches**)
an instrument for turning something on and off: *There is a* **switch** *on the wall for turning on the lights.*

switch[2] *verb*
1 to turn on or off with a switch: *Please* **switch off** *the lights. She* **switched on** *the radio.*
2 to change: *I used to cook on electricity, but I've* **switched** *to gas.*

swollen /'swəʊlən/ see **swell**

swoop /swuːp/ *verb*
to fly down very quickly: *The bird* **swooped** *down to the lake.*

sword /sɔːd/ *noun*
a sharp pointed weapon like a long knife

swore /swɔːʳ/ see **swear**

sworn /swɔːn/ see **swear**

swum /swʌm/ see **swim**

syllable /'sɪləbl/ *noun*
part of a word which can be said by itself: *The word surface has two* **syllables,** *"sur" and "face".*

symbol /'sɪmbl/ *noun*
a sign that stands for something: *The* **symbol** = *means "equals".*

sympathy /'sɪmpəθɪ/ *noun*
(*plural* **sympathies**)
a feeling of kind understanding of another person; a feeling of sharing someone's unhappiness: *I have been a prisoner, so I have a lot of* **sympathy** *with other people in prison.*
　sympathetic /ˌsɪmpə'θetɪk/ *adjective: When I told her why I was worried, she was very* **sympathetic.**

symptom /'sɪmptəm/ *noun*
a sign of something, especially an illness: *Fever is a* **symptom** *of many illnesses.*

syringe /sə'rɪndʒ/ *noun*
an instrument

needle
syringe

with a needle at one end for giving injections (medicine through the skin)

syrup /'sɪrəp/ *noun* (*no plural*)
sugar boiled in water or fruit juice

system /'sɪstəm/ *noun*
a group of things or ideas working together in one arrangement: *We have a large* **system** *of railways. What* **system** *of government do you have in your country?*

Tt

○**table** /'teɪbl/ *noun*
a piece of furniture with a flat top and legs: *We eat our meals at a* **table.**
　'tablecloth *noun* a cloth spread over a table

'table-tennis *noun* (*no plural*) a game in which you hit a small ball over a net across a table with a small wooden bat
　ping-pong is another word for **table-tennis.**

tablet /'tæblɪt/ *noun*
a hard flat piece or block of something: *The doctor gave me small white* **tablets** *to take when I have a headache. a* **tablet** *of soap*

tack /tæk/ *noun*
a small nail with a large head on it

tackle /'tækl/ *verb* (*present participle* **tackling**, *past* **tackled**)
1 to begin work on something: *I must* **tackle** *the work this evening.*
2 to try to stop someone: *He* **tackled** *the other player and kicked the ball across the field.*

tact /tækt/ *noun* (*no plural*)
the ability to do or say the right thing at the right time: *Ann was sad because she had failed her examination, so her friend used her* **tact** *and talked about something else.*
'**tactful** *adjective: She is very* **tactful**; *she always says the right things to people.* **tactfully** *adverb* '**tactless** *adjective: If you are* **tactless** *you will make people feel hurt or angry.*

tag /tæg/ *noun*
a small piece of paper or material fixed to something: *Look for a name* **tag** *on the coat to see who it belongs to.*

○ **tail** /teɪl/ *noun*
the part of an animal which sticks out at the end of its back (picture at **bird** and **horse**)

tailor /'teɪləʳ/ *noun*
a person who makes suits, coats, etc.

○ **take** /teɪk/ *verb* (*present participle* **taking**, *past tense* **took** /tʊk/, *past participle* **taken**)
1 to get hold of something: *The mother* **took** *her child by the hand.*
2 to carry something or go with someone to another place: '**Take**

this shopping home. Who has **taken** *my chocolate? Will you* **take** *me to town today?*
3 to swallow something: *I* **took** *the medicine.*
4 to travel in a vehicle: *to* **take** *a train*
5 to need: *I will* **take** *an hour to cook the dinner.*
6 (used in sentences like these): **Take down** (= write) *this sentence.* **Take off** *your clothes; they're very wet. The plane* **took off** (= left the ground) *at three o'clock.*
'**takeoff** *noun: The plane crashed five minutes after* **takeoff** (= after it left the ground).

tale /teɪl/ *noun*
a story

talent /'tælənt/ *noun*
the ability to do something well: *My sister has a* **talent** *for singing.* **talented** *adjective*

○ **talk**[1] /tɔːk/ *verb*
to speak or be able to speak: *The two men were* **talking**. *That child is too young to* **talk**.
talkative /'tɔːkətɪv/ *adjective* liking to talk a lot

○ **talk**[2] *noun*
spoken words: *We had a long* **talk**. *A doctor came to give our school a* **talk** *about his work.*

○ **tall** /tɔːl/ *adjective*
1 higher than other people or other things: *James is* **taller** *than Paul, but Richard is the* **tallest**.
2 having a height: *He is 1 metre 80 centimetres* **tall**.

tame[1] /teɪm/ *adjective* (**tamer**, **tamest**)
trained to live with man; not wild: *a* **tame** *monkey*

tame[2] *verb* (*present participle* **taming**, *past* **tamed**)
to make a wild animal tame

tangerine /ˌtændʒəˈriːn/ *noun*
a fruit like an orange, but with a skin that is easy to take off

tangle /ˈtæŋgl/ *noun*
a mixed-up and knotted mass of string, hair, or thread: *The string was* **in a tangle.** **tangled** *adjective*

tank /tæŋk/ *noun*
1 a container to hold liquids or gas: *The petrol* **tank** *in our car is empty.*
2 a heavy vehicle with guns on it, used in battle
tanker *noun*
a lorry with a tank or a ship with tanks on it
for carrying oil or other liquids

tanker

tap¹ /tæp/ *verb* (*present participle* **tapping**, *past* **tapped**)
to strike lightly: *He* **tapped** *on the door.* **tap** *noun*

tap² *noun*
an instrument on the end of a pipe which can be turned to let liquid or gas out (picture at **sink**)

tape /teɪp/ *noun*
a narrow piece of cloth or other material: *We use sticky paper* **tape** *to stick things together.*
'tape-measure *noun* a narrow band of cloth, plastic, etc. used for measuring
'tape-recorder *noun:* *A* **tape recorder** *is an instrument that can put sound onto long plastic tapes, and play it again so that we can hear it.*

tar /tɑːʳ/ *noun* (*no plural*)
a thick black liquid made from coal or wood: *We use* **tar** *to make roads.*

target /ˈtɑːgɪt/ *noun*
something we try to hit with a gun or an arrow: *The hunter's* **target** *was a wild animal.*

tarmac /ˈtɑːmæk/ *noun*
(*no plural*)
a mixture of tar (see) and very small stones, used to make the surface of roads

tart /tɑːt/ *noun*
a piece of pastry with fruit or jam (see) cooked on top of it

task /tɑːsk/ *noun*
a piece of work which must be done: *Washing the dishes is a* **task** *I do not enjoy.*

° **taste**¹ /teɪst/ *noun*
1 the special sense by which we know one food from another: *My sense of* **taste** *isn't very good; I have a cold.*
2 what food is like when it is in the mouth: *Chocolate has a sweet* **taste.**
3 the ability to see the goodness or badness of something: *She has good* **taste** *in clothes.*

° **taste**² *verb* (*present participle* **tasting**, *past* **tasted**)
1 to try food or drink by taking a little into the mouth: *Can I* **taste** *your drink?*
2 to have a feeling in the mouth: *This tea* **tastes** *sweet.*

tattoo /tæˈtuː/
verb
to make a pattern on
the skin by

tattoo

pricking it and putting colouring substances on it **tattoo** *noun*

taught /tɔːt/ see **teach**

° **tax**¹ /tæks/ *noun* (*plural* **taxes**)
money which must be paid to the government: *I pay* **tax** *out of my wages every week.*

° **tax**² *verb*
to make people pay taxes
tax'ation *noun* (*no plural*)

○ **taxi** /'tæksɪ/ *noun*
a car with a driver who will take you somewhere if you pay him: *to take a* **taxi** *to the station*

○ **tea** /tiː/ *noun*
1 (*no plural*) the dried leaves of a plant which we use to make the hot drink called tea: *a cup of* **tea**
2 a small meal in the late afternoon
3 a cup of tea: *Two* **teas**, *please.*
teaspoon *noun* a small spoon

○ **teach** /tiːtʃ/ *verb*
(*present participle* **teaching**, *past* **taught** /tɔːt/)
to help a person to learn: *Who* **taught** *you to ride a bicycle?*
'**teacher** *noun* someone who helps people to learn

○ **team** /tiːm/ *noun*
1 a group of people who play games against other groups: *a football* **team**
2 two or more animals which work together: *a* **team** *of oxen*

○ **tear**[1] /tɪəʳ/ *noun*
a drop of water from the eye: **Tears** *come to your eyes when you cry.*

○ **tear**[2] /teəʳ/ *verb* (*past tense* **tore** /tɔːʳ/, *past participle* **torn** /tɔːn/)
to pull into pieces; make a hole in: *She* **tore** *a page out of the book. He* **tore** *his trousers.*

tear[3] /teəʳ/ *noun*
a place in something which is torn: *a* **tear** *in his trousers*

tear

tease /tiːz/ *verb* (*present participle* **teasing**, *past* **teased**)
to make fun of a person playfully or unkindly: *You must not* **tease** *your little sister.*

technical /'teknɪkl/ *adjective*
1 having to do with machines: *a* **technical** *job*
2 having to do with special kinds of ability: *To build this machine, you must have* **technical** *ability.*
technician /tek'nɪʃn/ *noun* a person who works with machines or instruments: *Anne is training to be a* **technician.**

technology /tek'nɒlədʒɪ/ *noun* (*no plural*)
using the knowledge we get through science to make things in factories, build things, etc.: *the* **new technology** *of micro* (= very small) *computers*

teeth /tiːθ/ see **tooth**

telegraph /'telɪɡrɑːf/ *noun* (*no plural*)
a way of sending messages quickly by electric wire or radio
telegram /'telɪɡræm/ *noun* a message sent by telegraph

○ **telephone**[1] /'telɪfəʊn/ *or* **phone** /fəʊn/ *noun*
1 (*no plural*) a way of carrying the sound of a person's voice by electricity over a wire or by radio: *We told him the news by* **telephone.**
2 the instrument used to carry the sounds: *Please* **answer the telephone** (= pick it up when it rings and speak into it).
'**telephone** ˌ**box** *noun* a small building or room with a telephone **telephone kiosk** or **telephone booth** are other words for **telephone box.**
'**telephone di**ˌ**rectory** *noun* a large book with people's names and telephone numbers in it

○ **telephone**[2] *verb* (*present participle* **telephoning**, *past* **telephoned**)
to speak to someone by telephone: *I* **telephoned** *my sister last night.*

telescope /'telɪskəʊp/ *noun*
an instrument which we look through to see objects which are

far
from us

° **television**
/'telɪvɪʒn/
noun

telescope

1 (*no plural*)
the sending and
receiving of pictures by radio; the
pictures which are sent out: *to
watch* **television**
2 a large box-shaped apparatus on
which these pictures appear: *Do
you have a* **television? TV** is a
short way of saying and writing
television.

° **tell** /tel/ *verb* (*present participle*
telling, *past* **told** /təʊld/)
to speak to or advise someone: **Tell**
me what happened. I **told** *you not
to do it.*

° **temper** /'tempər/ *noun*
the way we feel: *Jane is* **good-
tempered;** *she never gets angry. He*
lost his temper (=became angry).

temperature /'temprətʃər/ *noun*
the amount of heat or cold: *In hot
weather the* **temperature** *gets very
high. When I was ill, I* **had a high
temperature;** *I felt very hot.*

temple¹ /'templ/ *noun*
a holy building

temple² *noun*
the part of the head above and in
front of the ear (picture on page
133)

temporary /'tempərərɪ/ *adjective*
lasting or meant to last for a short
time: *a* **temporary** *job*
temporarily /'temp(ə)rərəlɪ,
ˌtempə'rerəlɪ/ *adverb*

tempt /tempt/ *verb*
1 to try to make someone do
something wrong
2 to make someone want to do
something: *Can I* **tempt** *you to eat
some more of this cake?*

ten /ten/ *noun, adjective*
the number 10
tenth *noun, adjective* number 10
in order; 10th: *her* **tenth** *birthday*

tenant /'tenənt/ *noun*
a person who pays money to use
a house or land

tend /tend/ *verb*
to be likely to; usually do
something: *I* **tend to** *get tired in the
evening.*
tendency /'tendənsɪ/ *noun*
(*plural* **tendencies**): *Milk has a*
tendency *to go sour in hot
weather.*

° **tender** /'tendər/ *adjective*
1 easy to eat: *This meat is* **tender.**
2 easily damaged or hurt: *My
finger is* **tender** *because I cut it
yesterday.*
3 kind and gentle: *a* **tender**
expression on her face
tenderly *adverb*

tennis /'tenɪs/ *noun* (*no plural*)
a game played by two or four
people in which you hit a ball over
a net

tense¹ /tens/ *adjective*
1 full of excitement: *The players
were* **tense** *at the start of the game.*
2 tightly stretched: **tense** *muscles*
(see)

tense² *noun*
the form of a verb that shows
when the action of the verb
happens: *"I look" and "I am
looking" are* **present tenses;** *"I
looked", "I was looking" and "I
have looked" are* **past tenses;** *"I
will look" and "I am going to
look" are* **future tenses.**

tent /tent/ *noun*
a shelter made
of thick cloth
spread over
poles

tent

term /tɜːm/ *noun*

1 a fixed length of time: *He was made captain of the football team for a* **term** *of one year.*

2 a part of the school year: *There are three* **terms** *in a school year.*

terms *plural noun* the things you are asking for: *If you agree to my* **terms** — *free meals and good wages* — *I will work for you.*

terrace /'terɪs/ *noun*

1 a level area cut out from the side of a hill

2 a flat area outside a house: *We sat on the* **terrace** *in the evening.*

3 a row of houses joined together

terraced *adjective: a* **terraced** *house*

terrible /'terəbl/ *adjective*

1 causing fear: *We saw a* **terrible** *storm.*

2 very bad: *Your writing is* **terrible**.

terribly *adverb: It is* **terribly** (=very) *hot.*

terrify /'terɪfaɪ/ *verb*

(*present participle* **terrifying**, *past* **terrified**)

to fill with fear: *The animals were* **terrified** *by the storm.*

terror /'terəʳ/ *noun* (*no plural*) great fear: *a feeling of* **terror**

territory /'terɪtrɪ/ *noun*

(*plural* **territories**)

1 land ruled by one government: *This island is British* **territory**.

2 an area belonging to one person or animal: *Wild animals will not allow other animals to enter their* **territory**.

° **test**[1] /test/ *verb*

1 to look at something to see if it is correct or will work properly: *Before he bought the car, he drove it to* **test** *it.*

2 to ask someone questions: *The teacher* **tested** *the children on their homework.*

° **test**[2] *noun*

an examination: *I passed my* **driving test** *today.*

'test tube *noun*

a small thin glass tube: *We put chemicals in* **test tubes** *in our chemistry class.*

test tube

text /tekst/ *noun*

1 the words used in a book

2 a few words from a book

'textbook *noun: A* **textbook** *is a book we use to learn about something.*

° **than** /ðən; *strong* ðæn/

(used when we compare things, in sentences like these): *My brother is older* **than** *me. Mary sings better* **than** *anyone else in the class.*

° **thank** /θæŋk/ *verb*

to say we are grateful to someone: *I* **thanked** *her for the present she sent me.* **Thank you** *for the present you sent me.* **No, thank you,** *I don't want any more tea.*

'thankful *adjective* very glad; grateful

thanks *plural noun* words used to show that we are grateful: **Thanks** *for helping me. It was* **thanks to** *John* (=because of him) *that we won the game.*

° **that** /ðət; *strong* ðæt/

1 /ðæt/ (*plural* **those** /ðəʊz/) the one over there; the one further away than this one: *This is my bowl;* **that** *bowl is yours.*

2 /ðæt/ (*plural* **those**) (used to point out someone or something; used to mean the one known or mentioned already): *Did you bring* **that** *photograph? We played football and* **after that** (=next) *we went home.*

3 (used instead of **who, whom,**

which): *He's the person that sold me the bicycle.*

4 (used to join two parts of a sentence): *I think* **that** *it will rain.*

5 /ðæt/ so: *Please slow down — I can't walk* **that** *fast!*

6 (used to show the result of something): *The box was so heavy* **that** *I dropped it.*

7 (used to show why something is done): *Their father took them to the pool* **so that** *they could swim.*

thatch /θætʃ/ *noun*
(*no plural*)
roof covering
made of dry
glass or other
plants

thatch

thatched *adjective: a* **thatched** *cottage*

thaw /θɔː/ *verb*
to make or become soft or liquid, after something has been very cold and hard: *The sun* **thawed** *the ice and melted the snow.*

○ **the** /ðə, ðɪ; *strong* ðiː/
1 (a word used before another, when it is clear who or what is meant): *There's a boy outside; it's* **the** *boy from* **the** *house across* **the** *road.*
2 (used in front of the names of seas, rivers, deserts, etc.): **the** *Mediterranean Sea*
3 (used to talk about a class or group of people or things): **The** *cow is a useful animal* (=all cows are useful).

theatre /ˈθɪətəʳ/ *noun*
a building where plays are acted

theft /θeft/ *noun*
1 (*no plural*) the crime of stealing: *He was put in prison for* **theft.**
2 an act of stealing: *When she discovered the* **theft** *of her bag, she went to the police.*

○ **their** /ðəʳ; *strong* ðeəʳ/
belonging to them: *The children carried* **their** *bags to school.*

theirs /ðeəz/
something belonging to them: *They looked at our pictures, but they didn't show us* **theirs.**

○ **them** /ðəm; *strong* ðem/
(the word we use instead of **they** in sentences like this): *We gave* **them** *some food. We gave it to* **them.** *Did you have to wait for* **them?**

theme /θiːm/ *noun*
what we think, speak, or write about: *Stamp collecting was the* **theme** *of his talk.*

themselves /ðəmˈselvz/
1 (the same people, animals, or things as the sentence is about; the same as **they** in a sentence): *The travellers washed* **themselves** *in the river. They made a meal for* **themselves** (=without help). *They never go out* **by themselves** (=without another person).
2 (used to give **they** a stronger meaning): *They read us the stories which they* **themselves** *had written.*

○ **then** /ðen/ *adverb*
1 at another time; not now: *She lived in a village* **then,** *but now she lives in a town.*
2 afterwards; next: *I cooked the meat and* **then** *I washed the pot.*
3 if that is true: *"I have lost my ticket." "***Then** *you must pay again."*

theory /ˈθɪərɪ/ *noun*
(*plural* **theories**)
an idea that tries to explain something: *One* **theory** *about the moon is that it is a piece broken off the earth.*

○ **there** /ðeəʳ/ *adverb*
1 at or to that place: *Don't sit* **there** *by the door; come and sit here.*

therefore

2 (used with **be, seem,** and other verbs, in sentences like this): **There seems to be** *a big crowd in the street.* **Is there** *a market today?*

therefore /'ðeəfɔːʳ/ *adverb*
for that reason: *He has broken his leg and* **therefore** *he can't walk.*

thermometer
/θə'mɒmɪtəʳ/
noun
an instrument
that measures
heat and cold:
The doctor
put a **thermometer** *in my mouth to see if I had a fever.*

thermometer

° **these** /ðiːz/
the ones here; the ones nearer than that one or those ones: *I don't like* **these** *sweets; those are better.*

° **they** /ðeɪ/
those people, animals, or things: *My friends are playing football, and* **they** *want us to play too.* **They're** (= they are) *playing behind the houses.* **They've** (= they have) *got two teams.*

° **thick** /θɪk/ *adjective*
1 wide: *This piece of wood is* **thicker** *than that.*
2 close together: *a* **thick** *forest*
3 difficult to see through: **thick** *smoke*
4 not flowing easily: *This soup is too* **thick.** '**thickly** *adverb*

° **thief** /θiːf/ *noun* (*plural* **thieves**)
a person who steals: *The* **thief** *was sent to prison.*

thigh /θaɪ/ *noun*
the part of the leg above the knee (picture on page 133)

thimble
/'θɪmbl/
noun
a hard
covering for

thimble

the top of a finger which you use when sewing

° **thin** /θɪn/ *adjective*
1 not wide; not thick: *This string is too* **thin,** *I need a thicker piece. Grandfather's hair is very* **thin.**
2 not fat: *You should eat more; you're too* **thin.**
3 flowing easily: **thin** *oil*
'**thinly** *adverb: Spread the butter* **thinly.**

° **thing** /θɪŋ/ *noun*
an object; act or event: *What is that* **thing** *you are carrying? That was a good* **thing** *to do.*
things *plural noun* **1** belongings: *They packed all their* **things** *for the journey.* **2** conditions: *There used to be a lot of fighting in this area, but* **things** *are better now.*

° **think** /θɪŋk/ *verb*
(*past* **thought** /θɔːt/)
1 to use the mind: *Have you* **thought** *about what job you are going to do?*
2 to have an opinion; believe something: *What do you* **think** *of my singing? I* **think** *it will be hot today. I couldn't* **think** *of* (= remember) *his name.*

° **third** /θɜːd/ *noun, adjective*
1 number 3 in order; 3rd: *This is the* **third** *time I've asked you to be quiet!*
2 one of three equal parts of something; ⅓

° **thirst** /θɜːst/ *noun* (*no plural*)
the feeling of wanting or needing to drink something
'**thirsty** *adjective* (**thirstier, thirstiest**): *I often feel* **thirsty** *when it's very hot.*

thirteen /θɜː'tiːn/ *noun, adjective*
the number 13
thirteenth *noun, adjective*
number 13 in order; 13th

thirty /'θɜːtɪ/ *noun, adjective*
the number 30
  thirtieth *noun, adjective* number
30 in order; 30th

° **this** /ðɪs/
  1 (*plural* **these** /ðiːz/) the one
here; the one nearer than that one:
This *is my bowl; that bowl is yours.*
  2 the thing the speaker is talking
about: **This** *is what I want to do.*
  3 present; nearest to the present
time: *Shall we go out* **this**
afternoon, or wait till tomorrow?
This *is the 12th of May.*

thistle /'θɪsl/ *noun*
a plant with sharp pointed leaves

thorn /θɔːn/
noun
a sharp or
pointed part
of a plant

thorns

° **thorough** /'θʌrə/ *adjective*
with nothing missed out;
complete; careful: *They made a*
thorough *search for the lost ring,*
but didn't find it.
  thoroughly *adverb* completely;
carefully: *He always does his*
work **thoroughly.**

° **those** /ðəʊz/
the ones over there; the ones
further away than this or these
ones: *I don't like these sweets;*
those *are better.*

though /ðəʊ/
even if; in spite of: **Though** *he was*
poor he was happy. The animal
was walking **as though** (=as if) *it*
had hurt its leg.

thought[1] /θɔːt/ see **think**

° **thought**[2] *noun*
  1 (*no plural*) the act of thinking:
After much **thought** *he decided*
not to buy the car.
  2 something we think: *She's a quiet*
girl and doesn't share her **thoughts.**

thousand /'θaʊznd/
noun, adjective
the number 1,000
  thousandth *noun, adjective*
number 1,000 in order; 1,000th

° **thread**[1] /θred/ *noun*
a long single piece of cotton, silk,
or other material used in weaving
or sewing

thread[2] *verb*
to put a thread through a needle

threaten /'θretn/ *verb*
to say that you will hurt another
person if he does not do what you
want: *His father* **threatened** *to beat*
the boy if he stole again.
  ° **threat** /θret/ *noun: He took no*
notice of his father's **threat.**

three /θriː/ *noun, adjective*
the number 3: *I've got* **three** *sisters.*

threw /θruː/ see **throw**

thrill[1] /θrɪl/ *verb*
to fill with excitement: *The*
traveller **thrilled** *us with his stories.*

thrill[2] *noun*
an excited feeling: *It* **gave me a**
thrill *to know I had passed the*
examination.

° **throat** /θrəʊt/ *noun*
  1 the front part of the neck
(picture on page 133)
  2 the inside of the neck: *Food*
passes through our **throats** *and*
down into our stomachs.

throb /θrɒb/ *verb*
(*present participle* **throbbing,** *past*
throbbed)
to beat strongly: *Her heart* **was**
throbbing *after the race.*

throne /θrəʊn/ *noun*
the special chair of a king or queen

° **through** /θruː/
preposition, adjective, adverb
  1 from one side or end of
something to the other: *The nail*

went **through** *the wood. We* walked **through** *the market to the lorry park.*

2 by way of: *The thief got in* **through** *the window.*

3 because of: *I failed my examination* **through** *laziness!*

4 among; between: *She searched* **through** *the coats to find hers.*

throughout /θruːˈaʊt/ *preposition* through every part of: *He is famous* **throughout** *the world. It rained* **throughout** *the night.*

○ **throw**[1] /θrəʊ/ *verb* (*present participle* **throwing,** *past tense* **threw** /θruː/, *past participle* **thrown**)

throw

1 to send something through the air by moving your arm: *He* **threw** *the ball to me, and I caught it.*

2 to move one's body or part of one's body suddenly: *He* **threw** *his arms up. Don't* **throw away** *your old shoes, give them to me.*

○ **throw**[2] *noun* an act of throwing

thrust /θrʌst/ *verb* (*present participle* **thrusting,** *past* **thrust**) to push suddenly and hard: *We* **thrust** *our way through the mass of people.* **thrust** *noun*

thud /θʌd/ *noun* a sound made by something heavy and soft falling: *He fell out of the tree and landed on the ground with a thud.* **thud** *verb*

thumb /θʌm/ *noun* the short, thick finger on the hand which is separate from the others (picture on page 133)

○ **thunder** /ˈθʌndəʳ/ *noun* (*no plural*) the loud sound heard in the sky during a storm

'thunder-storm *noun* a storm with heavy rain, thunder, and lightning

○ **Thursday** /ˈθɜːzdeɪ, -dɪ/ *noun* the fifth day of the week

thus /ðʌs/ *adverb*

1 in this way: *He sold his farm and* **thus** *he had enough money for his journey.*

2 with this result; so: *There has been no rain* — **thus,** *the crops are dying.*

tick[1] /tɪk/ *noun*

1 the sound made by a watch or clock

2 a mark (✓): *All the correct answers had* **ticks** *beside them.*

tick[2] *verb*

1 to make the sound a clock makes

2 to make a mark (✓)

○ **ticket** /ˈtɪkɪt/ *noun* a small piece of paper or card which shows we have paid for something: *We buy a* **ticket** *to get a seat on a bus, train, or aeroplane.*

tickle /ˈtɪkl/ *verb* (*present participle* **tickling,** *past* **tickled**) to touch a person lightly and make him laugh: *I* **tickled** *her under her arms.*

tide /taɪd/ *noun* the rise and fall of the sea twice every day: *At* **high tide** *the sea covers the rocks, but at* **low tide** *it uncovers them.*

○ **tidy**[1] /ˈtaɪdɪ/ *adjective* (**tidier, tidiest**) in good order; neat: *a* **tidy** *room*

○ **tidy**[2] *verb* (*present participle* **tidying,** *past* **tidied**) to make something neat

tie[1] /taɪ/ *noun* a narrow band of cloth worn around the neck

tie

° **tie**[2] *verb*
(*present participle* **tying**, *past* **tied**) to fasten something with string or rope: *Can you* **tie up** *this parcel for me?*

tiger /'taɪgəʳ/ *noun*
a large fierce animal, one of the big cats, which has yellow fur with black stripes (=thin lines) (picture on page 17)

° **tight** /taɪt/ *adjective*
1 pulled or drawn closely together: *Tie the knot as* **tight** *as you can.*
2 not loose: **Tight** *shoes can hurt your feet.* **'tightly** *adverb*

tighten /'taɪtn/ *verb*
to make or become tight: *Will you* **tighten** *this screw; it's very loose.*

tile /taɪl/ *noun*
a flat piece of baked clay: *We use* **tiles** *to cover roofs and sometimes floors and walls.*

till[1] /tɪl/ *noun*
a container or drawer for money in a shop

till[2] see **until**

tilt /tɪlt/ *verb*
to move or cause something to move so that it is not level: *I* **tilted** *the cup to drink out of it.*

timber /'tɪmbəʳ/ *noun* (*no plural*)
wood prepared for building; trees to be used for building

° **time**[1] /taɪm/ *noun*
1 (*no plural*) minutes, hours, days, weeks, months, years: *How do you spend your* **time** *at home?*
2 (*no plural*) a special number of minutes, hours, etc.: *I hadn't* **time** *to finish my homework.*
3 a period or event: *How many* **times** *have you read this book?*
4 a special hour or day: *What* **time** *is it? She was* **in time** *for work; she was not late. The train arrived* **on time** (=not early and not late).

'timetable *noun* a list of the times when things will happen: *A school* **timetable** *tells us when different lessons begin.*

time[2] *verb* (*present participle* **timing**, *past* **timed**)
to measure how long it takes to do something

° **tin** /tɪn/ *noun*
1 (*no plural*) a soft, white metal
2 a container made of this metal: *Food which has been closed up in* **tins** *is called* **tinned** *food.*

tinkle /'tɪŋkl/ *verb* (*present participle* **tinkling**, *past* **tinkled**)
to make a sound like small bells: *The glasses* **tinkled** *as he carried them.*

tiny /'taɪnɪ/ *adjective*
(**tinier, tiniest**)
very small

tip[1] /tɪp/ *noun*
the pointed end of something: *the* **tip** *of a finger*

tip[2] *noun*
1 a small amount of money given to someone who has done something for you: *I gave a* **tip** *to the man who carried my cases.*
2 a useful piece of advice

tip[3] *verb* (*present participle* **tipping**, *past* **tipped**)
to give a small amount of money to someone

tip[4] *verb* (*present participle* **tipping**, *past* **tipped**)
1 to lean or cause to lean at an angle: *I* **tipped** *the*

tip

table and the glasses fell off it.
2 to turn over or cause something to turn over: *I* **tipped** *the bottle over and it broke.*

tiptoe[1] /'tɪptəʊ/ *verb* (*present participle* **tiptoeing**, *past* **tiptoed**) to walk on one's toes: *I* **tiptoed** *past the sleeping child.*

tiptoe[2] *noun*
on one's toes: *to walk* **on tiptoe**

° **tire** /taɪəʳ/ *verb* (*present participle* **tiring**, *past* **tired**)
to make someone feel that he needs rest: *Digging* **tires** *me.*
tired *adjective* needing rest or sleep: *I felt* **tired** *after work. Father is* **tired out** (= completely tired) *at the end of the day.*

tissue /'tɪʃuː/ *noun*
very thin cloth or paper: *She used paper* **tissues** *to blow her nose.*

° **title** /'taɪtl/ *noun*
1 the name of a story, a book, a film, etc.
2 a word used in front of a person's name: *A doctor has the* **title** *"Dr" in front of his name.*

° **to** /tə; *strong* tuː/ *preposition, adverb*
1 in the direction of: *He pointed* **to** *the clock. He sent a letter* **to** *his parents. We are driving* **to** *town.*
2 as far as: *When we got* **to** *the river, we sat down.*
3 on or against: *He fixed the shelf* **to** *the wall.*
4 until: *She works from two o'clock* **to** *ten o'clock. It is ten* (*minutes*) **to** *nine.*
5 (used to show why): *She worked hard* **to** *earn some money.*
6 to and fro one way then the other: *He walked* **to and fro** *outside the house.*

toad /təʊd/ *noun*
a small jumping animal like a large frog

toad

tobacco /tə'bækəʊ/ *noun* (*no plural*)
the dried leaves of a plant used for smoking in pipes and cigarettes

° **today** /tə'deɪ/ *noun, adverb*
1 (on) this day: **Today** *is Monday.*
2 modern times: *Many people use computers* **today.**

° **toe** /təʊ/ *noun*
1 one of the five end parts of the foot (picture on page 133)
2 the part of a shoe or sock that covers this end of the foot: *There is a hole in the* **toe** *of my sock.*

toffee /'tɒfiː/ *noun*
a hard brown sweet

° **together** /tə'geðəʳ/ *adverb*
1 one with another; in a group: *The children played* **together** *in the street. I stuck the two pieces of paper* **together.**
2 at the same time: *Don't all speak* **together!**

toilet[1] /'tɔɪlɪt/ *noun*
1 a container joined to a waste pipe, used for passing body waste **lavatory** is another word for **toilet.**
2 a room with this in it: *Where is the* **toilet,** *please?*

toilet[2] *adjective*
of washing, dressing, or using the toilet: **toilet** *soap/***toilet** *paper*

token /'təʊkən/ *noun*
a sign: *We shook hands as a* **token** *of our friendship.*

told /təʊld/ see **tell**

tomato /tə'mɑːtəʊ/ *noun* (*plural* **tomatoes**)
a red juicy fruit that we eat raw or cooked

tomb /tuːm/ *noun*
a hole in the ground where a dead person is put; a grave (see)
'tombstone *noun* a piece of stone put over a tomb, often with the name of the dead person on it

○ **tomorrow** /tə'mɒrəʊ/
noun, adverb
1 (on) the day after this day:
Tomorrow *will be Tuesday. It's my
brother's birthday* **tomorrow.**
2 the future: *What will the cars of*
tomorrow *look like?*

ton /tʌn/ *noun*
1 a measure of weight equal to
2,240 pounds
2 a measure of weight equal to
1,000 kilos: *1,000 kilos is a* **metric
ton.**

tone /təʊn/ *noun*
the sound of a voice or of a
musical instrument, etc.: *Her voice
has a pleasant* **tone.**

tongs /tɒŋz/ *plural noun*
an instrument used for picking
things up: *He picked up the hot
metal with* **a pair of tongs.**

○ **tongue** /tʌŋ/ *noun*
the part inside the mouth that
moves: *Our* **tongue** *helps us to talk
and to taste things.*

○ **tonight** /tə'naɪt/ *noun, adverb*
the night of today; on or during
the night of today: *We are going
to a party* **tonight.** *I hope that*
tonight *will be dry.*

tonne /tʌn/ *noun*
a measure of weight equal to 1,000
kilos; a metric ton (see)

○ **too** /tuː/ *adverb*
1 also: *I like bananas, but I like
oranges,* **too.**
2 more than is needed or wanted:
He drives **too** *fast.*

took /tʊk/ see **take**

○ **tool** /tuːl/ *noun*
an instrument
which helps us
to do work

⁾ **tooth** /tuːθ/ *noun*
(*plural* **teeth** /tiːθ/)
1 one of the white bony objects

tools

which grow in the mouth (picture
on page 133): *The children* **brush
their teeth** *after every meal.*
2 something which is shaped like
this: *The sharp parts of a comb or
a saw are called* **teeth.** (picture at
comb)

toothache /'tuːθeɪk/ *noun* (*no
plural*) a pain in a tooth: *I've had*
toothache *all day.*
'toothbrush *noun* (*plural*
toothbrushes) a small brush for
cleaning the teeth (picture at
brush)
'toothpaste *noun* (*no plural*) a
substance used for cleaning the
teeth

○ **top**¹ /tɒp/ *noun*
1 the highest part of something:
He climbed to the **top** *of the hill.*
2 the lid or cover of something: *He
took the* **top** *off the box. I wear
shoes* **on top of** (=over) *my socks.*

top² *adjective*
highest: *Put it in the* **top** *drawer.
Paul came* **top** (=had the best
marks) *in the examination.*

top³ *noun*
a toy which spins very quickly on
a point

topic /'tɒpɪk/ *noun*
something about which we talk or
write

topple /'tɒpl/ *verb* (*present
participle* **toppling,** *past* **toppled**)
to make or become unsteady and
fall down: *The pile of books*
toppled *onto the floor.*

torch /tɔːtʃ/
noun (*plural*
torches)
an electric
light that can
be carried: *He used a* **torch** *to see
into the dark cupboard.*

torch

tore /tɔːʳ/ see **tear**

tornado /tɔːˈneɪdəʊ/ *noun*
(*plural* **tornadoes** *or* **tornados**)
a storm with a strong wind which spins very fast

torpedo /tɔːˈpiːdəʊ/ *noun*
(*plural* **torpedoes**)
a weapon which is fired through the water from a ship to destroy another ship

torrent /ˈtɒrənt/ *noun*
a fast flow of water: *The river was a* **torrent** *after the storm.*
    torrential /təˈrenʃl/ *adjective*
    like a torrent: *The rain was* **torrential** *last night.*

tortoise /ˈtɔːtəs/ *noun*
an animal with a body covered by a round hard shell

tortoise

torture /ˈtɔːtʃəʳ/ *verb*
(*present participle* **torturing,** *past* **tortured**)
to cause great pain to someone on purpose **torture** *noun*

toss /tɒs/ *verb*
1 to throw: *They* **tossed** *the ball to each other.*
2 to move about or up and down: *The horse* **tossed** *its head in the air.*

° **total**[1] /ˈtəʊtl/ *noun*
everything added together: *Add up these numbers and tell me the* **total.**

° **total**[2] *adjective*
complete; whole: *"I want* **total** *silence," said the teacher. "No one must talk."* **totally** *adverb*

° **touch**[1] /tʌtʃ/ *verb*
1 to put the hand or another part of the body on or against something: *Don't* **touch** *that pot; it's very hot.*
2 to bring, put, or be on or against something: *The branches of the tree* **touched** *the water.*

° **touch**[2] *noun*
1 (*plural* **touches**) putting part of the body on or against something: *I felt the* **touch** *of his hand.*
2 (*no plural*) the sense which lets us feel the hardness, softness, etc. of something

tough /tʌf/ *adjective*
1 hard; not easy to bite or tear: *This meat is* **tough.** *Leather is a* **tough** *material.*
2 strong and brave

tour[1] /tʊəʳ/ *noun*
1 a journey during which several places are visited: *They have gone* **on a tour.**
2 a trip to or through a place: *We went* **on a tour** *of the city.*

tour[2] *verb*
to make a tour
    'tourist *noun* a person who travels for pleasure

tow /təʊ/ *verb*
to pull something along by a rope or chain: *We* **towed** *the car to the garage.*

° **towards** /təˈwɔːdz/ *preposition*
1 in the direction of: *She walked* **towards** *the door.*
2 facing: *He stood with his back* **towards** *us.*
3 near in time: **Towards** *evening, the day became cooler.*

towel /ˈtaʊəl/ *noun*
a piece of cloth for drying skin, dishes, etc.

tower /ˈtaʊəʳ/ *noun*
a tall narrow building or part of a building: *a church* **tower**

° **town** /taʊn/ *noun*
a large group of houses and other buildings where people live and work
    ˌtown 'hall *noun*: *A* **town hall** *is a building with offices for the government of the area around*

the town and with rooms for public meetings.

° **toy** /tɔɪ/ *noun*
something that children play with

trace[1] /treɪs/ *noun*
a mark or sign left behind by someone or something: *They searched the building but did not find any* **trace** *of the criminal.*

trace[2] *verb* (*present participle* **tracing,** *past* **traced**)
1 to copy a picture, plan, etc. by drawing on a thin piece of paper put over it
2 to try to find someone or something by looking for signs they have left behind: *They* **traced** *the criminal to a house in the city.*

° **track**[1] /træk/ *noun*
1 a rough path
2 marks on the ground left by an animal or person: *The hunter followed the animal's* **tracks.**
3 a special path for races

° **track**[2] *verb*
to follow an animal's track

tractor
/ˈtræktəʳ/
noun
a machine used for pulling heavy carts and farm machinery

tractor

° **trade**[1] /treɪd/ *noun*
1 (*no plural*) the buying and selling of goods: **Trade** *with other countries is important.*
2 a kind of business: *the clothes* **trade**
3 a job that needs special teaching: *She's a dressmaker* **by trade.**

trade[2] *verb* (*present participle* **trading,** *past* **traded**)
to buy and sell goods: *We* **trade** *with other countries.*

ˈ**trader** *noun* a person who buys and sells goods

ˈ**tradesman** *noun* (*plural* **tradesmen**) a person who buys and sells goods, especially a shopkeeper

tradition /trəˈdɪʃn/ *noun*
old customs or knowledge passed on from parents to their children: *It is a* **tradition** *that the young look after the old in their family.*
traditional *adjective*

° **traffic** /ˈtræfɪk/ *noun* (*no plural*)
the movement of cars and people in the streets, or of ships or planes: *The city streets are full of* **traffic.**
ˈ**traffic lights** *plural noun* lights which direct traffic: *A driver must stop when the* **traffic lights** *are red.*

tragedy /ˈtrædʒədɪ/ *noun* (*plural* **tragedies**)
1 something sad that happens: *Her son's death was a* **tragedy.**
2 a serious play
tragic /ˈtrædʒɪk/ *adjective: a* **tragic** *accident*
tragically *adverb*

trail /treɪl/ *noun*
1 the marks left by a person or animal: *The wounded animal left a* **trail** *of blood behind it.*
2 a path across rough country

trailer /ˈtreɪləʳ/ *noun*
a two-wheeled cart pulled by a car, etc.

° **train**[1] /treɪn/ *noun*
a number of cars for people or goods pulled along by an engine on a railway line: *Are you travelling* **by train**?

train

° **train**[2] *verb*
to make oneself, or someone or something else ready to do

something difficult: *I am training for the race. She is training to become a nurse.*

training noun (*no plural*): *Nurses have several years of* **training.**

traitor /'treɪtər/ noun

a person who helps people who are not friends of his country: *The* **traitor** *was sent to prison.*

tramp /træmp/ noun

a person with no home or job who wanders from place to place begging for food or money

trample /'træmpl/ verb

(*present participle* **trampling,** *past* **trampled**)

to walk heavily on something: *Don't* **trample on** *the flowers when you play in the garden.*

transfer[1] /træns'fɜːr/ verb

to move people or things from one place to another: *His employer* **transferred** *him to another office.*

transfer[2] /'trænsfɜːr/ noun

the act of transferring a person: *Can I have a* **transfer** *to a new office?*

transform /træns'fɔːm/ verb

to change completely in appearance or nature: *She* **transformed** *the room by painting it.*

transistor /træn'zɪstər/ noun

a small radio: *a* **transistor radio**

transitive /'trænzətɪv/ noun, adjective

a verb whose action is done to something or somebody; a verb that takes an object (see): *I gave the book to Jane. "Gave" is a* **transitive** *verb.* Look at **intransitive.**

translate /træns'leɪt/ verb

(*present participle* **translating,** *past* **translated**)

to give the meaning of words of one language in another language: *He* **translated** *the speech from Spanish into English.*

translation noun the act of translating; something that has been translated

transparent /træns'pærənt/ adjective

that we can see through: *Glass is a* **transparent** *material.*

transport[1] /træns'pɔːt/ verb

to carry from one place to another: *The goods were* **transported** *by train.*

transport[2] /'trænspɔːt/ noun

the act of transporting or of being transported: *the* **transport** *of goods by air*

trap[1] /træp/ noun

1 an instrument for catching an animal

2 a plan to catch a person; a position which you cannot escape from: *The police* **set a trap** *for the thieves.*

trap[2] verb (*present participle* **trapping,** *past* **trapped**)

to catch in a trap: *The police* **trapped** *the thieves. She was* **trapped** *in the burning house.*

○ **travel** /'trævl/ verb (*present participle* **travelling,** *past* **travelled**)

1 to go from place to place: *to* **travel** *round the world*

2 to move: *At what speed is he* **travelling**?

traveller noun a person on a journey

trawler /'trɔːlər/ noun

a boat for fishing

tray /treɪ/ noun

a flat piece of wood, metal, etc. on which things can be carried

tray

tread /tred/ *verb* (*present participle* **treading,** *past tense* **trod** /trɒd/, *past participle* **trodden**)
1 to stand on: *I* **trod** *on his foot by accident.*
2 to crush with the feet: *They get the juice out of the fruit by* **treading** *it.*

treason /ˈtriːzn/ *noun* (*no plural*)
an action which harms the king or leader of a country or its government: *The man was sent to prison for* **treason** *when he tried to kill the king.*

treasure /ˈtreʒəʳ/ *noun* (*no plural*)
a collection of gold, silver, etc.: *The* **treasure** *dug out of the earth was a box of gold coins.*

> **treasury** *noun* (*plural* **treasuries**): *The* **Treasury** *is the part of the government which collects and pays out the government's money.*

treat¹ /triːt/ *noun*
something which gives pleasure: *Her birthday* **treat** *was a visit to the theatre.*

° **treat²** *verb*
1 to behave towards: *He* **treated** *the animal cruelly.*
2 to handle: *Glass must be* **treated** *carefully.*
3 to give medicine as a doctor: *to* **treat** *an illness*

> **ˈtreatment** *noun: His* **treatment** *of the animal was cruel. The doctor's* **treatment** *cured him.*

treaty /ˈtriːtɪ/ *noun*
(*plural* **treaties**)
an agreement between two or more countries: *a peace* **treaty**

° **tree** /triː/ *noun*
a large plant with a trunk, branches, and leaves

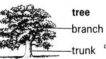

tree
branch
trunk

tremble /ˈtrembl/ *verb* (*present participle* **trembling,** *past* **trembled**)
to shake: *to* **tremble** *with fear*

tremendous /trəˈmendəs/ *adjective*
1 very large; very great
2 wonderful: *We went to a* **tremendous** *party.*

> **tremendously** *adverb*

trench /trentʃ/ *noun*
(*plural* **trenches**)
a long narrow hole dug in the earth

trespass /ˈtrespəs/ *verb*
to go on someone else's land without permission: *The farmer said we were* **trespassing.**

> **trespasser** *noun*

trial /ˈtraɪəl/ *noun*
1 when people in a court (see) of law decide whether a person is guilty of a crime: *The man was* **on trial** *for killing somebody.*
2 a test to see if something is good or bad

triangle /ˈtraɪæŋgl/ *noun*
a flat shape with three straight sides and three angles (picture on page 185)

> **triangular** /traɪˈæŋgjʊləʳ/ *adjective* shaped like a triangle

° **tribe** /traɪb/ *noun*
a group of people of the same race, language, customs, etc.

> **tribal** *adjective*

tributary /ˈtrɪbjʊtərɪ/ *noun*
(*plural* **tributaries**)
a small stream or river that joins a larger river

tribute /ˈtrɪbjuːt/ *noun*
something done, said, or given to show respect or admiration for someone: *The doctor* **paid tribute to** *his nurses by praising their work.*

° **trick¹** /trɪk/ *noun*
1 an action meant to deceive

someone: *He got the money from me by a* **trick**.

2 a clever act done to amuse people: *I can do magic* **tricks**.

3 something done to someone to make him look stupid and to amuse others: *The children* **played a trick** *on their teacher*.

° **trick**² *verb*

to deceive or cheat someone: *He* **tricked** *me into giving him the money*.

trickle /'trɪkl/ *verb* (*present participle* **trickling**, *past* **trickled**)
to flow in a thin stream: *Blood trickled from the wound.*
trickle *noun*

tricycle /'traɪsɪkl/ *noun*
a bicycle with three wheels

tried /traɪd/ see **try**

tricycle

trigger /'trɪɡə^r/ *noun*
a small part of a gun which you pull with your finger to fire it

trim /trɪm/ *verb* (*present participle* **trimming**, *past* **trimmed**)
to make neat by cutting: *She* **trimmed** *his hair*.

° **trip**¹ /trɪp/ *noun*
a short journey: *a* **trip** *to town*

° **trip**² *verb* (*present participle* **tripping**, *past* **tripped**)
to hit one's foot against something: *I* **tripped over** *the box on the floor and fell*.

triumph /'traɪʌmf/ *noun*
being successful; a feeling of happiness when you are successful: *It was a great* **triumph** *when our team won the race*.

trod /trɒd/ see **tread**

trodden /'trɒdn/ see **tread**

trolley /'trɒlɪ/ *noun* (*plural* **trolleys**)
a small light cart pushed by hand

troops /truːps/ *plural noun*
soldiers

trophy /'trəʊfɪ/ *noun* (*plural* **trophies**)
a prize given to a person who has won a game or race

tropics /'trɒpɪks/ *plural noun*
the hottest parts of the earth: *This plant only grows in* **the tropics**.
tropical *adjective* **1** of the tropics: *a* **tropical** *plant* **2** very hot: **tropical** *weather*

trot /trɒt/ *verb* (*present participle* **trotting**, *past* **trotted**)
to run with short steps: *The horse* **trotted** *along the road*.
trot *noun*

° **trouble**¹ /'trʌbl/ *noun*
a state of anxiety or unhappiness; pain: *The boy caused a lot of* **trouble** *to his parents; he was always* **in trouble** (=doing bad things).

° **trouble**² *verb* (*present participle* **troubling**, *past* **troubled**)
1 to cause someone unhappiness, anxiety, or pain: *Her child's bad behaviour* **troubled** *her*.
2 to annoy someone; give someone extra work: *Can I* **trouble** *you to shut the door?*

trough /trɒf/ *noun*
a long narrow wooden or metal container: *A* **trough** *is filled with food or water for animals*.

° **trousers** /'traʊzəz/ *plural noun*
a piece of clothing which covers the lower part of the body and the legs

a pair of trousers

trowel /'trauəl/ *noun*
a small tool used for digging small holes, taking plants out of the ground, etc.

truant /'truːənt/ *noun*
a child who stays away from school without a good reason: *The child was punished for* **playing truant** (=staying away from school).

truck /trʌk/ *noun*
1 an open cart used on a railway for carrying heavy goods
2 a lorry

° **true** /truː/ *adjective* (**truer, truest**)
1 correct: *Is it* **true** *that you are rich?*
2 real: *What I am saying now will* **come true** (=will happen).
'**truly** *adverb* really: *I am* **truly** *grateful for all your help.*

trumpet
/'trʌmpɪt/
noun
a brass
instrument **trumpet**
played by blowing through it

° **trunk** /trʌŋk/ *noun*
1 the main stem of a tree (picture at **tree**)
2 the human body without the head and limbs
3 a large box used for clothes when travelling
4 the long round nose of an elephant (picture on page 17)

trunks /trʌŋks/ *plural noun*
a piece of clothing like very short trousers worn by men for swimming

° **trust**[1] /trʌst/ *verb*
1 to believe that someone is honest or good: *Don't* **trust** *him — he's not telling the truth.*
2 to be sure that someone will do something: *Can I* **trust** *you to do this work well?*

trustworthy /'trʌst,wɜːðɪ/
adjective: A **trustworthy** *person is someone that you can trust.*

° **trust**[2] *noun* (*no plural*)
believing that someone is good or honest; being sure that someone or something will do something: *Don't* **put your trust in** *that man: he may trick you.*

° **truth** /truːθ/ *noun* (*no plural*)
what is true; the correct facts: *You should always* **tell the truth.**
'**truthful** *adjective: He is very* **truthful** *— he never lies.*

° **try**[1] /traɪ/ *verb* (*present participle* **trying**, *past* **tried**)
1 to do one's best to do something: *He* **tried** *to climb the tree, but he could not.*
2 to test something: *Have you* **tried** *this chocolate? She* **tried on** *the dress to see if it would fit.*

try[2] *noun* (*plural* **tries**)
an act of trying: *If you can't open the box, can I* **have a try?**

tub /tʌb/ *noun*
a round wooden or metal container for holding liquid: *She washed the clothes in a* **tub.**

° **tube** /tjuːb/
noun
1 a hollow
pipe made of
metal,
plastic, glass, **tubes**
or rubber, usually
used for liquids
2 a soft metal or plastic container with a cap: *a* **tube** *of toothpaste*

tuck /tʌk/ *verb*
to push or put something into or under something else: **Tuck** *your shirt into your trousers. She* **tucked in** *the covers on the bed.*

° **Tuesday** /'tjuːzdeɪ, -dɪ/ *noun*
the third day of the week

tuft /tʌft/ *noun*
a group of hairs, grass, etc. growing together: *The baby only had a few* **tufts** *of hair on its head.*

tug[1] /tʌg/ *verb* (*present participle* **tugging**, *past* **tugged**)
to pull hard: *The child* **tugged** *at my hand to make me go with her.*

tug[2] *noun*
a sudden strong pull: *I gave the loose tooth a* **tug.**

tug[3] *or* **'tugboat** *noun*
a small powerful boat used for guiding large ships into and out of a port

tumble /'tʌmbl/ *verb* (*present participle* **tumbling**, *past* **tumbled**)
to fall suddenly: *She* **tumbled** *downstairs.*

tumbler /'tʌmblə^r/ *noun*
a drinking glass with a flat bottom

tune[1] /tjuːn/ *noun*
a number of musical notes put together to make a pleasant sound: *Can you sing this* **tune?**

tune[2] *verb* (*present participle* **tuning**, *past* **tuned**)
to set the strings of a musical instrument so that it gives the right notes: *to* **tune** *a piano* (see)

tunnel[1] /'tʌnl/ *noun*
a large hole dug for a road or railway through a hill or under a river, town, or mountain

tunnel

tunnel[2] *verb* (*present participle* **tunnelling**, *past* **tunnelled**)
to make a tunnel: *They* **tunnelled** *for weeks before they reached the other side of the hill.*

turban /'tɜːbən/ *noun*
a length of cloth wound tightly round the head

turkey /'tɜːkɪ/ *noun*
a large farm bird that is used for food

○ **turn**[1] /tɜːn/ *verb*
1 to go or make something go round and round: *The wheels were* **turning.** *Will you* **turn** *the wheel to the right?*
2 to change or make something change position or direction: *She* **turned** *left at the end of the road. He* **was turning** *the pages of the book. She* **turned round** *to look at the boy behind her. She* **turned** (=changed) *her house* **into** *a shop. He* **turned down** (=said he didn't want) *the job.*

○ **turn**[2] *noun*
1 an act or turning: *the* **turn** *of a wheel*
2 a change of direction: *a* **turn** *in the road*
3 a chance to do something: *It's my* **turn** *to play.*
'turning *noun* a place where one road branches off from another

turtle /'tɜːtl/ *noun*
an animal which has a hard round shell over its body, and lives mainly in the sea

tusk /tʌsk/ *noun*
a long pointed tooth which grows outside the mouths of some animals (picture on page 17)

tutor[1] /'tjuːtə^r/ *noun*
a person who teaches one pupil or a very small class: *Her* **tutor** *teaches her at home.*

tutor[2] *verb*
to teach: *He* **tutored** *me in English.*

T.V. /tiː viː/ *see* **television**

tweezers /'twiːzəz/ *plural noun* an instrument

a pair of tweezers

made of two narrow pieces of metal joined at one end, used for picking up very small objects

twelve /twelv/ *noun, adjective*
the number 12
    twelfth /twelfθ/ *noun, adjective*
    number 12 in order; 12th

twenty /'twentɪ/ *noun, adjective*
the number 20
    twentieth *noun, adjective*
    number 20 in order; 20th

° **twice** /twaɪs/ *adverb*
two times: *You've asked me that question* **twice**.

twig /twɪg/ *noun*
a small branch from a tree

twin /twɪn/ *noun*
one of two children born of the same mother at the same time

twinkle /'twɪŋkl/ *verb* (*present participle* **twinkling**, *past* **twinkled**)
to shine with an unsteady light: *The stars* **twinkled** *in the sky.*

° **twist¹** /twɪst/ *verb*
1 to wind threads together or around something else: *String is made of threads* **twisted** *together. She* **twisted** *her hair round her fingers.*
2 to turn: **Twist** *the lid to open it.*
3 to turn in several directions: *The path* **twisted** *up the hill.*

° **twist²** *noun*
1 something made by twisting: *a* **twist** *in a piece of rope*
2 an act of twisting: *He gave the lid a* **twist** *to open the tin.*
3 a bend: *a road full of* **twists** *and turns*

twitch /twɪtʃ/ *verb*
to move suddenly and quickly

without control: *The horse* **twitched** *its ears.* **twitch** *noun*

two /tuː/ *noun, adjective*
the number 2

° **type¹** /taɪp/ *noun*
a special class or kind: *Cotton is a* **type** *of material.*
    typical /'tɪpɪkl/ *adjective* the same as other people or things of the same kind: *He is a* **typical** *pupil; he is like most of the other pupils.*

type² *verb* (*present participle* **typing**, *past* **typed**)
to use a machine to print letters on paper: *to* **type** *a letter*

    'typewriter
    noun a machine used to type letters

typewriter

    'typist *noun*
a person whose job is to use a typewriter

typhoon /taɪ'fuːn/ *noun*
a great storm

tyrant /'taɪərənt/ *noun*
a person with complete power who uses it cruelly
    tyranny /'tɪrənɪ/ *noun* (*no plural*) the rule of a tyrant

° **tyre** /taɪəʳ/ *noun*
a thick rubber part, often filled with air, which fits round the outside edge of a wheel:

tyre

My bicycle has a flat **tyre** — *I must mend it.*

Uu

° **ugly** /ˈʌglɪ/ *adjective*
(**uglier, ugliest**)
not beautiful to look at: *an* **ugly** *face*

umbrella /ʌmˈbrelə/ *noun*
a piece of cloth or plastic stretched over a frame, which you can hold over yourself to keep off the rain

umbrella

umpire /ˈʌmpaɪər/ *noun*
a person who decides about points in a game, especially in cricket (see)

unable /ʌnˈeɪbl/ *adjective*
not able to do something: *I am* **unable** *to come to school today.*

unanimous /jʊˈnænɪməs/ *adjective*
agreed by everyone: *There was a* **unanimous** *decision to go home.*

uncertain /ʌnˈsɜːtn/ *adjective*
not sure: *I am* **uncertain** *what to do.*

° **uncle** /ˈʌŋkl/ *noun*
the brother of one of your parents, or the husband of the sister of one of your parents

uncomfortable /ʌnˈkʌmftəbl/ *adjective*
not comfortable

uncommon /ʌnˈkɒmən/ *adjective*
not usual: *an* **uncommon** *plant*

unconscious /ʌnˈkɒnʃəs/ *adjective*
not knowing what is happening or feeling anything: *After she hit her head she was* **unconscious** *for several minutes.*

uncover /ʌnˈkʌvər/ *verb*
1 to take something from on top of: *He* **uncovered** *the dish and showed us the food.*
2 to find out: *The police* **uncovered** *a plan to steal some money.*

° **under** /ˈʌndər/ *preposition, adverb*
1 in or to a lower place; below: *She sat in the shade* **under** *a tree. The dog crept* **under** *the bed.*
2 less than: *My shirt cost* **under** *two pounds. All the children are* **under** *twelve (years old).*
3 working for or obeying: *The children worked well* **under** *the kind teacher.*

undergo /ʌndəˈgəʊ/ *verb* (*present participle* **undergoing**, *past tense* **underwent** /ʌndəˈwent/, *past participle* **undergone** /ʌndəˈgɒn/)
to bear; have done to you: *These people have* **undergone** *many difficulties to get here.*

undergraduate /ˌʌndəˈgrædjʊət/ *noun*
a student at a university

underground[1] /ˈʌndəgraʊnd/ *adjective, adverb*
under the ground: *There is an* **underground** *room in the old house. They went* **under'ground.**

underground[2] *noun*
a railway which goes under the ground: *to travel by* **underground**

undergrowth /ˈʌndəgrəʊθ/ *noun* (*no plural*)
thickly growing plants underneath trees: *They pushed their way through the* **undergrowth.**

underline /ˌʌndə'laɪn/ *verb* (*present participle* **underlining**, *past* **underlined**)
to put a line under a word or words: *This sentence is **underlined**.*

underneath /ˌʌndə'niːθ/ *preposition, adverb*
under: *She sat **underneath** the tree in the shade. They looked down from the bridge at the water **underneath**.*

° **understand** /ˌʌndə'stænd/ *verb* (*present participle* **understanding**, *past* **understood** /ˌʌndə'stʊd/)
to know the meaning of: *Do you **understand** every word on this page?*

understanding *noun* (*no plural*): *His **understanding** of English is very good.*

undertake /ˌʌndə'teɪk/ *verb* (*present participle* **undertaking**, *past tense* **undertook** /ˌʌndə'tʊk/, *past participle* **undertaken**)
to promise; say that you will do: *I **undertook** to teach the children English.*

underwear /'ʌndəweəʳ/ *noun* (*no plural*)
clothes worn next to the skin, under your shirt, trousers, dress, etc.: *She **changes her underwear** (=puts on clean underwear) every day.*

° **undo** /ʌn'duː/ *verb* (*present participle* **undoing**, *past tense* **undid** /ʌn'dɪd/, *past participle* **undone** /ʌn'dʌn/)
to untie or unfasten: *He **undid** the string round the parcel. Her buttons were **undone**.*

undoubtedly /ʌn'daʊtɪdlɪ/ *adverb*
for sure; surely: *He is **undoubtedly** too busy to write me a letter.*

undress /ʌn'dres/ *verb*
to take clothes off

uneasy /ʌn'iːzɪ/ *adjective* (**uneasier, uneasiest**)
a little afraid: *I had an **uneasy** feeling that someone was watching me.* **uneasily** *adverb*

unemployed /ˌʌnɪm'plɔɪd/ *adjective*
having no paid work: *He was **unemployed** for two months after leaving college.*

unemployment *noun* (*no plural*): *There is high **unemployment** (=many people without work) in this town since the factory closed.*

uneven /ʌn'iːvn/ *adjective*
not level or flat: *an **uneven** road*

unexpected /ˌʌnɪk'spektɪd/ *adjective*
not expected
unexpectedly *adverb*: *She arrived **unexpectedly** early.*

unfair /ʌn'feəʳ/ *adjective*
not fair; not just: *It's **unfair** to punish Peter and not James — they were both behaving badly.* **unfairly** *adverb*

unfasten /ʌn'fɑːsn/ *verb*
to stop being unfastened; undo: *She **unfastened** her belt.*

unfold /ʌn'fəʊld/ *verb*
to open out: *She **unfolded** the cloth.*

unfortunate /ʌn'fɔːtʃənət/ *adjective*
having bad luck; unlucky
unfortunately *adverb*: ***Unfortunately**, I can't come to your party.*

unfriendly /ʌn'frendlɪ/ *adjective*
not friendly: *Why is she so **unfriendly**?*

ungrateful /ʌn'greɪtfəl/ *adjective*
not grateful: *The **ungrateful** child took her present and ran off without saying anything.*

unhappy /ʌnˈhæpɪ/ *adjective*
(**unhappier, unhappiest**)
not happy; sad: *She looked* **unhappy** *after she read the letter.*

unhealthy /ʌnˈhelθɪ/ *adjective*
(**unhealthier, unhealthiest**)
not healthy; not good for health: *She looks* **unhealthy.** *This is an* **unhealthy** *place to live.*

uniform
/ˈjuːnɪfɔːm/
noun
clothes worn
for a special
job or for
school: *The*
soldiers were
wearing **uniform.**

uniform

union /ˈjuːnjən/ *noun*
1 (*no plural*) coming or joining together: ·*the* **union** *of states to form a country*
2 a group of people joined for a special reason: *A* **trade 'union** *is a group of workers such as miners or teachers, who have joined together.*

unique /juːˈniːk/ *adjective*
being the only one: *That building is* **unique** *because all the others like it were destroyed.*

unit /ˈjuːnɪt/ *noun*
1 one complete thing or set: *This lesson is divided into four* **units** — *speaking practice, writing practice, new words, and a word game.*
2 an amount or sum: *We measure distance in* **units** *called kilometres.*

unite /juːˈnaɪt/ *verb* (*present participle* **uniting,** *past* **united**)
to join together: *We are* **united** *in what we believe. the* **United** *States of America*

universe /ˈjuːnɪvɜːs/ *noun*
all the stars, space, etc. that we know about

uni'versal *adjective* of or for everyone: *Micro-computers are of* **universal** *interest; everyone is learning how to use them.*

university /ˌjuːnɪˈvɜːsətɪ/ *noun*
(*plural* **universities**)
a place where you can study when you have left school for a degree (=special paper that you have to pass many examinations to get)

unjust /ʌnˈdʒʌst/ *adjective*
not just; unfair: *an* **unjust** *punishment*
unjustly *adverb*

unkind /ʌnˈkaɪnd/ *adjective*
not kind; rather cruel: *That was an* **unkind** *thing to say!*

unknown /ʌnˈnəʊn/ *adjective*
not known: *An* **unknown** *person wrote this story.*

unless /ənˈles/
1 if not: **Unless** *you go at once you will be late.*
2 except when: *My baby sister never cries* **unless** *she is hungry.*

unlike /ʌnˈlaɪk/ *preposition*
not like; not the same as: *She is* **unlike** *her mother; she is tall and her mother is very short.*
unlikely *adjective* not expected: *They are* **unlikely to** *come since the weather is so bad.*

unload /ʌnˈləʊd/ *verb*
to take something off a vehicle, from a person, etc.: *Two men* **unloaded** *the lorry.*

unlock /ʌnˈlɒk/ *verb*
to open with a key: *to* **unlock** *a door*

unlucky /ʌnˈlʌkɪ/ *adjective*
(**unluckier, unluckiest**)
not having or giving good luck: *Some people think that 13 is an* **unlucky** *number. I was* **unlucky** — *I missed the bus by just one minute.*

unnecessary /ʌn'nesəserɪ, -srɪ/ *adjective*
not necessary: *All those clothes are* **unnecessary** *on such a hot day.*

unpack /ʌn'pæk/ *verb*
to take things out of boxes, baskets, etc. where they have been stored: *She* **unpacked** *(her clothes) when she arrived home from her holiday.*

unpleasant /ʌn'pleznt/ *adjective*
not nice or pleasant: *That drink has an* **unpleasant** *taste, I don't like it.*

　unpleasantly *adverb*

unreasonable /ʌn'riːznəbl/ *adjective*
not reasonable: *He's being* **unreasonable** — *he wants more money and more free time.*

unreliable /ˌʌnrɪ'laɪəbl/ *adjective*
that you cannot depend on: *I wouldn't ask him to help — he's very* **unreliable.**

unsafe /ʌn'seɪf/ *adjective*
not safe

unsatisfactory /ˌʌnsætɪs'fæktrɪ/ *adjective*
not good enough: **unsatisfactory** *work*

unsteady /ʌn'stedɪ/ *adjective*
not safe or sure: *This chair is* **unsteady,** *will you hold it while I stand on it?*

　unsteadily *adverb: The old woman walked* **unsteadily** *down the stairs.*

unsuitable /ʌn'suːtəbl/ *adjective*
not suitable: *A knife is an* **unsuitable** *toy for a baby.*

untidy /ʌn'taɪdɪ/ *adjective*
(untidier, untidiest)
not tidy: *Her room was* **untidy** — *there were clothes all over the floor.*

　untidily *adverb*

untie /ʌn'taɪ/ *verb* (*present participle* **untying,** *past* **untied**)
to undo string, a knot, etc.: *She* **untied** *the parcel and looked inside.*

° **until** /ən'tɪl/ *or* **till** /tɪl/
up to the time when something happens: *We can't go* **until** *Thursday. I couldn't sew* **until** *I was six.*

untrue /ʌn'truː/ *adjective*
not true

unusual /ʌn'juːʒʊəl/ *adjective*
not usual; strange: *an* **unusual** *hat*
　unusually *adverb: She is* **unusually** *quiet.*

unwell /ʌn'wel/ *adjective*
not well; ill: *He has been* **unwell** *since Sunday.*

unwilling /ʌn'wɪlɪŋ/ *adjective*
not willing: *I was* **unwilling** *to leave the party but I had to go home.* **unwillingly** *adverb*

unwind /ʌn'waɪnd/ *verb* (*present participle* **unwinding,** *past* **unwound** /ʌn'waʊnd/)
to undo (something that has been wound): *She* **unwound** *the wool from the ball.*

unwise /ʌn'waɪz/ *adjective*
not reasonable or wise: *It is* **unwise** *to go out in this cold weather.*

° **up** /ʌp/
adverb, preposition, adjective
1 to or in a higher place; to or in a standing position: *The boy climbed* **up** *the tree. The village is high* **up** *in the hills. Is Maria* **up** *yet, or is she still in bed? Stand* **up** *so that I can see how tall you are.*
2 (used in some phrases, often to make the meaning stronger): *Before you go out,* **lock up** *the house. The boy* **ate up** *all his dinner. Go and see what those children* **are up to** (=are doing).

,up to 'date *adjective* modern; having the latest information: *I like wearing* 'up-to-date *clothes. I keep* up to date *with the news by listening to the radio.*

'upwards *adverb* from a lower to a higher place; towards the sky or top of anything: *The plane flew* upwards. *The people were all looking* upwards.

uphill /ˌʌpˈhɪl/ see hill

upon /əˈpɒn/ *preposition* on: *The village stands* upon *a hill.*

° upper /ˈʌpəʳ/ *adjective* in a higher position; further up: *The* upper *part of your arm is the part above your elbow.*

upright /ˈʌpraɪt/ *adjective* straight up and down: *Put the bottle* upright, *not on its side.*

upset /ʌpˈset/ *verb* (*present participle* upsetting, *past* upset)
1 to knock over: *I* upset *the soup all over the table.*
2 to make unhappy or worried: *James was* upset *because he had lost his ticket.*
3 to spoil something that was planned: *The storm* upset *our plans for a party outside.*

° upside-down /ˌʌpsaɪd ˈdaʊn/ see down

upstairs /ˌʌpˈsteəz/ see stairs

urge¹ /ɜːdʒ/ *verb* (*present participle* urging, *past* urged)
to try and make someone do something: *He* urged *her to rest.*

urge² *noun* a strong wish: *I had an* urge *to see him.*

urgent /ˈɜːdʒənt/ *adjective* needing to be done without delay; very important: *I must post this letter; it's* urgent.
urgently *adverb*

° us /əs; *strong* ʌs/ the person who is speaking and some other person or people, used in sentences like this: *The teacher told* us *to be quiet. Please give the book to* us.

° use¹ /juːz/ *verb* (*present participle* using, *past* used)
to do something with; have a purpose for: *How do you* use *a telephone? What do you* use *this thing for?*
used *adjective* not new: used *cars*

° use² /juːs/ *noun* a purpose; being used; using: *What is the* use *of waiting for her? The earth is ready for* use. *I was given the* use *of their swimming pool.*
'useful *adjective* having a good purpose; helpful: *That is a* useful *knife.* 'usefully *adverb*
'useless *adjective* having no good purpose: *This is a* useless *knife — the handle has broken!* 'uselessly *adverb*

used to¹ /juːst tə/ *adjective* knowing what something or someone is like, so that it does not seem strange or unusual or difficult: *He* is used to *traffic because he often drives in town. He* is used to *driving in town.*

used to² *verb* (used with another verb to show that something was done often in the past, but is not done now): *He* used to *play football every Saturday when he was young. My father* didn't use to *smoke, but now he does.*

° usual /ˈjuːʒʊəl/ *adjective* done or happening regularly; by custom: *Are you coming home at the* usual *time? Yes, I shall leave the office at the same time* as usual. *My* usual *chair had been moved from its* usual *place.*

usually *adverb: I'm* **usually** *at school early, but today I was late.*

utensil /juːˈtensl/ *noun*
an instrument or container used in everyday activities: *cooking* **utensils**

utmost /ˈʌtməʊst/ *adjective, noun*
the most possible: *He* **did his** utmost *to stop his sister marrying that man.*

utter¹ /ˈʌtəʳ/ *verb*
to say: *He looked at me without* **uttering** *a word.*

utter² *adjective*
complete: *What he is doing is* **utter** *stupidity!* **utterly** *adverb*

Vv

vacant /ˈveɪkənt/ *adjective*
empty: *a* **vacant** *seat on the bus*
vacancy *noun (plural* **vacancies***)*
an unfilled place or job: *The hotel has no* **vacancies** *— it's full. He's looking for a* **vacancy** *in an office.*

vacation /vəˈkeɪʃn/ *noun*
a holiday: *She is* **on vacation.**

vacuum
/ˈvækjʊm/
noun
a space with
no air in it: *A*
'vacuum flask
*keeps liquid
hot or cold*

vacuum flask

vacuum cleaner

for a long time. A **'vacuum cleaner** *cleans things by sucking the dirt into a* **vacuum.**

vague /veɪg/ *adjective*
not clear: *I have only a* **vague** *idea where the house is.* **vaguely** *adverb*

vain /veɪn/ *adjective*
too proud of yourself, especially of what you look like: *She is very* **vain** *— she's always looking at herself in the mirror.*
vanity /ˈvænətɪ/ *noun (no plural)*: *What* **vanity** *— he thinks all the girls like him!*

valley /ˈvælɪ/ *noun*
low ground between two hills or mountains

○ **value**¹ /ˈvæljuː/ *noun*
what something is worth: *What is the* **value** *of your house? Your help has been of great* **value.**
valuable *adjective: This house is very* **valuable;** *it would cost you a lot of money.*

value² *verb (present participle* **valuing,** *past* **valued***)*
1 to think that something is worth a lot: *I* **value** *your advice.*
2 to say how much something is worth: *He* **valued** *the ring at £100.*

van /væn/
noun
a small
covered lorry
for carrying
goods

van

vanish /ˈvænɪʃ/ *verb*
to go from where you could see it: *I thought it would rain, but the clouds have* **vanished** *and it's a fine day.*

vapour /ˈveɪpəʳ/ *noun (no plural)*
a gaslike form of a liquid, like steam

varnish

varnish[1] /'vɑːnɪʃ/ *noun*
a hard shiny clear covering that you put on wood, metal, etc.: *The varnish protected the table from being damaged.*

varnish[2] *verb*
to put varnish on something

vary /'veərɪ/ *verb (present participle* **varying,** *past* **varied)**
to change: *The weather* **varies** *from day to day.*
    va'riety /və'raɪətɪ/ *noun* a lot of different things: *At school we learn a* **variety** *of things.*
    various /'veərɪəs/ *adjective:* *There are* **various** *colours to choose from — which do you like best?*

vase /vɑːz/ *noun*
a pot for putting cut flowers in

vast /vɑːst/ *adjective*
very big: *The city is* **vast** *compared to our village.*
    'vastly *adverb*

vault[1] /vɔːlt/ *noun*
an underground room: *The money was kept in the bank's* **vault.**

vault[2] *verb*
to jump over: *He* **vaulted** *the fence.*

° **vegetable**[1] /'vedʒtəbl/ *noun*
a plant that people eat

° **vegetable**[2] *adjective*
of or from plants: *We use* **vegetable** *oil for cooking.*

° **vehicle** /'viːəkl/ *noun*
something which carries people or goods: *Cars and lorries are* **vehicles.**

veil[1] /veɪl/ *noun*
a covering for the head and (part of) the face: *In many Muslim countries, the women wear* **veils.**

veil[2] *verb*
to put a veil on or over: *She* **veiled** *her face before she went out.*

vein /veɪn/ *noun*
one of the tubes in your body that carries blood to the heart

veld /velt/ *noun (no plural)*
wild or dry country in southern Africa

velvet /'velvɪt/ *noun (no plural)*
a type of cloth with a soft surface

verandah /və'rændə/ *noun*
a roofed area built onto a house, with no outside wall

verandah

verb /vɜːb/ *noun*
a word or words that tells us what someone or something does or is: *In the sentence "We are going home", "are going" is a* **verb.**

verdict /'vɜːdɪkt/ *noun*
what is decided, especially by a law court (see): *The* **verdict** *was that the prisoner was guilty.*

verge /vɜːdʒ/ *noun*
edge: *a grass* **verge** *beside the road*

verse /vɜːs/ *noun*
1 lines of writing which have a rhythm (= musical beat) and often a rhyme (= the words at the end of the lines sound alike)
2 a few lines of this from a longer piece (called a poem)
3 a small part of the Bible (= Christian religious book) or Koran (= Muslim religious book)

version /'vɜːʃn/ *noun*
a story told by one person compared with the same story told by another: *I have heard two* **versions** *of the accident.*

versus /'vɜːsəs/ *preposition*
against: *a football match* **versus** *St Paul's College In lists,* **versus** *is usually written* **v.:** *St Paul's College* **v.** *Greenwood School.*

vertical /'vɜːtɪkl/ *adjective*
standing upright; at right angles to: *Walls are usually* **vertical.**

° **very**[1] /'verɪ/ *adverb*
1 (used to make another word stronger): *It is* **very** *hot in this room. I am* **very** *well, thank you.*
2 (used with **not** like this): *The boy is* **not very** *big* (=he is rather small). *They did* **not** *stay* **very** *long* (=they stayed a short time).

very[2] *adjective*
the same; the one that is right: *I found the* **very** *thing I had been looking for.*

vessel /'vesl/ *noun*
1 a container: *A pot is a* **vessel** *for holding food.*
2 a ship or boat: *There were many* **vessels** *in the harbour today.*

vest /vest/ *noun*
a piece of clothing worn next to the skin and under other clothes

vest

veterinary /'vetrɪnərɪ/ *adjective*
treating animals: *A* **'veterinary surgeon** (*or* **vet**) *is an animal doctor.*

via /'vaɪə/ *preposition*
travelling through: *I went to London* **via** *Paris.*

vibrate /vaɪ'breɪt/ *verb* (*present participle* **vibrating,** *past* **vibrated**)
to shake quickly backwards and forwards: *The bus* **vibrated** *when the driver started the engine.*
vi'bration *noun*

vicar /'vɪkər/ *noun*
a Christian priest who looks after one church

vice- /vaɪs/
a word used with a title, to mean that the person is next below the person with the title: *The* **vice-president** *is the next person in importance below the president.*

vicinity /vɪ'sɪnətɪ/ *noun* (*no plural*)
surrounding area: *The market is* **in the vicinity of** (= near) *the school.*

victim /'vɪktɪm/ *noun*
someone who suffers from an illness or action: *She was the* **victim** *of a road accident.*

victorious /vɪk'tɔːrɪəs/ *adjective*
winning: *a* **victorious** *team*

victory /'vɪktərɪ/ *noun*
(*plural* **victories**)
winning a fight or a game: *The school football team has had three* **victories** *this month against other schools.*

video /'vɪdɪəʊ/ *noun*
1 film for showing on a television set: *You can copy the football game from the television onto* **video tape** *by using the* **video recorder.**
2 a machine for copying plays, sport, etc. from the television **video recorder** is another name for **video.**

view /vjuː/ *noun*
1 something you see: *The house has a* **view** *over the sea.*
2 an opinion: *What is your* **view** *on school punishments?*

vigorous /'vɪgərəs/ *adjective*
very active or strong: *The* **vigorous** *young plants grew fast.*

vile /vaɪl/ *adjective* (**viler, vilest**)
very unpleasant: *a* **vile** *smell*

° **village** /'vɪlɪdʒ/ *noun*
a small place where people live, not so large as a town

villager *noun*
someone who lives in a village

villain /'vɪlən/ *noun*
the chief bad character in a play or film

vine /vaɪn/ *noun*
a name given to some plants with climbing stems, like a **grape vine**

vinegar /'vɪnɪgə^r/ *noun* (*no plural*)
a very sour liquid used in cooking

violent /'vaɪələnt/ *adjective*
having great force: *a violent storm*
violence *noun* (*no plural*)

violet /'vaɪələt/ *noun*
1 a small flower with a sweet smell
2 the colour of the violet, which is a mixture of blue and red

violin /vaɪə'lɪn/ *noun*
a musical instrument with four strings, played with a bow (=tightly

bow

violin

stretched threads which are drawn across the strings to make a sound)

viper /'vaɪpə^r/ *or* **adder** *noun*
a snake with a dangerous bite

virtue /'vɜːtjuː/ *noun*
a good quality of someone's character: *Honesty is a virtue.*

visible /'vɪzəbl/ *adjective*
able to be seen: *The smoke from the fire was visible from the road.*
vision /'vɪʒn/ *noun* **1** (*no plural*) sight: *She has good vision — she can see well.* **2** something we imagine; dream: *He had a vision of himself as a rich businessman.*

° **visit**[1] /'vɪzɪt/ *verb*
to go and see: *We visited our friends in town.*

° **visit**[2] *noun*
an act of visiting: *We had a visit from your teacher. She paid us a visit.*
visitor *noun*

vital /'vaɪtl/ *adjective*
necessary for life; very important: *a vital examination*

vivid /'vɪvɪd/ *adjective*
1 bright: *a vivid colour*
2 clear and lifelike: *She gave the police a vivid description of the accident.*

vocabulary /və'kæbjʊlərɪ/ *noun* (*plural* **vocabularies**)
1 all the words you know: *He has a very large vocabulary.*
2 a list of words in a book: *The vocabulary used in the course book is printed at the back.*

° **voice** /vɔɪs/ *noun*
the sounds you make when you speak or sing: *a high voice/ a loud voice*

volcano /vɒl'keɪnəʊ/ *noun* (*plural* **volcanoes**)
a mountain from which burning and melted rock sometimes comes

volleyball /'vɒlɪbɔːl/ *noun* (*no plural*)
a game in which a large ball is knocked back and forwards across a net by hand

volt /vəʊlt/ *noun*
a measure of electricity

volume /'vɒljʊm/ *noun*
1 (*no plural*) the space something contains or takes up: *What is the volume of this box?*
2 the amount of sound that something makes: *She turned down the volume on the radio.*
3 a book, especially one of a set

volunteer[1] /ˌvɒlən'tɪə^r/ *noun*
a person who offers to do something: *We want some volunteers to help paint the house.*
voluntary /'vɒləntrɪ/ *adjective* acting or done willingly, without payment: *She is a voluntary worker at the hospital.*

volunteer[2] *verb*
to offer to do something: *We all volunteered to paint the house.*

vomit /ˈvɒmɪt/ *verb*
to bring food up from the stomach: *The child **vomited** after eating the bad meat.*

vote[1] /vəʊt/ *verb* (*present participle* **voting**, *past* **voted**)
to state a choice from among several, especially to choose someone secretly during an election (see): *Three people **voted for** a music club, but ten people **voted for** a football club, so we started a football club.*
ˈvoter *noun* someone who votes

vote[2] *noun*
a choice made by voting: *He won the election* (see) *because he got most **votes**.*

vow[1] /vaʊ/ *verb*
to promise something important: *He **vowed** to look after his mother when his father died.*

vow[2] *noun*
a very important promise

vowel /ˈvaʊəl/ *noun*
a written letter, or the sound of a letter, which is one of *a, e, i, o,* or *u.* Look at **consonant**.

voyage /ˈvɔɪ-ɪdʒ/ *noun*
a long journey, often by sea

vulgar /ˈvʌlɡəʳ/ *adjective*
rude or rough in behaviour, taste, etc.

wade /weɪd/ *verb* (*present participle* **wading**, *past* **waded**)
to walk through water: *We **waded** across the river, because there was no bridge.*

wag /wæɡ/ *verb* (*present participle* **wagging**, *past* **wagged**)
to move or cause to move from side to side or up and down: *The dog **wagged** its tail.*

° **wage** /weɪdʒ/ *noun*
money given to us for the work we do: *He earns a low **wage**. he gets his **wages** on Fridays.*

waggon *or* **wagon** /ˈwæɡən/ *noun*
1 a cart: *The horses pulled the **waggon**.*
2 an open container used on a railway: *The train was pulling many **waggons**.*

wail /weɪl/ *verb*
to make a long cry showing sadness or pain: *The child was **wailing** unhappily.* **wail** *noun*

waist /weɪst/ *noun*
the narrow part of the body between the chest and the legs: *Ann wore a belt around her **waist**.* (picture on page 133)

° **wait**[1] /weɪt/ *verb*
to stay somewhere until someone comes or something happens: *Please **wait** here until I come back. I was **waiting** for the bus.*
ˈwaiter *or* **ˈwaitress** *noun* a person who brings food to people eating at a table
ˈwaiting room *noun* a room for people who are waiting: *a doctor's **waiting room***

wait² *noun*

a time of waiting: *He had a long* **wait** *for the train, as it was late.*

○ **wake** /weɪk/ *verb*

(*present participle* **waking**, *past tense* **woke** /wəʊk/ *or* **waked**, *past participle* **woken** *or* **waked**) to stop or make someone stop sleeping: *I* **woke** *early this morning. Be quiet, or you* **will wake** *the baby. Please* **wake** *me* **up** *at 8 o'clock.*

○ **walk¹** /wɔːk/ *verb*

to move on the feet at the usual speed: *We* **walk** *to school each day.*

○ **walk²** *noun*

a journey on foot: *Shall we go for a* **walk** *this afternoon? It is a long* **walk** *to the town.*

○ **wall** /wɔːl/ *noun*

1 something built especially of bricks or stone which goes round a house, town, field, etc.: *There was a* **wall** *around the park.*
2 one of the sides of a building or room: *We have painted all the* **walls** *white.*

'**wallpaper** *noun* (*no plural*) special paper used to cover the walls of a room

wallet /'wɒlɪt/
noun
a small flat case for papers or

wallet

money, usually carried in a pocket

○ **wander** /'wɒndə^r/ *verb*

to move about without purpose: *The children* **wandered** (**about**) *in the woods.*

○ **want¹** /wɒnt/ *verb*

1 to wish to have something: *I* **want** *a bicycle for my birthday.*
2 to need: *I* **want** *someone to help me.*

want² *noun* (*no plural*)

need; lack; not having something necessary: *The children were* **in want of** *food. The corn was dying* **from want of** *rain.*

○ **war** /wɔː^r/ *noun*

fighting between nations: *The two countries were* **at war** *for two years. One country* **declared war on** (= said they were going to fight) *another.*

warfare /'wɔːfeə^r/ *noun* (*no plural*) the fighting which happens in a war
'**warship** *noun* a ship used for war

ward /wɔːd/ *noun*

a room in a hospital

warden /'wɔːdn/ *noun*

a person who looks after a large building where people live, a public place, etc.: *Where is the* **warden** *of the college? A* **traffic warden** *makes sure that people park their cars in the correct places in a town.*

wardrobe /'wɔːdrəʊb/ *noun*

a cupboard in which clothes are hung up

warehouse /'weəhaʊs/ *noun*

a large building for storing things

wares /weəz/ *plural noun*

goods for selling: *The man spread his* **wares** *on the table.*

○ **warm¹** /wɔːm/ *adjective*

1 not cold but not hot: **warm** *water*
2 able to keep out the cold: **warm** *clothes*

warmth *noun* (*no plural*): *the* **warmth** *of the sun/the* **warmth** *of her welcome*

○ **warm²** *verb*

to make or become warm: *The hot drink* **warmed** *him. He* **warmed** *himself by the fire.*

○ **warn** /wɔːn/ *verb*

to tell someone of something bad

which might happen: *She* **warned** *me about the dangerous road, so I crossed it carefully.*

'**warning** *noun: Because of her* **warning,** *I was careful.*

warrant /'wɒrənt/ *noun*

a paper saying that one may do something: *The police must have a* **search warrant** *to search a house.*

was /wəz; *strong* wɒz/ *verb*

past tense of the verb **be** that we use with **I, he, she,** and **it**: *The sun* **was** *shining but it* **wasn't** (= was not) *too hot.*

◦ **wash**[1] /wɒʃ/ *verb*

1 to make clean with water: *Have you* **washed** *your shirt? Will you* **wash up?** (= clean the dishes after a meal)

2 to flow over continually or carry in a flow of water: *The bridge was* **washed away** *in the storm.*

'**washing** *noun* (*no plural*) clothes to be washed or already washed

'**washing ma,chine** *noun* a machine for washing clothes

◦ **wash**[2] *noun*

1 an act of washing or being washed: *Have you had a* **wash**? *Go and give the car a* **wash.**

2 things to be washed or being washed: *My shirt is in the* **wash.**

washbasin

/'wɒʃbeɪsn/ *noun*

a large bowl or basin, often fixed to a wall for washing

washbasin

wasp /wɒsp/ *noun*

a flying insect like a bee

◦ **waste**[1] /weɪst/ *verb* (*present participle* **wasting,** *past* **wasted**)

to use something wrongly or use too much of something: *Don't* **waste** *the flour; there isn't much.*

◦ **waste**[2] *noun*

1 an act of wasting: *It is a* **waste** *to throw away good food.*

2 used, damaged, or unwanted things: *The* **waste** *from the factory was taken away in lorries.*

◦ **watch**[1] /wɒtʃ/ *noun* (*plural* **watches**)

1 a small clock worn on the wrist or carried in a pocket

watch

2 a person or people told to keep their eyes on a place or a person: *The police* **kept watch on** *the criminal's house.*

'**watchman** *noun* (*plural* **watchmen**) a guard, especially of a building

◦ **watch**[2] *verb*

1 to look at; keep one's eyes on: **Watch out** *for the cars when you cross the road.*

2 to look after: *Will you* **watch** *the baby?*

◦ **water**[1] /'wɔːtəʳ/ *noun* (*no plural*) the liquid in rivers, lakes, and seas, which animals and people drink

'**waterfall** *noun* a place where water falls over rocks from a high place to a lower place

'**waterproof** *adjective* which does not allow water to go through: *a* **waterproof** *coat*

water[2] *verb*

to put water onto land or plants

watt /wɒt/ *noun*

a measure of electrical power: *a 60* **watt** *electric light*

◦ **wave**[1] /weɪv/ *noun*

1 one of curving lines of water on the surface of the sea which rise and fall

2 a movement of the hand from side to side: *She gave a* **wave** *as she left the house.*

wave

wave² *verb* (*present participle* **waving**, *past* **waved**)
to move or cause to move from side to side or up and down: *She* **waved** *her hand to say goodbye.*

wax /wæks/ *noun* (*no plural*)
a solid substance made of fats or oil which melts when it is heated: *Candles* (see) *are made from* **wax.**

way /weɪ/ *noun*
1 direction: *Which is the* **way** *to the station? Look both* **ways** *before you cross the road.*
2 distance: *We have to go a long* **way** *to school. I fell* **on the way** (= while I was going) *to school.*
3 a path: *I can't see because you are* **in my way** (= where I want to see).
4 how a thing is done or works: *Show me the* **way** *to use this camera, please.*

we /wɪ; *strong* wiː/
the person who is speaking and some other person or people: *When my friend comes to see me,* **we** *play football.* **We're** (= we are) *all in the same class at school. Next year,* **we'll** (= we shall *or* we will) *be in a higher class. My sister and I didn't go to the film because* **we'd** (= we had) *seen it before. The hill was so steep we thought* **we'd** (= we should *or* we would) *never get to the top. I've got a bicycle and my friend has one too —* **we've** (= we have) *each got a bicycle.*

weak /wiːk/ *adjective*
1 not strong in body or character: *She was* **weak** *after her illness.*
2 containing a lot of water
'weakness *noun* (*plural* **weaknesses**) being weak; a fault: *Spending too much money is her* **weakness.**

weaken /'wiːkən/ *verb*
to make or become less strong

wealth /welθ/ *noun* (*no plural*)
riches; owning a lot of houses, land, etc.: *The father passed on the family's* **wealth** *to his son.*
'wealthy *adjective* (**wealthier, wealthiest**) rich: *a* **wealthy** *family*

weapon /'wepən/ *noun*
a thing with which we fight: *A gun is a* **weapon.**

wear /weə^r/ *verb* (*past tense* **wore** /wɔː^r/, *past participle* **worn** /wɔːn/)
1 to have or carry on the body: *She* **wore** *a pretty dress.*
2 to change because of continual use: *My shoes are* **worn** *out; they are full of holes. You've* **worn** *a hole in your sock.*
3 to last; remain unchanged: *This dress has* **worn** *well; it is three years old and it still looks new.*

weary /'wɪərɪ/ *adjective* (**wearier, weariest**)
tired: *I felt* **weary** *after work.*
wearily *adverb*

weather /'weðə^r/ *noun* (*no plural*)
the state of the wind, rain, sunshine, etc.: *I don't like cold* **weather.** *The* **weather** *has been dry this week.*

weave /wiːv/ *verb* (*present participle* **weaving**, *past tense* **wove** /wəʊv/, *past participle* **woven**)
1 to make threads into cloth, by moving a thread over and under a set of longer threads on a loom (see): *The boy learnt how to* **weave.**
2 to make something in this way: *I* **wove** *a mat.*
'weaving *noun* (*no plural*): *She is very good at* **weaving**; *the cloth she makes is beautiful.*

web /web/ *noun*
a net of thin threads spun by a spider

web

wedding /'wedɪŋ/ *noun*
the ceremony when people get married: *I'm going to my brother's* **wedding** *tomorrow.*

○ **Wednesday** /'wenzdeɪ, -dɪ/ *noun*
the fourth day of the week

weed[1] /wiːd/ *noun*
a wild plant which grows where it is not wanted

weed[2] *verb*
to remove weeds from the ground: *They* **were weeding** *the field.*

○ **week** /wiːk/ *noun*
a period of seven days, especially from Sunday to Saturday: *I play tennis twice a* **week**. *Will you come and see us next* **week**?

'**weekday** *noun* any day except Sunday

'**week'end** *noun* Saturday and Sunday: *I don't work* **at the weekend**.

'**weekly** *adjective, adverb: This is a* **weekly** *paper; it is printed every Friday. It is printed* **weekly**.

weep / wiːp/ *verb*
(*past* **wept** /wept/)
to cry: *She* **wept** *when she heard the bad news.*

○ **weigh** /weɪ/ *verb*
1 to measure how heavy a thing is: *He* **weighed** *the fish.*
2 to have a weight of: *The fish* **weighed** *two kilos.*

weight *noun* (*no plural*) the heaviness of anything: *The baby's* **weight** *was four kilos.*

weird /wɪəd/ *adjective*
strange; unusual: **weird** *clothes*

○ **welcome**[1] /'welkəm/ *adjective*
wanted; happily accepted: *You are always* **welcome** *in my home.*

○ **welcome**[2] *verb* (*present participle* **welcoming**, *past* **welcomed**)
to greet someone with pleasure: *My aunt* **welcomed** *me.*

○ **welcome**[3] *noun*
a greeting when someone arrives: *Mother gave our visitor a kind* **welcome**.

○ **well**[1] /wel/ *adjective*
in good health; not ill: *I hope you are* **well**. *I had a fever, but now I am better, thank you.*

○ **well**[2] *adverb*
(**better** /'betə[r]/, **best** /best/)
1 in a good or satisfactory way: *Mary can read very* **well**. *"* **Well done!**" *the teacher said, when I did my sums correctly.*
2 completely; thoroughly: *Wash your hands* **well** *before you eat.*
3 (used with other words to mean completely, fully, much): *If the room is* **well-'lit**, *it's easier to read. That writer is* **well-'known**.

○ **well**[3] *noun*
a deep hole in the ground from which we take out water or oil

went /went/ see **go**

wept /wept/ see **weep**

were /wə[r]; *strong* wɜː[r]/ *verb*
past tense of the verb **be** that we use with **you, we,** and **they**: *You* **were** *born in this town, but your brothers* **weren't** (= were not).

○ **west** /west/
noun, adjective, adverb
the direction in which the sun goes down: *We travelled* **west** *for two days. There is a* **west** *wind* (= coming from the west).

'**western** *adjective* in or of the west

'**westwards** *adverb* towards the west: *to travel* **westwards**

○ **wet**[1] /wet/ *adjective*
(**wetter, wettest**)
1 covered with or containing liquid; not dry: *My hair is* **wet**. *Don't touch the* **wet** *paint.*
2 rainy: *a* **wet** *day*

wet² *verb* (*present participle* **wetting,** *past* **wet** *or* **wetted**)
to make something wet

whale /weɪl/ *noun*
a very large animal that lives in the sea; it is not a fish but feeds its young with milk

wharf /wɔːf/
noun (*plural*
wharfs *or*
wharves
/wɔːvz/)
a place built
on the edge of
water where
ships load and unload

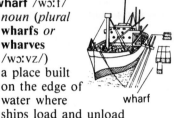

wharf

° **what** /wɒt/
1 which thing or things: **What** *is your name?* **What** *did you say?*
2 which: **What** *time is it?* **What** *tools do I need for this job?*
3 (used in sentences like this): *She told me* **what** *to do. I didn't know* **what** *had happened.* "**What** *are you using those scissors* **for?**" "*To cut paper.*"
4 (used to show surprise or other strong feelings): "**What** *a silly thing to do!*"

whatever /wɒ'tevəʳ/
anything at all that; no matter what: *You may do* **whatever** *you want to do.* **Whatever** *you do, I won't tell you my secret.*

° **wheat** /wiːt/ *noun* (*no plural*)
a grass plant with grain seeds that are made into flour

° **wheel** /wiːl/ *noun*
an object made of a larger circle which turns around a smaller circle, to which it is joined: **Wheels** *make cars, lorries, and bicycles move.* (picture at **bicycle**)
'**wheel,barrow** *noun* a cart with a wheel at the front and two handles at the back

° **when** /wen/
1 at what time: **When** *will the bus come?*
2 at the time at which: *I lived in this village* **when** *I was a boy.*

whenever /we'nevəʳ/
1 at any time at all that; every time: *Please come to see me* **whenever** *you can.* **Whenever** *I see him I speak to him.*
2 (used to make **when** stronger): **Whenever** *did you have time to do all that work?*

° **where** /weəʳ/
1 at or to what place: **Where** *is that train going? He doesn't know* **where** *his friends are.*
2 (used to tell what place, like this): *The house* **where** *I live has a green door.*

wherever /weə'revəʳ/
1 at or to any place at all that: *I will drive you* **wherever** *you want to go.*
2 (used to make **where** stronger): *You are very late;* **wherever** *have you been?*

° **whether** /'weðəʳ/
if: *I don't know* **whether** *he'll come or not.*

° **which** /wɪtʃ/
1 what person or thing: **Which** *child knows the answer?* **Which** *of you is bigger, Mary or Jane?*
2 that: *The book* **which** *I like best is the one* **which** *you gave me.*

° **while** /waɪl/
all the time that; during the time that: *I met her* **while** *I was at school.* **While** *the child played, her mother worked.*

whine /waɪn/ *verb* (*present participle* **whining,** *past* **whined**)
to make a high sad sound: *The dog* **whined** *at the door.*
whine *noun*

○ **whip**¹ /wɪp/ *noun*
a long piece of leather or rope fastened to a handle, used for hitting animals or people

○ **whip**² *verb* (*present participle* **whipping**, *past* **whipped**)
to beat with a whip: *He* **whipped** *the horse to make it run faster.*

whirl /wɜːl/ *verb*
to move or make something move round and round very fast: *The wind* **whirled** *the leaves into the air.* **whirl** *noun*

whisker /ˈwɪskəʳ/ *noun*
1 hair growing on the sides of a man's face
2 one of the long stiff hairs that grow near the mouth of dogs, cats, rats, etc.

○ **whisper**¹ /ˈwɪspəʳ/ *verb*
to speak very quietly: *The two girls* **were whispering** *in the library.*

○ **whisper**² *noun*
words which are whispered: *She spoke* **in a whisper**, *so I could not hear what she said.*

○ **whistle**¹
/ˈwɪsl/ *noun*
1 an instrument which makes

whistle

a high sound when one blows through it: *The teacher blew a* **whistle** *to start the race.*
2 a thin high sound made by putting the lips together and blowing through them or by blowing through an instrument: *When he gave a* **whistle**, *his dog ran to him.*

○ **whistle**² *verb* (*present participle* **whistling**, *past* **whistled**)
1 to make the sound of a whistle: *He* **whistled** *to his dog.*
2 to make music by doing this: *He* **whistled** *the song.*

○ **white**¹ /waɪt/ *adjective*
1 of the colour of the paper in this book; very light: *a* **white** *dress*
2 with light-coloured skin: *Some of the children were* **white,** *the others were* **black.**

○ **white**² *noun*
1 (*no plural*) white colour: *She was dressed* **in white.**
2 a person with light-coloured skin
3 the white part of the eye, or of an egg (picture at **egg**)

○ **who** /huː/
1 what person or people: **Who** *gave you that book?* **Who** *are those people?*
2 that: *The man* **who** *lives in that house is my uncle.*

whoever /huːˈevəʳ/
1 any person that; no matter who: **Whoever** *wants a banana may have one.* **Whoever** *those people are, I don't want to see them.*
2 (used to make **who** stronger): **Whoever** *told you that silly story?*

○ **whole**¹ /həʊl/ *adjective*
complete; total: *They told me the* **whole** *story.* **'wholly** *adverb*

○ **whole**² *noun* (*no plural*)
the complete amount or thing: *Two halves make a* **whole.** *He put the* **whole** *of his money into the bank. The weather this month has been good* **on the whole** (=most days were fine).

whom /huːm/
(used instead of **who**, in sentences like this): **Whom** *did you speak to at the market today? The boy* **whom** *we call Tom is really called Thomas.*

whose /huːz/
of who or whom; belonging to who or whom: **Whose** *coat is that? It's my coat. This is the woman* **whose** *little boy was ill.*

○ **why** /waɪ/
for what reason: **Why** *is she crying? I can't tell you* **why** *she is crying. No one knows* **why.**

wicked /'wɪkɪd/ *adjective*
very bad: *a* **wicked** *person*
wickedly *adverb*

○ **wide**¹ /waɪd/ *adjective*
(**wider, widest**)
1 large from side to side; broad
2 fully or completely open: **wide** *eyes*
width /wɪdθ/ *noun* the distance from one side of something to the other; how wide something is: *What is the* **width** *of this material?* (picture on page 185)

○ **wide**² *adverb*
completely: *The door was* **wide** *open. He stood with his legs* **wide apart.**

widow /'wɪdəʊ/ *noun*
a woman whose husband is dead

widower /'wɪdəʊəʳ/ *noun*
a man whose wife is dead

○ **wife** /waɪf/ *noun*
(*plural* **wives** /waɪvz/)
the woman to whom a man is married

wig /wɪg/ *noun*
a covering for the head, made of hair from other people or animals

○ **wild** /waɪld/ *adjective*
1 not trained to live with man: **wild** *animals*
2 living in the natural state: *We picked the* **wild** *flowers in the woods.* **'wildly** *adverb*

○ **will**¹ /wɪl/ *verb*
1 (used with other verbs to show that something is going to happen): *Peter* **will** *carry the books, and* **we'll** (=we will) *carry the paper and pens. We* **won't** (=will not) *be late home.*
2 (used in questions when asking to do something or used when offering to do something): **Will** *you help me, please? Yes, I* **will** *help you.*
Look at **would, shall,** and **should.**

○ **will**² *noun*
power in the mind or character; what we want to do: *She has a strong* **will**, *and she does what she wants no matter what people say.*

will³ *noun*
a piece of paper that says who will have a person's belongings after he is dead: *The man left his farm to his son in his* **will** (=his will said that his son should have his farm).

○ **willing** /'wɪlɪŋ/ *adjective*
1 ready: *Are you* **willing** *to help?*
2 given or done gladly: **willing** *help*
willingly *adverb*: *I will* **willingly** *help you.*

○ **win** /wɪn/ *verb* (*present participle* **winning**, *past* **won** /wʌn/)
1 to be first or do best in a competition, race, or fight: *Who* **won** *the race? I* **won** *but David came second.*
2 to be given something because one has done well in a race or competition: *He* **won** *the first prize in the competition.*
winner *noun*

○ **wind**¹ /waɪnd/ *verb*
(*past* **wound** /waʊnd/)
1 to turn round and round: *He* **wound** *the handle. He* **wound up** (=turned the handle on) *the clock because it had stopped.*
2 to make into a ball or twist round something: *She* **wound** *the rope around her arm.*
3 to bend and turn: *The path* **wound** *along the side of the river.*

○ **wind**² /wɪnd/ *noun*
air moving quickly: *The* **wind** *blew the leaves off the trees.*

'**windmill** *noun* a building containing a machine which is turned by the force of the wind: *A* **windmill** *is used to crush grain into flour.*

'**windscreen** *noun* the piece of glass across the front of a car

'**windy** *adjective* (**windier, windiest**) with a lot of wind

windmills

° **window** /'wɪndəʊ/ *noun*
an opening in the wall of a building to allow light and air to enter: *Please shut the* **window.**
'**window-sill** *noun* a flat shelf below a window

wine /waɪn/ *noun* (*no plural*)
an alcoholic drink made from a small round juicy fruit (**grape**)

° **wing** /wɪŋ/ *noun*
one of the two limbs of a bird (see) or insect with which it flies

wink /wɪŋk/ *verb*
to close and open one eye quickly: *He* **winked** *at me.*
wink *noun*

° **winter** /'wɪntəʳ/ *noun, adjective*
the season in cool countries when it is cold and plants do not grow

wipe[1] /waɪp/ *verb* (*present participle* **wiping,** *past* **wiped**)
to make dry or clean with a cloth: *Will you* **wipe** *the table? She* **wiped** *the marks* **off** *the table.*

wipe[2] *noun*
a wiping movement: *She gave her face a* **wipe.**

° **wire** /waɪəʳ/ *noun*
1 (*no plural*) thin metal thread: *a* **wire** *fence*
2 pieces of wire: *electric* **wires**

wireless /'waɪəlɪs/ *noun* (*plural* **wirelesses**)
a radio

° **wise** /waɪz/ *adjective* (**wiser, wisest**)
having or showing good sense and cleverness: **wise** *advice*
wisdom /'wɪzdəm/ *noun* (*no plural*)
wisely *adverb: to act* **wisely**

° **wish**[1] /wɪʃ/ *verb*
1 to want what is not possible: *I* **wish** *I could go to America.*
2 to want: *I* **wish** *to see you now!*
3 to hope that someone has something: *We* **wish** *you success in your new job.*

° **wish**[2] *noun* (*plural* **wishes**)
1 a feeling of wanting especially what is not possible: *She had a* **wish** *to see the world.*
2 what is wished for: *It was my mother's* **wish** *that I should go.*

wit /wɪt/ *noun* (*no plural*)
1 cleverness; quickness of the mind: *He had the* **wit** *to telephone the police.*
2 the ability to talk in a clever and amusing way
'**witty** *adjective* (**wittier, wittiest**) clever and amusing: *a* **witty** *person* '**wittily** *adverb*

witch /wɪtʃ/ *noun* (*plural* **witches**)
a woman who is believed to have magic (see) powers

° **with** /wɪð/
1 in the company of: *She comes to school* **with** *her sister.*
2 using: *He opened the door* **with** *his key. Simon filled the bucket* **with** *water.*
3 having: *a white dress* **with** *red spots*
4 because of: *They smiled* **with** *pleasure.*
5 (used in sentences like these): *I*

don't agree **with** *you. She quarrelled* **with** *her friend.*

withdraw /wɪð'drɔː/ *verb*
(*past tense* **withdrew** /wɪð'druː/, *past participle* **withdrawn**)
1 to take away or back: *She* **withdrew** *all her money from the bank.*
2 to move or make something move away or back: *The soldiers* **withdrew.**

wither /'wɪðəʳ/ *verb*
to make or become dry or colourless: *The plants* **withered** *in the dry weather.*

within /wɪ'ðɪn/
preposition, adverb
1 in less than: *He learned to speak English* **within** *six months!*
2 in; inside: **Within** *these old walls there was once a town.*

○ **without** /wɪ'ðaʊt/ *preposition*
1 not having: *You can't see the film* **without** *a ticket.*
2 (used in sentences like these): *Can you carry these glasses* **without** *dropping them* (=and not drop them)? *Why did you go out* **without** *telling me?*

witness /'wɪtnɪs/ *noun*
(*plural* **witnesses**)
a person who sees something happen: *She was a* **witness** *at the accident.*

wives /waɪvz/ see **wife**

wobble /'wɒbl/ *verb* (*present participle* **wobbling,** *past* **wobbled**)
to move or make something move unsteadily: *The table* **is wobbling.**

woke /wəʊk/ see **wake**

woken /'wəʊkən/ see **wake**

○ **woman** /'wʊmən/ *noun*
(*plural* **women** /'wɪmɪn/)
a fully grown human female

won /wʌn/ see **win**

○ **wonder**[1] /'wʌndəʳ/ *verb*
1 to express a wish to know: *I* **wonder** *why James is always late for school.*
2 to be surprised: *We all* **wondered** *at his rudeness.*

○ **wonder**[2] *noun*
1 (*no plural*) a feeling of surprise and admiration: *They were filled with* **wonder** *when they saw the spaceship.* **No wonder** (=it is no surprise) *he is not hungry; he has been eating sweets all day.*
2 something or someone causing this feeling
wonderful *adjective* unusually good: **wonderful** *news*
wonderfully *adverb*

won't /wəʊnt/ see **will**

○ **wood** /wʊd/ *noun*
1 (*no plural*) the material of which trunks and branches of trees are made
2 a small forest: *He was lost in the* **wood.**
'**wooden** *adjective* made of wood: **wooden** *furniture*

○ **wool** /wʊl/ *noun*
(*no plural*)
1 the soft thick hair of sheep and some goats
2 the thread or material made from this hair: *The dress was made of* **wool.**

wool

'**woollen** *adjective:* a **woollen** *dress*

○ **word** /wɜːd/ *noun*
1 a letter or letters, a sound or sounds which together make something we can understand: *Home is the* **word** *for the place we live. She* **had a word** *with me* (=talked to me).
2 (*no plural*) a message: *Send me*

word *as soon as you get home.*
3 (*no plural*) a promise: *I* **give** *you* **my word** *that I will return.*

wore /wɔːʳ/ *see* **wear**

° **work**[1] /wɜːk/ *verb*
1 to do an activity, especially as employment: *He* **works** *in a factory. Are you* **working** *or playing, children?*
2 to be active; move or go properly; *Does this light* **work**?
3 to make someone or something do something: *Can you* **work** *this machine? She* **worked out** (=found an answer to) *the sum.*

° **work**[2] *noun* (*no plural*)
1 activity: *It takes a lot of* **work** *to build a house.*
2 a job or business: *to go to* **work**
3 what is produced by work: *He sells his* **work** *in the market.*
  '**worker** *noun*
  '**workman** *noun* (*plural* **workmen**) a person who works with his hands, especially in a trade
  works *plural noun* **1** the moving parts of a machine **2** a factory: *the steel* **works**

° **world** /wɜːld/ *noun*
1 the earth: *This car is used all over the* **world**.
2 all human beings thought of together

° **worm** /wɜːm/
noun
a long thin creature with a soft body without bones or legs

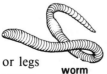

worm

worn /wɔːn/ *see* **wear**

° **worry**[1] /'wʌri/ *verb* (*present participle* **worrying**, *past* **worried**)
to feel or make someone feel anxious: *My parents* **worry** (*about me*) *if I come home late. The news*
of the fighting **worried** *us.*
  worried *adjective*

° **worry**[2] *noun*
1 (*no plural*) a feeling of anxiety: *The* **worry** *showed on her face.*
2 (*plural* **worries**) someone or something that makes us feel worried: *My father has a lot of* **worries**.

° **worse** /wɜːs/ *adjective, adverb*
1 more bad: *My writing is bad, but yours is* **worse**. *She was ill yesterday, but today she's* **worse** (=more ill).
2 more badly: *My brother sings* **worse** *than me.*

worship[1] /'wɜːʃɪp/ *verb* (*present participle* **worshipping**, *past* **worshipped**)
to pray to and show great respect to: *Christians* **worship** *God.*

worship[2] *noun* (*no plural*)
worshipping: *A church is a place of* **worship**.

° **worst** /wɜːst/
adjective, adverb, noun
1 most bad: *Your spelling is the* **worst** (*spelling*) *I've seen.*
2 most badly: *They were all very bad, but you behaved* **worst** *of all.*

worth[1] /wɜːθ/ *preposition*
with a value of: *How much is this bicycle* **worth**? *It's* **worth** *£50.*

° **worth**[2] *noun* (*no plural*)
value: *When she was in trouble, she discovered the* **worth** *of her friends* (=how good they were).
  '**worthless** *adjective* without worth; useless
  worthy /'wɜːði/ *adjective* (**worthier, worthiest**) deserving: *He is* **worthy** *of our praise.*

° **would** /wəd; *strong* wʊd/
1 (the word for **will** in the past): *They said they* **would** *play football on Saturday, and* **they'd** (=they

would) *win the game, but I said they* **wouldn't** (=would not) *win.*
2 (used when we are not sure enough to say **will**): *It's pretty, but* **would** *it be big enough?*
3 (used as a polite way of asking someone something) **Would** *you like a cup of tea?* **I'd** (=I would) *rather have coffee, please.*

wound[1] /waʊnd/ see **wind**

° **wound**[2] /wuːnd/ *verb*
to cause harm to the body: *The soldier was* **wounded** *in the arm.*

° **wound**[3] /wuːnd/ *noun*
a damaged place in the body

wove /wəʊv/ see **weave**

woven /'wəʊvən/ see **weave**

° **wrap** /ræp/ *verb* (*present participle* **wrapping,** *past* **wrapped**)
to put something all round an object: *I* **wrapped** *the book in paper and posted it.*

wreath
/riːθ/ *noun*
a ring of flowers and leaves

wreath

° **wreck**[1] /rek/ *noun*
a ship, car, building, etc. which has been partly destroyed
'wreckage *noun* (*no plural*)
broken parts: *the* **wreckage** *of the plane after the crash*

° **wreck**[2] *verb*
to destroy or cause to destroy: *The ship was* **wrecked** *on the rocks.*

wrench /rentʃ/ *verb*
to pull or turn suddenly and with force: *He* **wrenched** *the door open.*
wrench *noun*

wrestle /'resl/ *verb* (*present participle* **wrestling,** *past* **wrestled**)
to fight a person and try to throw him to the ground
wrestler *noun* a person who

wrestles as a sport
wrestling *noun* (*no plural*)

wriggle /'rɪgl/ *verb* (*present participle* **wriggling,** *past* **wriggled**)
to twist from side to side: *He* **wriggled** *on the hard chair. The snake* **wriggled** *through the grass.*

wring /rɪŋ/ *verb*
(*past* **wrung** /rʌŋ/)
to twist; remove water by twisting: *She* **wrung** *the wet clothes.*

wrinkle /'rɪŋkl/ *noun*
a line or fold on a surface: *Grandfather has many* **wrinkles** *on his face.*

° **wrist** /rɪst/ *noun*
the joint between the hand and the lower part of the arm (picture on page 133)
'wrist-watch *noun* a watch which fastens around the wrist

° **write** /raɪt/ *verb* (*present participle* **writing,** *past tense* **wrote** /rəʊt/, *past participle* **written** /'rɪtn/)
1 to make letters or words on paper, using a pen or pencil: **Write** *your name and then* **write down** (=put onto paper) *this sentence.*
2 to produce and send a letter: *He* **writes** *to me every day.*
'writer *noun* a person who writes books
'writing *noun* (*no plural*) **1** the activity of writing: *I enjoy* **writing.** **2** the way someone writes: *What beautiful* **writing!** **Handwriting** is another word for **writing.**

° **wrong**[1] /rɒŋ/ *adjective*
1 not good: *Telling lies is* **wrong.**
2 not correct: *I gave the* **wrong** *answer.*
3 not suitable: *This is the* **wrong** *time to visit her.*
'wrongly *adverb*: *I wrote your name* **wrongly.**

° **wrong**² *adverb*
incorrectly: *You've spelt the word*
wrong.

° **wrong**³ *noun* (*no plural*)
something bad: *Small children do
not know right from* **wrong.**

wrung /rʌŋ/ see **wring**

x-ray¹ /'eks reɪ/ *noun*
a photograph of the inside of your
body, taken with a special unseen
light: *The* **x-ray** *showed that the
boy's leg was broken.*

x-ray² *verb*
to photograph by x-ray

yacht /jɒt/ *noun*
a boat with sails (= large pieces of
cloth which catch the wind and
make it move)

° **yard** /jɑːd/ *noun*
1 a piece of ground next to a
building with a wall or fence round
it: *the school* **yard**
2 a measure of length, the same as
three feet; nearly a metre

yawn /jɔːn/ *verb*
to open the mouth wide and
breathe deeply as if tired: *I felt so
sleepy I couldn't stop* **yawning.**

° **year** /jɪəʳ/ *noun*
a measure of time, 365 days (or 12
months, or 52 weeks): *She is seven*
years *old. On January 1st, the* **New
Year** *begins.*
  '**yearly** *adjective, adverb* every
  year; once a year

yeast /jiːst/ *noun* (*no plural*)
a living substance which is added
to flour and water to make bread
rise

yell /jel/ *verb*
to shout or cry very loudly

° **yellow** /'jeləʊ/ *adjective, noun*
(of) the colour of the sun, or the
middle part of an egg

° **yes** /jes/
a word we use to answer a
question, to show that something
is true or that we agree with
something: *Can you read this?* —
Yes, *I can.*

° **yesterday** /'jestədeɪ, -dɪ/
noun, adverb
(on) the day before this day: *It was
very hot* **yesterday.**

° **yet** /jet/
1 up to now: *Has he come* **yet?** *No,
not* **yet.**
2 but: *He was poor,* **yet** *happy.*

yield /jiːld/ *verb*
1 to give way when force is used:
The army **yielded** *when it was
attacked.*
2 to give fruit, etc.: *The trees*
yielded *a large crop of fruit.*

yoghurt /'jɒgət/ *noun* (*no plural*)
milk treated in a special way to
make it thick and a bit sour but
not bad

yoke /jəʊk/ *noun*
a piece of wood put across the necks of cattle when pulling carts

yolk /jəʊk/ *noun*
the yellow part inside an egg (picture at **egg**)

° **you** /juː/ (*plural* **you**)
the person or people that the speaker is talking to: **You** *can swim fast.* **You're** (=you are) *a good swimmer. If I watch* **you,** *I'll learn to swim too. I hope that* **you'll** (=you will) *teach me.* **You've** (=you have) *got a lot of books.* **You'd** (=you had) *already gone when I arrived — I thought that* **you'd** (=you would) *still be there.*

° **young**[1] /jʌŋ/ *adjective*
not having lived very long; not old: *His children are* **young** *— four and two years old.*

young[2] *plural noun*
young people or animals: *She teaches the* **young.** *Animals protect their* **young.**

° **your** /jər; *strong* jɔːʳ/
belonging to you: *Put* **your** *books on* **your** *desks.*

° **yours** /jɔːz/
something belonging to you: *Are all these pencils* **yours?**

° **yourself** /jəˈself/
(*plural* **yourselves** /jəˈselvz/)
1 the same person as the one that the speaker is talking to: *Look at* **yourself** *in the mirror. You can't lift that* **by yourself** (=without help). *Why are you playing* **by yourself** (=alone)?
2 (used to make **you** have a stronger meaning): *You told me the story* **yourself.**

youth /juːθ/ *noun*
1 (*no plural*) the time when a person is young: *In his* **youth** *he was a soldier.*
2 (*plural* **youths** /juːðz/) a young man
3 (*no plural*) young people: *the* **youth** *of this country*

Zz

zebra /ˈzebrə, ˈziːbrə/ *noun*
(*plural* **zebra** *or* **zebras**)
an African wild animal like a horse which has brown and white lines all over its body (picture on p.17)

zero /ˈzɪərəʊ/ *noun*
(*plural* **zeros** *or* **zeroes**)
the number 0. **nought** is another way of saying **zero.**

zigzag
/ˈzɪgzæg/
noun
a z-shaped
pattern

zigzag

zinc /zɪŋk/ (*no plural*)
a white metal often mixed with other metals

zip[1] /zɪp/
noun
a fastener
that is often
used on

zip

clothes, and has two sets of teeth which can be joined together

zip[2] *verb* (*present participle* **zipping,** *past* **zipped**)
to shut with a zip: *She* **zipped up** *her dress.*

zone /zəʊn/ *noun*
an area

zoo /zuː/ *noun*
a place where different animals are kept for people to look at